M000159297

COVERING
GLOBALIZATION

ACS76@ columbia.edu

COVERING

GLOBALIZATION

A HANDBOOK FOR REPORTERS

EDITED BY ANYA SCHIFFRIN
AND AMER BISAT

COLUMBIA
UNIVERSITY
PRESS

NEW YORK

COLUMBIA UNIVERSITY PRESS
Publishers Since 1893

New York   Chichester, West Sussex

Library of Congress Cataloging-in-Publication Data

Covering globalization : a handbook for reporters /
   edited by Anya Schiffrin and Amer Bisat.
      p. cm.
   Includes bibliographical references and index.
   ISBN 0–231–13174–7 (cloth : alk. paper)—
   0–231–13175–5 (pbk. : alk. paper)
   1. International finance. 2. Globalization.
3. International economic relations.
I. Schiffrin, Anya, 1962– II. Bisat, Amer.
HG3881.C67437 2004
337—dc22   2004049382

Columbia University Press books are printed
on permanent and durable acid-free paper.

Printed in the United States of America
c   10 9 8 7 6 5 4 3 2 1
p   10 9 8 7 6 5 4 3 2 1

For Joe and for Nadia

CONTENTS

DOZENS OF PEOPLE contributed to this book in many different ways. The idea of the book grew out of a Web site that a number of people have written for and supported. Nicholas Rosen, Trond Gabrielsen, and Sara Silver were the first writers on the site; Alejandro Bianchi and Peter Green came on soon after. Alex Fishman did the first postings. Deidre Sheehan did a fantastic job of editing the texts on the Web site and so helped improve the pieces that are in this book. Jane Folpe did a typically thorough job of research, and I am very grateful to Susan Schneider for her editing and Dao Thu Hien for the job she did on researching the book. Shari Spiegel, Anton Korinek, Kim Andreassen, and Shana Hofstetter all worked on various aspects of administering and designing the Web site. The Open Society Institute and the Ford Foundation funded the project, so special thanks are due to Butch Montes, Laura Silber, and George Soros. Chrystia Freeland, Mark Clifford, Abid Aslam, Darren McDermott, Roman Frydman, Grainne McCarthy, Anne Nelson, Sheridan Prasso, Tim Carrington, and Graham Watts were among the first people to understand my idea and encourage me to pursue it. Frydman helped with marketing the site, as did Tim Karr. The site itself came out of conversations with reporters in countries as diverse as Argentina, Bolivia, Ecuador, Bulgaria, Moldova, Uruguay, and Vietnam. A number of people in those countries (and others) gave me help and ideas including My Ha Nguyen, Fang Wang, Mary Campbell, Monica Almeida, Petko Shishkov, and Tanja Jakobi.

Terri Thompson is the director of the Knight-Bagehot Fellowship at Columbia University's Graduate School of Journalism, where I learned an enormous amount about what makes a successful business/economics journalism program and a great deal from the experience of fellow journalists such as John Authers and Kim Allers. Much of what I know formally about economics and finance came from studying with Mary Ellen Carter, Graciana del Castillo, Ann Harrison, Hugh Patrick, and Matt Rhodes Kropf at Columbia University. My editors at Dow Jones Newswires and at the Asian *Wall Street Journal* gave me the chance to write about economics and business: John Hitchcock gave me my first full-time job as a business reporter and sent me to Amsterdam and Hanoi for five years. Once I got there, Michael Bergmeijer, George Thomas, Rod Alvarez, Kambiz Foroobhar, Roger Malone, Rob Fischer, David Plott, Aki Sato, and Reginald Chua urged me on. Samantha Marshall and Jesse Pesta taught me an enormous amount about good business writing. At the *Industry Standard*, Jane Goldman, Jim Ledbetter, Thomas Goetz, Rich Turner, and Jonathan Weber were wonderful bosses; Megan Barnett, Matt Yeomans, Hugh Garvey, Greg Dalton, Bill Brazell, and Susan Orenstein were terrific colleagues; and Kevin Kelleher was a tireless editor and a dream to work for. My partner, Joseph E. Stiglitz, read many of the drafts and contributed his comments. Ravi Kanbur and Michael Orszag also shared their ideas and suggestions, and Frederic Mishkin's writing informed much of my work. While I was overseas, I learned a lot from my sources: Raymond Salet at the Netherlands Ministry of Finance, Andrew Steer and Nisha Agrawal at the World Bank office in Hanoi, Tony Foster at Freshfields, Elizabeth Dahlin at the Embassy of Sweden, and countless Vietnamese sources who asked for anonymity. My Hanoi colleagues, Adrian Edwards, Jonathan Birchall, Kevin Bubel, Tim Larimer, Kristin Huckshorn, and Dean Yates were endlessly supportive and creative, as were Paul Alexander, Ian Stewart, Dao Thu Hien, Bo Hong Mai, Ho Binh Minh and Nguyen Trinh Thi, Nguyen Pham Muoi, Mila Rosenthal, Huynh Quoc, and Nguyen Hung.

At Columbia University, Robert Garris, Lisa Anderson, David Klatell, Robin Lewis, Nick Lemann, Arlene Morgan, and Michelle Steer have been enormously helpful. I'd like to thank my editor, John Michel, as well as his Columbia University Press colleagues Jeanie Lu and Michael Haskell and Claire Wellnitz for all their efforts.

COVERING
GLOBALIZATION

CHAPTER ONE

THE IMPORTANCE OF CRITICAL THINKING

JOSEPH E. STIGLITZ AND
ANYA SCHIFFRIN

GLOBALIZATION HAS BECOME a major subject of interest in both developing and developed countries. Reporters are now being asked not only to cover major events, such as the annual meetings of the International Monetary Fund and the World Bank and the periodic meetings of the World Trade Organization, but also to interpret what happens at those meetings within the broader debate on globalization. Indeed, media coverage already has played an important role in shaping the recent evolution of globalization. The media spotlight, including reporting trade agreements after the riots in Seattle at what was supposed to be the inauguration of a new round of trade negotiations in December 1999, helped validate many of the criticisms that had been leveled by the critics of globalization and provided some of the impetus for having the new round of trade negotiations focus on development.

While economic and business reporters naturally focus on *economic* globalization—the closer integration of the economies of the world as a result of the reduction of transportation and communication costs and the reduction of manmade barriers to the movements of goods, services, and capital throughout the world—there are other important dimensions to globalization: the spread of knowledge, ideas, ideology, civil society, and culture. These dimensions represent both some of the greatest virtues and some of the most important criticisms of globalization. Advocates of globalization see not only the increases in incomes but also the spread of democratic values. Opponents of globalization worry not just about the loss of jobs but about the loss of local culture.

Supporters of globalization point out that it enables each country to learn from the lessons of others. Critics point out that it has resulted in

3

international economic institutions imposing the same policies around the world, regardless of their appropriateness to the situation at hand. They worry that global institutions do not have the detailed local knowledge required to tailor closely economic policies to individual countries. For example, responses to economic crises are often similar, whether these crises arise in Latin America—where there has been a history of large budget deficits and loose monetary policy (resulting in high inflation)—or in East Asia—where governments have been running surpluses and inflation has not been a problem—and whether or not the countries affected have a high level of private indebtedness. In all of these cases, countries having economic problems have been told to cut deficit spending and raise interest rates. Much of this advice is meant to bring these nations in line with global economic policies, such as trade liberalization or privatization, which can lead to foreign ownership of local companies.

Because the advice of global institutions is often poorly adapted to the country at hand and is often insensitive to the social and political context, it has often failed and has often generated intense domestic opposition. This opposition itself has now become a global phenomenon: protests against the reduction of food subsidies and suspicion toward foreign ownership of local businesses have occurred in many countries around the world. The opposition has now spread from developing countries, where it has long been present, to the developed world: the antiglobalization movement itself is a global one.

Today, domestic economic policies have global impacts. This is particularly true of the policies of the advanced industrial countries: U.S. and EU subsidies of agriculture mean that developing countries such as those in Africa find it harder to export their products. In adopting its four-billion-dollar cotton subsidies, America meant only to help its 25,000 (mostly well-off) cotton farmers; the unintended consequence was to lower further the living standards of ten million African cotton farmers, many of whom were already living at subsistence levels. But this global impact is even occasionally true of developing countries: when Vietnam decided to expand its coffee exports, it was so successful that coffee prices around the world were depressed, leading to economic difficulties in Brazil, Colombia, and Central America.

Of course, the international economic institutions (the IMF, the World Bank, and the WTO) have profound effects on local economies—effects that are never fully anticipated and are often quite different from those intended. Joining the WTO can mean opening up local industries to foreign competition, with a resulting loss of jobs. The intellectual-property regime that was part of the last round of trade negotiations completed in 1994 (the Uruguay Round) was meant to encourage innovation. But one unintended side effect was that the resulting higher prices of drugs effectively denied access to life-saving medicines to many of the world's poorest people. The pact has also led to concerns about biopiracy, the patenting of traditional medicines, foods, and other products by West-

THE IMPORTANCE OF CRITICAL THINKING

ern companies (among the most famous or infamous instances was the attempt by a Texas company to patent Basmati rice). The IMF's policies can also have a destabilizing effect on the countries it advises. In the 1990s, it urged developing countries to open their capital markets to short-term capital flows, hoping to encourage economic efficiency. But this opening made countries vulnerable to speculative capital flows (speculating on short-term changes in exchange rates), and hot money rushed in and out of these countries, leading to increased global instability.

Most important for economic and business reporters is understanding that much of the opposition to globalization is not so much to globalization itself but to the way that it has been managed and, in particular, to the imposition of a particular set of ideas and ideologies on developing countries. The end of the Cold War has also meant the global expansion of economic ideologies, such as that of the Washington Consensus, which argues for "market fundamentalism" (the belief that markets are by and large self-regulating and that governments, therefore, should play a minimal role in their maintenance) and advises countries to focus on liberalization, privatization, and stabilization—which usually means keeping inflation low even at the expense of economic growth. Globalization has also helped spread the idea of "global capitalism," which accepts that economic globalization and the domination of large multinational firms is inevitable and beneficial and that countries should be working on how to live with it. This in turn has helped spawn antiglobalization as a global movement.

The antiglobalization movement is concerned not only about *what decisions* have been made by the international economic institutions but *how* they are made. Their contention is that the institutions are undemocratic and nontransparent, that they are dominated by the advanced industrial countries, in particular by the United States. The debate about "unilateralism" versus "multilateralism," raised so often in the economic globalization debates, has recently become central to other global discussions—the Kyoto accord on global warming, the International Criminal Court, and, most recently, the war in Iraq.

In economics as well as in politics, there is an intertwining of the global and the local. For journalists this means that reporters everywhere cover global issues and that local economic stories have become global ones. This has placed a huge burden on reporters all over the world. It is not enough to know about your local company anymore. You also need to know about global trends in the sector in which your local company operates. You cannot write about labor in Jakarta or Hanoi without knowing about the Nike boycotts in the United States and Europe. Writing effectively about a local privatization or banking crisis means having to know about what has happened in other countries. The experiences in other countries inform much of the debate.

Unfortunately, reporters around the world are covering these often complex topics with very little background information, either about the experiences in other countries or the alternative interpretations that have been given to them. We have met with reporters around the world and found two things: they are mostly (with some notable exceptions) ill prepared to write about the complex economic issues facing their countries, and they lack information about what has happened in other countries. In Ecuador we met reporters who needed to know about privatization because Ecuador was thinking of privatizing electricity and they had never covered a privatization before. A few months later we went to Bulgaria and found that reporters there were also supposed to be covering electricity privatization. They did not know much about the subject, and they had no idea that it had been discussed in Ecuador. In Turkey, a country beset by financial crises, reporters asked us about the debt crises in Argentina and Brazil.

In Brazil reporters we met wanted to know how Korea had done so well and what lessons they could draw on as they wrote about the Brazilian economy. When we were in Bulgaria, the government had just restructured its foreign debt, and reporters were unsure of the consequences—they knew that Russia had restructured its debt, just before its crisis of 1998, under the advice of the same people who had encouraged Bulgaria to restructure. They naturally worried about whether there would be similar consequences. In Moldova, one of the poorest of the former Soviet Union republics, which had seen its income decline 75 percent since it began its move to a market economy, most of the meager public funds were spent on servicing the international debt. It faced imminent default or debt restructuring. Reporters wanted to know how these things happen and what the consequences would be: Would it lead to an even further decline, or, as in Russia and Argentina, would it signal the beginning of a turnaround?

Inevitably, this lack of knowledge hurts coverage. Business and economics reporters are especially vulnerable because the subjects they write about are so technical and require so much knowledge. Naturally, reporters will turn to the nearest available sources and, regrettably, they sometimes report what they learn uncritically, not realizing the biased perspectives. When journalists are on deadline and writing about topics that are unfamiliar to them, it is all too easy to take the nearest press release and repeat it verbatim. The problem is that those who devote resources to public relations usually have a motive for doing so. They typically want to convince others to support the positions that they advocate. But too often reporters take press releases as "facts" rather than as "advocacy."

The international economic institutions, for instance, have well-honed and well-funded public relations departments. If they are urging a country to privatize its water supply, they naturally will explain why this will enable more investment and therefore greater access to clean water. They will typically not mention the enormous opposition to water privatization in other countries, and if the issue gets raised in a press conference, they will either quickly dismiss such opposition or explain why it was misguided. They are unlikely to emphasize the problems that have occurred elsewhere, including increasing prices, which make clean water unavailable to some people that previously had access. They are also apt to leave out the one-sided renegotiations, wherein if the foreign concessionaire bids in a way that leads to low profits, it insists on new terms—often with pressure brought to bear by its foreign government—but if the foreign concessionaire has high profits, pressure from the local government to renegotiate is strongly resisted. If there are discussions of an electric-power agreement, the emphasis will be on the increased availability of electricity not on the price of the power or on the large risks that the government may assume. The companies that obtain concessions or make power agreements also have well-functioning and well-financed public relations departments that attempt to shape public opinion.

These problems were illustrated in the debate about capital market liberalization. The IMF tried to change its charter to enable it to push capital market liberalization on countries around the world at its Hong Kong meeting in September 1997 (though it had long been using its economic power to "encourage" recipients of its money to do so). It put forward arguments that capital market liberalization would enhance growth and stability, and the IMF was supported in this by Western financial firms that stood to gain from the increased access that such liberalization would provide for them in the developing world. Many of the reports and editorials in leading business organs in the West, with their conservative bias and close ties to the business and financial communities, supported this view. In short, economic and business reporters in the developing world were often left with the impression that there was a broad global consensus on the desirability of capital market liberalization; only "backward" politicians in the developing world opposed it, typically because they simply did not understand market economics. Many well-intentioned reporters in developing countries, wanting to do what they could to advance the development of their countries, adopted strong "reform" positions. The IMF and the World Bank were at the vanguard of the reform movement, and if they advocated capital market liberalization, if they put such stress on it, it *must* be a central to successful reform, or so these reporters thought. They were simply unaware of the studies inside the research department of the World Bank of the hundred or so crises of the last thirty years—studies that showed that one of the most important factors contributing to these crises was premature, excessive, and excessively rapid financial and capital market liberalization. They were unaware, too, of the academic studies which suggested that capital market liberalization did not enhance economic growth. The academics who did these studies had other academics as their audience; they certainly did not have the large public relations departments to disseminate their findings. It would be another five years before the IMF would release a study confirming that capital market liberalization did not enhance stability or growth and for *The Economist* magazine to recant its position. If reporters had been well informed, they would have been able to present the different sides of the debate far earlier; it is even possible that policies would, as a result, have been changed and that some of the countries that experienced crises, with the deep recessions and depressions that typically followed, would have been spared the misery that ensued.

In some cases, nongovernmental organizations may attempt to provide counter-information. But they are typically nowhere near as well-financed as the private companies and global economic boards, and sometimes in their zeal, accuracy is lost. If the views of the NGOs are presented, reporters are seldom in a position to do more than simply report; they can provide little assistance in understanding the sources of such marked differences in opinion.

While the biased and advocative nature of major sources of information available to reporters in developing countries presents a major problem, it is not the only problem for these reporters; national bias is another. U.S. reporters often write patronizingly about the foreign economies and the need for reform and restructuring in the labor market. U.S. coverage of Enron's activities in India mostly took the view that India was lucky to have Enron investing there; most U.S. reporters did not question why prices at the Dabhol power plant in the Indian state of Maharashtra were so high or why the Indian government should have to bear the risk in the deal. As a result, they did not see the real story: that protests against the plant would grow and that the deal would fall apart.

National bias in the more advanced industrial countries has often presented a problem for those in the less developed countries. Stories published elsewhere are major sources of information for reporters. The greater resources of media in more developed countries enables them to provide seemingly more comprehensive and in-depth coverage, and many reporters in developing countries are accordingly tempted simply to repeat these perspectives. In fact, in many cases reporters from developed countries get their information from the same sources available to those in the developing world, for example, the international economic institutions and major financial institutions.

Coverage of the Argentinean crisis is illustrative. According to the IMF and the Western bankers who were worried about what a devaluation of the Argentinean peso or a default on Argentinean bonds would do to them, the explanation of the crisis was simple: a corrupt and profligate government. Few stories noted that the IMF had brought President Carlos Menem of Argentina to its annual meeting in Washington in 1999, displaying him as an example of the kind of leader to be emulated. Few noted that even if there were no governmental corruption, it was unlikely that the country's economy could have withstood an exchange rate that started so badly out of line and became increasingly so with the appreciation of the dollar, to which it was tied, and the depreciation of the currency of its neighbor, Brazil. The press also missed the fact that Argentina's deficit was not out of line. Even at the culmination of the crisis, Argentina's deficit was 3 percent of its GDP, which is smaller than the 5 percent deficit seen in the United States in its last recession. And the so-called full-employment or structural deficit—what the deficit would have been had the country's workforce been fully employed and what most economists argue should be used in assessing a country's budgetary performance—was almost surely zero. Argentina had in fact succeeded in reducing its expenditures net of interest payments by 10 percent in two years, a truly impressive record, and the deficit it did have was caused by the privatization of social security, urged upon it by the IMF. Had Argentina not privatized its social security program, its deficit would have been zero, and it would have had a large structural or full-employment surplus. The press missed these factors and failed in many cases to note that the excessive fiscal stringency in Argentina was in fact a major part of the country's poor economic performance. More balanced coverage by the media would have put less blame for the country's problems on a "corrupt and profligate" government and more blame on the IMF and might have led to different policies being pursued by the country and advocated by outsiders.

The Internet has provided new opportunities for *all* reporters, in both developed and developing countries, to be more aware of the dangers of "national bias." Those with access to the Internet can see how the same story is being reported in different countries. They can attempt to identify the reasons for the difference in perspectives, and, even if they cannot fully sort out which view "right," they can at least make their readers aware of these differing perspectives.

It is, of course, neither surprising nor alarming that most sources of information and most reporting is biased, incomplete, or distorted. One should expect that those who spend money to provide information often have an "agenda." The responsibilities of the reporter are to try to understand the biases, to detect the agendas, to let readers be aware of the possible distortions, and to help readers unravel the conflicting interpretations.

To do this, reporters need to understand the *incentives* for those providing information and to recognize that good advocacy entails persuasion, which in turn entails trying to understand what a reporter "wants" to hear. When the source of information is someone in the political process, a natural question is: Which faction of the government are they in? Are they trying to send a message to someone? In the Cold War, Western reporters took a highly critical approach to the "news" provided by both official and unofficial sources in the communist countries. But they often failed to note that, on a more limited scale, such problems occur in all democracies. Today, most reporters are aware of the desire of well-oiled political machines to provide "spin" on every potential news story. The government is always ready to supply a positive interpretation of even adverse economic news. When jobs are falling, they may emphasize that the rate of decrease in jobs is slowing, indicating that a turnaround is right around the corner. There are always special circumstances that can be identified for job loss—a snow storm, a power outage, a strike—and these *may* be relevant. But reporters need to ask the hard questions: Have they, for instance, calculated precisely how much of the job loss is due to these events? Are there other "special circumstances" that may imply that the job-loss number is underestimating the seriousness of the situation?

Increasingly, governments have resorted to "leaking" good news stories to reporters that are likely to provide the favorable spin they want. Those who must rely on others for their primary sources of information need to be aware of the distortions that result. These "connected" reporters know that their continued access to "breaking" news requires that their stories be favorable to those providing the inside information, or at least as favorable as the facts allow. There is a symbiotic relationship between these reporters and the government officials that provide them the inside information. The symbiotic relationship between the press and sources of information extends to the private sector as well as the public. Reporters covering markets are especially vulnerable, not only because they provide the information that reporters require but also because it is the experts and market traders who train the reporters, as they are the ones know the materials. Their agendas and biases get naturally imbued into the reporter.

Approaching the information provided by news sources with strong skepticism creates its own bias: a press that is highly, perhaps overly, doubting. It may believe that information filtered through conflicts of interest or incentives suffers from distortion when in fact none exists. Doing so often plays well to readers who often want to question "authority," to believe in the pervasiveness of corruption. Good reporting needs to be as aware of these biases in the media, of the incentives to overplay certain types of stories, as it is of the biases in those providing information to it.

Another problem in much of the economic and business reporting in developing countries is a hectoring and moralistic tone that undermines the dispassionate, analytic voice that is the hallmark of good reporting. The moralistic tone is especially prevalent when discussing corruption and cronyism. Reporters see one of their responsibilities as uncovering wrongdoing, and it is natural that they take aim at corruption and cronyism. Yes, developing countries have a lot of corruption, and research at the World Bank and elsewhere has shown that such corruption can have a strong adverse effect on developing country's growth prospects. But corruption is often blamed for all of a country's ills, as the example cited earlier of Argentina illustrates. As a too facile explanation, one which readers can easily understand, it diverts attention from harder issues.

Similarly, the 1997 East Asian crisis was often blamed on cronyism by reporters, who picked up their cues from the IMF and U.S. Treasury Department. But the IMF and the U.S. Treasury had a strong incentive for picking this victim: to shift blame away from what many economists view as the true culprit—capital market liberalization, which had been pushed by both organizations. Reporters again failed to ask the hard questions: To what extent was cronyism and corruption to blame? Would there

THE IMPORTANCE OF CRITICAL THINKING

likely have been a crisis even if there were no cronyism or corruption? If cronyism and corruption were as rampant as claimed and had such a distorting effect on the economy, how was it that these countries had had the most rapid growth of any region of the world over the previous three decades? Why was it that the crisis occurred just as corruption was being reduced in many of the countries in East Asia? Why was it that countries that were far more corrupt (by any of the standard measures) did not have crises? Why was it that only a few years earlier, the Scandinavian countries, Norway, Sweden, and Finland, viewed as the nations the least susceptible to corruption, all had had crises? Many economists do not believe that corruption was a major cause of the 1997 crisis in Asia. Some economists feel that corruption is essentially a tax and that its economic impact is insubstantial.

Worse, this moralistic tone does little to contribute to an understanding of the underlying forces behind corruption, the multiplicity of forms in which it can be displayed, and to the design of policies and programs to root out corruption. For instance, for every bribe, there is a briber and a bribed. It is often companies from richer countries who pay the big bribes. BP's attempt to reduce corruption by publishing what it paid to the Angolan government was unmatched by other oil producers. The governments of the advanced industrial countries have it within their powers to force such transparency by simply not allowing tax deductibility for any payments that are not so disclosed.

When readers perceive a double standard, this moralistic tone may undermine the credibility of the media. During the East Asian crisis, many in the media talked about the need for Asian countries to adopt American accounting practices and American-style corporate governance. The Enron, Arthur Anderson, and Wall Street scandals make clear that American accounting practices and corporate governance were not all that they seemed. The problems should have been apparent—the Financial Accounting Standards Board had complained about the treatment of executive options years before. But most in the media failed to note this—until the scandals broke out. The "moralistic" approach led the media to "scold" the developing countries, rather than delving more deeply into what good corporate governance or good accounting entailed. Had they done that, they would have recognized the failings in America.

There are many other instances of seeming double standards. Developing countries are:

- Told that they need to dismantle their subsidies or tariffs, but subsidies or trade protection in America or Europe is defended as necessary to safeguard jobs. But problems of unemployment are even worse in most developing countries than they are in developed countries.

- Urged to privatize entities and institutions that the West will not privatize, such as pensions.

- Advised to lift capital market controls and open their markets even though the West, with its much stronger markets, had them until the 1970s.

- Pushed to sign trade agreements even though they may lose jobs or wind up opening markets to foreign companies while not getting equal benefits.

Particularly problematic is reporting where moralistic tones are used to advance hidden agendas—often of those who "control" the main sources of information. Such messages are often expressed with a standard set of clichés (which, in any case, good reporting attempts to avoid.) Reporters talk about "market discipline" or the importance of "reform" to set forth a set of measures by which the success of a government is to be measured. They often cover debates about government "commitment" to reform and suggest that those who oppose the government measures are either corrupt and beholden to special interest groups or just playing politics. But reporters often do not ask the hard questions: To what extent are these "reform measures" simply symbolic? To what extent will they make a *big* difference? Most important, to what extent are the so-called reform measures consonant with ideology or special interests themselves? How would such reform measures fare, say, in the United States?

Reporters often talk about how, if the reform measures fail, markets will be "disappointed" and "punish" the country through higher interest rates. The problem is that there is often a self-fulfilling nature to such reporting: if everyone believes that failing to enact reform measures will lead to higher interest rates, it will happen—regardless of the economic significance of those measures. Reporters often do not give full play to the legitimate arguments against the "reforms."

Consider, for instance, some of the "reforms" by which Mexico's new government in 2000 was to be judged. The fiscal reforms included extending the Value Added Tax to medicines and lowering income tax rates. The U.S. has consistently rejected the VAT, because it is a regressive tax (that is, it imposes a higher burden on the poor than on the rich). Putting more weight on the VAT and less on income tax thus reduces the progressiveness of the tax system, making it less fair. There is a large literature dealing with the desirability of taxing necessities like food and medicines at lower rates than luxuries; there is by no means a consensus that moving toward a uniform tax system is a desirable reform. Such so-called reforms would—and should—have a hard time politically in any democracy. Reforms that reduce the progressiveness of taxes in America are often criticized. Yet most reporters simply assumed that the fiscal reform was desirable because it was labeled "reform." Few reporters asked: Are there tax reforms that could increase the progressiveness of the tax system? Why did the government not focus its efforts on increasing enforcement (collection) or on taxing monopoly or oligopoly profits? When the fiscal reform failed, the government was criticized for its lack of political astuteness in

THE IMPORTANCE OF CRITICAL THINKING

pushing the reform through Congress; it was not criticized for having designed the wrong reform package.

Another reform entailed what was viewed as a move toward the privatization of electricity. The developing world is replete with examples of "failed" attempts at privatization that have not led to increases in efficiency, or worse have led to increases in prices. Even in the United States, deregulation has not worked out as its proponents had hoped, at least in California. Given the failures of privatization in other sectors of Mexico (banking, roads), and given the problems elsewhere, the lack of enthusiasm toward privatization should hardly have been a surprise. Yet, again, the failure of the reform was blamed on a lack of political skills in pushing the policy. Reporters sometimes emphasized the consequences of the failure — the lack of needed investment that might result — without noting the cause of this lack: IMF accounting rules that treat the borrowings of state corporations for investment as if they were borrowings by the government for ordinary consumption (which differs from the treatment of European state-owned enterprises.) And the media did not explore other ways by which the public interest could have been maintained while the state seeks better economic treatment, for example, the establishment of a state corporation in which the state itself was a minority shareholder but in which other public bodies (NGOs, independent state authorities) held the swing votes, so that private interests, domestic or foreign, remained in the minority.

Thinking critically about these reforms — or economic policy more generally — means asking why? Who will benefit? Who will lose? What is really going on? What are the parties involved in any issue really thinking or planning? To what extent are the arguments disingenuous? Are they a "cover-up" for another agenda? One also needs to push the enquiry back further: Where are they getting their information? Who is lobbying for the "reform"? Who are they talking to and what agendas do those people have?

THE IMPORTANCE OF THE MEDIA

We want to conclude with a few words on the central importance of the media — of good reporting — for developing countries.[1] One of the ways in which developed countries are different from developing countries is the "information density": In developed countries there are a large number of channels through which information flows between government and the citizens, between markets and consumers, between individuals in one part of the country and those in another. With so many channels underdeveloped or blocked in developing countries, it is all the more important that those channels work well; that they disseminate information that is accurate and unbiased. The absence of think tanks puts additional burdens on reporters to interpret the information. Thus, reporters need to get the information that will help them become more informed *and* think critically about this information.

There are by now a large number of studies that show the critical importance of the media in both corporate and public governance. Nobel laureate in economics Amartya Sen's work shows, for instance, that countries with a free press are less likely to have famines; other work shows that a free press helps to limit corruption and ensure individual rights are not abused. The press played a central role in exposing the corporate scandals in the United States and continuing pressures for reform. Interestingly, there is some evidence that a foreign press may be particularly effective, less likely to suffer from what we referred to earlier as "national bias" and less beholden to powers within the country that would resist exposure. The *Financial Times*, for instance, was particularly active in exposing the problems in the New York Stock Exchange; even though the *Wall Street Journal* first noted the excessive salary of the board's CEO, it did little to push the story.

Development is a process of transformation, and such change is best effected through the creation of a national dialogue on the need for change and a consensus behind what changes are required. Countries are too large for everyone to sit together in such a dialogue; it is largely through the media that such a national dialogue occurs. The media help frame the issues and provide the information that forms the basis of such a dialogue. How they characterize a reform may doom even a good reform to a premature death or may enable the debate over a "bad" reform to continue. As participants in the debate increasingly realize the power of the press to help shape the debate, pressures will inevitably be brought to bear; reporters will be increasingly confronted with information and arguments by those wishing to shape the debate in particular ways.

It is our hope that the discussions of the following chapters will provide reporters with some of the background information, some of the tools, that will enable them to interpret the events and policy debates in their countries, both for themselves and for their readers, who are so dependent on them. And we hope that out of this will emerge policies that promise stronger, more democratic, sustainable, and equitable growth for the future.

NOTES

1. For a broader discussion of the issues raised here, see Alisa Clapp-Itnyre, Simeon Djankou, and Roumeen Islam, eds., *Right to Tell: The Role of Mass Media in Economic Development* (Washington, D.C.: World Bank, 2002).

CHAPTER TWO

CAPITAL MARKETS

CATHERINE MCKINLEY

C APITAL MARKETS are markets in which equity (shares) and debt (bonds) are traded. If they exist at all in less developed countries, they are typically small and do not have much effect on the country's broader economy. Most financing in those countries is conducted, instead, through bank financing rather than through capital markets. Over the past decade or so, an "emerging markets" capital market has developed. Based primarily in New York and London, this market has permitted developing countries' governments ("sovereigns") and the occasional company to borrow funds in the international markets.

In developing countries in general, companies prefer to raise. money from banks rather than through the sale of shares. Why? A share offering forces the company to offer a higher degree of transparency than would otherwise be necessary. Having their shares traded by the public, in addition, makes managers accountable to shareholders, something not all managers want. On the demand side, investors in developing countries often eschew the market due to the weak regulatory framework and because of the market's typically thin liquidity. Meanwhile, corporate bond issues are rare if a company has not already sold shares.

When stock markets open in less-developed countries, they usually have a small number of shares listed on the exchange, limited hours, and often rules about how much share prices can rise or fall on a given day. Disclosure is usually a problem, as companies—more often than not family owned—are not accustomed to disclosing details of their finances. Because the markets are so illiquid they, tend to be volatile. Moreover, the thinness of the markets as a whole means that the multitude of institutions, like analysts, that provide information to potential investors are scarce, reinforcing a vicious cycle associated with information asymmetry.

There are a number of other reasons why developing countries do not have stock markets (as in Laos, Somalia, or Sudan) or have ones that are small compared to the size of the economy (Vietnam, Ecuador). Low economic growth, high inflation, and low savings rates all discourage the creation of strong markets. Also, weak regulations on investment, inadequate bankruptcy laws, and a lack of protection for investors all work against the development of robust capital markets in developing and transitional countries.

A key constraint on growth and prosperity in developing countries is the absence of financing for productive enterprises. A deepening of stock markets, as such, is broadly seen as helping overall economic growth. This is because stock markets:

- Give companies an avenue outside the banking system through which to raise investment capital. In addition, when capital markets are working well, capital market financing is both cheaper and longer-term than bank lending;

- Widen the investment base for savers thus bringing private savings into the public arena;

- Increase the efficiency with which private savings can be efficiently used;

- Raise corporate accountability;

- Facilitate foreign capital inflows.

To take advantage of these benefits, some less-developed countries are now working on plans to launch or deepen their stock markets. Cambodia is one. The World Bank and International Monetary Fund generally view capital markets as important and urge countries to set them up. Foreign financial firms also benefit from the creation of new markets and get involved in the process; Japanese banks provided assistance to Vietnam when it set up its stock market, which opened in Saigon in July 2000.

However, while most economists agree that stock markets help countries develop, many would argue that they are not a first priority. In most developed countries, after all, capital markets emerged decades (if not centuries) after the development of a mature banking sector. Even today in the United States and the United Kingdom, a relatively small fraction of new funds for investment are raised through the stock market. So in terms of developing new business, having a strong banking system is far more important. But while having a robust capital market may not do much to help a country grow, having a poorly regulated one prone to corruption and abuse can certainly cause major problems—the pyramid schemes found in eastern Europe in the mid-1990s are a testament to this fact.

A major prerequisite for an effective stock market is a well-functioning legal and regulatory framework. This is never an easy feat. In particular, creating a stock market before there are effective shareholder protections is an invitation to disaster down the line: if abuses occur, as they have so often, there will be a backlash against equities markets that may be long lasting. Even when the necessary reforms are made, larger and more successful firms, those with good corporate governance with a willingness to meet the standards of more advanced countries, tend to want to be listed on major international exchanges. This means that local exchanges tend to be dominated by smaller firms. Companies that want to be listed in the United States can do so by issuing American Depository Receipts (ADRs), which are listed on the New York Stock Exchange and on the NASDAQ.

BOND MARKETS

Like stocks, bonds help companies and governments raise capital. Unlike stocks, however, bonds (1) offer a fixed and well-defined income stream for investors (that is, a "coupon") and (2) are repaid back to the investor at the end of a prespecified period (that is, "maturity"). Instead of the unlimited profitability that a stock offers, a bond offers its owner seniority: if the company goes bankrupt, bondholders have first access to available assets, and stockholders receive the residual. Bonds are also known as "fixed income" assets.

Bonds trade in fixed income markets. Such markets tend to develop domestically before borrowers attempt to raise money overseas. There are good reasons. For one thing, international bonds are issued in hard currencies (for example, in dollars or euros) rather than in local currencies. Also, bonds issued in international markets are governed by international contract law rather than by the law of the issuing country. Governments in less-developed countries may shy away from the risks associated with an international debt sale for as long as possible. Instead, they tend to first rely on concessional lending from donors and multilateral agencies (such as the World Bank, the IMF, or regional development banks) and bilateral donors. However, this money is sometimes tied to promises of economic reform and can be limited in its scope. Countries then tend to try to issue short-term treasury bills in local currencies. Access to international capital markets tends to occur at a later stage of development.

EQUITY MARKET COVERAGE

Stocks, or equity, represent ownership in a company. Theoretically, it is possible to buy and sell stocks that are not listed on a stock exchange (see "over the counter trading," below). However, many investors find it easier to trade through an exchange because of the high level of corporate transparency that listed companies must offer, the strict regulations that usually accompany exchange-based trading, and the higher liquidity found on exchanges. Such trading, in addition, offers investors a way to deal with cumbersome and expensive issues related to settlement, delivery, and payment systems. When a less-developed country sets up a stock exchange, it may differ from exchanges in more developed countries in the following ways:

- *Government influence.* Governments in many less-developed countries tend to micromanage their economy, and this can reflect on their stock market as well. How independent is a country's exchange and the regulatory body that governs it? Does the government try to influence trade? If so, how?

- *Trade regulation and policing.* Some emerging market regulators impose few rules on equity trading when a market first opens in order to attract investors. China did this in the early 1990s and saw phenomenal growth in its two stock markets. However, many investors were burned during the inevitable crash that followed each bull rush, and China is now trying to tighten its regulatory environment. In the long run, trading migrates to markets that are better regulated. This is perhaps why other countries, like Vietnam, Egypt, and, to a lesser extent, countries in central Europe, have taken the opposite tack, imposing strict rules from the outset. Markets in these countries will probably take longer to develop but, the argument goes, may fare better in the long run. So it's important to look at the regulatory framework in the country a reporter covers. What is relevant are not only the rules governing trading itself but those having to do with corporate governance, the protection of minority shareholders, and voting rights. For instance, the New York Stock Exchange has regulations, which greatly restrict nonvoting equity shares. What impact will that framework have on investor sentiment and on companies' willingness and ability to list? Whatever the rules appear to be, many less-developed countries lack the legal and administrative infrastructure to enforce them. Reporters should watch out for broken rules: Who is doing the breaking, listed companies or investors? Do regulators try to rectify the situation? How effective is this?

- *Limits on trade.* Some less-developed markets will impose limits on various aspects of trade. These can include: the degree to which a stock price can rise or fall each day; the number of shares an investor can buy in a single trade or own in a single listed company; the degree to which a foreign investor can access the market; and so on. These rules serve a variety of purposes, for example, limiting stock market volatility, preventing someone from cornering the market, and making sure that there is a "level playing field."

- *Government ownership in listed stocks.* Reporters should ask how large a percentage, if any, a government retains in a listed company. In China, the government holds a 51 percent majority in most listed companies (which are usually partially privatized state-owned companies) and thus retains majority-voting rights. But even if the government retains majority control, it may not exercise those rights, leaving the management to the company, or it may intervene only through the appointment of members of the board. Reporters need to look at the experience of their own governments and the impact of governmental "control." Each time another company lists its stock, it will provide a slew of new stories: What type of company is it? How is it preparing for its debut? Will it sell shares through a private placement or will it offer an initial public offering (IPO) to the public? How much interest is its debut creating in the investment community? IPOs often are issued at a substantial discount, giving those who are lucky enough to get an allocation a bonanza but effectively depriving the old shareholders of money that should be theirs. What is the magnitude of the IPO discount? Who gets the bonus?

■ *Investment Banks.* In more-developed countries, investment banks play an important role in the issuing of stocks (and bonds and other securities). Generally speaking, they help "make markets." That is, they bring together suppliers of stock (firms that needed capital) and suppliers of funds (potential investors). They also structure, market, and distribute IPOs. Even in countries with active exchanges, investment banks "make markets" in secondary trading by aggregating small transactions before bringing them to the exchange. Investment banks also play an important role in providing information to the issuer of the stock about how and when to issue the securities, and in "placing" the securities, that is, finding buyers. Many believe that investment banks help make the market by providing certification services; that is, investors are more willing to buy shares issued by a reputable investment firm that has advised a company on a "fair" price at which to issue the shares. However, the lack of informed and reputable investment banks in many developing countries may be an impediment to the workings of an effective securities market.

A less-developed stock market may face problems that developed markets generally avoid. Issues to watch for include:

■ *Technical problems*, such as a failure to process orders, loss of information because of a computer failure, lack of communication between the trading floor and brokerage offices, and so on. "Technical glitches" in stock market registration may be used to inhibit takeovers.

■ *Insider trading*, through which company executives, underwriters (see "Investment bank" in the glossary), and others with intimate knowledge of a company's operations use that knowledge to trade shares. This gives them an unfair advantage over the public.

■ *Lack of corporate disclosure* as companies fail to provide the information demanded of them in a timely manner or at all. This may be deliberate or may be the result of a lack of understanding of the rules. It may also be due to weakness in the country's accounting system. Are reforms underway?

■ *High volatility* typically occurs in young markets that lack liquidity and have a limited number of investors. In such an illiquid market, one or two trades by such concentrated investors can cause the overall market to rise or fall significantly and cause a snowball effect as other investors follow, creating an even stronger gain or decline.

■ *Bubbles* grow when investors do not understand the basic value of the companies in which they are investing. If prices begin to rise (sometimes because of a large single trade) some investors will anticipate further gains and buy stock in order to take advantage of those gains. Others will follow until the stocks have become overvalued or, put differently, until the share's market price materially deviates from its fundamental value (see "Price-Earnings Ratio" in the glossary). This creates a bubble. When investors realize how overvalued the market has become, they start to sell, taking profits while they can. Again, others will follow and the bubble will burst. This happened in the Japanese stock market in the late 1980s and early 1990s and, more recently, in the United States.

■ *Investment and mutual funds,* which buy shares in firms, are often absent in new, smaller, stock markets because there are too few stocks to make it worth their while to invest or because no regulation exists to allow them access. They allow greater diversification on the part of investors. In some larger countries, such as Russia, they developed quite rapidly. Some of the investment funds in Eastern Europe have been a source of major problems, as the managers of those funds used their power to funnel money out of the companies over which they had managed to get effective control and divert these assets for their own benefit.

BOND (DEBT) MARKET COVERAGE

The sale of bonds allows governments and corporations to borrow money from the public and from institutional investors (for example, pension funds and insurance companies) rather than from a bank. Such borrowing enables greater diversification and liquidity, allowing, in turn, increased competition among borrowers. The creation of a government bond market with bonds of different maturities may serve one other purpose: the information on the yields of different maturities helps the pricing of corporate debt of different maturity. Borrowers may choose to go to the debt markets because the amount of money they need to borrow is higher than any single bank is willing or able to lend or in order to spread the risk associated with their debt between a number of lenders.

(However, banks often address these problems by forming a lending consortium.) The issuer (debtor) will sell the bonds for a certain number of years and will pay interest to the buyer (creditor) for the duration of the bond's life. Interest can be paid annually or when the bond expires (matures). Interest rates are determined by the market, which will demand a higher rate of return from risky debtors (to compensate bondholders for the risk of default) than from relatively safe debtors. Some bonds, such as *zero coupon bonds*, do not pay interest but instead are sold at a discount to their face (par) value. The "return" is the difference between the sale price and the face value at which the creditor will redeem the bond on maturity.

Bonds can be issued by governments and companies and can be traded domestically or on an overseas market. Domestically traded bonds are usually denominated in the local currency and sold to domestic investors, both individual and institutional (although it may be possible for foreign investors operating in the country to buy the bonds). Bonds that are sold overseas are denominated in a major foreign currency, usually U.S. dollars, and are sold to banks, investment funds, and other institutional investors. They are not usually targeted at individual retail investors, though those sometimes form an important source of demand for bonds. Bonds, of course, carry with them the risk of default—more so for international bonds, since the issuing country must service the bond in a foreign currency and must ensure it has enough foreign exchange resources to cover that cost at the right time.

Sovereign bonds are sold by governments. Their price is usually quoted in terms of basis points above the price of U.S. Treasury bonds with the same maturity. A fifteen-year $750-million sovereign bond sold by the Philippines in January 2002 was priced at 437.5 basis points above Treasury bonds, for example. This practice attempts to quantify the riskiness of a country relative to a "riskless" asset, that is, the U.S. Treasury. The higher the quoted spread, the more the perceived risk of the creditor. Once on the secondary market, the higher the spread (that is, the higher the interest rate the country has to pay), the lower the price of the bond. For example, in a crisis situation in which investors eschew a bond, bond prices could drop to twenty cents on the dollar—a level typically associated with a extremely high spread levels.

When reporting a sovereign bond issue, there are several things to watch for:

- *Does the country have a sovereign rating?* Ratings, which will include a current rating and a future outlook, try to quantify in a standardized fashion the issuing country's credit worthiness. Ratings are based on "solvency" indicators (for example, debt-to-GDP and debt-to-exports ratios) as well as "liquidity" indicators (for example, level of international reserves, level of current account deficit). A change in ratings tends to be news because it will impact how the market views a bond

PYRAMID SCHEMES

TYLER MARONEY

A pyramid scheme is a fraudulent investment maneuver in which unscrupulous promoters intentionally mislead unsophisticated people by promising "guaranteed" high returns on their "investment." They are most often found in developing countries and flourish where there is corruption, a weak regulatory framework, little public understanding about how capital markets are supposed to work, and a lack of alternative investment vehicles. The most famous in recent years was in Albania in 1997 when a pyramid scheme there proved disastrous for the larger economy. They have been found in Europe and the United States, but since the fall of communism they have been a real problem in the former Soviet Union. Millions of victims in such countries as Bulgaria, Latvia, Slovakia, and Romania have watched their life savings, their mortgages—even money borrowed from loan sharks—disappear into byzantine pyramid schemes.

Pyramid schemes inevitably end in financial ruin due to their inherent insolvency: a pyramid scheme's liabilities always outweigh its assets. Only those who invest money at the early stages of a pyramid scheme stand to gain, and this is only because the promoters must create this initial "profit" to get the plan into action. Those profits do not come from interest earned on the initial investments, the appreciation of securities into which the creators invested the money, or any other kind of real revenue, but from taking the money from new investors and declaring it "profit" to the earlier investors. The entire system depends on the continuous flow of new deposits. When the scheme fails to attract newcomers, its only source of revenue disappears and it collapses.

HOW THEY WORK

In a typical pyramid scheme, a company—which may be disguised as a bank, a mutual fund, or some other kind of private investment business—lures investors with promises of high returns, either capital gains from claimed special situations or unnaturally high interest rates due to a special system the promoters have invented. To survive, the scheme, often called a "nonbanking institution," must maintain a steady stream of deposits from new investors who, unknowingly, take their place at the bottom row of the pyramid. Since such schemes are rarely supported by real assets and sell no actual products, payments to those at the peak, called interest or dividends, are contingent upon the recruitment of new investors.

Early investors often make money. The promoters use the new deposits to give the promised high returns to the first investors so that tales of exorbitant windfalls and the promise of even higher returns are advertised in local media outlets and spread through word of mouth. It is this return that attracts the new investors, making the ruse possible.

The scheme mushrooms until the interest and principal owed to the early investors exceeds the money that is paid in by new recruits. Eventually, the deceptive returns attract suspicion and the scheme finds itself unable to make any interest payments. In a move of desperation, even higher yields are promised, in some cases as high as 50 percent a month. When depositors try to make withdrawals, they discover how insolvent the scheme is, panic ensues, and it crumbles quickly.

In most cases, there is little that governments or judiciaries can do to prevent or alleviate the havoc wreaked by pyramid schemes. This is, in part, because the schemes often operate outside the law or exploit existing legal loopholes to flourish for a brief time before the authorities can enforce poorly written laws. In Eastern Europe, it is difficult to prove that such schemes are illegal and that they are intended to mislead, since the code-based system requires a higher standard of proof than a common-law system. Once pyramid schemes collapse, the founders often liquidate any assets, stash them in offshore accounts, and flee.

WHO HAS HAD THEM

Although pyramid schemes have afflicted everyone from housewives in Glasgow to Internet addicts in Minneapolis, most have been concentrated in Eastern Europe. In the former communist bloc, experiments in laissez-faire economics are still in their seminal stages. People there have only a vague understanding of what capitalism is. They believe all capitalists are wealthy, and they are under the illusion that the high promised return of a pyramid scheme is a part of the capitalist system to which they so desperately want to belong. After being mired for decades in strict state-controlled politics and economics, Eastern Europeans have little understanding of the risks that accompany the potential for prosperity that capitalism affords. It is the vulnerable, the poor, the greedy, and often the elderly who are most susceptible to the empty promises of these sophisticated, get-rich-quick swindles.

Probably the most famous single pyramid scheme was the MMM scandal. Run by Sergei Mavrodi, a notorious Russian entrepreneur, MMM ran a massive advertising campaign that lured money away from hungry investors with promises of unprecedented returns. At its peak in 1994, MMM was valued at roughly $1 billion. The MMM scheme was founded in the wake of the collapse of the Soviet Union when poor Russians were at their most vulnerable.

When the bubble burst, massive losses followed that sparked skepticism of capitalism itself.

In 1997, both the Albanian government and the entire financial structure caved in following the implosion of the myriad pyramid schemes. Roughly two-thirds of the population suffered massive losses, and hundreds of thousands were left penniless and debt-ridden. In the ensuing anarchy, entire battalions of military and police officers deserted; over a million guns and mortars were looted from army depots; foreigners fled the country; and the president, whose government had failed to intervene in time, was forced to resign. To add to the chaos, most government revenues were never collected because customs buildings and tax offices were looted and burned. After months of rioting and panic-induced heart attacks, more than 2,000 people were dead.

issued by that country and will effect its interest rate. (The major rating agencies are Moody's and Standard and Poor's)

■ *How much money does the issuing country hope to raise and how much demand is there for new debt?* Countries usually announce their "financing programs" along with the budget document. A ministry of finance will usually announce an "envelope" of borrowing but will keep the precise timing and terms of bond issuance vague so as to better "time" market conditions. If there is high demand for bonds from a country, then the government may be able to borrow a lot of money relatively cheaply. Reporters should try to assess available liquidity by talking to investment funds. They should keep in mind that some funds tend to specialize in certain countries' debt and talk to these, as other investors tend to follow their lead. Investment banks also publish *flow of funds reports* that discuss major investment trends; these can create interesting stories. It is also worth finding out how much comparable debt is already on the international market, as this will impact investor appetite for new debt.

■ *For how long will the country borrow?* A bond's maturity can affect its interest rate. Usually, but not always, creditors will demand a higher rate of return for a longer loan because of the increased risk it carries. Occasionally, a country's curve gets inverted (that is, rates on short-term debt exceeds rates on long-term debt: this phenomenon tends to reflect intensive market concerns that a default is imminent.

Other concepts related to bonds include:

■ *Brady bonds* are named after former U.S. Treasury Secretary Nicholas Brady. Their creation in the late 1980s, in exchange for previously restructured commercial bank loans from the 1970s, introduced a renewed access to capital markets by emerging economies—after more than a decade of absence. A Brady bond's principal, and typically one-coupon payment, is backed by zero-coupon U.S. Treasury bonds. Virtually all Latin American countries have issued Brady bonds (the two main exceptions are Chile and Colombia). Elsewhere, Bulgaria, Nigeria, and the Ivory Coast have also issued such bonds.

- *London and Paris Club debt.* London Club debt is a forum through which *private sector foreign creditors* can reschedule or restructure overdue debt that is owed by foreign governments. It is an informal group of banks and private sector creditors that meet to restructure the private sector debt owed by a country. The Paris Club is a group of wealthy governments that meet to reschedule *official debt* owed to developing countries. Both forums exist to facilitate eventual payment by countries that are not able to repay outstanding debt on time. Paris Club reschedulings are always formally linked to the country having an IMF agreement in place.

- *Regional and Municipal bonds* are issued by different provinces or municipalities. These are less common in developing or transitional countries, and one typically finds them in countries whose fiscal structure is highly decentralized and in which regional governments run into deficits and need to raise capital internationally. Notable examples include Russia (the cities of Moscow and St. Petersburg) and Argentina.

- *Internationally traded corporate bonds* are issued by companies abroad. Such issuance typically occurs either because domestic capital markets are too small to facilitate a big enough bond issue or because rates abroad are more favorable than at home. Internationally traded corporate bonds are rare in less-developed countries because foreign investors require a degree of corporate transparency that few can offer. There are some exceptions to this rule, mainly associated with developing countries that are at a more advanced stage of development. The list includes Korea and Mexico and, to a lesser extent, Thailand and Brazil. Also, a company typically (but not always) must wait until its government has sold at least one sovereign eurobond before it can raise money overseas. This is because potential investors need a government benchmark against which they can price the risk of a particular company. Traders almost always price corporate bonds in comparison to a similar-maturity sovereign bond. You will often hear them speak of "such-and-such company" trading "through" (that is, with a lower interest rate) or "wide" (with a higher interest rate) to a sovereign. Vietnam is currently preparing a sovereign bond issue that bankers say will set a benchmark from which its companies can borrow overseas.

As your market develops you should watch for stories in the following areas:

■ *Changes to the regulatory and accounting systems.* Will the changes strengthen or weaken the system? Will they benefit investors, listed companies, or both?

■ *Price manipulation* either by insider traders or by large investors with a big enough stake to influence the entire market.

■ *Are local companies listing overseas?* High-quality companies in less-developed countries may list their shares overseas using American depository receipts or global depository receipts. Why have they chosen to do so?

■ *The role of foreign investors.* This may change (probably increasing) over time as investment rules are relaxed or as the market grows and becomes more attractive to foreign capital. The large-scale arrival of foreign investors can help stabilize trade because it brings a degree of professionalism few domestic investors have had time to develop. On the other hand, by virtue of their size foreign investors can often overwhelm domestic markets, exacerbating rallies and, when they exit, deepening slumps. Adverse conditions abroad may thus quickly impact domestic markets. Therefore, international contagion becomes an important determinant of an economy's health. How large a share do foreigners account for in a given stock market? Are their investments speculative "hot money" or long-term in nature? Some foreign investors have announced that they will only invest in countries with good corporate governance standards. Major institutional investors, like Calpers, have blacklisted certain countries. Reporters should determine if this has happened to their countries and, if so, why?

■ *Who is investing?* Is the market dominated by institutions or by retail investors? Is the profile of a typical investor changing? If so, why?

■ *How are donor funds being used?* Often, donors will give a country money to help set up its stock exchange. Reporters can check with the donor communities in their countries to find out how (and how effectively) those funds are being used.

■ **AMERICAN DEPOSITORY RECEIPTS.** ADRs are issued by a U.S. bank and represent shares of a foreign corporation held by the bank. They are traded on the NYSE as if they were stock in that corporation.

■ **ASSETS.** All items of value owned by a company. They can include current assets (cash or liquid assets that can be easily converted in to cash), long-term assets (buildings, equipment, and other assets that will depreciate over time), deferred assets (costs, such as insurance, that are paid in advance but will benefit the company in the future), and intangible assets (assets that cannot be valued exactly, such as a company's brand name, copyrights, and so on).

■ **BALANCE SHEET.** A financial statement that balances a company's assets against its liabilities.

■ **BARGAIN HUNTING.** The purchase of shares while they are trading at a distressed level on the assumption that their value will rise.

■ **BEAR/BULL MARKETS.** In a bear market stock prices fall, and investor sentiment is low. In a bull market the opposite is true.

■ **BID AND ASK PRICES.** The bid is the highest price a buyer is willing to pay for a security (stock or bond), while the ask price is the lowest a seller will accept. The two together make a quote.

■ **BLUE CHIP.** A high-quality listed company.

■ **BOOK VALUE.** The value of a company's shares calculated by deducting its liabilities from its assets (as reported in the company's financial statements) and then dividing the figure by the number of common outstanding shares the company has issued. See market value.

- **CAPITAL STOCK.** A company's total outstanding stock. See common stock; preferred stock.

- **COMMON STOCK.** The stock issued to the majority of shareholders. Shareholders have the right to vote on company business and to receive dividend payments. If a company does not make enough money to pay dividends to all shareholders, then common stock holders will be paid only after preferred stock holders.

- **CLOSED-ENDED INVESTMENT FUND.** A type of mutual fund in which investors put their money for a fixed period of time, allowing the fund's manger to then invest that money on their behalf. After the initial offering, the fund "closes" and no longer accepts investments. Investors are given shares in the fund in return for their contributions. Once the fixed time period is up the fund will be dissolved, and all money will be distributed among investors according to the number of shares they held in the fund. See open-ended investment fund.

- **CONVERTIBLE BOND.** A bond that can, subject to some conditions, be exchanged for common stock in the company that issued it. Some preferred stock is also convertible into common stock.

- **DEPRECIATION.** A physical asset's loss of value over time.

- **DIVIDEND.** The distribution of profits to shareholders. For common shareholders dividends will vary as the company's profits vary; for preferred shareholders it is fixed.

- **EARNINGS PER SHARE (EPS).** A measure of a company's earnings on a per-share basis. It is calculated by dividing total earnings by the number of shares outstanding. Companies usually use their most recent earnings figure to calculate EPS. Analysts will also use predicted future earnings in order to give investors an idea of a stock's future worth.

- **EARNINGS REPORT.** A statement of earnings and expenses over a given period of time. A listed company is required by its stock exchange to issue earnings reports on a regular basis, as the report will be used by investors to value stock.

- **EQUITY.** Ownership of a company through shares.

- **FACE VALUE.** The value of a stock or a bond as it appears on the security's face. A bond's face value will differ from its actual (i.e., market) value if the bond's yield varies from its coupon rate.

- **FISCAL YEAR.** A twelve-month period after which a listed company must consolidate and publish its accounts. The fiscal year does not have to be a calendar year.

- **GLOBAL DEPOSITORY RECEIPTS.** GDRs are similar to ADRs but are issued in currencies other than U.S. dollars and allow companies from developing countries to list on exchanges in countries other than the United States.

- **GRAY MARKET.** An unofficial market in which investors can buy shares in unlisted companies. Gray market trading is usually discouraged by market watchdogs because it is unregulated and therefore perceived to be more risky than on-market trading.

- **INDEX.** All stock markets will have at least one index, used to track the performance of a group of listed shares. The index takes into account price fluctuations of the shares and averages them out to give an aggregate change. While some indexes will include all listed shares on the particular exchange, most indexes focus only on a small group. For example, indexes will include representatives of a certain industry, all blue chip stocks, or a cross-sector representation of the whole market.

- **INITIAL PUBLIC OFFERING (IPO).** The first public sale of stock by a company. Its shares are sold to one or several investment banks who then resell them to the public. An IPO is the method through which a privately owned company transforms itself into a publicly owned one.

■ **INSTITUTIONAL INVESTORS.** Companies whose business is to manage funds for institutions such as pension funds, insurance companies, and banks. Institutional investors tend to specialize in stocks, bonds, or foreign exchange, though some invest in all asset classes.

■ **INVESTMENT BANK.** A bank that serves as a middleman between companies wishing to sell shares or bonds and the investing public. They are also known as underwriters.

■ **LIABILITIES.** All the claims on a company. These typically include loans that the company has raised, bonds it has issued, trade credits and short-term debt, and accounts payable. Accrued but unpaid wages, interest payments, and dividends also count as liabilities.

■ **LIQUIDITY.** A measure of how easily buyers and sellers can trade with each other in a market. It can also be used to describe the ease with which a company can access its assets. For example, cash is considered extremely liquid (i.e., it can be accessed on short notice), but real estate is illiquid.

■ **LONG TERM INVESTMENT.** An investment that aims to take advantage of a company's long-term core growth. See speculation.

■ **MARKET VALUE.** The value investors are willing to pay for a company. It is calculated by multiplying the most recent price of the company's stock by the number of shares outstanding. Market value often materially varies from face value.

■ **NET ASSET VALUE PER SHARE.** The total value (assets minus liabilities) of a company or investment fund divided by its total number of shares.

■ **OPEN-ENDED INVESTMENT FUND.** A type of mutual fund that continually sells new shares to investors as long as there is demand for those shares. Like closed-ended funds, the managers invest the money raised on behalf of the shareholders. Because there is no fixed date on which the fund will be liquidated, shareholders sell their shares in the fund whenever they want to cash out.

■ **OVER THE COUNTER (OTC) TRADING.** The transfer of shares between buyers and sellers outside a formal exchange. Such trading is usually mediated by investment banks who act as "market makers."

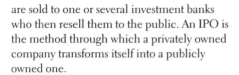

■ **PAR VALUE.** The face value of a security. For bonds, par value is 100.

■ **PREFERRED STOCK.** A stock that gives the owner a fixed dividend regardless of the company's performance and has priority over common stock in the payment of those dividends. Preferred stocks, however, do not give shareholders voting rights.

■ **PRICE-EARNINGS (PE) RATIO.** Offers investors a way to compare the relative merits of listed stocks. It is calculated by dividing a stock's price per share by its earnings. The higher the PE ratio, the more investors are willing to pay for a stake in a company and the greater their confidence that the company will perform well in the future. The PE is most useful when comparing companies in similar industries, as they are likely to face similar growth prospects, all other factors being equal. A company with a higher PE than others in its industry is either a much better company or is being overvalued by investors. Entire industries can also become overvalued, as was the case in 2000 and 2001 with technology companies.

■ **PRIMARY MARKET.** When companies or governments sell stock or bonds for the first time. See secondary market.

■ **PRIVATE PLACEMENT.** The sale of shares under a private agreement with the buyer (who can be an institutional investor or a group of company employees, for example). A company selling shares through a private placement does not invite public bids for its stock, which differentiates a private placement from an IPO.

- **PROFIT TAKING.** The sale of shares once they have risen in value above the price the investor originally paid for them. It is designed to realize immediate financial gain. Large-scale profit taking can pull a market's index lower if enough investors sell shares in enough companies.

- **PROSPECTUS.** A document issued by a company before a public offering that outlines the company's financial position, business plan, and other information of interest to potential investors. A prospectus tends to be a regulatory requirement for an issuing company.

- **RATE OF RETURN.** The amount of money investors receive from their investment in stocks and bonds. A rate of return measures the change in price adjusted for any dividend and/or interest received during a particular period.

- **RETAIL INVESTOR.** An individual investor, as opposed to an institutional investor such as a fund or bank.

- **RIGHTS ISSUE.** The offer made by a company for its existing shareholders to buy new shares at a predetermined price before those new shares are offered to the public. The number of shares that existing shareholders can buy is fixed according to the number of shares they already own.

- **SECONDARY MARKET.** The trade among investors after securities (i.e., stocks and bonds) has been sold by an issuer.

- **SECURITY.** Any financial product of value. It commonly refers to listed stocks or bonds.

- **SPECULATION** or **SHORT TERM INVESTMENT.** Trading in stocks and bonds to make money from short-term (hourly, daily, weekly)

changes in their price. Investors who are speculating may buy a share or bond not because of a belief in the fundamentals of the issuing company or government but rather because they may be trying to make a quick profit based on how they expect the market to move.

- **STOCK DIVIDEND.** A dividend paid in the form of stock rather than cash.

- **STOCK SPLIT.** The division of a company's outstanding shares to either increase or decrease the number of those shares. Usually, this will increase the number of total shares and is designed to facilitate future trade in those shares by raising their liquidity and making each share cheaper. It does not impact the relative ownership of existing investors as the number of shares owned by each investor will increase by the same ratio as the split.

- **TREASURIES.** Debt obligations of the U.S. government. These are viewed as the safest debt investments in the world. Treasury bills have maturities of one year or less; Treasury notes, between one and ten years; and Treasury bonds have maturities of over ten years.

- **VOLATILITY.** A measure of the fluctuation in a stock or bond's market price. Generally, the safer the investment the lower its volatility, as it will tend to attract long-term investors.

- **VOLUME.** A measure of the number of stocks and bonds traded on a market during a given period. It is usually calculated on a daily basis.

- **VOTING RIGHT.** The right held by owners of common stock to have a say (via the right to vote on major decisions) in the operations of the company they have invested in.

- **ZERO COUPON BOND.** A bond that does not offer interest payments. The bond, instead, is sold to an investor at a discount to its face value. At maturity, though, the investor receives the whole face value.

MAJOR STOCK EXCHANGES

1. New York Stock Exchange. http://www.nyse.com.

2. London Stock Exchange. http://www.londonstockexchange.com.

3. Tokyo Stock Exchange. http://www.tse.or.jp/english/index.shtml.

4. Livedgar, a Web site run by the U.S. Securities and Exchange Commission, publishes regulatory filings by publicly-traded companies in the United States (subscription required). http://login.gsionline.com.

5. Stockcharts.com carries tools for analyzing trends and data on stocks (subscription required). http://stockcharts.com.

SECURITIES REGULATION

6. The U.S. Securities and Exchange Commission is the federal regulatory body for the industry and has the authority to enforce rules and impose penalties on violators. http://www.sec.gov/index.htm.

7. NASD is a self-regulatory group overseeing its members in the Nasdaq Stock Market. http://www.nasd.com.

8. The Center for Corporate Law at the University of Cincinnati College of Law publishes a comprehensive list of securities acts in the United States. http://www.law.uc.edu/CCL/sldtoc.html.

9. The London-based International Accounting Standards Board is a privately funded organization with board members from nine countries. http://www.iasc.org.uk/cmt/0001.asp.

10. The Institutional Investor's Web site (subscription required) publishes highly rated annual rankings of capital markets analysts in the United States. http://www.institutionalinvestor.com.

11. The Milken Institute, a not-for-profit research organization based in Santa Monica, California, publishes studies on a range of issues from corporate finance to capital access to the high-yield markets. http://www.milkeninstitute.org/research.

12. The European Capital Markets Institute, based in Madrid, has a number of research papers on issues pertaining to the capital markets in Europe. http://www.ecmi.es/asp/tpv/productos.asp#ShortPapers.

CHAPTER THREE

FOREIGN EXCHANGE MARKETS AND FOREIGN EXCHANGE CRISES

SARA SILVER

BRIEF HISTORY

THE CONCEPT OF MONEY is probably as old as humanity itself, but it has not always existed in the forms with which we are most familiar. Barter was long used as a means of exchanging goods—and in some cases it still is—but over time people began using more uniform means for trade. From cattle to shells to precious metals like gold and silver, money has had many forms throughout the ages. The paper currency now used widely across the globe was but one of these countless forms of money and traces back hundreds of years to China. In the United States, paper currency made its first appearance in the colonies in the seventeenth century, setting the stage for the introduction of paper money issued by the U.S. Treasury during the Civil War.

With the advent of paper currency came the challenge of keeping its value stable since the paper itself did not contain a built-in value like the precious metals that preceded it. Some nations tried to stabilize their currencies by fixing them to an anchor, such as the gold standard used for several decades and the Bretton Woods system, under which many countries fixed their currency to the dollar, which was fixed to gold between World War II and 1973. In this context, a nation that could not sustain its fixed exchange rate or left the system altogether would face a currency crisis, but unless there was a simultaneous banking disaster, the country generally did not face a full-scale economic collapse or financial crisis.

In the past two decades, however, the liberalization of financial markets in developing nations—often referred to as emerging markets—and increasing global financial integration have set the stage for a new, frightening kind of implosion: the collapse of both a nation's currency and its banks. This twin meltdown can wreak havoc on a country by unleashing a mass exodus of capital, soaring interest rates, and a hemorrhaging of the real economy, and this destructive process can leave an economy crippled for years. South America saw the first of what scholars call "modern" financial crises from 1981 to 1983, when Chile, Argentina, and Uruguay all suffered. More recently, Russia, Mexico, Thailand, Indonesia, Malaysia, and Argentina have endured economic disasters when currency crises combined with banking collapses.

The modern-day currency crisis is a cycle that can begin with an event or a series of events that prompt anxious investors to begin removing their money from a nation's foreign exchange market. One such event occurs when a government decides to *devalue* its currency by taking steps to reduce its value or halting its efforts to support its value. This process is known as a "devaluation." But often investors can spark a drop in a currency in domestic and global markets through concerns about real or rumored political instability, possible interest rate hikes, a spectacular company failure, or an unexpected decline in an economy's performance, to name but a few.

As investors sell more of the local currency, the market gets flooded, and the currency loses value. A central bank can attempt to make the local currency more attractive by increasing the supply of dollars, which is known as "foreign exchange intervention," or by raising interest rates on the local currency. But if, and when, it becomes obvious that the government has insufficient monetary reserves, or willpower, to finance imports, pay its debts, and still support its currency, *capital flight*—the selling of a local currency for dollars in order to invest the funds abroad—accelerates.

This departure of investors en masse can trigger a currency crisis. Governments, banks, and companies that have taken out debt denominated in dollars, euros, or another strong and stable currency may have trouble making payments on these obligations because their income is in the local currency and more and more of this currency is required to meet the debts in foreign currencies. On the other hand, this provides a real boon to exporters, whose goods are suddenly cheaper to produce and whose foreign income rises dramatically in relative terms.

Real interest rates—the current interest rate minus inflation—can rise before and during the currency crisis to compensate investors for the risk of further currency weakness. These elevated rates can hurt borrowers—especially those who have taken out flexible-rate loans—strangle whole sectors of the economy, and contribute to widespread loan delinquencies, which in turn can damage the finances of the banks that issued the loan. After Mexico's 1994 currency devaluation, for example, some middle-class families lost their homes, their cars, and all of their savings trying to keep up with credit card debt when interest rates reached more than 50 percent.

LIQUIDITY CRUNCH

A currency crisis is often associated with a *liquidity crunch*, in which the economy runs out of liquidity precisely when it needs it most. Liquidity shortages typically occur when capital flows into a country dry up and/or capital flight escalates. In these circumstances, companies that had relied on foreign cash for their financial survival find it difficult to refinance their debt. Local currency liquidity also declines when the central bank, trying to defend the currency, drains money from the local system. Ironically, it can be the strongest and most promising countries—for example Mexico in 1994 and East Asian nations in 1997—that are subject to liquidity crises. Because these countries attract the strongest capital inflows, they can fall into a cycle of overborrowing, leaving them most vulnerable to capital flight when investor angst strikes. It is important to note, however, that not all sudden devaluations lead to broader financial crises.

Britain's sudden exit from the European Monetary System in 1992 and the resulting devaluation of the British sterling against the currency of other nations, for example, seemed like a national humiliation at the time. But in retrospect, the domestic economy appears to have benefited from the sudden improvement in competitiveness and lower interest rates that paved the way to an impressive economic recovery. The 1994 devaluation of the Mexican peso, meanwhile, led to the write-off of more than 50 percent of the nation's bank loans and the bailout of the entire banking system. Wages in certain sectors have still not recovered.

Why the different outcomes? Reporters trying to discern when a currency devaluation might lead to a full-fledged financial crisis should ask questions about the health of the banking and corporate sectors. Telltale signs that an economy is ripe for disaster include increasing corporate indebtedness or leverage (especially in foreign currency), which can be seen on the balance sheet of public companies by comparing the amount of debt to total capital, which is debt plus equity. Another factor is the growth of *nonperforming loans*, or loans that cannot be collected, on banks' balance sheets. Poor supervision of banks and companies, particularly when banks are allowed to develop economic ties to the companies they fund, let these problems fester and deepen. The link between currency and banking crises is also strong if the private sector has overborrowed in dollars or if the banking sector has aggressively extended the lengths of its loan payments.

David Beim and Charles Calomiris, professors at the Columbia Business School in New York, cite four prerequisites for a full-blown financial collapse. Any of them can touch off the vicious cycle, but all must be present for a currency crisis to prompt an economic disaster.

1. Financial liberalization

2. A fixed currency value

3. Large, optimistic capital inflows

4. Underlying weakness in banks and firms

GAUGING CURRENCY MOVEMENTS

The movement of currency can be measured in two ways: nominal or real terms. Nominal comparisons track the level of a local currency against the U.S. dollar, the euro, or another strong currency. When this rate of exchange steadily loses value on the open market, it is said to depreciate. This depreciated currency now buys fewer imports—sold in the foreign country's currency—and helps the country sell more exports, since a country's products are relatively cheaper for foreign nations. Real comparisons, meanwhile, measure the goods and services a currency can purchase. But to gauge a currency's value in real terms it is important to consider inflation, or the rate at which domestic prices rise.

Moderate inflation can be the byproduct of a growing economy since it causes excess demand for goods and services. But a growing amount of money in a country's monetary system can also spark inflation. Because it is difficult for many nations to collect taxes or reduce spending, printing money has seemed a relatively painless way for many governments to finance their deficits. But printing money, which increases the *money supply*—usually defined as the amount of currency in circulation plus deposits—without a commensurate increase in money demand, can cause inflation to occur. A nation needs enough currency to keep the economy going, but there is sometimes too much of a good thing.

Inflation and a depreciation of the exchange rate are closely related over the long term but can vary widely over the short term. For example, if a country expands the money supply—or prints money—faster than the economy itself is growing, inflation picks up. Inflation reduces, or depreciates, the real value of a currency, causing it to be worth less both inside and outside the nation. It is important to note also that exchange rates do not only fluctuate in line with current inflation. They can factor into expectations of future inflation, and, if the outlook is bleak, the currency can weaken in anticipation. An inflation/depreciation spiral can also develop, in which an increase in inflation leads to a slide in the currency and, as the latter happens, prices of imports rise and inflation, in turn, increases even more.

TYPES OF EXCHANGE RATE REGIMES

In order to understand exchange rate crises and the financial crises they can spur, reporters should understand the various exchange rate regimes found around the world.

FREE FLOAT   In this scheme, governments let the market determine the currency's value and expend no resources to prop up its value. This is mainly meant to allow the local currency—rather than the economy as a whole—to absorb economic turbulence. While this can stave off the violent collapse of a currency, the nation's imports and exports become subject to the often-volatile swings of the currency markets. Developing countries that maintain freely floating exchange-rate regimes also tend to experience higher and more volatile inflation rates. Brazil, for example, saw its inflation swing sharply higher in 2002–3 after its currency, the real, took a beating from investors' fears about the 2002 presidential elections that brought Lula Inacio da Silva to power.

DIRTY FLOAT This regime means that government intervention is decided on a case-by-case basis, and intervention is often used as a way of smoothing out otherwise desirable movements in the currency. While many developed nations profess to be "free floaters," they will sometimes intervene to change their exchange rate. For example, the U.S. and Japanese central banks have coordinated actions to change the dollar-yen exchange rate, while the pound sterling "shadowed" the German mark for several years in the 1980s.

CRAWLING PEGS AND TRADING BANDS The pegged exchange rate moves slowly, but it stays in line with inflation. The moves are often permitted within prescribed ranges and bands—hence the regime's name. This can work well if inflation is mild and the exchange rate is relatively constant. Chile, Colombia, Ecuador, and Israel have all maintained crawling bands.

FIXED EXCHANGE RATES Countries trying to control inflation can anchor the value of their currency to another, stronger currency. Central banks do so by announcing their willingness to buy and sell the local currency at a specific exchange rate with an eye to maintaining its price close to a stated value. If the exchange rate is fixed, then inflation can actually cause the real value of the currency to rise. This is known as a "real exchange rate appreciation." For example, if local wages rise but the exchange rate does not, then wages are now higher when measured in U.S. dollars. As a result, domestic production, when measured in U.S. dollars, becomes costlier. This means that it is more expensive for other nations to import the country's goods, leading to a loss of competitiveness.

CURRENCY BOARD This is an extreme version of a fixed exchange rate regime and not very common. Hong Kong has had one for years and a number of smaller countries such as Estonia and Bulgaria have tried similar setups. A currency board is a legal framework ensuring that local currency is always backed by reserves of U.S. dollars or another strong currency, which in effect makes the latter a substitute currency. Domestic money supply is allowed to rise only if there is an inflow of dollars into the system. By the same token, a net outflow of dollars automatically causes the money supply to fall, forcing the real economy to adjust by forcing a liquidity crunch. Currency boards are motivated by a desire to prevent the government from printing money to finance government operations. Ecuador, Panama, and El Salvador have all "dollarized"—or replaced their local currency with the dollar—but currency boards are used by countries that want a separate currency whose value is entirely determined by the dollar or another strong currency. In Argentina, the currency board was credited with reining in inflation that had soared to four and five digits in the late 1980s. The system collapsed in 2001, partly because the government could neither control nor cover spending by provincial governments.

MARKET VALUATIONS

When writing about a country's currency, it is vital to watch its performance on world markets, where banks, traders, and investors are constantly evaluating its value. Strong currencies are generally found in economies with an open monetary policy that leads to a stable money supply growing in tandem with the rest of the economy, low and stable inflation, adequate international reserves, a nearly balanced budget, and a solid balance of payments.

Since few countries meet this ideal, psychology plays a vast role in determining the value of currencies. For example, the markets can—and have—long ignored large trade deficits and budget deficits in the United States and maintained great confidence in the dollar, preferring to believe that capital flows into the country will continue. When Asian currencies came under attack in the markets in the autumn of 1997, many of these countries boasted strong reserves with trade balances either in surplus or with small deficits. But analysts thought banks were weak and worried that their currencies would be vulnerable in the future.

When the market determines, correctly or not, that a domestic currency is worth less than its traded value, demand for dollars or another strong currency rises and capital flight can ensue. At the same time, an *overvalued* currency can also take its toll on the economy by making it less competitive, since the overvalued currency can make it too costly for exporters to compete internationally. In both cases, a country's finances come under pressure: exports shrink, imports rise, and demand for the foreign currency increases. When this happens, the economy loses dollars. Sometimes, the central bank decides that it must absorb excess demand for the foreign currency, so it buys its own currency on the open market by using its international reserves, held in U.S. dollars or another hard currency. Obviously, this policy of intervention can only work for so long. If sustained indefinitely, reserves can dwindle to nothing. Once the central bank stops intervening, the excess demand for dollars translates into a cheaper local currency.

Central banks do not always intervene by selling dollars—they sometimes buy them. This results in an increase in international reserves. Central banks can undertake such an intervention when there is a spurt of capital flows from abroad that, if left sloshing around the system, would cause the local currency to appreciate, hurting competitiveness.

When analyzing a currency's movement, and whether it might be ripe for a sharp movement one way or the other, here are some tips to consider:

- Many central banks refuse to say whether they are intervening in the market, but a reporter can get a get a sense of this after the fact by checking for changes in the level of international reserves. In 1994, Mexico's reserves dropped from $17.2 billion at the end of October, to $12.5 billion at the end of November, to $6.1 billion at the end of December. As international reserves dwindled, the central bank was forced to widen the range in which the peso traded on December 20, allowing a de facto devaluation of 15 percent. The widening of the peso's band proved inadequate and forced more intervention with reserves. Eventually, the central bank was forced to let the peso float on December 22 of the same year.

- Financial analysts look at the *current account* to predict future exchange rates. The current account measures the amount of money flowing in and out of a country through trade in goods and services, interest payments, and aid. A current account surplus indicates that a nation has excess hard currency on hand, and it can prompt a strengthening of the domestic currency as plentiful foreign currency bolsters confidence in the local currency. A current account deficit means a country must come up with additional funds to cover a shortfall in the money flowing into the country, the absence of which can lead to a weakening of the domestic currency. The current account makes up part of the balance of payments.

- It is also important to watch the *trade balance*, which is part of the current account. If imports are rising while exports are shrinking, this suggests that the currency may be overvalued, since imports are cheap and exports are too expensive for other nations to buy. In 1979, Chile had opened much of its economy, but it was plagued by inflation. It fixed the exchange rate at 39 pesos per dollar and succeeded in nearly eliminating inflation over the next two years. But in the interim, domestic inflation caused the currency to strengthen in real terms. A trade deficit of more than 10 percent of gross domestic product suggested that the currency had become grossly overvalued. The currency peg broke in 1982, causing a massive contraction in the real economy.

SPECULATION AND DERIVATIVES

Once a government exhausts its reserves—and its capacity to borrow to increase them—it can no longer prop up its currency. An entire class of traders is always on the prowl for hints that this may be on the verge of happening. This group, known as "speculators," tries to make money by betting the currency will decline or by hastening its fall. Unregulated hedge funds, which borrow heavily so that bets on small moves in exchange rates can be magnified many times over, are often the vehicles for such speculation, but speculators can also be the trading departments of large banks or other institutional investors. To understand speculation in the market, a reporter should understand two kinds of currency contracts:

SPOT RATES The amount a currency sells for now.

FORWARD CONTRACTS An agreement to buy or sell the currency for a given amount sometime in the future.

If the Mexican peso, for example, is now trading at nine per dollar and people believe it to be overvalued, an exporter may only commit itself to selling a dollar for ten pesos a year from now. If speculators believe a currency to be overvalued, they sell both the spot and forward contracts. Selling spot contracts can create an immediate excess of supply, as investors hope there is too much supply for the government to buy back. By selling the forward contracts, if a forward market exists, at the fixed price, investors stand to gain an enormous profit if the peg breaks and its value drops. With little chance of a currency gaining strength, there is very little risk, unless the Central Bank dramatically raises rates or floods the market with massive amounts of dollars.

In the middle of a crisis, governments and the media often blame foreign speculators for bringing down a currency. Indeed, the Hungarian-born investor and philanthropist George Soros made more than $1 billion of his fortune by attacking the pound sterling and the Italian lira in 1992, just before they dropped out of the European Monetary System. But more often, local banks, companies, and government officials are among the first to see a crisis brewing. This rush to sell local currency holdings is what was referred to above as capital flight.

There is also a new generation of investment instruments, *derivatives*, so named because their price is derived from the value of another instrument. Derivatives make it much easier for speculators to swap risks with others and to make heavy bets, which have made markets more volatile.

In Mexico, for example, U.S. banks bought high-interest-rate government securities, like treasury bonds known as Tesobonos, which paid out in pesos at a rate linked to the dollar. But they then hedged their risks through derivative contracts with Mexican banks. Although there were laws preventing Mexican banks from speculating against the peso, they signed derivative contracts to accept the proceeds of the Tesobonos in exchange for an up-front dollar deposit and regular dollar payments. This effectively reduced the return of the U.S. banks to a normal dollar loan yield and gave the higher returns to Mexican banks in exchange for accepting the risk. Thus, when the peso lost strength, it was the Mexican banks that had to sell ever more pesos to meet their obligations under the Tesobono currency swaps.

When covering currency markets in all their complexity, here are some questions reporters should ask:

- Who is doing the selling?

- If the pressure is coming from foreign investors, is it really speculators, such as hedge funds? Or is it, more dangerously, an exit by large, long-term institutions like mutual funds? How much of the pressure is by domestic players and how much is due to foreign players?

- If the pressure is coming from domestic investors, is it wealthy people moving their money out of the country? Or is it local banks meeting derivatives contracts?

- Who holds dollar debt? Who holds debt in local currencies?

- Is the currency crisis spilling over into the financial/banking system?

- Which foreign banks did the lending and how much exposure do they have?

- Besides exporters, who will benefit from devaluation? For example, what company borrowed in domestic currency even though it exports for hard currency? Besides importers, who will suffer? Are there many savers in the local currency who will now see the value of their wealth eroded?

- What happens to domestic credit? Which people and businesses hold loans denominated in the foreign currency?

- What is the role of the International Monetary Fund, the World Bank, and the U.S. Treasury? Is the country considered too big to fail?

GLOSSARY

- **CAPITAL FLIGHT.** The process by which investors, often en masse, rush to sell their investments in a country because of fears they will sharply lose their value.

- **CURRENT ACCOUNT.** The amount of money flowing in and out of a country through trade in goods and services, interest payments, and aid.

- **DEVALUATION.** The process by which a government reduces the value of its currency; one way to do this is by ceasing to support its value through intervention in the local market.

- **FOREIGN EXCHANGE INTERVENTION.** The process by which a nation's central bank attempts to support the local currency by selling U.S. dollars or another benchmark currency in the open market.

- **LIQUIDITY CRUNCH.** The lack of hard currency by a government; it typically occurs when capital flows into a country dry up and/or capital flight escalates.

- **MONEY SUPPLY.** The amount of currency in circulation plus deposits; some measures of this include money market accounts and other liquid assets.

- **NONPERFORMING LOANS.** Loans that have not been paid by the borrower, leaving the lending bank unable to recover the money.

- **OVERVALUED.** When investors believe a domestic currency is worth less than its traded value.

- **REAL INTEREST RATES.** A nation's current interest rate minus the current inflation rate.

LINKS FOR MORE INFORMATION

1. The Washington, D.C.–based liberal think tank Center for Economic and Policy Research publishes many papers on macroeconomic issues, including the Argentina debt crisis. http://www.cepr.net/argentina_crisis.htm.

2. The Derivatives Study Center in Washington, D.C., has written primers on sovereign debt restructuring, derivatives, hedge funds, employee stock options, and other subjects. http://www.econstrat.org/dscbriefs.htm.

3. The Chicago Mercantile Exchange is the largest foreign-exchange-futures trading market in the United States. http://www.cme.com/prd/fx/index.html.

4. Forex-Markets.com offers regular updates on foreign exchange news, currency prices, research reports on foreign exchange, and links to some of the largest currency brokerages. http://www.forex-markets.com.

5. The International Monetary Fund published a paper by Atish Ghosh, Jonathan Ostry, Anne-Marie Gulde, and Holger Wolf entitled "Does Exchange Rate Regime Matter for Inflation and Growth?" http://www.imf.org/external/pubs/ft/issues2.

6. The Bank for International Settlements' Web site carries a paper by Marc Klau entitled "Exchange Rate Regimes and Inflation and Output in Sub-Saharan Countries." http://www.bis.org/publ/work53.htm.

7. The Asia Recovery Information Center Web site has a policy forum, which publishes working papers covering topics ranging from financial crises and fiscal and monetary policy to managing short-term capital flows. http://aric.adb.org.

8. Currency Boards and Dollarization, a Web site maintained by Kurt Schuler, a senior economist in the U.S. Senate, has lots of reference materials about currency boards and related topics. http://www.dollarization.org.

9. Jeffrey Frankel, a professor of capital formation and growth at the Kennedy School of Government at Harvard University, has written extensively on foreign exchange and other macroeconomic issues. http://ksgnotes1.harvard.edu/people/jeffrey_frankel.

10. The Hong Kong Institute for Monetary Research publishes papers on various issues including monetary policy, the sovereign debt markets, and inflation in Asia. http://www.hkimr.org/index_2.htm.

CHAPTER FOUR

COVERING
CENTRAL BANKS

MARJORIE OLSTER

WHAT IS A CENTRAL BANK?

C ENTRAL BANKS are among the most influential and closely
watched financial authorities in virtually any country. They have
the overarching responsibility of maintaining a country's "economic stability." Some central banks define economic stability broadly:
they see themselves as inflation fighters, growth promoters, lenders of last
resort, and exchange-rate defenders. Others prefer a much narrower focus,
usually emphasizing price stability. However they define their mandates,
central banks try to achieve their objectives using a unique set of instruments: they are the ones who control a country's money supply and interest rates and have the power to buy or sell domestic or foreign currency to
affect exchange rates.

Central banks are usually made up of a board of directors or governors
and a body of staff. The latter prepares the groundwork while the former
has periodic meetings to discuss its country's economic outlook and set
monetary policy. The board members in the United States are appointed
by the president and are accountable to Congress. Increasingly, central
bankers are being granted "independence" so as to shield them from political pressure.

Markets carefully monitor central banks' operations. Their decisions
move asset prices. Consequently, decisions are shrouded in secrecy and
the policy-making meetings are closed to the press. That said, transparency and process-predictability (as opposed to decision-predictability) is the
sign of a mature and respected central bank.

The central bank has a large research staff that investigates current topics in the economy and monetary policy. Their work is usually very analytic and staffers often publish their papers in academic circles. Their reports are closely followed and carry great weight in the economic community and often make terrific analytic stories for a central bank reporter. Reporters should try to follow the central bank's research as closely as possible and line up interviews with research economists on their areas of expertise.

Monetary policy tries to influence economic behavior in the future. Therefore, a central bank always has a forecasting framework that is used when making monetary-policy decisions. Central bank research departments put out periodic forecasts on major economic indicators. These are important stories because a forecast can also be seen as a target and can indicate what the central bank sees as the most desirable levels for inflation, growth, and employment.

A central bank reporter should closely follow the statements and speeches of key central bank officials for any hints on the direction of policy or assessments of the economy. Whenever possible, the reporter should try to obtain exclusive interviews with officials or economists at the central bank to learn more about how this powerful institution makes its decisions.

WHAT ARE THE CENTRAL BANK'S MANDATES OR OBJECTIVES?

In many countries there are laws that set out a central bank's objectives or mandates. Some countries have inflation rules, which mandate that the level of inflation must not rise above a certain percentage point. In the United States, the Federal Reserve has a much-debated dual mandate, which calls for maintaining low and stable inflation while promoting maximum sustainable growth and employment; there is no specific inflation target. But many other central banks have just a single mandate: to keep inflation low.

Setting "monetary policy" means keeping interest rates and/or the money supply (currency in circulation plus deposits) at a targeted level. While details can be complicated, the actual theory behind monetary policy is fairly straightforward. Inflation, the theory goes, increases if the supply of money exceeds the demand for it. At its most basic, monetary policy involves estimating how much money the economy desires (that is, demands) and then deciding how much money to inject (that is, supply) into the system. If inflation is too high, the central bank creates a liquidity shortage by withdrawing money from circulation. If deflation is the risk, the central bank floods the system with liquidity.

Money can also have an impact on growth. Liquidity is to an economy what grease is to an engine. Few transactions can occur if liquidity is constrained. As economic activity falls, demand drops—and so does inflation. Recessions, unfortunately, are an effective way of controlling runaway inflation. A good central bank is one that never allows economies to overheat. To use a cliché, it does so by removing the punch bowl before the party turns rowdy.

In writing about a central bank, reporters should make sure they know whether the bank has an inflation rule and whether its mandate extends to growth as well as price stability.

WHAT TOOLS DO CENTRAL BANKS USE TO CONTROL INFLATION OR STIMULATE GROWTH?

A central bank has many tools at its disposal to steer an economy. It can control any number of policy levers, including interest rates, the money supply, foreign-exchange sales, and the reserve ratio—or the percentage of checking deposits that banks are required to hold on reserve.

A good way of thinking of central bank instruments is to distinguish between "immediate" tools and "intermediate" ones. As the names suggest, immediate tools are the ones over which a central bank has immediate control. For example, a central bank controls its policy interest rate (for example, the federal funds rate in the United States), the amount of foreign exchange it sells, and the amount of base money (that is, the part of the money supply over which it has complete control). Intermediate tools are those over which the central bank has no direct control but can be reasonably expected to strongly influence. Consider, for example, the structure of interest rates. The Fed changes the federal funds rate (the immediate tool) and expects that market-determined interest rates (for example, mortgage rates and prime rates, both of which are intermediate tools) will move in tandem.

The precise tool (or set of tools) that a central bank uses depends on what economists label the "monetary policy transmission mechanism." What matters is how effective the tool is in achieving the ultimate objective of the monetary policy, be it inflation, growth, or exchange-rate stability. In the 1980s, the U.S. central bank targeted a rate of growth in the money supply, but it later decided that the correlation between money-supply growth, on the one hand, and economic growth and inflation, on the other, was not strong enough. So it switched to targeting interest rates. Today, the most prevalent tool used by central banking in setting monetary policy is the manipulation of interest rates.

What is the "transmission mechanism" from interest rates to inflation and growth? Raising interest rates increases the costs of borrowing for consumers and businesses and tends to curb demand and eventually drive down rising inflation or keep inflation from rising further. If supply exceeds demand, producers can lose the power to raise prices or maintain profitable prices for their goods, causing deflation, which can devastate an

economy. Lowering interest rates can encourage consumers and businesses to borrow money, which they then invest in items like homes, computers, or office furniture, stimulating demand and growth in the economy.

As mentioned above, central banks tend to control "policy rates." In
most countries, the policy rate is the overnight bank-lending rate—that is,
the rate banks charge each other to borrow money for one night. That rate
does not directly affect the rate of borrowing for consumers or businesses,
but it serves as a benchmark or a standard that affects borrowing costs
throughout the economy. Other rates normally follow the direction of the
overnight lending rate. For example, after a central bank rate hike, credit
card rates and mortgage rates normally rise too, even though the central
bank does not directly affect those rates.

SOME KEY ISSUES IN COVERING CENTRAL BANKS

Interest rate predictions are the bread and butter of any journalist watching over a central bank. The direction, timing, and magnitude of interest
rate changes are of keen interest to domestic and foreign markets and
investors. Many news services poll an elite group of senior economists reg-
ularly to get a consensus view on interest rate predictions and then write
stories and analyses of the poll findings. These experts are usually pretty
adept as a group at predicting upcoming changes.

Markets' expectation of interest rate moves is also an interesting topic
for a financial journalist. Markets are always "pricing" the probability of
interest rate moves. These probabilities are implicit in the pricing of
bonds. In advanced capital markets, for example, there are futures contracts whose prices move in line with the market's expectation of central
banks' changing monetary policy. While central bankers do not like to
have their actions dictated by markets, they nonetheless listen carefully to
what markets (implicitly) say.

Bonds are also useful as way for journalists to gauge what the market is
thinking about future inflation. If traders are expecting inflation to rise, they
often drive up rates on longer-term government and corporate bonds to
reflect the increased risk of inflation over time. This can also give a sense of
where shorter-term interest rates set by the central bank might be headed.

One key question to ask when covering a central bank is: Does the central bank have credibility with the markets and the public? Do they believe
in the central bank's resolve to fight inflation? If not, this can be reflected
in the market pricing. For example, government- and corporate-bond-
market interest rates, which are determined by market participants, do not
always follow in lockstep with central bank rates. If the markets believe the
central bank is not doing a good job at fighting inflation, they might drive
up rates for long-term debt securities to reflect the increased risk of inflation in the future. Gaining credibility, however, can be very costly. In the
early 1980s, and after years of inflation, the U.S. Federal Reserve pushed

interest rates to record highs, throwing the United States into a deep recession. Since then, the Fed has gained credibility and no longer needs to "overshoot." A central bank may want to keep interest rate expectations in the market under control by showing it is active in keeping inflation low.

TIPS FOR INTEREST RATE PREDICTIONS

Financial journalists often interview professionals whose job is to predict interest rates. It is important therefore to know which economic indicators the central bank is looking at when it makes its decisions on raising or lowering rates.

The first place to look is at inflation indicators. Measures of current inflation are helpful but perhaps more important are inflation forecasts for the future. That is because economists believe changes in interest rates affect the macroeconomy with a lag of months or even a year. So in making a decision on rate changes, the central bank needs to have an idea of where inflation is headed, as well as what it did in prior months. Reporters should look for measures of "inflation in the pipeline": for example, an exchange rate weakening today increases the prices of imports and can be a precursor of higher inflation tomorrow. By the same token, higher oil prices today will often put pressure on transportation costs in the future, causing inflation to rise.

Central banks will also look at measures of economic growth, including indicators of production, on the one hand, and demand for goods, on the other. They also consider consumer confidence when making monetary-policy decisions. In examining indicators or components of indicators, central banks focus on those that have some predictive power for the future. For example, Federal Reserve Chairman Alan Greenspan likes to look at an indicator called supplier delivery time, which is one component of a monthly manufacturing report, to see whether bottlenecks are developing in the supply chain. If delivery times slow, it could be a sign that demand is outpacing production and supply.

Financial journalists should try to find out what indicators the central banks they are covering look at. This is not always easy because central banks can be secretive about their decision-making processes. Knowing a central bank and its priorities is key. In Vietnam, as in the United States, the central bank also focuses on economic growth. In both places, economists often believe that falling inflation is a sign that growth is slowing, and the central bank is likely to ease interest rates (or at least less likely to raise them).

The story of how a central bank makes its decisions can also be an interesting one if it can be brought to light. How transparent is that decision-making process? Do the central bank officials give clear signals to the markets on what they are planning to do to minimize the element of surprise, or does it want to surprise the markets so that its move has a bigger impact? These are all questions worth asking.

In the United States, there has been a gradual movement toward greater transparency at the Federal Reserve Bank over the past decade. The Fed began announcing specific changes in target interest rates in 1994. Before that, it only signaled changes through daily money market operations. In the late 1990s, the Fed began making statements after each policy meeting on where it saw the balance of risks in the economy, either tilting toward higher inflation, that is, higher interest rates, or toward risk of recession, that is, lower interest rates, or an even balance between the risks. The statements were meant to signal markets as to the likely direction of future interest rates. Not everyone was happy with the change. Some complained that the complicated phrasing of the balance-of-risk statements were even more confusing than having no statement at all. The Fed has continued to try to refine the process. The Fed has also started to release minutes of its meetings, though it does so with a lag of more than a month. Some would like to see the minutes released in a more timely fashion.

Central bank independence is always an interesting topic for journalists. What degree of independence does the central bank have from the political authorities? Who has the power to appoint central bankers, and who are the bankers accountable to? Is there ever political pressure on the central bank to act in a way that perhaps is not consistent with its mandate of maintaining low and stable inflation? For example, let's say it's an election year, unemployment is up, and the party in power would very much like to see interest rates lowered to spur on the economy. But the central bank has forecasts showing the economy is poised to pick up and inflation expectations are rising. A decision by the central bank not to lower rates further could be unpopular with the political powers but would show a commitment to an inflation-fighting mandate. Some studies have shown a correlation between high degrees of central bank independence and low inflation.

The central bank is not monolithic; its board is made up of members with sometimes widely varying points of view on the economy and on how to set monetary policy. In the United States, journalists who cover the central bank try to identify the "hawks"—those bankers who want to be aggressive about fighting inflation, even at the cost of slower growth—versus the "doves," who favor a slightly looser monetary policy in favor of faster growth and greater employment. The composition of the board can influence the direction of policy and should not be overlooked.

These are just a few examples of topics worthy of journalistic exploration.

HOW EFFECTIVE ARE INTEREST RATE CHANGES?

Economies do not always work according to the textbook theories of monetary policy. A central bank can indeed change an instrument, but that is no guarantee that the instrument will be effective. Much, as mentioned above, depends on the strength of the "monetary policy transmission mechanism." In Japan in 1999, the central bank effectively lowered interest rates to zero, but Japanese consumers and investors did not react, preferring, instead, to save at very high rates while spending conservatively.

Transmission mechanisms also operate against other backdrops. A number of South American countries suffered from hyperinflation in the 1980s, and economic agents lost all trust in the local currency. Demand for the local currency simply evaporated and nothing—even extremely high interest rates—could restore confidence. A few of the countries took the drastic step of "dollarization," or pegging their currencies one-to-one to the U.S. dollar, to get inflation under control. In doing so, they essentially gave up their central banks' autonomous ability to control monetary policy.

CRISIS MANAGEMENT

A crisis can throw even a well-guided monetary policy off course. The central bank is often called the lender of last resort, which means that in a crisis such as a large bank failure or a credit crunch, the central bank steps in to assure that there is no systemic threat that could paralyze the entire financial system of the country.

How does this work? In the first trading session after the U.S. stock market crash of 1987 and the September 11, 2001, attack on the World Trade Center, the U.S. central bank dramatically eased monetary policy. It was an instant reaction to a major financial or political crisis intended to shore up public confidence in the stability of the banking system. The Fed issued similar statements on both occasions, assuring the financial markets that it stood ready to provide as much liquidity to banks as needed to get through the crisis. This was reassurance, in effect, that the Fed would provide all the money and credit needed to smooth out the bumps and help the banks weather the storm. The tactic was considered successful in both cases.

In 1998, Russia defaulted on its debt payments in the wake of a serious currency crisis in Asia. The U.S. stock market fell sharply and a major U.S.-based hedge fund collapsed, threatening the integrity of the U.S. financial system. Risk appetite disappeared, and it became difficult for anyone except for the highest-rated companies to get credit in the private debt markets. A classic credit crunch developed. The Fed recognized that the trend could do serious damage to the economy, and so it cut rates three times in quick succession in the fall of 1998. This worked, and credit eased up.

Very infrequently, the central banks of the world's biggest economies will act together in concerted interest rate cuts if there is a major global financial crisis. In December 1998, twelve European Union countries cut their rates. In the weeks prior, countries around the world cut their rates too. Even if there is no crisis, central banks often cut rates together. Before the European Central Bank was founded, the Netherlands and other European central banks adjusted their rates when the German central bank changed theirs.

CAPITAL MARKETS

What is the mandate of the central bank of the country at issue? Is it to keep inflation at bay, or are there other goals? If inflation is a key element of the mandate, what inflation indicator does the central bank look at most closely to guide policy? (Many countries have a number of inflation indicators that come out weekly or monthly, but the central bank usually has one or more it watches most closely)

■ What do private economists covering the country forecast for the direction of interest rates and growth? If a reporter does not have access to the surveys put out by news wires or other media, he should conduct his own poll of a few economists to get an idea. This will be less scientific, but reporters can at least get a sense of how the market sees the economy.

■ If there is a domestic bond market, what are the rates for longer-term government and corporate debt? These rates can be a tip-off as to whether investors are betting interest rates will go up or down.

■ Reporters should try to follow the central bank's research as closely as possible and line up interviews with research economists on their areas of expertise.

■ When does the central bank hold meetings on monetary policy or interest rates, and when does it release the results of these meetings? Is it possible to obtain the minutes of the meetings? These are often looked at by economists and other people in the market for hints about future decisions.

■ What is the general state of the economy? Is there a chance of recession that the central bank might have to confront with changes in interest rates? Is the economy growing too fast? Is borrowing strong or tepid?

■ Does the central bank of the country ever coordinate its economic policies with those of its neighbors or major trading partners?

■ Are there any signs of financial trouble in the country's banking industry or at a particular bank, such as runs on deposits, a high percentage of defaulted loans, or rumors of fraud? Is there a chance the central bank may intervene to take over the troubled bank or banks? Could the financial difficulties be broad enough to endanger the nation's banking system as a whole? What will the central bank need to do to keep the industry afloat?

■ Are there any signs of deep-seated financial trouble elsewhere in the economy, such as in the corporate sector? Is the trouble acute enough that it could have repercussions for the economy as a whole? Will the central bank need to respond to the crisis with interest rate changes?

■ Is it possible to conduct off-the-record interviews with central bank officials? Even if they only speak off-the-record, they can give valuable insights into the workings of the central bank, the direction of policies, and so on.

■ Have there been any recent changes to the board of the central bank or rumors of changes in the board or at the next tier? If so, how would these changes affect the bank's policies? Reporters should get to know the people who may some day move up to the board or to the job of governor.

- **FEDERAL FUNDS RATE**. The interest rate on the overnight lending of federal funds, which are deposits made by banks with the Federal Reserve system to satisfy their reserve requirements. The Federal Reserve sets a target for the widely watched federal funds rate and decides on this target level at its regular monetary policy meetings.

- **FEDERAL RESERVE**. The central bank of the United States; it is typically referred to as "the Fed."

- **HAWKS AND DOVES**. Hawks are the central bankers viewed as aggressive in the fight against inflation, while doves are those bankers favoring a slightly looser monetary policy that aims for faster growth and greater employment.

- **INFLATION**. The rate, expressed in percent, at which prices rise; created when the demand for goods and services exceeds their supply. Excessive inflation is largely viewed as negative to an economy because it erodes consumers' purchasing power.

- **MONEY SUPPLY**. Currency in circulation plus liquid deposits; central banks generally attempt to keep this at a target level at which the bank believes supply of and demand for money will be in relative balance.

- **NAIRU (NON-ACCELERATING INFLATION RATE OF UNEMPLOYMENT)**. A belief often used to guide monetary policy that holds that if unemployment is below a certain level (e.g., 6 percent), inflation will accelerate.

- **OVERNIGHT BANK-LENDING RATE.** The rate banks charge one another to borrow money for one night.

- **TAYLOR RULE**. A theory often cited in the United States as a guideline for how the central bank should set the overnight federal funds rate; it says the correct level for the real (i.e., inflation-adjusted) federal funds rate should be based on the relationship between growth and inflation levels or, in other words, on whether inflation is above or below some target and on whether there is a gap between actual and potential growth in the economy.

1. The Bank for International Settlements is an international body that fosters cooperation among central banks and other agencies to ensure monetary and financial stability. http://www.bis.org/index.htm.

2. The Federal Reserve, the U.S. central bank, has four major tasks: deciding the country's monetary policy, supervising and regulating commercial banks, ensuring that the U.S. financial system is stable, and serving the U.S. government's and certain institutions' banking needs. http://www.federalreserve.gov.

3. The European Central Bank works with central banks of member countries in the euro area to maintain price stability and watch the value of the euro. http://www.ecb.int.

4. The Central Banking Resource Center is a global guide to central banking and central banks. It includes links to central banks, treasuries and ministries of finance, central-banking research and training institutes, multilateral monetary institutions, resources on monetary and central-banking history, plus much more. http://adams.patriot.net/~bernkopf/index-nf.html.

5. The Center for the Study of Central Banks, based at the New York University School of Law, sponsors seminars, encourages research, and collects and shares information relating to 'mail discussion digest, an online collection of central bank charters, and listings of central-banking books in its library. http://www.law.nyu.edu/centralbankscenter.

6. The Bank of England's Centre for Central Banking Studies conducts seminars and technical assistance for central banks and similar institutions throughout the world. It is a center for comparative study and collaborative research on issues at the forefront of central banking. http://www.bankofengland.co.uk/ccbs/index.htm.

7. The Group of Thirty is a private, nonprofit, international body composed of representatives of the private and public sectors and academia. Under "Publications," many interesting research papers can be found on issues pertaining to central banking and financial regulation. http://www.group30.org.

8. Central Banking Publications Ltd. carries information about published materials, workshops, and seminars on central-banking issues. It also has the most comprehensive list of Web sites for central banks around the world, from Armenia to South Africa to Thailand. http://www.centralbanking.co.uk/index.htm.

9. Central Banking Publications' affiliate, Centralbanknet.com, is a collection of the latest news, event listings, and a history of central banking. http://www.centralbanknet.com.

10. The Monetary Policy Rule page on the Web site of Stanford University's Professor John B. Taylor offers a database of news articles, research papers, speeches, and technical articles on monetary policies. http://www.stanford.edu/~johntayl/PolRulLink.htm.

CHAPTER FIVE

CAPITAL CONTROLS

ANYA SCHIFFRIN

HISTORY

FROM THE 1940s to the late 1980s, capital controls, or restrictions on the flow of money across borders, were the norm around the world. In Europe, anyone who needed a foreign exchange to trade with another country (so-called current account transactions) to buy goods or services could get it. But it was not so easy to get money that could be used for financial transactions such as currency speculation or buying and selling stocks in another country's equity markets. Often there was a special, less-favorable exchange rate for such transactions. Ordinary individuals confronted these capital controls when they wanted to take a trip abroad: typically, they were allowed only a limited amount of foreign exchange.

It hadn't always been this way. In the nineteenth century there were no man-made restrictions on the flow of capital. But, at least partly because of the lack of technology, capital moved far more slowly than it does today. Until the 1930s, the world was on the gold standard—a system by which all domestic money had to be backed, in full, by the government's gold reserves. This meant that for every dollar in circulation, you had to have one dollar's worth of gold sitting in the central bank's vault. In essence, the government promised to convert any or all of the country's local currency for gold at a constant rate of exchange. The idea behind the system was easy: if a country ran a balance-of-payments deficit, which meant it needed to borrow to pay for imports, gold would leave the country as payments for imports went out faster than payments for exports came in. To maintain full backing, the government would have had to respond by taking money out of circulation, which would, in turn, cause the money supply to fall. A shrinking money supply, theory suggests, contributes to a decline in the prices of goods and services. This would make local goods more attractive and imported goods less so. Exports would climb and imports would fall and the balance-of-payment deficit would, in theory, turn into a surplus. The process reverses as gold returns and equilibrium is restored. Thus, for the gold standard to work, the capital account had to be liberal. Otherwise, gold could not be shipped from one country to another.

The gold standard broke down and was abandoned by the United States during the Great Depression: maintaining the system required a process of declining prices (i.e., deflation) that was simply too painful to sustain, especially during a period of deep economic contraction. Other countries, such as Great Britain, France, Ireland, Scandinavia, Iraq, Portugal, Thailand, Japan, and a number of countries in Latin America, abandoned the system in droves, each hoping that freeing the exchange rate from the gold standard's "straitjacket" would increase exports. But, of course, when all countries tried to do this simultaneously, nobody's exports rose; imbalances remained and currencies weakened. Capital controls had to be imposed.

As World War II came to an end and the advanced industrialized countries tried to reestablish the global economic order, a system of fixed exchange rates was again set up, and the International Monetary Fund was created to help make it work. The idea was to set up a system that would make it easy to finance trade in goods and services rather than in mere financial transactions. The system, in other words, centered on reducing the foreign-exchange restrictions associated with trade, a process known as current-account liberalization. It was designed to maintain stability in exchange rates and a ready availability of foreign exchange, both of which were required to facilitate trade. Today, almost all countries have fully liberalized their current account. While current-account liberalization was being aggressively pushed, however, the system was much more cautious about pushing for the liberalization of capital account. (Current-account liberalization refers only to loosening restrictions on money used to pay for imports and exports; capital-account liberalization means allowing the free flow of money that can be used for things like buying stocks, speculation on the foreign exchange markets, and purchasing assets. Typically there is more worry about the effects of taking capital out of the country than allowing it in.) The United States was an exception to this globally cautious attitude toward capital-account liberalization. Indeed, the United States had open capital markets throughout most of the twentieth century, except for two brief periods: the Great Depression of the 1930s and in the 1970s.

It was only in the 1960s that some European countries began to gradually ease restrictions. Since then, the trend spread gradually until, by the 1990s, most developed countries in the world had full capital-account liberalization. In countries that liberalized global financial transactions, anyone could buy and sell any other currency that was fully liberalized, for whatever purpose. Supposedly, the only reporting requirements were those designed to ensure compliance with tax laws. Money could travel to buy stocks in other countries, to invest in other countries, or to buy other currencies. Soon, enormous markets in foreign exchange developed with New York, London, Frankfurt, and Tokyo becoming the major money-market centers and with active trade also in Hong Kong and Singapore. The UK lifted controls in 1979 and then Germany in 1984. Spain lifted theirs in 1992 and Greece in 1994. At first, a number of European countries pegged their currencies to one another and traded in a band known as the European Exchange Rate Mechanism. Later many countries abolished their currencies in favor of the euro.

Some developing countries, such as China, India, and Sri Lanka, largely kept their controls, but others, especially in Latin America and East Asia, began to liberalize. In the developing countries, the process started with Chile in the early 1970s and soon spread to almost all Latin countries. Asia was a latecomer to the game of liberalizing capital accounts a decade or so later, mostly in the 1980s, although China retained its controls. Malaysia reimposed capital controls after the 1997 Asian economic crisis, and, in the last couple of years, capital controls have come back in some parts of Latin America such as Chile, Argentina, and Venezuela.

As barriers were removed, money began to flow into many of these developing countries. Foreign investors eagerly bought the stocks and bonds issued by companies in developing countries and lent them money directly. Indeed, by September 1997, at its annual meeting in Hong Kong, the IMF lobbied member-states to change its charter to allow it to push countries toward full capital-account liberalization.

The trend toward full capital account liberalization was part of a larger push for economic liberalization that began in the United States with the election of President Ronald Reagan and in the UK with the election of Prime Minister Margaret Thatcher—both of whom were great believers in free markets. Economists did not do much research, either theoretical or empirical, as to whether liberalization was a good idea. Nonetheless, many believed that the free flow of capital would enrich countries all over the world. After all, trade and investment had helped wealthy countries develop in the nineteenth century.

The arguments for capital-account liberalization and against capital controls are:

- Developing countries save little but need to invest heavily. They also have a wealth of opportunities but little capital. Foreign capital, though, will not flow into a country unless investors are assured that, should they need to, they can freely repatriate their capital—hence the importance of capital-account liberalization.

- Flows of foreign capital into a country can help improve productivity, and this, in turn, brings about a major increase in living standards. It

The IMF and Capital-Account Liberalization

NICHOLAS ROSEN

The issue of financial market liberalization has been a difficult and controversial one for the International Monetary Fund. Throughout much of the 1990s, the IMF aggressively pushed nations to open their countries to the flow of international financial capital. But they have since reversed their position—at least in theory.

The IMF originally argued that by removing barriers to foreign inflows, perennially capital-short developing countries could harness a powerful engine for growth, diversify risk, and increase welfare while creating new investment opportunities for international investors. These convictions were so strong that in 1997 the fund's executive board launched a campaign to have the IMF charter amended to include the promotion of capital market liberalization as part of the fund's mandate.

In the meantime, numerous countries, including Russia and the Asian "new industrializers," followed the IMF's prescription for capital-markets reform. Some of those countries were, with hindsight, simply not ready for open capital accounts. They relied heavily on short term borrowing to finance inefficient and uneconomical investments. In July 1997, the "chickens came home to roost." Thailand, for instance, which was running huge current-account deficits that were financed with extremely short-term external borrowing had to abandon its fixed exchange rate regime. The baht—the Thai currency—collapsed, and financial contagion spread from Thailand to South Korea, Indonesia, and eventually Russia and Brazil. The bonanza of capital inflows these countries had enjoyed was quickly reversed as a stampede of panicked investors fled the region. A decade of solid growth and rising incomes screeched to an abrupt halt as bank failures, unemployment and poverty gripped the region.

In the wake of the crisis, many observers blamed the capital-account policies championed by the IMF and the U.S. Treasury for opening financial markets too fast and rendering them vulnerable to unpredictable shifts in short-term capital flows. The IMF itself adopted a more cautious tone after the crisis and now stresses the need for extensive preparation before starting the liberalization process—though it's certainly not advocating capital-market controls as a long-term solution.

A March 2003 paper authored by then IMF chief economist Kenneth Rogoff concluded that liberalization should be "approached cautiously, with good institutions and macroeconomic framework" as important prerequisites. He has said that developing countries should not rush to liberalize their capital markets, and, in many cases, the IMF has actually conceded that controls on capital mobility—particularly those that curb inward flows, like the ones used by Chile—may be advisable. Meanwhile, plans to add capital-account reform to the IMF's charter mandate appear dead.

also promotes the integration of economies into the world financial system; the increased availability of capital from a wide range of sources is good for growth.

- Open capital accounts promote good policies: countries that have stable governments, fair and consistent regulations, and attractive investment climates will draw more funds. Capital-market liberalization provides both a carrot and a stick: countries that pursue such policies will find that they can attract more capital; those that do not will find capital rapidly leaving.

- Capital controls are microeconomically inefficient in that they hinder the optimal allocation of resources; that is, money is not allowed to flow naturally to the most efficient or successful companies or investments. Controls also have large administrative costs, are widely evaded, and give rise to corruption.

But the downside of the process proved to be painful. True, the heavy inflow of capital into developing countries that liberalized their capital accounts initially triggered a period of rapid economic growth. It is also true that the inflows pushed the value of those countries' currencies upward against the U.S. dollar. But when foreign investors lost confidence in the economies of these countries, they began to pull their money out. The value of the currencies then fell sharply against the U.S. dollar, making it ever more difficult for the developing countries to pay back their debts and causing foreign investors to lose even more confidence. The years after capital-market liberalization spread were punctuated by a series of financial crises, including the Asian crisis in 1997, the Russian crisis in 1998, the Brazilian crisis in 1999, and the crises in Turkey and Argentina in 2001. Over a hundred countries have faced crises in the past thirty years.

While a number of different factors have contributed to each of those crises, capital-market liberalization has usually been an important one. Most of the crises have been precipitated by the rapid and disruptive flow of money out of the country—what a number of economists, including Rudiger Dornbusch and the Inter-American Development Bank's chief economist, Guillermo Calvo, have called the "sudden stop."

In 1997, the Asian crisis began when foreign-exchange speculators began selling off Asian currencies. The countries were stuck in a tight place. The way to stop money going out of a country is to raise interest rates, but raising interest rates rapidly is terrible for the banking sector of any country and poses especially difficult problems for banks in developing countries. For one thing, banks face maturity mismatches between the deposits they attract and the loans they have made—a mismatch that is at the core of banking but whose balance sheet impact can be fatal when interest rates rise. Banks borrow short term (that is, their depositors can withdraw their money at any time) but lend long term (for mortgages, for example). This means that when interest rates rise suddenly, what banks pay to depositors may rise suddenly, though what they receive adjusts very slowly. This can be seen another way. The market value of a long term loan (such as the mortgage) that has a fixed interest rate falls dramatically as market interest rates rise. If market interest rates are 10 percent, a mortgage paying only 5 percent interest will sell at a deep discount. But meanwhile, the bank's commitment to its depositors remains unchanged. In short, the value of its assets plummets, while the value of its liabilities remains relatively unchanged. A bank with a positive net worth can suddenly become a bank with a negative net worth. The sudden rise in interest rates by the Federal Reserve Board in the early 1980s brought on the failure of the savings and loan associations. But the problem is particularly severe in developing countries, where banks are more likely to be undercapitalized and where markets are thin, so that banks will find it more difficult to raise additional capital At the same time, higher interest rates mean that people and companies who have borrowed money find it harder to pay back. When they stop repaying, banks go out of business and stop lending. Less-developed countries do not have strong stock markets and so rely far more on bank finance to grow the economy and create jobs. Bank closures can mean that the economy stops growing. After currencies collapsed in Thailand, South Korea, and Indonesia, so did their banking systems. As things got worse, commercial banks with long-term relations with many of the affected countries also reduced their credit lines. The end result was massive bankruptcies and an increase in unemployment. Ultimately, flows equivalent to some 12–15 percent of gross domestic product left these countries.

Of course, Thailand, South Korea, and Indonesia did not have perfect economies, and there were problems with some of their companies and banks, including shaky lending practices; over-investment in bubble assets, such as real estate; and lack of regulation and oversight, all of which contributed to the weakness in the region's banks. But despite these serious flaws, the crisis itself was triggered by the massive outflows of capital. Many people began to question whether rapid capital-market liberalization was really a good idea—what was the point of bringing in millions of dollars of foreign capital, driving up the value of your own currency, and then seeing it leave again? They noted that countries such as China, India, and Vietnam that have capital controls were relatively unaffected by the crisis. In 1998, Malaysia imposed controls on hot money and, to some extent, was vindicated when it turned out that these worked far better than people had predicted before they were imposed.

Criticisms of rapid capital account liberalization market include:

■ There is a difference between foreign direct investment (that is, foreign investment in factories, businesses, and things that produce goods and services) and portfolio investment in stocks and bonds, which tends to be more speculative. FDI money is sunk into ownership of companies and property and so can not be pulled out of a country overnight. Early supporters of capital-account liberalization did not really think about the differences between these two kinds of capital flows, but, now while most people agree that FDI is important, they worry about unregulated portfolio investment and the effect it has on developing countries.

■ Many advocates of capital-market liberalization claim that without it countries will not be able to attract foreign direct investment, but there is little evidence to support that conclusion. China, for example, is the largest FDI recipient in the world and has a closed capital account. (The Chinese government has made verbal commitments to liberalize, but few measures have yet been taken.)

■ Capital market liberalization was pushed even on countries where there was no shortage of capital. For example, in East Asia there were very high savings rates. Indeed, the problem there was where to invest successfully these savings. This is not necessarily a problem if a country has a strong regulatory framework and a robust financial sector.

The G-7 developed countries, for example, have liberalized capital accounts and have not suffered major crises as a result.

■ Free capital mobility makes macroeconomic management difficult not only in bad times but also in good ones. In prosperous times, the rush of money into a country can lead to an overvalued exchange rate, which has a negative impact on exports. Flows also swell the country's liquidity, which, in turn, fuels inflation. To avoid inflation, countries often raise interest rates, but this simply makes matters worse, as more capital is attracted into the country. Finally, surges in inflows can over-tax the ability of banks to mediate the capital prudently, often contributing to bad investment decisions and to speculative and sometimes even corrupt transactions.

■ While many countries have had problems implementing capital controls, some have done so with remarkable success, such as Chile and Malaysia. Even if controls are imperfect and partially evaded, they still may help stabilize the economy (as Paul Volcker, former chairman of the U.S. Federal Reserve, put it, a leaky umbrella still may provide some protection on a rainy day). But it's important to distinguish between controls that stop capital from coming in, as in Chile, and those that stop capital from flowing out, as in Malaysia. The two types of controls have very different implications.

■ International financial markets are capricious. Even countries that have reasonably good economic policies may find themselves suddenly facing higher interest rates or a broader loss of confidence as money is quickly pulled out.

■ Changes in technology have exacerbated the increase in volatility associated with capital-market liberalization. When capital movements were first liberalized, foreign-exchange trading was far less developed and communications were slower, so it was hard to imagine that it would be possible for speculators and banks to take hundreds of millions of dollars out of a country overnight.

The debate over capital controls has remained highly contentious, but even mainstream economists have began to say that capital market liberalization should be done slowly and only after certain conditions had been met, such as

■ the development of a strong banking sector that is able to handle large inflows and channel them into productive investments;

■ a restructured and efficient corporate sector that can use inflows effectively and not throw "good money after bad";

■ a strong regulatory and legal regime that restricts monopolistic practices, ensures prudential banking practices, and, when needed, regulates bankruptcy of debt-burdened corporations;

- a sound macroeconomic environment that avoids large fiscal deficits, which exacerbate the overheating associated with capital inflows, and inflexible exchange rate regimes, which cannot handle the volatility of capital flows;

- a strong system of prudential regulation and laws that mandate proper accounting, auditing, and reporting;

- no implicit government guarantees that encourage excessive inflows of short term capital.

As well, the idea of using controls on inflows as a preventive measure—to stop the buildup of excessive short-term liabilities—has become increasingly accepted by some top economists:

- Columbia University professor Jagdish Bhagwati, a top economist in the field of trade, asserts that although free trade helps developing countries, the risks from unfettered capital-market liberalization are high. He points out that there is no evidence that capital-market liberalization provides more benefits then you would get from opening up to foreign investment, and that the benefits that do come from the free movement of capital can be wiped out by crises that cause growth to collapse.

- Harvard economist Dani Rodrik, who has also criticized excessively rapid trade liberalization, concluded that there is no statistical evidence supporting the view that capital-market liberalization boosts economic growth or leads to more real investment.

- Studies at the World Bank and elsewhere showed that capital-market liberalization has been systematically related to instability and crises.

TYPES OF CONTROLS

- *Taxes.* Chile imposed taxes on capital flowing into the country, Malaysia on capital leaving the country. The point of these taxes is that they affect the incentives to borrow abroad, and they can be fine-tuned, for instance, to discourage short-term borrowing without discouraging long-term borrowing.

- *Bank (prudential) regulations.* Bank regulations can make sure that banks limit foreign borrowing as a ratio of their foreign-denominated assets. It is this so-called currency mismatch that often gives rise to problems. Restrictions can also be placed on the extent to which banks concentrate their lending to particular firms and/or sectors. Liquidity regulations that restrict the ratio of short-term liabilities to banks' assets have also become fairly common. Such regulations are today typically considered part of prudential bank regulations and thus are not as subject to as much criticism.

- *Direct controls.* China, India, and many other countries continue to impose direct controls on foreign-exchange transactions. For many years in Vietnam, companies needed to get permission to buy foreign exchange and had to show why they needed it. Companies involved in infrastructure construction got a higher priority than companies that sold consumer goods.

There are examples of success and failure. Critics of capital controls point to the failures, suggest that controls can be and often are easily circumvented, and note that success requires a high level of sophistication. Advocates argue that we now know much more about how to make controls work. Bank regulations in Malaysia succeeded in limiting the foreign-exchange exposure of domestic companies and banks, resulting in Malaysia's having a shallower downturn than neighboring countries while being left with less debt. But critics say that Malaysian capital controls were imposed "after the horse left the barn." In other words, by the time the controls were imposed, capital had already flowed out and the controls were superfluous. For example, South Korea and Malaysia ended with a similar postcrisis outcome, even though the former did not impose controls and the latter did. Chilean controls succeeded in reducing inflows of short-term capital, with little adverse effect on long-term flows. But Chile later abandoned the system, at a time when its problem was a shortage of flows rather than an excess. Ultimately, while the capital controls did not isolate the country from the vagaries of the international market place, it did reduce the impact.

RAPID LIBERALIZATION CAN BE DANGEROUS

Economists now generally agree that rapid liberalization of capital markets can be dangerous for developing countries unless they have a stable macroeconomy, strong banking sectors, and developed ways of overseeing the financial sector. The idea of controls on short-term borrowing has also become increasingly accepted, even if the idea of imposing controls during a crisis is still controversial. However, it is unlikely that the trend of liberalization will be reversed. Countries that have liberalized will find it difficult to go back to the old system, but it seems likely that countries that have not fully liberalized (China, Vietnam, Laos, Malaysia) will not rush to do so.

THE ARGUMENTS FOR AND AGAINST CAPITAL CONTROLS

Pro

- Can prevent crises from happening by stopping large inflows

- Give countries flexibility so they can lower interest rates and promote growth without worrying about their currency collapsing

- Give countries breathing room during a crisis so they can reorder the financial sector in an orderly fashion

- Ensure domestic savings are used locally. Countries like Vietnam and Laos do not want to see local savings invested abroad, as these countries need capital to grow their own economies

CON

- Hard to enforce

- Ineffective even when they are enforced; Sebastian Edwards and other opponents say that countries that stepped up capital controls after crises, such as Argentina, Brazil and Mexico, experienced slower growth

- Produce distortions

- Encourage smuggling and other "rent-seeking activities"

- Lull countries into a false sense of security whereby they refrain from changing their policies because they feel protected from market discipline and from capital flight

TIPS FOR REPORTERS

- What kinds of controls govern a country's currencies now, and are they effective?

- Is there a need to change the rules? If so, why?

- What would the consequences be if the regulations were changed? What would the consequences be if they were not changed?

- What is the level of short-term borrowing in the country?

- What is the level of dollar-denominated debt the country owes?

- Are banks in the country excessively exposed to short-term dollar-denominated loans? Will they suffer if there was to be a large movement in the currency?

- Do firms in the country face a currency mismatch? Have they borrowed heavily in dollars even though their earnings are predominantly in local currencies?

- What are the major vested interests in the country that would benefit from freer capital movements? Which will be hurt?

- Are there sufficiently advanced institutional frameworks that could monitor capital flows and, if needed, influence them through direct and indirect controls?

- What is the level of foreign direct investment in the country compared to the level of portfolio investment?

LINKS FOR MORE INFORMATION

1. Professor Ross Levin, who teaches finance at the Carlson School of Management of the University of Minnesota, has written extensively on banking issues. http://legacy.csom.umn.edu/ WWWPages/FACULTY/RLevine/Index.html. His work on capital controls can be found at http://econpapers.hhs.se/paper/wopwobadc/ 1622.htm.

2. The online library of the Friedrich Ebert Foundation published a case study of Chile's economic liberation and control of foreign capital. http://library.fes.de/fulltext/iez/ 00766.htm.

3. University of California at Berkeley's Professor J. Bradford DeLong has written about the history of capital controls on this Web site. Www.j-bradford-delong.net/comments/ USIA.html.

4. Professor Jagdish Bhagwati's remarks prepared for the 7 November 1998 NBER conference on Capital Controls in Cambridge, Mass., titled "Why Free Capital Mobility May Be Hazardous to Your Health: Lessons from the Latest Financial Crisis." http://www.columbia.edu/ ~jb38/papers/NBER_comments.pdf).

5. "Capital Control Freaks, How Malaysia Got Away with Economic Heresy," Paul Krugman, *Slate*, 27 September 1999. http://slate.msn .com/ id/35534.

6. "An Introduction to Capital Controls," Christopher J. Neely, *Federal Reserve Bank of St Louis Review*, November/December 1999. http://research.stlouisfed.org/econ/cneely.

7. "Capital Flow and Capital Control," Ana Maria P. G. Pontes, George Washington University, Washington D.C., Minerva Program, Fall 1999. http://www.gwu.edu/~ibi/minerva/ Fall1999/Pontes.Ana.pdf).

8. "The Mirage of Capital Controls," Sebastian Edwards, University of California in Los Angeles' Anderson Graduate School of Management, May 1999. http://www.anderson.ucla.edu/faculty/sebastian.edwards/ for_aff.pdf).

9. The World Bank's page on international capital flows. http://www.worldbank.org/research/ projects/capflows.htm.

10. "Capital Flows in Crisis and the International Financial Infrastructure: An Indonesian Review," remarks by J. Soedradjad Djiwandono, professor of economics at the University of Indonesia, at a World Bank conference in Washington, D.C., in 1998. http://www.pacific .net.id/pakar/sj/capital_flow_crisis_1.html.

CHAPTER SIX

DOLLARIZATION

TYLER MARONEY

DOLLARIZATION IS the process by which a country abandons its own currency and adopts the currency of a more stable country as its legal tender. Though the concept was coined in reference to the U.S. dollar, the conversion to any foreign, stable currency —the European euro and the Japanese yen, for example—is usually known as dollarization.

In many countries, such as those with weak currencies and underdeveloped banking systems, there is a natural move toward the dollar. People who are afraid of inflation or who do not trust their domestic central bank keep their money in hard currency. If hard-currency bank accounts are restricted (often because the government wants to discourage the use of the dollar), they may keep their savings at home under the proverbial mattress. In much of Eastern Europe, the Deutsche mark was considered a safer bet than the local currency and was used commonly in daily transactions. In many parts of the world, the dollar has the same function and people often prefer to be paid in dollars when they can get them or convert their savings into dollars. This is especially true of countries with high inflation—there dollars are considered to be more reliable and prices may even be denominated in dollars. This tendency often extends to imported goods and luxuries that get priced in dollars and to the tourist sector. Indeed, tourists in countries like Vietnam—where there is a weak banking system—and Cuba—where dollar shops stock items that are not found in government-run stores—often find they can go for weeks without using local currency.

When dollarization is done on a formal basis, it is politically often associated with conservative ("orthodox") politicians. Such politicians and economists advocate dollarization because of their overall belief in strong currencies and because of their desire to boost confidence in the local economy. They hope that by formally dollarizing, the country will be rid of inflation and the economy will be put on a sounder footing.

In this chapter, and for simplicity, we will be referring only to the U.S. dollar. The analysis for other major currencies is identical. There are two types of dollarization: full (or statutory) and unofficial.

FULL (STATUTORY) DOLLARIZATION

This occurs when a government makes the official decision to use a foreign currency for all transactions, including government and private debt—both public and private bank accounts are converted to dollars. The outgoing domestic currency becomes extinct; the U.S. dollar becomes the "legal tender." In full dollarization, businesses pay their employees in dollars and all transactions, whether commercial of financial, are conducted in dollars. In a dollarized economy, central banks may not cease to exist in a legal sense, but, in a practical sense, they *effectively* lose relevance: monetary policy is relegated to the U.S. Federal Reserve.

UNOFFICIAL DOLLARIZATION

Sometimes known as "currency substitution," unofficial dollarization is common in developing countries. Most emerging-market countries have some degree of unofficial dollarization, which occurs when the value of the local currency becomes volatile and people shift to the more dependable dollar for making purchases, valuing assets, and personal savings.

In both Havana, Cuba, and Lima, Peru, for example, tourists often pay for taxi cabs and Coca Colas in dollars, which coexist with the local currencies. Similarly, while Argentina had never officially dollarized, almost the entire economy had turned on the greenback; most major transactions—such as car loans and mortgages—were conducted in dollars. In January 2001, Argentina broke its hard peg to the dollar and "pesofied." As the peso fell precipitously after the devaluation, what has become known as "green fever"—a desperate rush to buy dollars—struck the nation.

WHY DOLLARIZE?

In virtually all cases, dollarization occurs as a response to massive macroeconomic imbalances, which usually take the form of uncontrollably high inflation and a precipitously depreciating currency. The "informal" or spontaneous dollarization usually starts with depositors who simply refuse to save in the unstable local currency. Given the local currency's

CAPITAL MARKETS

instability, owners of assets like real estate also start quoting values in dollars and, eventually, using dollars for their transactions. As confidence in the local currency falls because of the rampant inflation, interest rates naturally rise on the local currency (nominal interest rates always need to keep ahead of inflation. In cases of rampant inflation, moreover, real interest rates on the affected currency rise even more due to the risk premium). Consequently, many businesses begin borrowing in dollars so as to benefit from their lower rates. Soon, large parts of the economy are turning on the dollar.

Dollarization usually, but not always, occurs when the monetary authorities—generally central banks—try to stabilize inflation and a sliding currency by instituting tight monetary policies. However, after years of instability, such policies are typically not credible and often fail. The authorities, in that case, opt for a "nominal anchor" that ensures credibility. A decision to dollarize is an extreme case that ties the hand of the central bank so that it completely gives up control over monetary policy.

But formal dollarization does not only follow cases of economic collapse and chaos. There is also a "currency union" argument for dollarization. Small countries that are geographically close and economically highly integrated with a large country sometimes find it beneficial to eschew their own currencies and simply adopt those of their giant neighbors. Panama is a case in point. Some Central American countries (El Salvador, for example) have considered dollarization precisely on the view that a currency union will deepen trade relations with the anchor country: the United States. The decision to adopt the dollar in central America also reflects the fact that the countries are receivers of dollar-denominated remittances from their oversees laborers residing in the United States. The whole euro experiment is an ambitious and comprehensive manifestation of the "currency union" theory.

It must be stressed that dollarization, as a system of currency exchange, does not guarantee stability and economic growth in and of itself. When a country makes the decision to formally dollarize, it adopts the monetary policy of the U.S. central bank. This is because a domestic central bank conducts monetary policy by changing the quantity and price (that is, the interest rate) of the domestic money. Clearly, if there is no domestic money, there is no scope for monetary policy. Instead, in a dollarized economy, the quantity and price of money is determined by the authority that issues the legal tender: the U.S. Federal Reserve.

Although dollarization did not become fashionable until the 1990s, it is not a new exchange-rate system. Panama has been dollarized for almost a century. Economists have long debated the merits of dollarization, but in recent years it has attracted more attention, particularly when Argentina talked about the idea in the late 1990s. It has also become more relevant because of the adoption of the dollar in Ecuador and El Salvador.

ECUADOR AND THE DOLLAR

NICHOLAS ROSEN

Ecuador, a poor, mountainous nation of 12 million, arrived at dollarization on an economic roller coaster. The early 1990s brought the tiny economy a hopeful surge of growth fueled by oil, Ecuador's principal export, as high crude prices and a new pipeline allowed for an impressive expansion in oil sales. But by the late 1990s, a glut of oil on world markets brought on the collapse of prices, and economic crises sweeping through Asia, Russia, and neighboring Brazil further poisoned the waters for emerging markets as a whole. Trade disputes between the United States and Europe, meanwhile, hurt Ecuador's banana exports. And then there were the destructive forces of nature: first drought, then devastating rains brought by the El Niño weather pattern.

In the fallout of this turbulent chain of events, Ecuador's economy contracted 7 percent in 1999. Government revenues, already hit by reduced oil proceeds, contracted in line with the economy. Having borrowed heavily in the boom years, the government found itself laden with debt it could not afford to service. Ecuador joined the ranks of the world's financial outcasts by defaulting on $6 billion in loans. The banking system was also on a precipice. Ecuadorian banks, heavily exposed to corporations hurt by the oil price decline and natural disasters, were clearly insolvent, and a bank run inevitably developed, prompting the government to virtually take over the banking system.

Naturally, Ecuador's currency, the sucre, bore the burden of the default and the banking collapse. Within one year it lost two-thirds of its value while inflation soared to 90 percent, levels reminiscent of the bleak days of hyperinflation in the 1970s and 1980s.

Although Ecuadorians had turned to the U.S. dollar as a stable medium of exchange well before the crisis, President Jamil Mahuad rejected official dollarization as a "leap into the void." Adopting the dollar would mean relinquishing control over monetary policy, a key economic tool. Printing money would no longer be a way to stimulate growth, finance public spending, or bail out banks in crisis.

But as the clamor of business interests, indigenous groups and labor unions rose, Mahuad realized his political future was in jeopardy. So on January 9, 2000, he reversed his stance, calling for legislation to legally replace the sucre with the U.S. dollar. The plan gave Mahuad some political breathing room, as many Ecuadorians supported dollarization, but the respite proved brief. Two weeks later, anti-Mahuad protesters, backed by dissident military officers, stormed the presidential palace and ousted him. A ruling junta of officers and opposition leaders was hastily established. After twenty-four hours, the junta ceded power to Gustavo Noboa, Mahuad's vice president.

With civilian rule restored and the opposition in disarray, Noboa announced his resolve to continue with dollarization. He argued the move was Ecuador's only hope to avert economic collapse: the dollar would arrest inflation, prevent devaluation, and stabilize the economy.

Soon after, the International Monetary Fund led a group of lenders that granted Ecuador $2 billion in emergency loans, a turning point for the country.

But not everyone was happy. The same labor and indigenous groups that drove Mahuad from power were horrified by the surge in the cost of living that initially accompanied dollarization, which also prompted drastic cuts in social spending and price supports.

Exporters from the non-oil sectors were equally alarmed. Ecuador, like most developing countries, was occasionally hit by "exogenous" shocks such as a financial crisis in a neighboring country. Left unattended, these shocks have a detrimental economic impact on the local economy. The advantage of a freely flexible currency is that it cushions the blow: as the currency devalues in the face of a shock, exports become more competitive and import substitutes more profitable; both help support the local economy. Dollarization, by contrast, is the least flexible foreign exchange arrangement. Ecuadorian exporters reasonably feared dollarization would leave the economy with virtually no "shock absorber."

But with his political fortunes staked on dollarization and international lenders waiting expectantly, Noboa shrugged off the resistance, and in March 2002 the country fixed the exchange rate to 25,000 sucres. The Central Bank, stripped of its monetary policy duties, was reduced to overseeing the banking system and minting coins of subdollar values.

Ecuador's first year under dollarization brought ups and downs. Investment rose, although this was partly the result of higher oil prices and pent-up demand from years of recession. Capital flight eventually subsided. But inflation persisted, rising to 91 percent in 2000. A large segment of the population opposed the plan, complaining they were earning less and their buying power had shrunk.

At first the indicators seemed to vindicate dollarization. The economy expanded 5.5 percent in 2001—the fastest rate in Latin America at the time—on the back of rising consumer spending and investment, and the economy continued to grow in 2003. Interest rates were down and inflation appeared more or less under control, falling to 6.1 percent in 2003 from nearly 38 percent in 2001. But looking forward, the program's ultimate success remains an open question. Recent growth was propped up by a stretch of high oil prices, while exports have been hit hard as agriculture, tourism, and textiles have become less competitive.

At this writing, Ecuador is extremely vulnerable to market shifts since it can no longer devalue its currency to respond to outside shocks. Falling oil prices, for instance, would hit the country with unmitigated force. Any sudden economic blow would threaten the weak banks, and there is great concern that without the liquidity of the Central Bank, domestic banks will be unable to extend the credit necessary for growth and job creation.

Lacking monetary policy, one of Ecuador's only means of staying competitive is through tough microeconomic reforms that can increase the economy's efficiency and allow it to adjust to external shocks with greater flexibility. But these reforms are always controversial, and the population remains restive: more than 70 percent still live below the poverty line, and dollarization has been slow to benefit the poor since wages have yet to catch up with prices. President Lucio Gutierrez, a leader of the 2000 coup d'état who took power several years later, has found his own administration imperiled by more political unrest. Many Ecuadorians wonder whether the dollar will bring long-term prosperity or merely a brief rest on an increasingly uncertain road.

CONDITIONS FOR SUCCESSFUL DOLLARIZATION

For dollarization to succeed, a number of prerequisites are necessary. First, any country that wishes to dollarize must have the resources to do so. The country needs to exchange all local currencies into dollars at a certain exchange rate. At that exchange rate, enough dollars have to be available. Otherwise, a dollar shortage will develop. Alternatively, if there is not enough hard currency to cover all the local currency, the government may have to accept a weaker exchange rate.

The second prerequisite is for the country to have a strong banking sector. Weak banking sectors are susceptible to collapse. The severe economic impact of a collapsing banking sector can be staved off, usually, by the central bank printing money and providing it as emergency liquidity to the sector. This option is simply not available to a dollarized economy in which the central bank has no control over monetary policy. Of course, the dollarized economy's central bank can ask the "anchor" country's central bank (the Fed) to provide it with emergency financial assistance; however, the Fed is on the record as refusing to commit to helping a dollarized country's banking sector. The central bank could also use its own reserves of dollars to assist a faltering banking sector; however, this option, unlike the free option of simply printing money, is expensive and uses "real" resources.

Finally, it is best to have a strong fiscal position. In a dollarized economy, a government often does not have the luxury of running a large deficit, that is, of spending much more than it makes. This is because large deficits, in a dollarized economy, can no longer be financed by printing money.

PANAMA

The first country to fully dollarize was Panama. Since 1904, the year after the country separated from Colombia, Panama's economy has run on the greenback. This has had many positive effects on the economic health of the country. For example, in the 1990s, inflation barely exceeded 1 percent per year. And yet, reliance on the dollar has not alleviated Panama's dependence on outside help. Since 1973, Panama has had more than fifteen International Monetary Fund programs, and dollarization did not prevent Panama from defaulting on its foreign debt in the mid-1980s.

EL SALVADOR

In late November of 2000, El Salvador's legislature passed a law mandating the full dollarization of the country. On New Year's Day, 2001, automated teller machines were programmed to dispense dollars and bank accounts were converted. The move was not made under the same desperate circumstances as in, for example, Ecuador. In fact, the Salvadoran inflation rate had been low, about 1.3 percent, for the previous decade, and the economy had been performing relatively well. Rather, the move was aimed at making El Salvador, a country already highly integrated with the United States, more attractive to international investors. Salvadorans were not as stunned when their country dollarized as Ecuadorians were because the colon, El Salvador's former currency, had already been fixed to the dollar for eight years. The Salvadoran central bank has estimated that almost 70 percent of the money in use today is dollars.

Again, it is still too early to weigh the benefits of dollarization. But there are some promising signs: the day after El Salvador adopted the new currency, the interest rate on consumer loans and mortgages fell from 17 to 11 percent, giving a much-needed boost to the economy. As such, the economy continued to perform well and has, partly as a result of deep integration with its northern neighbor, weathered the dual shocks of September 11 and of the dot-com bubble's bursting relatively well.

OTHER CASES

A few years ago, the United Nations announced that the dollar would become the official currency of East Timor, which had just gained its independence from Indonesia. In December 2000, Guatemala passed a law allowing the free circulation of dollars, although it stopped short of full dollarization. And a host of other countries have considered dollarizing—Costa Rica, Honduras, and Nicaragua, to name a few. Some have proposed that Afghanistan dollarize as well, but only as a temporary measure until a more stable political regime assumes control of the government. No country has ever reversed a policy of full dollarization, and it is generally considered a permanent move.

THE BENEFITS

- Probably the biggest advantage to dollarization is the economic stability that comes with it. A dollarized economy imports its inflation from the United States; as such, high inflation is brought almost immediately under control. The U.S. dollar is the most trusted currency in the world and any country that formally adopts it also adopts the monetary policy of the Federal Reserve Board. Dollarizing, therefore, eliminates the risk of sharp devaluations, reducing, in turn, local interest rates.

- Furthermore, dollarization attracts foreign investors, who know that the monetary value of their assets is safe. If credible, dollarization causes domestic interest rates to fall to those prevailing in the United States. Lower rates, in turn, contribute to growth and further investment.

THE COSTS

- Although dollarization can make a country more stable, it is, by no means, a panacea. A dollarized economy becomes vulnerable to changes in the value of the dollar, even though those fluctuations are the result of U.S. domestic economic conditions. When and if the dollar fluctuates against international currencies, which it often does, sometimes wildly, there is no way to respond to such a crisis. This is because any (formally) dollarized country forfeits control of its centralized, independent monetary policy to the central bank of the country whose currency has been adopted. What is more, the Federal Reserve Board acts with the interests of the United States in mind, without particular concern for the international fallout on dollarized economies.

- For the same reason, it is *impossible to respond to economic shocks*, such as the volatile price of oil on the international market, by tweaking exchange rates. Dollarization leads to the loss of the exchange rate as a policy instrument. For example, take a country whose major export is timber. Say the global price of timber falls sharply. Export proceeds fall, causing the economy to contract. Had the currency been flexible, however, a depreciation would have occurred. The country would have regained lost competitiveness and the real economy would have been, at least to some extent, shielded from the shock. Put differently, in a dollarized economy, external shocks are no longer absorbed by the local currency but now get transmitted through the real economy.

- In addition, a dollarized country *loses seignorage benefits*. Seignorage, essentially, is revenue earned from issuing currency. This is a profitable business because the costs of printing and circulating bills (essentially worthless pieces of paper) are much lower than the value of the goods that paper will buy. The U.S. government makes about $25 billion a year in net seignorage, and, when residents of another country hold dollars, they are creating income for the U.S. Treasury Department. There has been talk of sharing seignorage benefits with a dollarized country, but, to date, the United States has not allowed that to happen.

■ Further disadvantages of dollarization include the *fear of counterfeiting*, given that fake bills are hard enough to identify in the United States. In addition to producing cocaine, Colombia is notorious for its dollar "factories." There is also the political risk. When El Salvador dollarized, opposition politicians blasted the government for selling out to economic imperialism. For many countries, the biggest obstacles to dollarization is cultural: dollarizing is seen as akin to surrendering national sovereignty.

■ It should be stressed that dollarization, while it may help stabilize hyperinflation, plays *no direct role in financial and political reform*. In other words, many economists argue, it has almost no effect on socioeconomic distortions such as tax evasion, poor living standards, unemployment, and corruption. Those who disagree with this say that an economically stable environment is much more conducive to reform than one that is not. Dollarization, therefore, is a necessary but not sufficient condition for a sustainable development strategy.

CONCLUSION

In the final analysis, it is important to stress that dollarization is no cure-all. As many students of dollarization have pointed out, it is difficult to weigh the true costs and benefits for one simple reason: lack of precedent. There is virtually no historical record with which to contrast and compare the results of an adopted currency. Most analysis is theoretical. Only a handful of countries have fully dollarized, and each one was different in size and made the conversion for different reasons and under different circumstances. Panama is the only country with a long history of dollarization, and it has a close political and economic relationship to the United States. Many economists believe that dollarization will succeed best in small, open, flexible economies that have strong trading and economic relationships with the United States or other giant economies. El Salvador is one such guinea pig. It may take years, however, to measure its success.

What is more, dollarization is virtually permanent. After a country officially adopts the dollar, trying to revert back to a local currency would surely be chaotic. This is one of the problems with the proposal that Afghanistan dollarize. It cannot be temporary. Until more countries have lived under the dollar for at least a few decades, it will be difficult to assess the effectiveness of full dollarization.

Look out for:

- *The level of "unofficial" dollarization.* Understanding this will help reporters figure out the potential difficulty a country would have in making the transition to a more stable currency. Argentina, for example, would be able to dollarize relatively easily because the greenback is already a pillar of the economy. And El Salvador, as noted, had already pegged its currency to the dollar, making the transition smoother. As a quantitative measure, look at the percentage of total banking deposits denominated in dollars. This indicator is usually published by the central bank.

- *The severity of inflation.* In 1989, Argentina suffered from hyperinflation that reached 5,000 percent annually, which, at the time, was the highest rate in the world. When Ecuador made the decision to dollarize, inflation was completely out of control.

- *The rate of dollarization.* When a country decides to formally dollarize, the government announces a "rate of dollarization"—that is, the rate at which domestic monies can be transferred into the newly adopted dollar. That decision has crucial socioeconomic and political implications. A generous exchange rate can make holders of local monies richer but would make the cost of local production too expensive when measured in dollar terms.

By contrast, too onerous an exchange rate makes people poorer in dollar terms but renders a country's exports competitive. Learning the dynamics of how (and why) the rate of dollarization was decided upon is a worthwhile journalistic endeavor.

- *How closely linked is the local economy to the United States?* This question has two parts. First, reporters should look at how closely linked the local currency is to the dollar. El Salvador and, until recently, Argentina had pegged their currencies to the dollar. This makes for an easier transition to full dollarization. Reporters should look to see if a currency board or some kind of peg exists and how long that system has been in use. The second part is slightly more difficult: Is the United States a major trading partner for the country in question? Does the country have a large expatriate labor pool working in the United Sates? Does the country heavily rely on dollar-denominated capital? Answers to those questions are often published in central bank bulletins.

- *Reserves of dollars in the central bank and the private financial system.* Sustainability of dollarization depends on how many dollars come into the country every year as well as how many dollars both local banks and the central bank hold. Reporters should research these topics and keep an eye on remittances from abroad.

1. Currency Boards and Dollarization, a Web site maintained by Kurt Schuler, a senior economist at the U.S. Senate, has lots of reference materials about dollarization and related topics. http://www.dollarization.org.

2. Andrew Berg and Eduardo Boreinsztein's paper titled "The Dollarization Debate" talks about the costs and benefits of dollarization and countries that are likely to benefit from it. *Finance and Development,* March 2000. http://www.imf.org/external/pubs/ft/fandd/2000/03/berg.htm.

3. Professor Nouriel Roubini at the Stern School of Business runs a Web site that carries a large number of papers on a range of economic topics, including currency and dollarization. http://pages.stern.nyu.edu/~nroubini/asia/dollarize.htm.

4. Many working papers published by the National Bureau of Economic Research on currency union and dollarization can be downloaded from the Ideas' Web site. http://ideas.repec.org/p/nbr/nberwo/8879.html.

5. The seach engine on the Institute for International Economics' Web site will produce a series of papers on dollarization and related issues. http://www.iie.com/homepage.htm.

6. The Cato Institute in Washington, D.C., published an interesting case study on dollarization in Argentina. http://www.cato.org/pubs/fpbriefs/fpb-052es.html.

7. Professor Guillermo Calvo, director of the Center for International Economics at the University of Maryland, writes a lot about dollarization. His papers and policy notes are on his Web site. http://www.bsos.umd.edu/econ/ciecalvo.htm.

8. The World Bank's Web page on dollarization has some useful information. http://lnweb18.worldbank.org/External/lac/lac.nsf/Sectors/Economic+Polic.

CHAPTER SEVEN

DERIVATIVES

RANDALL DODD

INTRODUCTION

DERIVATIVES SERVE an important and useful economic function, but they also pose several dangers to the stability of financial markets and the overall economy. They are often employed for the useful purpose of hedging and risk management, and this role becomes more important as financial markets grow more volatile. However, they can also be associated with massive market failings whose consequences can be tragic. Most remember the LTCM episode, when this major hedge fund's derivative holdings imploded, nearly bringing down with them the global capital market as we know it.

As the name suggests, a derivative is a financial contract whose value is linked ("derived") to the price of an underlying commodity, asset, rate, or index. Derivatives markets also serve to determine the prices of many assets and commodities and the economic value of nonmarket events such as the weather. However, they are also used for unproductive purposes such as avoiding taxation, outflanking regulations designed to make financial markets safe and sound, and manipulating accounting rules, credit ratings, and financial reports. Derivatives are also used to commit fraud and to manipulate markets.

Derivatives are powerful tools that can be used to hedge the risks normally associated with production, commerce, and finance. Derivatives facilitate risk management by allowing a person to reduce his exposure to certain kinds of risk by transferring those risks to another person who is more willing and able to bear such risks. Farmers use derivatives to hedge against a fall in the price of their crop *before* the crop can be harvested and brought to market. Banks use derivatives to reduce the risk that the short-term interest rates they pay to their depositors will rise above the fixed interest rate they earn on their loans and other assets. Utility companies can hedge the (typically volatile) price at which they purchase gas, oil, and other source fuels as well as the (also typically volatile) price at which they sell electrical power. International businesses hedge their foreign-exchange risk from trade and investment.

As a testament to their usefulness, derivatives have played a role in commerce and finance for thousands of years. Derivatives contracts have been found written on clay tablets from Mesopotamia that date to 1750 B.C. Aristotle mentioned an option type of derivative and how it was used for market manipulation in the fourth century B.C. (*Politics*, chapter 9). Derivatives trading on an exchange can be traced back to twelfth century Venice. In the early seventeenth century, futures and options were traded on stocks and commodities such as tulips in Amsterdam. The Japanese traded contracts similar to futures on warehouse receipts for rice in the eighteenth century. In the United States, forward and futures contracts have been formally traded on the Chicago Board of Trade since 1849.

Today, derivatives are traded in most parts of the world, and the size of these markets is enormous. Data for 2002 by the Bank of International Settlements puts the amount of outstanding derivatives in excess of $165 trillion and the trading volume on organized derivatives exchanges at $693 trillion. By comparison, the IMF's figure for worldwide output, or GDP, was $32.1 trillion.

WHAT ARE DERIVATIVES?

As noted above, a derivative is a financial contract whose value is linked to the price of an underlying commodity, asset, rate, index, or the occurrence or magnitude of an event. The term "derivative" refers to how the price of these contracts is *derived* from the price the underlying item. Typical examples of derivatives include futures, forwards, swaps, and options, and these can be combined with traditional securities and loans in order to create structured securities which are also known as "hybrid instruments."

The simplest and perhaps oldest form of a derivative is the *forward contract*. This is the obligation to buy (or sell) a certain quantity of a specific item at a certain price or rate at a specified time in the future. For example, a foreign-exchange forward contract requires party A to buy (and party B to sell) 1 million euros for U.S. dollars at $1.0865 per euro, say, *a year from now*. A forward rate agreement on interest rates requires party A to borrow (and party B to lend) $1 million for three months at a 2.85 percent annual rate beginning *a year from now*.

Futures contracts are like forwards, except that they are highly standardized. The futures contracts traded on most organized exchanges are

CAPITAL MARKETS

so standardized that they are fungible—meaning that they are substitutable one for another. This fungibility facilitates trading and results in greater trading volume and market liquidity. This allows the buyer of a futures contract to extinguish his obligations by selling an identical contract instead of having to take delivery of the underlying item at the expiration of the contract. The public trading of futures in a transparent environment means that everyone can observe the market price throughout the trading day.

Swap contracts are one of the more recent innovations in derivatives contract design. The first currency swap contract was between the World Bank and IBM and began in August of 1981.[1] The basic idea in a swap contract is that the counterparties agree to swap two different types of payments. A payment is either fixed or is designed to float according to an underlying interest rate, exchange rate, index, or the price of a security or commodity.

Take the "vanilla" interest rate swap as an example. This is a transaction structured so that one series of payments is based on a fixed interest rate and the other series is based on a floating interest rate such as LIBOR or a U.S. Treasury bill yield. Why would the two parties enter into such an agreement? One possible explanation has to do with different interest rate expectations: the party agreeing to pay off the variable interest rate loan must be expecting interest rates to be falling while that agreeing to pay the fixed interest rate must be worried that rates will be rising in the future.

A second example is a foreign-exchange swap that comprises two transactions; the first involves buying (or selling) a foreign currency at a specific exchange rate, and the second involves selling back that currency at another specific exchange rate. A foreign currency swap is structured so that one party makes a series of payments based on an interest rate in one currency and then receives a series of payments in another currency based on that currency's interest rate. Here again, parties enter into such transactions because they need to hedge existing foreign exchange exposures or they have differing views about how the exchange rates will be moving in the future.

Consider an example of a foreign-exchange swap of a U.S. dollar for Mexican peso. A Mexican investor enters a swap to buy $100,000 with an exchange rate of $0.1000 per peso (thus paying 1,000,000 pesos). Simultaneously, the same investor commits to selling, in 180 days, the same $100,000 dollars (that is, buying pesos) but at an exchange rate of $0.0952 (thus receiving 1,050,000 pesos). Put differently, the investor is guaranteeing himself a 50,000 peso profit in six months!

Two questions arise from the above example. First, is this a risk-free trade in which the investor is guaranteed a profit? Of course not. While the investor is indeed making a profit in pesos, he may well be making a loss when the trade is denominated in dollars. For example say the actual exchange rate in six months turns out to be $0.08 instead of the contracted

HOW DERIVATIVES MARKETS WORK

RANDALL DODD

Derivatives are traded in two kinds of markets: in exchanges and in over-the-counter markets. Exchange trading has been traditionally organized in "pits," where trading occurs through "open outcry" of bids and offers. Pit trading is increasingly augmented and sometimes replaced by electronic trading systems that automatically match bids and offers.

OTC markets are organized along various lines. The first is called a "traditional" dealer market, the second is called an electronic brokering market, and the third is called a proprietary trading platform market. In the first, dealers act as market makers by maintaining bid and offer quotes. Dealers communicate these quotes, and the negotiation of execution prices, over the telephone and sometimes with the aid of an electronic bulletin board. This is known as bilateral trading because only the two ends of the phone observe prices at any one time.

The second type of OTC market, an electronic brokering market, is essentially the same as the electronic trading platforms used by exchanges. They are considered OTC because the contracts are less standardized, and the EBM does not necessarily clear the derivatives transactions.

The third OTC market type, exemplified by Enron Online, is a combination of the first two in which a dealer sets up its own proprietary electronic trading platform. In this arrangement, bids and offers are posted exclusively by the dealer so that other market participants observe only the dealer's quotes but not one another's. In this electronic trading, the dealer is the counterparty to every trade, so that the dealer holds half of the credit risk in the market.

$0.095. In this case, the original investment, when valued in dollars, would actually be worth $80,000 rather than the original $100,000. In this event, the investor would have lost 20 percent.

The second question is why would the other side agree to such transaction? That party either thinks the peso will weaken by even more over the next six months (that is, he is willing to pay off the 50,000 pesos since he expects to make much more once the contract expires) or because his revenue stream is in pesos but he has a dollar-denominated loan (that is, he is willing to pay a 50,000-peso "insurance" to protect against a sharp weakening in the peso and a much higher debt service payment).

An *option* contract gives to its holder the right to buy (or sell) the underlying item at a specific price at a specific time period in the future. There are two basic kinds of options. Buying a *call option* provides an investor the right to *buy* an asset while a *put option* gives the investor the right to *sell* the asset. For instance, a call option will give the investor the right to buy, say, crude oil at $28 a barrel over a three-month period. If the market price rises above the strike price of $28 before the option expires (that is, before the three months are over), then the investor can exercise the option and capture a profit equal to the market price less $28. Say for example the price of oil rises to $30. The investor will exercise the option by buying oil at $28 and then sells it in the open market at $30, thus pocketing the $2 profit. If, on the other hand, the price never rises above $28 or even falls below that level, then the option expires worthless or "out of the money" and the investor loses the money (known as the *option premium*) he paid for the option.

A put option is similar. Take the example of coffee. A put option would provide an investor the right to sell coffee at a strike or exercise price of

$0.65 per pound; if the price were to fall to say $0.60, then the investor would be able to exercise the put option (that is, sell the coffee at $0.65 while buying from the open market at $0.60) and gain $0.05 for every pound of coffee covered by the options contract.[2]

Just like in any financial transaction, there are two sides to every contract. Whereas the buyer of a call option has the *right* to buy an asset to profit from a favorable price movement, the seller of the same option (known as the "short options" position) has the *obligation* to sell the same asset if the option is exercised. The option writer is essentially selling price protection to the buyer, who pays a "premium" for the insurance.

Employee stock options are currently a financial-policy issue. They are nothing more than call options that are paid or granted by the corporation to an employee. The corporation is the option writer in that, if the employee decides to buy the company stock at a certain price, the corporation has the obligation to sell it at that price.

Credit derivatives permit the transfer of credit exposure between parties. Each contract has two parties: the credit-protection buyer and the credit-protection seller. The buyer of protection is typically an owner of an asset that is vulnerable to a credit event (for example, bankruptcy). To protect himself against this possibility, the asset holder buys "protection" by entering a credit-default swap so that if the bankruptcy actually does occur, the derivatives counterparty compensates him for the asset's loss of value. The seller of the protection essentially believes that the risk of a bankruptcy is low and that the payment he receives from selling the protection will more than compensate him for the risk he takes on.

Structured securities are a rapidly growing segment of the derivatives markets. They typically combine features of conventional securities and with those of derivatives. The term "structured" refers to attached or embedded derivatives. Familiar examples of structured securities include *callable bonds* (that is, bonds that the borrower has the right to redeem even before they mature) and *convertible bonds* (that is, bonds that are convertible into a company's stock).

In the 1990s, "putable" bonds and loans, used to structure lending to developing countries, gained notoriety for their role in financial crises. The attached put options allowed the lender to demand repayment of the debt in the event of a financial crisis or other "credit event." Most of these structures were entered into during times of stability when the chances of a crisis seemed remote. Borrowers agreed to them since they reduced the cost of debt (that is, lowered interest cost). However, when the crises hit, borrowers ended up facing massive and unexpected debt obligations precisely at a time when they were least able to afford those obligations. The IMF estimated in 1999 that there were $32 billion in debts putable through the end of 2000 for all emerging countries. Of the total, $23 billion was to East Asian borrowers, and $8 billion was to Brazil.[3]

As an indication of the dangers derivatives pose, it is worthwhile to recall a shortened list of recent disasters. Long-Term Capital Management froze U.S. credit markets when it collapsed with $1.4 trillion in derivatives on its books. Sumitomo Bank in Japan used derivatives to manipulate global copper markets from 1995 to 1996. Barings, one of the oldest banks in Europe, was quickly brought to bankruptcy by over a billion dollars in losses from derivatives trading. Both the Mexican financial crisis in 1994 and the East Asian financial crisis of 1997 were exacerbated by the use of derivatives to take large speculative positions on fixed exchange rates. Most recently, derivatives played many roles in the collapse of Enron — the largest bankruptcy in U.S. history at that time.

In addition to disasters, there are public concerns with credit risk, the lack of transparency, and the abuse of derivatives for fraud and manipulation. Derivatives trading, especially in the over-the-counter market, results in many payment obligations between firms. A large price movement can generate large payment requirements that increase the likelihood of default. A default at one firm affects the ability of other firms to meet their obligations and possibly leads to systemic failures. Warren Buffett described this as "daisy chain risk."

Derivatives markets and corporations' derivatives positions are also less transparent than other financial assets and financial transactions. It is hard for all but derivatives dealers to know the price and trading volumes in OTC derivatives markets. Investors cannot observe a firm's derivatives position and thus cannot make an informed judgment as to whether it is hedged or speculating or whether it is speculating long or short.

ABUSE OF DERIVATIVES

The same powerful tools that are used for risk management can be used for unproductive, if not destructive, purposes. The flexibility and unregulated nature of OTC derivatives makes them highly effective instruments to abuse for the purpose of *avoiding taxation*, dodging or *out-flanking prudential market regulations*, and for *distorting or manipulating accounting rules and reporting requirements*. They can also be employed in the commission of criminal acts of fraud and *market manipulation*.

Derivatives can also be used to avoid, or evade taxation by restructuring the flow of payments so that earnings are reported in one period instead of another or in one country instead of another. They can also be used to transform interest and dividend income into capital gains, or vice versa.

Derivatives played an important role in the financial crises of Mexico and East Asia. Regulators in both cases set limits on banks' exposure to foreign-exchange risk; however, the restrictions applied only to foreign exchange positions held "on" the balance sheet. Banks (ab)used derivatives to out-flank these restrictions by moving positions into an "off-balance sheet" status.

The collapse of Enron and the revelation of other corporate scandals in the U.S. have disclosed other abusive practices. Derivatives were used to hide debt that should have been reported in regular corporate reports, to fabricate income on the same corporate reports, and to dodge taxes to the government. A series of derivatives between the same counterparties can be abused to create a loan from one firm to another that is not reported as debt but rather as income in one period when the "loan" is made and then a loss in a later period when the "loan" is repaid.

Derivatives can be an effective weapon for market *manipulation*. *Information-based manipulation* involves insider trading or making false reports on the market. *Action-based manipulation* involves the deliberate taking of some actions that changes the actual or perceived value of a commodity or asset. For example, investors may take a position on the stock and then pursue legislation or regulatory changes that might be passed to change the value of the assets.

Trade-based manipulation is the classic case of using one market to capture the gains from creating a price distortion in another interrelated market. How does this work? A manipulator acquires a large position in the derivatives market for crude oil through a long position in forward or swap contracts for future delivery or future payments based on the future price of oil. The manipulator next goes into the spot or cash market and buys enough crude oil to push up the price. This raises the value of the long derivatives positions, and these can be sold at a profit without driving the oil price back down. Then if the manipulator can sell off its inventory of oil without incurring substantial losses, the manipulation will be profitable.

Some recent cases of market manipulation using derivatives:

- Avista Energy, electricity, 1998.

- Enron, electricity, 1998.

- Enron, et al., electricity and gas, 2000 and 2001.

- Arcadia, crude oil, 2001.

- Fenchurch, U.S. Treasury securities, 1993.

- Ferruzzi, soybeans, 1989.

- Sumitomo, copper, 1995 through 1996.

POLICY SOLUTIONS

The three pillars of prudential regulation of financial markets should apply to the derivatives market, especially OTC derivatives markets, as well. These are: (1) registration and reporting requirements; (2) capital and collateral requirements; and (3) orderly market rules.

Registration requirements help prevent fraud by requiring key individuals to pass competency exams (for example, as stock brokers and insurance agents are currently required to do) and background checks for criminal records for fraud. If someone is convicted of securities fraud, he or she is barred for life from securities brokering, but under current law he or she can go to work for an unregistered derivatives dealer the next day.

Reporting requirements make markets more transparent by giving all market participants equal access to prices and other key information. It also gives to regulators the ability to observe markets in order to detect problems before they become a crisis.

All derivatives transactions should be adequately *collateralized*. Enron's failure exposed several bad industry practices. The current practice is to "super-margin" a firm if its credit rating drops (that is, if rating agencies downgrade the firm). This immediately raises the amount of collateral the firm must post against its derivatives positions just at the time the firm is experiencing problems with inadequate capital. This amounts to a *crisis accelerator*. Adequate collateral requirements should be set in the beginning, not after the trouble has started.

Derivatives dealers should have *adequate capital*. Dealers who are banks or securities broker-dealers already face capital requirements—although they do as banks and broker-dealers and not as derivatives dealers per se. However, entities such as Enron do not face any capital requirements. Capital is important because it reduces the incentive for risk taking and serves as a buffer to dampen losses at the dealer from becoming defaults and translating into losses for other trading partners.

Orderly market rules are the third pillar of market safety and soundness. One basic rule is to require OTC derivatives dealers to act as market makers. Dealers are in a privileged position in the market, and so they should bear the responsibility—like security dealers—of ensuring market liquidity by maintaining bid-ask prices continuously through trading hours. Another basic rule, borrowing from futures exchanges, is to set position limits and price-movement limits. Lastly, OTC markets should be encouraged to establish clearinghouses in order to increase the efficiency of the clearing and settlements process. The latter, in addition to improving trading liquidity, reduces the threat of system failures that can quickly reverberate across the financial system.

CONCLUSION

The enormous derivatives markets are both useful and dangerous. Current methods of regulating these markets are not adequate to assure that the markets are safe and sound and that disruptions from these markets do not spill over into the broader economy.

- There are not a lot of data on derivatives. Futures and options exchanges provide the most information (see links, below), but there is far less information on OTC derivatives. Official sources of data on OTC derivatives include the BIS, the U.S. Treasury, the Bank of England, and the U.S. Federal Reserve Board for interest rates on swaps. Some additional information is included as footnotes to 10q and 10k SEC filings, however, this is most likely to be distilled down through aggregation.

- It is important to ask market participants how they manage collateral (what assets are accepted as collateral, whether there is a threshold before collateral is required, and how quickly must changes to collateral be met). A critical feature of collateral management is whether counterparties must post substantially more collateral if their credit rating drops—this can accelerate a crisis as firms get into trouble for one reason and then are pushed into further trouble by their collateral obligations.

- A good line of follow-up questioning concerns how the firm is assessing the credit risk of their trading counterparties. They should be mak-

ing evaluations of the ability of their counterparties to perform on derivatives contracts, and they will look at official credit ratings as well as their own credit analyses in order to make these assessments. The problem is that the use of credit derivatives has made it much more difficult to judge the credit exposure of other participants in the market.

- Another important question is whether a firm is a market maker (dealer) or an end user. Dealers engage in a large volume of trading by going long and short against their customers and other dealers. As a result, the amount of their outstanding contracts is much larger than their net position on the market. Their role is critical because if they cease maintaining bid and offer prices throughout the trading day, the market loses liquidity and can become illiquid.

- If the firm is not a dealer but an "end user," then it is important to ask how the firm observes prices and makes trades with the dealers in the market—this is likely to be over the telephone and sometimes enhanced with an electronic bulletin board, but it increasingly involves an electronic trading platform where traders observe market prices and directly execute trades.

1. Bank for International Settlements. http://www.bis.org/publ/index.htm.

2. Office of Comptroller of the Currency, U.S. Treasury. http://www.occ.treas.gov/deriv/deriv.htm.

3. Bank of England. http://www.bankofengland.co.uk.

4. Derivatives Study Center. http://www.financialpolicy.org.

5. U.S. Federal Reserve Board of Governors. http://www.federalreserve.gov/rnd.htm.

6. H.15 Release: data on U.S. dollar interest rate swap rates. http://www.federalreserve.gov/releases/h15.

7. CFTC: Commodity Futures Trading Commission. www.cftc.gov.

8. CBOT: Chicago Board of Trade. www.cbot.com

9. CME: Chicago Mercantile Exchange. www.cme.com

10. NYMEX: New York Mercantile Exchange. http://www.nymex.com.

11. CBOE: Chicago Board Options Exchange. http://www.cboe.com.

12. Eurex: now the world's largest derivatives exchange. http://www.eurexchange.com.

13. Euronext and LIFFE: London International Financial Futures and Options Exchange. http://www.liffe.com.

14. LME: London Metal Exchange. http://www.lme.co.uk.

1. The design of the swap is thought to have originated from the practice of hedging cross-currency interest rates by making back-to-back loans. See Charles W. Smithson, Clifford W. Smith Jr., and D. Sykes Wilford, *Managing Financial Risk: A Guide to Derivative Products, Financial Engineering, and Value Maximization* (New York: Irwin, 1995).

2. The New York Board of Trade futures and options contracts are for 37,500 pounds.

3. IMF, *Involving the Private Sector in Forestalling and Resolving Financial Crises* (Washington, D.C.: Policy Development and Review Department, 1999).

CHAPTER EIGHT

HEDGE FUNDS

AMER BISAT

INTRODUCTION

ASK THE EDUCATED layperson about hedge funds, and the answer will involve descriptions of colorful names (Tiger, Jaguar, Quantum); of men (and yes, the managers are almost always men) with little taste for restraint; and, of course, of the 1990s financial crises. Hedge funds have entered the collective psyche as financial behemoths that sow the seeds of destruction wherever they tread. George Soros's hedge fund is famed for forcing the pound sterling's exit from the European Monetary System, and the 1998 collapse of Long-Term Capital Management nearly brought down the global financial system as we know it. Many are convinced that hedge funds exacerbated—if not caused—Asia's multiple crises in the 1990s as well as the subsequent ones in Argentina and Brazil.

As with all stereotypes, the above is not without truth. Hedge funds are flexible and unregulated financial structures that, through leverage (see below), channel large flows into concentrated investments. The combination of size and flexibility can be insurmountable. When hedge funds target a certain asset (for example, an exchange rate or a company share), their force can be overwhelming and difficult to resist.

The term "hedge fund" covers a number of very different financial structures. While some funds have been responsible for crises, others, by being the first to buy distressed assets, have stopped the hemorrhage after a crisis. Hedge funds play an important liquidity-providing role, eliminate market distortions, and offer hedging to those who need it.

Journalists writing about hedge funds should be familiar with their history, the techniques they use, the various types of hedge funds in existence, what distinguishes them from traditional financial institutions, their role in causing (and reversing) crises, and proposals to regulate them.

WHAT ARE HEDGE FUNDS?

At their most basic, hedge funds are limited financial partnerships that manage money for high net-worth individuals. They are flexible, aggressive, profit from asset prices going up *or* down, and magnify their investment positions by borrowing against their capital.

Hedge funds are a recent financial phenomenon. Their start is credited to an Alfred Winslow Jones, a journalist who, in 1950, set up a fund that combined "shorting" with "leverage" to produce relatively high returns and limited volatility. ("Shorting" and "leverage" will be defined below). According to Tremont-CSFB (a consultancy that monitors hedge funds), there are around 7,000 hedge funds in operation today managing some $600 billion. Hedge funds tend to become popular during bear markets: their number rose by a third since the U.S. equity market bubble burst in 2001.

HOW DO HEDGE FUNDS OPERATE?

To understand how hedge funds operate, keep in mind an important distinction: the return on an investment comprises "market" and "idiosyncratic" components. Take the example of a company share. Its price can rise either because the overall market rose (higher confidence and economic growth, lower interest rates) or because of stock-specific reasons (a new contract, a new invention, higher earnings). Theory tells us that "market" movements are difficult to predict but "idiosyncratic" ones are easier to foresee.

The basic insight into hedge funds' operations is that they isolate the "market" component and focus their investments on the "idiosyncratic" one. They do so by "short selling."

■ *Short selling* is a technique that permits investors to turn a profit when asset prices fall and lose money when they rise. The idea is fairly simple. An investor sells an asset he or she does not own (usually after borrowing it). If the asset's price falls, the investor buys it from the open market (at the now cheaper price), returns it to the lender, and pockets the profit.

Consider an example. You conclude that the share price of "Disaster," now trading at $15, is overvalued and that the price will soon fall. What would you do? You would go to somebody who owns the share but has a temporary need for cash. You lend him the money and, in return, borrow the share. You also promise that, within three months, you will deliver back the stock in return for your cash. (This process is known as a "repurchase agreement" or a "repo operation"). You sell the borrowed stock for $15 in the open market. If you are proved right and Disaster's shares trade down (say, to $10), you go out to the open market, buy the share for $10, hand it over to the lender who, in turn, gives you back your $15. And voila: you made a $5 profit. Obviously, had the price rallied to $18, you would have lost $3 on your investment.

Lets get back to hedge funds, which, as we noted, "isolate" market components. Hedge funds buy assets they like and short others that serve as a market proxy. In this way, they "hedge" overall market moves but benefit from changes that are particular ("idiosyncratic") to the assets they like.

- Consider an example. Say a hedge fund likes the prospects for a firm (called Reckless) but is less certain about those for the overall market. The hedge fund manager buys a share of Reckless, say for $100, and "shorts" the same amount of another stock that proxies the market (for example, a basket of stocks that mimics the S&P 500). The manager makes no profit if the overall market, *including Reckless*, rallies by 10 percent since the profit made on owning Reckless is offset by losses incurred by shorting the market. By contrast, if Reckless rallies by 10 percent (for a profit of $10) but the overall market rallies by only 8 percent (for a loss of $8), the manager pockets a $2 profit.

It should be clear that the profit/loss associated with a hedged investment is smaller than the one from an unhedged investment.

- For example, if the manager had held an unhedged position in Reckless, the profit from a 10 percent rally would have been $10. Instead, by hedging the position, the profit was only $2.

To make a hedged position particularly profitable, hedge funds magnify it. This is where leverage comes in. Leverage is the process of borrowing against capital to concentrate an investment position.

- For instance, had the investor in the above example borrowed ten times his capital and bought ten shares of Reckless rather than the one share we assumed above, his or her profit would have been $20 rather than the $2 calculated above.

Key to keep in mind when thinking about leverage is that, just like it magnifies profits, leverage can also magnify losses. Leverage can be very risky.

- Consider the following example. Say our investor had a $10 capital. He or she borrows another $90 (that is, a 9 to 1 leverage) and buys one share of Reckless. Let's say he or she hedges the investment by shorting $100 worth of the S&P 500. If the price of Reckless falls by 10 percent while the whole market stays unchanged, the investor's loss ($10) will completely wipe out his capital. Think of it this way: thanks to leverage, a relatively modest fall in the stock price (10 percent) translated into a 100 percent loss in capital.

TYPES OF HEDGE FUNDS

Despite popular belief, there is no one type of hedge fund. Some trade fixed-income instruments, others equity or foreign exchange. Some focus on one geographic area, others invest worldwide. Some are generalists while others are extremely specialized. A few manage hundreds of million of dollars, while others oversee only a few millions. Some invest money for outsiders, others (including bank "proprietary desks") invest insider capital. Some have multiple autonomous portfolio managers, while others focus all decisions on one trader. Some employ massive leverage, while others borrow only a relatively small multiple of their capital. Some employ derivatives while others use only spot transactions.

These differences notwithstanding, one can distinguish between two broad categories of hedge funds:

- *Macro hedge funds* are those that bet on large market moves. Their analysis is "top down," in that they analyze macrodynamics (hence the name), including growth, inflation, balance of payments, and demographics. Such funds are less interested in particular securities and more in the general market direction. If, for example, they assess that a country is close to trouble, they would short any liquid asset, including the currency and the largest share in the local stock market. Contrary to the name, macro funds do not hedge but typically take on "naked" positions. George Soros's hedge fund is perhaps the most famous example of a macro fund having bet (successfully) that the UK will not be able to maintain its European Monetary System membership. Julian Robertson's Tiger Fund is another famous macro fund.

- *Relative-value funds* emphasize security selection. Such funds are much less interested in the overall market direction—indeed, they completely hedge out the market component. Their profit/loss comes from the performance of a particular security *relative* to the overall market. Relative-value hedge funds use mathematical models to identify "cheap," as opposed to "expensive," securities. They typically buy the cheap security and short (as a hedge) the expensive security. They make money when the difference between the two securities converges. Relative-value hedge funds employ leverage intensely. LTCM is the most famous of relative-value hedge funds, having bet (unsuccessfully) on "convergence" trades in the fixed-income markets; its losses were magnified by massive leverage.

Hedge funds differ from other traditional financial institutions in important ways.

- *Short selling*. Hedge funds can bet on asset prices going up as well as down. Most traditional money managers are allowed "long only" strategies.

- *Leverage*. Hedge funds, especially relative-value funds, leverage their investments often multiple times. Most traditional money managers are not allowed to employ leverage.

- *Total return vehicles*. Traditional money managers are measured against an index (for example, the S&P 500 or the EMBI). By contrast, hedge funds are "total-return" vehicles whose performance is measured in absolute terms. This distinction alters incentive structures in important ways. Traditional money managers may not care if their fund registers negative returns so long as the loss is smaller than that of the index. By contrast, a hedge fund tries hard to avoid absolute losses. In a similar vein, a traditional money manager may have the incentive to "hug" the index by mimicking its components. A hedge fund manager has, by contrast, the incentive to take on more aggressive bets.

- *The client base*. Hedge funds attract high-net-worth investors who seek high-return, high-risk investment vehicles. The number of investors in a hedge fund has to be small for the fund to maintain its unregulated status (see below). By contrast, traditional money managers market their funds to the retail sector and institutional investors (for example, pension funds, insurance companies, university endowments). The nature of the client bases explains, to a large extent, the differing attitudes toward risk between the two types of money managers.

- *Capital structure*. Hedge fund managers are almost always obliged to invest their own capital in the fund; some are even required to reinvest part of their performance fees (see below). This is meant to align the incentive structure of managers with those who invest in the fund. By contrast, traditional money managers are employees—rather than partners—whose own capital is not at risk.

- *Profit-sharing arrangements*. Hedge funds are rewarded based on their performance. A typical hedge fund charges an annual administrative fee (usually 1 percent of assets under management) *and* keeps a certain percentage of the profit (usually 20 percent). Hedge funds employ the concept of "water marks," whereby if the fund loses money, it will not receive a performance fee until that amount is recuperated (that is, if the profit level reverts back to the watermark). By contrast, traditional money mangers are paid a constant fee regardless of performance.

- *Flexibility*. Hedge funds are more flexible than traditional money managers. Partly because they are unregulated (see below), and partly because their clients are wealthy individuals with a high appetite for risk and tolerance for volatility, hedge fund investment guidelines are lightly worded. In practice, this means that hedge funds can invest in all asset classes, can use derivatives and leverage, and have liberal position-size limits. Traditional money managers, by contrast, invest money for more conservative clients who impose strict operational guidelines. Flexibility allows hedge funds to be quick to the draw and aggressive in expressing investment views.

- *Quality of managers*. Reflecting profit-sharing arrangements, hedge fund managers are generally better remunerated than traditional money managers. As a result, hedge funds tend to attract the "best and the brightest."

- *Regulatory framework*. Hedge funds are much less regulated than traditional money managers. This issue is covered in detail below.

ARE HEDGE FUNDS RESPONSIBLE FOR CRISES?

Hedge funds always seem to be at the center of crises. They are fast. They are aggressive. They are usually the first to come in and the first to balk when signs of trouble appear. The role of hedge funds became politicized when Malaysian Prime Minister Mahathir Mohamed blamed them for the Asian crisis. Hedge funds have also become lightning rods for the antiglobalization movement. Politicians of all stripes, often cheered on by the media, equate hedge funds with crises.

There are four issues to think through when assessing the role of hedge funds in crises:

- *Herd activity*. Hedge funds are flexible and fast. When they zero in on a target, they tend to lead and are then followed by the much larger, but slower, traditional financial institutions. This has given the impression that investors move in a herd. This impression is sometimes correct—but not always. In the Indonesia and Brazil crises, for example, local banks were the first to sell local assets, with hedge funds jumping on the bandwagon afterwards.

- *Size*. Leverage is powerful. Through it, a hedge fund mobilizes multiples of its capital. Moreover, hedge funds are not governed by diversification rules and, as such, can concentrate their investments in one position. Large and concentrated positions are visible and give the (sometimes correct) impression that hedge funds cause dramatic asset price movements. For instance, some estimate that George Soros's Quantum fund mobilized a whopping $15 billion against the UK sterling in 1992, eventually forcing its floatation. The investment—as well as the $1 billion profit the financier reportedly reaped—made headline news and became one of the most famous financial transactions in modern history.

- *Self-fulfilling prophecies.* Market pressures can cause crises even if there is no "fundamental" reason. Consider Asia in 1997. The crisis countries were not indebted and boasted prudent fiscal stances. However, as their currencies devalued, their debt levels (much of which was dollar denominated) rose dramatically and what started off as low-debt countries suddenly became highly indebted. As creditworthiness deteriorated, a vicious cycle emerged, with more risk-averse investors selling Asian assets. Some argued that, had the currencies not depreciated so dramatically, the crises would not have occurred or, at worst, would have been contained. And since hedge funds were behind the exchange rate pressures, the argument went, they were responsible for the crises. (This argument, of course, ignores the fact that Asia's problems were not fiscal but banking-related and that in some cases, especially in Indonesia, local banks initiated the currency selling rather than hedge funds).

- *Interconnectivity and contagion.* Hedge funds work within a complicated web of financial linkages. If those linkages are severed, what could start off as a localized crisis can turn into a systemic and global one.

    The Russia crisis and the eventual collapse of LTCM are good cases in point; they triggered a global financial meltdown that went well beyond the economic size of Russia and the financial prowess of LTCM. Why this disproportionate effect? Leverage explains much. For one thing, before the crises, hedge funds had bought Russian assets and financed them through leverage. As the price of Russian bonds collapsed, lenders asked for more collateral ("margin calls"). To raise the required amounts, hedge funds sold positions in assets unrelated to Russia. Indeed, the leverage was so large that the ensuing distressed selling caused price collapses in virtually all fixed-income assets, with the largest price drops accounted for by the riskiest *and most illiquid* assets.

    Enter LTCM. The hedge fund itself was not a particularly large holder of Russian assets. Instead, it had invested hundreds of billion dollars in so-called convergence plays, whereby the fund bought *illiquid* but cheap assets and shorted virtually identical but more expensive *liquid* assets, hoping that the two prices, usually different by miniscule amounts, will eventually come closer together. To magnify the profit from these miniscule price differentials, the hedge fund leveraged its positions dramatically. Now, as the Russia crisis hit and as hedge funds sold their illiquid positions and piled into the safer (and more liquid) assets, price differentials, instead of converging, diverged, and LTCM's losses ran into the billions—every day! Banks that had lent LTCM money had, themselves, borrowed the funds elsewhere. As LTCM approached bankruptcy, the specter of a chain of financial defaults emerged. Faced with the threat of a systemic collapse, the U.S. government was forced to intervene.

DO THE HEDGE FUNDS PLAY A STABILIZING ROLE?

The role of hedge funds in crises receives extensive coverage. Less has been written about their stabilizing roles.

- *Provide liquidity.* Hedge funds are very active traders, getting in and out of positions at sometimes-breakneck speed. While not "market makers" in the classic sense, the trading activity of hedge funds increases the depth of otherwise illiquid markets. Put differently, in markets where hedge funds are active, traditional money managers usually find it easier to sell their position or build a new one whenever they need to.

- *Ensure efficiency.* Asset markets can be inefficient. Why, for example, should a U.S. Treasury bond that matures in March 2013 be priced any differently than one that matures three months earlier? Sometimes, there are fundamental reasons for such anomalies. But at other times, there are none. Hedge funds are extremely good at spotting such dislocations and "arbitraging" them away.

- *Stop hemorrhage.* When crises start, they take on a life of their own. Vicious cycles develop, and asset prices "overshoot" (see the point on "self-fulfilling prophecies," above). When the traditional investor base is balking en masse, hedge funds—fast, efficient, and contrarian— step in. As the Indonesia rupiah reached the absurd level of 16,000 to the dollar in June 1998, hedge funds bought it, taking it up to the more reasonable 8000 to the dollar. The rally reversed the, until then, unstoppable wave of (dollar-indebted) corporate bankruptcies.

SHOULD HEDGE FUNDS BE REGULATED?

A feature of hedge funds that most find striking is that they are unregulated. This is so since they are private partnerships catering to a limited number of rich and financially sophisticated investors who require little protection. Formally, regulation is not necessary if a money manager has a small number of investors and if each investor is an "accredited investor" (defined as an investor with either $1 million in net worth or an income of more than $200,000 per year). Funds that satisfy these conditions are not registered (in the United States; they are in the UK); they face minimal capital requirements; they are not subject to information disclosure rules; they are not prohibited from engaging in any lawful financial investment; and they are subject to relatively light tax regimes.

CAPITAL MARKETS

Attitudes toward hedge funds have changed materially since the mid-1990s. The role of hedge funds in crises has raised their public profile; their regulation has become a political imperative. The interlinking nature of leverage, moreover, has turned hedge funds from localized vehicles to ones whose failure can cause systemic crises. In addition, hedge funds have recently become popular among the retail sector, whose wealth and sophistication are much less than that of the traditional hedge fund investors. These reasons have generated calls for strengthening oversight over hedge funds.

To this end, there are many proposals being debated.

- *Increasing transparency and information disclosure.*

- *Requiring commercial and investment banks to carry out detailed credit analysis* on their hedge fund clients before they are allowed to extend credit to them. Banks would also be required to modulate the lending size, its cost, and collateral ("margin") on the basis of the hedge fund's credit quality.

- *Restrict hedge funds' ability to short sell.* A less radical proposal is to preclude the practice of "naked" shorting: that is, when the hedge fund sells an asset it does not even possess as opposed to when it sells a security it had borrowed.

- *Require hedge funds to register.* Registration—already a requirement in the UK but not in the United States—would require hedge funds to provide the SEC with biographic information on their managers and agree to occasional audits.

- Strengthen oversight over hedge funds' potential money-laundering activities and abuse of off-shore tax deferral schemes.

The push to regulate hedge funds has intensified in recent years. In the United States (where the majority of hedge funds operate), the effort is being led by the Securities and Exchange Commission. State-level district attorneys (especially in New York) are also active in the process. The U.S. congress has held a number of hearings on the topic. Hedge funds are understandably resistant to excessive regulations. They see them as increasing operational costs and curtailing their flexibility and nimbleness. Hedge funds are also resisting information-disclosure proposals on the ground that they make their investment positions public inviting counterparty threats.

- The best source on the amount of a "short" in a particular asset is the "repo" desk at investment banks. Those desks arrange for lending securities to hedge funds that engage in short selling.

- "Financing" desks in investment banks arrange for "leveraging" for hedge funds. Reporters should talk to them about prevailing margin requirements (that is, "collateral"), which tend to rise during periods of instability.

- The Chicago Board of Trade publishes, on a daily basis, the amount of "shorting" on particular assets and commodities. A spike usually suggests increased hedge fund activity.

- Tremont-CSFB, a consultancy that monitors hedge funds, publishes a monthly index on hedge funds' performance. The results can make for interesting stories.

- The ongoing debate on regulating hedge funds is intense. It involves myriad regulatory bodies and working groups from both the public and private sectors. Politicians have jumped on the cause. This will likely be an evolving story that may be worth keeping an eye on.

- Depending on the story a reporter is working on, he or she should make sure to know whether the fund is a macro or a relative-value hedge fund. Reporters should wear their "economist" hats with the former and their "finance" hats with the latter.

- Hedge funds are extremely secretive. Getting quotes on their particular positions is virtually impossible. However, hedge fund managers may not mind talking about what they are doing—so long as it is on deep background. These "chats" can be extremely useful in getting a sense of what hedge funds are thinking about.

For extensive background and analysis of hedge funds, see IMF Occasional Paper 166, *Hedge Funds and Financial Market Dynamics*, by Eichengreen et al. A summary of that book is available electronically at http://www.imf.org/external/pubs/ft/issues/issues19/index.htm.

1. Economist and columnist Paul Krugman wrote extensively about hedge funds during the Asia crisis. These, and newer writings, can be found on his Web site. http://www.wws.princeton.edu/~pkrugman.

2. Tremont-CSFB publishes an index and other extensive data on hedge funds, including monthly returns. http://www.hedgeindex.com/index.cfm.

3. Magnum.com is a useful Web site that offers background on various hedge funds and updates, definitions, and links to official sites with find policy papers on the hedge fund regulation debate. http://www.magnum.com.

4. Nouriel Roubini, an NYU professor, publishes an excellent "Global Macroeconomic and Financial Policy Site." In it, you will find a page on hedge funds that updates relevant academic, policy, and journalistic writings on the topic. http://www.stern.nyu.edu/globalmacro.

5. The Hedge Fund Association is a trade group that represents hedge fund managers. http://www.thehfa.org.

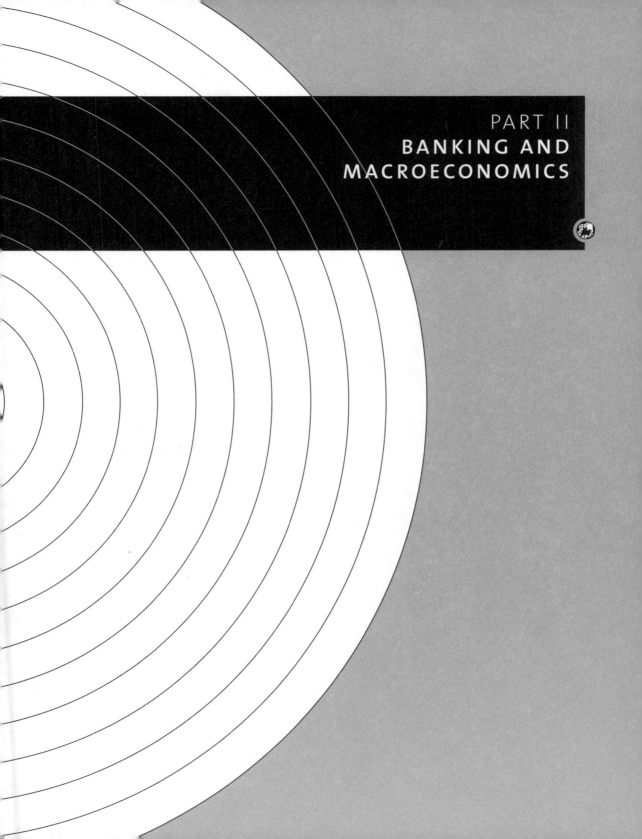

PART II
BANKING AND MACROECONOMICS

CHAPTER NINE

BANKING CRISES
CAUSES AND SOLUTIONS

ANYA SCHIFFRIN

THE BANKING system is the heart of a country's economy. It is the major savings vehicle for the population. It also pumps the money that is required for the economy to grow and for businesses to develop. This intermediation role is especially true for developing countries, as they typically do not have developed capital markets and so bank credit makes up most of the funds that small businesses need to expand. Without such funds, companies cannot develop and jobs can not be created. And yet banking crises are endemic, for it is much easier to lend money than to get it back. And when banks run out of money, they cannot lend, and the broader economy may come to a standstill. This is why the repercussions of banking crises are so severe. The Mexican banking crisis in 1994 and 1995 and the Asian banking crises of 1997 and 1998 tipped those countries into serious recessions that affected the broader community. Today there are many countries that fear banking crises. China, Japan, and Burma are just some of the countries where the banks have large amounts of bad debt.

Once a banking crisis starts, it spreads. If problems in one bank are made public, small depositors get scared and they take their money out of that bank. This causes the bank to fail, which generates bigger headlines and scares even more people, who then withdraw their funds and cause even more banks to fail. Suddenly, you have a massive run on the banks. As a result, governments and bankers fear panics and do their best to keep information secret. This can make it hard for reporters to cover banking. In 1997, the Vietnamese government issued rules requiring journalists to "consult" with the central bank before writing about a number of topics that were on an official list of banking secrets. The list was not made public, but it was thought that the level of nonperforming loans held by the state-run banks was classified as a state secret. Apparently the Communist Party felt that hiding this type of information was essential to safeguard the stability of the banking system.

Banking crises essentially stem from the same problem—large amounts of nonperforming loans. In a healthy banking system, such as that presently found in the United States, "problem loans"—loans that are nonperforming or close to nonperforming—account for about 9 percent of outstanding loans. During the Asian banking crises, the numbers were as high as 47 percent in Thailand and 75 percent in Indonesia.

There are several reasons why banks can end up with bad debt:

■ *State-directed lending* to unprofitable government-run businesses, also known as "policy lending." During the era of state socialism, many countries did not have a private banking sector. In countries such as Russia, China, and Vietnam, banks existed only to finance government activities, and state-owned enterprises and their lending was rarely based on sound financial criteria. Many of these state companies were overstaffed and inefficient and were not required to make a profit. Governments did not subsidize these businesses directly. Instead, they used the banking system to channel funds to these companies. A direct subsidy would have been a more clear way of supporting the businesses and the jobs they created. As it happened, funding companies through the banking system meant that the banks were also put into danger. In many of these countries, there were designated banks that funded different types of industry, farmers, and foreign trade. In the 1990s, governments in many developing countries (for example, Brazil, Morocco, Poland) compelled banks to stop this sectoral lending and phased out regional, specialized development banks altogether.

■ Nonfinancially based lending is but one step away from a second problem: *corrupt lending*. In Vietnam the small, semiprivate banks lent money to their friends. There was no control over such lending, the friends' companies did not post collateral, and there were no strict requirements guaranteeing that the money would be paid back. But these problems can also exist in capitalist countries. In the Texas savings and loan scandal of the early 1980s, for instance, federal regulators accused bank directors of making loans to "insiders" in excess of the regulatory limits.

■ Excessive exposure to sectors experiencing "*bubbles*." Some banks have gotten into trouble by excessively lending to particular sectors. Debtors often use the borrowed funds to speculate, causing asset prices to rise to extreme levels that outstrip their "reasonable" value. For their part, banks lend using the assets as collateral. As asset prices "come down to earth," banks end up having, on their books, overvalued collateral. Real estate is the most common example of a bubble, but throughout history there have many different kinds of bubbles. In the 1990s in the United States, Internet companies experienced a bubble, while in the Nethlerands the "tulipmania" bubble in the seventeenth century caused a dramatic economic downturn when it burst in 1638. Before the Asian crisis of 1997, Thai and Vietnamese banks lent money to companies that built or bought office buildings. Soon there was too much office space, and when the price of the buildings fell the companies were no longer able to repay their loans. During the crisis, a number of Thai banks were hurt by loan defaults, and Bangkok wound up with hundreds of empty office buildings.

■ Banks have a close relationship to *fluctuations in currency*. Currency crises can lead to banking crises, and vice versa. Sometimes the two emerge simultaneously, an event referred to as the "twin crisis phenomenon." If banks in developing countries have dollar-denominated loans and the local currency is devalued, then it becomes more expensive to repay loans that are dollar-denominated and banks' balance sheets deteriorate. This was a major problem in Korea and Indonesia during the Asian crisis and Turkey in 2001. It was also one of the reasons that Argentina postponed devaluing the peso during the crisis in 2001.

■ A *rise in interest rates* also affects banks, for the simple reason that high interest rates make loans more expensive to repay. During the Asian crisis, the IMF encouraged countries to hike up interest rates to support their currencies, which were in freefall. As soon as interest rates went up (reaching above 30 percent in Indonesia) the banks started to fail.

Also, reporters should look out for *portfolio mismatches of long-term and short-term debt*. If interest rates go up, the bank must begin paying a higher interest rate to its depositors. But its long-term loans cannot be rolled over to a new interest rate. Thus the value of its assets (loans) goes down while the value of its liabilities (deposits) goes up—a recipe for insolvency. This was a major cause of the Texas savings and loan crisis, when the Federal Reserve raised interest rates dramatically to stave off inflation. Savings and loan banks were faced with rapidly rising cost of deposits while heavily invested in home mortgages, which were fixed at a lower interest rate. The high interest rates also caused a recession and loan defaults, eventually amounting to billions in losses for the S&Ls.

■ *Adverse selection*. According to economic theory, high interest rates encourage bad borrowing. This sounds strange but it works like this: when interest rates are 5 percent it is not expensive to borrow money. When rates rise to 15 percent, only the companies that are the most desperate will borrow at such a high rate. The strong companies will get money somewhere else. So the companies that borrow at 15 percent are, by definition, the least creditworthy and the most likely to default on loans. The process becomes a vicious cycle. Banks, which cannot differentiate very well between the weak and the strong borrowers

INDONESIA—
A BANKING CRISIS

GRÁINNE MCCARTHY

Casting around Southeast Asia in the 1990s, one would have been hard pressed to hear warnings of impending doom. The Asian tigers were clocking up the kind of growth that made most rich countries jealous. Economists were speaking of the twenty-first century as the one that would belong to Asia. Foreign investment was pouring into the region.

Even when the dominoes began to fall after the devaluation of the Thai baht on 2 July 1997, economists—in both the public and private sectors—predicted that Indonesia would weather the storm. How wrong they were. In the end, Indonesia was the hardest hit of all of the former Asian Tigers. Its economy, which had grown 5.6 percent in 1997, contracted by a staggering 14 percent in 1998 as the country underwent its worst political and economic upheaval in more than thirty years. Inflation soared to over 80 percent in 1998, and short-term interest rates hit a high of just over 70 percent by September 1998 while the rupiah collapsed.

Long-standing problems in the banking sector played a major role in the havoc wreaked on the Indonesian economy. Corruption, lax banking supervision, perverse links between borrowers and lenders, government interference, and heavy foreign borrowing that was not hedged against the possibility of exchange-rate fluctuation left a mountain of debt after the rupiah plunged. As a result, the ratio of foreign-bank debt to gross domestic product jumped to 140 percent in 1999 from around 35 percent before the crisis, render-

ing most of the banking system technically bankrupt.

As the economy began to unravel, consumers panicked and rushed to pull money out of the banks. Huge deposit runs put the banks' capital bases under severe pressure. Bank Indonesia continued to print money rapidly—the base money supply jumped 36 percent in December 1997, 22 percent in January 1998, and a further 11 percent in May 1998—and pumped it into the flailing banking system in the form of liquidity support. It ultimately injected around 144 trillion rupiah into Indonesian banks at the height of the currency crisis.

The economic crisis ultimately caused the local currency to collapse and began a spiral into a political crisis that would eventually pile enough pressure on President Suharto to end his thirty-two-year reign. He stepped down on May 21, after bloody riots in Jakarta that left as many as 1,200 dead.

The key factor driving the collapse of the rupiah, and indeed other currencies in the region, was capital flight. If investors suspect that the government will not or cannot maintain the peg, they often flee the currency, just as they did across Asia in 1997. This capital flight deletes hard-currency reserves and forces the devaluation the investors feared. Analysts reckon up to $40 billion fled Indonesia offshore, some to Singapore, some elsewhere. The rupiah's slide undermined local confidence in the currency also—many ordinary Indonesians changed their rupiah into dollars and stashed the hard currency under their mattresses.

The currency crisis, in turn, became a banking crisis. Because of the loan-maturity mismatch and the currency mismatch—the use of short-term debt for fixed as-

sets and unhedged external debt—banks and firms were vulnerable to sudden swings in international investors' confidence. In many ways. even apart from this fundamental problem, the Indonesian banking crisis was inevitable, as local banks were used to funding a number of enterprises that did not make money but were run by friends of President Suharto. The entire economic and legal system was designed to perpetuate this kind of corruption. While Indonesian legislation—in particular the bankruptcy law—has been recognized as respectable by international standards, the problem was always in the implementation. It was routine for judges to be bribed so that cases often never even got to court.

The system began to crumble, and by October 1997, Indonesia became the second Asian tiger to turn, in desperation, to the International Monetary Fund for help. In return for a $43 billion IMF-led package, Indonesia had to agree to reform its legal system, abolish monopolies, improve corporate governance, make the central bank independent, overhaul its banking system, raise interest rates to stabilize the rupiah, privatize businesses, and address a host of other issues.

The package was supposed to help restore confidence in the currency and the government, but it did not work. A major step included in the conditional IMF agreement was the decision to liquidate sixteen banks, some of which were owned by well-connected businessmen and members of Suharto's family. The IMF's Asia Pacific director at the time, Hubert Neiss, described the banks as "rotten to the core." When the banks were closed, however, it sparked a massive rush by depositors who were fearful that their money was not guaranteed. It was, by all accounts, the textbook case of how not to close banks. The situation was only partly remedied in January 1998 by a government guarantee of domestic bank deposits and liabilities and the establishment of the Indonesian Bank Restructuring Agency to rehabilitate the banking system.

The government closed as many as seventy banks and nationalized many others. When the smoke cleared, the total number of banks had declined from 238 before the crisis to 162 in 1999.

Looking back, there were glaring warning signals, not least the woefully weak, corrupt, and overcrowded banking system. Moral hazards also played a role, under which the governments effectively offered guarantees to encourage bankers to make loans to borrowers who were incapable of paying them back. And many foreign bankers were encouraged to make highly imprudent loans to overleveraged Indonesian companies.

More than four years after Suharto's government signed its

first agreement with the IMF, Indonesia—now ruled by the democratically elected President Megawati Sukarnoputri—remains a fragile place. Still, foreign banks are investing, and the government exited the IMF program at the end of 2003. But while many banks that survived are doing much better, they rely heavily on interest income from the government bonds issued to refinance them. That means they have not effectively functioned as intermediary institutions helping to stimulate growth.

(asymmetric information), worry that they will not get paid back, so they raise rates to 20 percent. The companies that borrow at 20 percent are even more desperate and the process continues.

- *"Macroeconomic imbalances"* are typically associated with loose monetary and fiscal policies. Sometimes governments or central banks decide to loosen the supply of money by, for example, lowering interest rates or increasing government spending. In these cases, consumption increases and economies overheat. Imbalances, such as large current-account deficits and inflation, develop. Banks, in the meantime, also wind up lending a lot of money as well—often without taking sufficient precautions as to the creditworthiness of their clients. In good times, this is not a problem. But eventually, imbalances need to be reversed. The central bank hikes rates and the government tightens its fiscal purse. The economy slows, and, inevitably, the number of non performing loans rises. This was the precisely the dynamic behind the Mexican peso crises in 1994/95.

- *Weak banking supervision and regulations* by central banks. Typically, developing countries lack adequate regulations, and those they have are not consistently enforced. There may be poor credit controls in place, a lack of deposit insurance, and few capital-adequacy requirements. It may be hard for banks to collect collateral, and courts may not support the banks when they try to collect on debts. The role of regulation can de debated, but there is no question that banking crises can be exacerbated by lack of good regulation.

CRISIS PREVENTION

The last century has been marked by frequent banking crises. The Great Depression was in part a result of bank failures in the United States and elsewhere. The 1980s and 1990s saw banks fail in Latin America, and trouble in postcommunist transition economies, as well as the East Asian financial crisis, have brought financial stability to the forefront of global concern. Banking crises, in addition, have been extremely expensive. The cost of recapitalizing a banking sector can easily exceed 10 percent of GDP—a figure that does not even include the "cost" of the inevitable postcrisis recession. As a result, policy makers have developed many safeguards to stop crises from occurring in the first place. Policy makers try to tread a delicate balance with those safeguards. They need to be tight enough to ensure banking sector stability but not too tight so as to restrict banking activity.

- *Capital-adequacy requirements.* The Basel Committee and the Bank for International Settlements (BIS), which designs financial-regulation accords among advanced industrialized nations, have established standards for capital-adequacy requirements. Currently, in every nation that follows the committee's guidelines, the banks must keep 8 percent of (risk-weighted) assets aside to "provision" against loans that may not be repaid. The Basel rules are currently being revised amid great controversy, and China has refused to go along with the new rules. *Capital-adequacy ratios* are defined as a measure of a banks' capital expressed as a percentage of its risk-weighted credit exposures. This ratio is used to protect depositors and promote the stability and efficiency of financial systems around the world. Two types of capital are measured: tier-one capital, which can absorb losses without a bank being required to cease trading, and tier-two capital, which can absorb losses in the event of a winding-up and so provides a lesser degree of protection to depositors.

- *Liquidity requirements.* Banks sometime fail not because they are insolvent but because they, at a particular moment, become illiquid, that is, they do not have enough—usually short-term—funds they can easily get their hands on to honor deposit withdrawals. This (illiquidity) risk is inherent to the business of banking, which revolves around attracting short-term (liquid) deposits and lending them in (illiquid) loans. Bank regulators try to mitigate this risk by requiring banks to maintain, at all times, a certain portion of their deposits in liquid instruments such as cash and very short-term government paper—"dry powder" for "rainy days."

- *Open foreign-exchange position limits.* During boom periods, demand for loans picks up at a faster pace than deposits. To fill the gap, banks tend to borrow overseas. Banks also do so to benefit from lower international interest rates. This, though, creates a foreign-currency mismatch (also known as an "open fx position"), which renders banks vulnerable to a large movement in the exchange rate. To mitigate this risk, bank regulators often impose a limit on the size of the banks' open position. Put differently, banks are allowed to borrow abroad (in foreign currency) no more than the amount of their own lending at home in the same currency.

- *Deposit Insurance*. In the wake of bank failures during the Great Depression of the 1930s, the U.S. government created the Federal Deposit Insurance Corporation, in June 1933, an independent federal agency that serves to protect depositors in the event of a crisis, as well as monitor the banks. The FDIC backs deposits as large as $100,000 and derives income from payments by insured banks and interest on government securities. In part, deposit insurance is meant to protect small investors against unexpected banking crises. But it also has a more ambitious objective: Banks fail because of "runs." The existence of a deposit-insurance scheme makes such runs less frequent and reduces the chance of systemic bank failures.

  Many nations around the world have developed deposit-insurance schemes, hoping to protect against bank runs and strengthen their overall financial systems. Some, as in Germany, function privately and with a minimum of government involvement. But there is energetic debate surrounding a "one-size-fits-all" approach to deposit insurance, especially in nations with weak financial infrastructures. Critics claim that deposit insurance pushes down interest rates and thus reduces market discipline. For years the World Bank urged developing countries to put deposit-insurance schemes in place, but now new research from the World Bank suggests that deposit insurance actually raises the risk of banking crises. The research is controversial, but the World Bank is arguing that knowing that the deposits are covered, banks have every incentive to make riskier loans and depositors have very little incentive to be careful about which banks they place their money in. However, many argue that the new stance of the World Bank is wrong, in part because small investors lack information about which banks are likely to have problems and so need to be protected; they certainly are not carelessly putting their savings into troubled banks because they know there is deposit insurance that will cover their accounts.

  The worry that deposit insurance contributes to moral hazard has generated new approaches to deposit-insurance design. These approaches focus on encouraging depositors to monitor banks (for example, by restricting the amount of deposits covered and by narrowing the type of deposits covered) while making certain that insured banks lend prudently (for example, by applying higher prudential regulations on insured banks). New schemes have also been experimenting with co-insurance designed to shift the insurance burden toward other creditors (for example, by using subordinated debt—see below).

- *Subordinated debt*. Some argue that banks should be required to sell subordinated debt, a market-based approach that can help keep banks in line. Subordinated debt is high-interest debt that by law cannot be paid back until all other liabilities are satisfied. Investors holding the debt have the most to lose from a default and will thus monitor the banks closely.

- *Categorizing loans*. This requirement increases transparency and helps regulators and depositors better monitor the health of the banking sector. Banks are required to keep strict categories of overdue loans, indicating how long loan payments have been delinquent (that is, 30 days overdue, 60 days, 120 days, and so on). When interest payments are overdue for a significant period of time (this varies country to country), the loan is classified as nonperforming. Banks also are often required to classify even performing loans as "doubtful." Regulators can use these classifications to identify the stability of individual banks and the banking system as a whole. Regulators are supposed to keep a close eye on the process of classification: Many banks try to hide problem loans. One way banks do so (the so-called evergreening process) is by treating unpaid interest as new lending (that is, "recapitalizing interest") rather than by declaring the whole loan nonperforming.

- *Arms-length lending laws*. To avoid conflict-of-interest problems, U.S. federal law prohibits banks from lending excessively large amounts of money to officers, directors, principal shareholders, and their related interests. Banks are also subject to limits on how much to lend to particular entities and sectors; these are called "exposure limits."

- *Bank–firm relationships*. Countries have different traditions regarding how their financial systems operate. Under a market-based system like that in the United States. and the UK, big businesses access capital largely through the markets for stocks and bonds. In Germany and Japan, on the other hand, companies tend to rely on a single, large, "main" or "universal" bank, which lends them money and may even become a large equity shareholder. In this system, the bank plays an active monitoring role and can minimize moral-hazard problems, which is why some argue that the main-bank system is more stable. But others contend that the Anglo-Saxon system, with its reliance on the capital markets, leads to a more efficient allocation of capital and can detect approaching crises with "price signaling." Price signaling works since capital markets, unlike banks, "mark to market" asset prices (that is, they reprice the asset on a daily basis rather than keeping it on the books at historical price levels). As an asset becomes riskier, its price immediately falls, thus sending investors an instantaneous signal that all is not well.

SOLUTIONS TO BANKING CRISES

- *Recapitalizing banks*. There are many ways to go about patching up the damage of a banking crisis and replenishing dried-up banks with fresh capital. The most common is for the government to take control of failed banks and opt for straight capital injections. The cost of the recapitalization tends to be too high to be financed from current financial sources. Printing money to pay for recapitalization causes inflation. Governments often issue bonds to finance the effort.

- *Stripping off bad loans.* In Malaysia, nonperforming loans were first transferred to an asset-management company and then sold off, leaving the banks healthier. (This is nearly always done in conjunction with recapitalizing the banks. Otherwise, the governent strips the bank of its assets and leaves it only with liabilities).

- *Sale to foreign banks.* Countries that have sold off their ailing banks to foreign competitors usually end up with stronger banking systems. But there can be downsides, too. For instance, foreign banks do not tend to do much local lending. Citibank in Ecuador is more likely to lend to the local branch of IBM or another big U.S. company then to a small local company. Also, if the local bank gets into trouble later, there is no guarantee it will be bailed out by its big foreign parent. A foreign bank could just decide to pull out and take a write-off on their accounts.

- *Shutting banks down.* In countries where there is a lot of corruption this can seem like the best solution. Shutting down a few seriously troubled banks sends a signal that the government is serious about reform and lets depositors know they have nothing to be afraid of. If the worst banks are not closed, it is likely they will go back to their old habits and get into trouble again. However, shutting down banks can cause panic and thus send the opposite signal. Depositors start to look around and worry that other banks are in trouble and rush to pull out their money before they get shut down as well. In Indonesia, the IMF pressured the government to shut down sixteen financial institutions in November 1998, and by the end of the month nearly two-thirds of all Indonesian banks suffered a run on deposits.

When reporters evaluate different options for resolving a banking crisis, they should ask detailed questions about the actual situation in the country:

- Are local businesses highly dependent on bank finance? Would a credit crunch be a disaster for them? Are there alternate forms of finance for local firms?

- What is the public mood like? Would bank closures create a panic?

- Does the government have persuasive advisors? Do the economists from the IMF and the World Bank who are dealing with the country really seem familiar with the banking sector? Are they making a big effort to familiarize themselves with the domestic situation, or are they holed up in the central bank crunching numbers? Are they being lied to by local officials?

- Are steps really being taken so the crisis does not happen again, or is it likely the scenario will be repeated in a few years?

■ What is the level of nonperforming loans in the banking system and banks of the country in question? What is considered a healthy level? If this information is kept secret, reporters should try to figure out how NPLs are defined and how lax or tight the credit controls are. Do the banks have any overdue loans, and how generous is the definition of overdue? In the Vietnam crisis, for instance, interest on a loan had to be a year overdue before the principal was considered to be at risk. Thus, official pronouncements about there being few "bad loans" in the Vietnamese banking sector were hardly credible. Though by the government's definition everything was okay, their loan classification did not meet international norms. By international standards it was clear there was a high level of NPLs in the system.

■ The executives at the top of the banks are not likely to speak frankly about their banks, so reporters need to go far down the chain of command. Managers and credit officers at the local branches are a good start. They should be asked how they feel about their loan portfolios, whether they look solid, whether the government-run companies are good at paying back their loans. Many countries now have local credit-rating agencies that monitor bank balance sheets. Finally, international institutions (especially the World Bank and the IMF) put out periodic reports on the health of the banking sector in various countries.

■ Reporters should write from the other side of the problem. If the banks will not talk, the companies that borrow from the banks should be examined to get a sense of how strong they are and whether they are in a position to repay their bank loans. If the country has a bank that specializes in lending to agricultural businesses, it is important to visit it and see how profitable it is.

■ Reporters should find out what sort of collateral has been pledged and look at how easy it is to collect. If the collateral is real estate and the country has a real estate bubble, then chances are the banks will have a problem. If the court systems in the country are slow and inefficient (or corrupt), it may be unlikely that a bank will be able to collect and resell the collateral.

■ Reporters should have a local accountant or banker to go over a profit-and-loss account and a balance sheet and explain what to look for. Tell-tale signs include major write-downs and off-balance-sheet exposures.

■ In the event of a devaluation, reporters should pay attention to what percentage of loans and deposits are held in foreign currencies. Also important is the currency mismatch from the borrower's perspective: for example, if a large share of loans is in foreign currency but the borrower's revenues tend to be in local currency, then a devaluation could well cause corporate failures and, in turn, banking problems.

■ Reporters need to monitor interest rates. If interest rates go up, loans are more difficult to repay, and there may be defaults. Also, it is important to know which banks have long-term loans with fixed rates, like mortgages. Because bank deposits are short term, this may lead to serious balance sheet problems.

1. World Bank's page on banking research. http://econ.worldbank.org/programs/finance.

2. Web site of Professor Franklin Edwards of Columbia University; provides access to a host of his research papers on finance. http://www-1.gsb.columbia.edu/faculty/fedwards.

3. Web site of Professor Frederic Mishkin, also of Columbia University; offers access to his research on financial crisis and emerging-market finance. http://www-1.gsb.columbia.edu/faculty/fmishkin.

4. IDEAS, an electronic database maintained by the University of Connecticut, carries a number of research papers on the Japanese banking crisis. http://ideas.repec.org/p/nbr/nberwo/ 7250.html.

5. The Basel Committee on Banking Supervision. http://www.bis.org/bcbs.

6. Cornell University's Legal Information Institute's Web site offers access to U.S. laws regulating banks. http://www.law.cornell.edu/topics/banking.html.

7. The U.S. Federal Deposit Insurance Corp. insures deposits in U.S. banks and promotes safe and sound banking practices. http://www.fdic.gov/about/index.html.

8. The Institute of International Banking and Finance, based at the SMU School of Law, maintains a Web site that provides access to research papers on banking issues around the world. http://iibf.law.smu.edu/index.htm.

9. The Institute of International Finance, a global association of financial institutions created in 1983 in response to the international debt crisis, publishes numerous reports on regulatory and policy issues concerning banks around the world. http://www.iif.com/pub/index.quagga.

10. Global Banking Law Database, maintained by the World Bank and the International Monetary Fund. http://www.gbld.org.

GLOSSARY

■ **NONPERFORMING LOAN (NPL)** A loan on which a borrower has not made a payment for an extended period of time.

■ **CAPITAL ADEQUACY RATIO** A measure of the amount of a bank's capital expressed as a percentage of its risk-weighted credit exposures. This ratio is used to protect depositors and promote the stability and efficiency of financial systems around the world. Two types of capital are measured: tier-one capital, which can absorb losses without a bank's being required to cease trading, and tier two capital, which can absorb losses in the event of a winding-up and so provides a lesser degree of protection to depositors.

■ **MORAL HAZARD** A phenomenon encountered whenever there is a disjunction between "actions" and "consequences." In a perfect market, an investor should be penalized for making a bad decision, just as he or she is rewarded for a good one. In "failed markets," this causality breaks. Economists ascribe failing markets to myriad causes including, in particular, incomplete information, that is, when two parties engaging in an economic transaction do not share the same information set.

■ **LIQUIDITY** A concept that assesses the speed and ease with which an asset's value can be realized. Cash is by far the most liquid asset: one can use it to buy virtually anything, and its "value" (in terms of purchasing power) is well defined. Checking accounts are slightly less liquid than cash but more so than term-deposits, which can be accessed only at the end of a particular period. At the other end of the liquidity spectrum lie assets such as fine art, jewelry, and real estate. Bonds and stocks are somewhere in the middle. Banks, almost by definition, face liquidity mismatches since their assets are tied up in long-term investments (e.g., loans) but their sources of financing (e.g., deposits) can be easily called. This mismatch can create crises if depositors decide to withdraw their deposits in a rush. Regulators try to limit this risk by requiring banks to hold a minimum amount of liquid assets.

CHAPTER TEN

SOVEREIGN DEBT CRISES

SUZANNE MILLER

S OVEREIGN COUNTRIES have been borrowing money from foreign creditors since colonial times. Argentina, for instance, slid
into debt even before it achieved independence, turning to England for money to fight Spanish colonial rule. In 1915, the United States
sent troops to Haiti after the government failed to pay its debt. In 1902,
Great Britain, Germany, and Italy sent a joint naval expedition to the
Venezuelan coast, where they blockaded seaports and captured Venezuelan gunboats. Argentina's foreign affairs minister, Maria Luis Drago,
protested, laying the groundwork for the Drago Doctrine—in essence an
extension of the Monroe Doctrine—which maintained that no public
debt could be collected from a sovereign Spanish American state by
armed force or occupation by a foreign power. A modified form of the
Drago Doctrine was approved at the Hague Conference of 1907.

More often, though, debt crises are resolved when creditors agree to big
write-offs and debt restructuring. Often restructuring is followed by fresh
loans. How do countries get caught in these debt cycles to begin with?

Countries borrow for many reasons. Those in the developing world, for
instance, often turn to international financial institutions for help in
building their economies. In doing so, debtor countries often find that
their fortunes become entwined with those of the international markets.
This is what happened to Latin America in the 1960s and early 1970s,
when multinational corporations built big in Southern Hemisphere countries because money and labor were cheap. Much of this government-
and industry-fueled expansion was financed with commercial bank loans.
So when OPEC oil prices shot higher in 1973, many Southern countries

found they were already hooked on oil imports and had to borrow more money to keep the oil flowing. When the second OPEC crisis hit in 1979, debt levels were nearing intolerable levels, just when the U.S. economy was starting to contract and close to imports. And so began the infamous debt crisis of the 1980s. Latin American countries suffered massive economic setbacks, and banks lost billions of dollars in loans.

All this suggests that the international financial community has a stake in making the process of working out sovereign bankruptcy more manageable, as many financial institutions have tremendous credit exposure to sovereign countries that borrow bank debt and bonds. For one thing, when a country falters, creditors are often forced to write off millions of dollars in losses.

That, of course, is not supposed to happen in the first place. During the boom years of the early 1990s, some insisted that buying the bonds issued by governments, known as sovereign bonds, made good sense for investors in search of secure returns because of the inherent strength in the underlying guarantee. For example, a business may collapse and disappear, but how often does that happen to an entire country? In the case of a rich, developed nation, such as the United States, the servicing of debt is virtually assured. That is why the bonds issued by the U.S. government are sought as a safe haven in uncertain times.

But the same does not apply to all countries. Naturally, the stronger a country's economic health, the stronger the underlying guarantee of repayment. Yet sometimes a country's entire economy becomes too weak for the government to meet its obligations to investors at home and abroad. When a country does not have the money to pay its debts when they come due, it defaults on the debt. A country—just like a business—that cannot pay its debts is considered bankrupt.

This problem famously occurred in the 1980s during the Latin debt crisis, mentioned earlier, when loan defaults by several countries, led by Mexico, totaled $251 billion by the end of 1989. More recently, Argentina defaulted on debts of more than $130 billion in November 2001. That was 25 percent of the emerging-market debt outstanding at the time—making it the single biggest sovereign default ever.

WHY DO COUNTRIES DEFAULT?

There is no one hard and fast reason why countries default on their debt. Economists have distinguished between two types of default: those caused by "liquidity" and those caused by "solvency." Liquidity crises happen not because the country is overly indebted but rather because, at a particular moment in time and for myriad reasons, it suddenly loses access to enough financing to cover debt servicing as it comes due. Solvency crises are more complicated. They usually occur when a country becomes so indebted that the likelihood of continuous servicing of debt well into the future becomes slim. Fearing that eventuality, lenders "boycott" the insolvent country by cutting lines of credit and refusing to roll over the debt that comes due. As funding is cut, the insolvent country faces a liquidity crunch, which, at the limit, can cause default.

At a less theoretical level, defaults usually occur as a result of a combination of factors that include:

- a high level of debt

- sluggish domestic growth

- problems in domestic economic policy

- rising interest rates

- currency devaluations

- collapse in commodity prices for commodity-exporting countries

When industrialized countries experience an economic slowdown, they stop importing from developed countries. Commodity prices—a staple of production in many developing nations—also fall. As export earnings fall, domestic recessions develop, and the country's ability to service its debt suffers.

Currency instability can be a big factor on its own. Domestic currencies pegged to the dollar sometimes become massively overvalued as domestic inflation outstrips international inflation. Pressures develop and the currency regime eventually collapses. The problem, however, is that a sharp devaluation can have disastrous effects on the corporate sector, especially if that sector had borrowed a lot in foreign currencies. As companies collapse, the overall economy goes into recession. Tax revenues fall, and the government's ability to service its debt evaporates. Indeed, many ascribe Argentina's accelerated collapse in late 2001 to the breakdown of its rigid currency board and the subsequent big devaluation in the country's currency, the peso.

Sovereign defaults, though, are rarely caused by only one reason. They are often caused by a cumulative set of events. In August 1982, the Mexican government was suddenly unable to roll over its commercial debt as a series of economic and political problems came to a head. The government had borrowed heavily to fuel growth at home—and the borrowing was increasingly short term in nature. That plan unraveled when the U.S. government raised interest rates to slow its own domestic inflation. Higher interest rates made the servicing of Mexico's foreign-exchange debt that much more difficult. So Mexico had to borrow new funds to replace loans that were due. Overnight it went from being a net borrower to a net repayer. The turnaround was too disruptive, and Mexico eventually approached its creditors, asking for rescheduling. Shortly thereafter, other sovereign debtors in Latin America sought rescheduling agreements, too. Meanwhile, exports were hurt as developing countries struggled with falling commodity prices after a decade-long rise in the 1970s.

WHAT HAPPENS WHEN COUNTRIES DEFAULT?

When a business defaults on its debt, it generally either declares bankruptcy voluntarily in court or its creditors have it declared bankrupt, also by a court. Bankruptcy laws vary from country to country, but they all tend to have the legal system at the center. This is done for two reasons: First, the bankrupt firm needs a legal cover to shield it from lenders while it reorganizes. Second, creditors need the legal system to rule on intracreditor issues. The legal system, in other words, is meant to give creditors a chance to recoup some of the money they are owed while allowing the business an opportunity to reorganize and get back on its feet. The court in different ways will oversee the process of rescheduling debt payments, restructuring the debts, or reorganizing the business.

When countries default, there is not much creditors can really do about it. Unlike companies, sovereign countries do not have assets that can be turned over to their creditors, and there is no universally accepted legal procedure for coping with the default or applying standard penalties. In a similar vein, legal injunctions on sovereigns, even when obtained, can be very difficult to enforce. Creditors can, in the future, raise the interest rates they charge the borrowing country, for instance, making it tougher for the borrower to raise fresh debt. In the long run, some economists believe this is a good thing because it prevents these countries from falling deeper into debt. Even so, the short-term consequences can be painful.

What generally happens is that countries that cannot pay their debts try to have them rescheduled or try to negotiate a write-down, or reduction, of the total amount of debt. The majority of negotiations and workouts have historically been done on an ad hoc basis between creditors and the government. To renegotiate official debts, or the money owed by one country to another, debtor nations have to deal with the so-called Paris Club, a group of rich creditor nations. To renegotiate commercial debt, or money owed to private creditors, such as banks, countries deal with a group known as the London Club. The London Club does not include bondholders. Indeed, while informal associations exist, there is no formal club that represents bondholders. Many consider this to be part of the problem.

BAILOUTS

In some cases, where a country appears to be rapidly approaching default or the size of the debt means a default could disrupt the financial markets and the stability of the country itself, the International Monetary Fund may step in. This multilateral institution has in the past made emergency loans to help countries in such situations, in a move often referred to as a bailout. In theory, the IMF has three roles when assisting a country in distress: First, it provides the "bridge financing" for countries facing liquidity crises. Second, it forces the country into the kinds of fiscal and structural adjustments needed to put it back on a more solid footing.

Third, by providing a seal of approval, IMF loans are supposed to act as "catalysts" for the private sector to return with its flows.

The IMF does not help all countries that default. For instance, in 1999 Ecuador defaulted on $6 billion in Brady bonds and received no help from the IMF. But it does have a history of paying big money to help others. So far it has paid out some $250 billion. The IMF has been heavily criticized for its long track record of bailouts that have failed to show discernable long-term benefits or even failed in their immediate objective of stabilizing the exchange rate, as happened in East Asia in 1997, Russia in 1998, and Brazil in 1999. IMF critics contend bailouts typically prolong and exacerbate economic problems. The fund counters by noting that, by the time it arrives, the problems are so serious that the best the fund can do is to mitigate the crises rather than stop them from occurring.

MORAL HAZARD

A persistent criticism of bailouts has also been the moral hazard problem, where the creditor lends money carelessly, knowing that if things go wrong, there is a good chance of a bailout. This excessive lending, critics claim, has played an important role in bringing on some of the recent crises. This was the widely held view in the case of Russia, which defaulted on its debt in August 1998. Creditors believed it was "too big to fail," especially since the West would be worried about instability in a nuclear power. But this logic failed to hold when the IMF issued a big bailout in July of that year. Despite the cash infusion, the ruble collapsed and the country defaulted on its loans. This triggered a sell-off in the emerging markets and underscored the limitations of bailouts.

A NEW PROPOSAL

Things took a new twist, however, when Argentina defaulted on more than $130 billion of debt in November 2001. The IMF declined to give the country more money as the economy collapsed, marking a major policy shift. The IMF had been closely tied with the policy stances of Argentina throughout the 1990s, often trotting out Argentina as it's A+ student. Even when the new Bush administration came in strongly questioning bailouts, the IMF continued to lend to Argentina. In part, this reflected a sense that the Argentine government was trying hard to avoid a default and that the official community must do its share by helping out. The official community also wanted to avoid the potentially disruptive fallout from an Argentine collapse and its effects on Brazil, especially. Finally, noneconomic considerations also played a role: major governments allegedly put political pressure on a skeptical IMF management to continue disbursing funds to Argentina. Eventually, though, the IMF declined to give more money as it believed that further funding would not be enough to avert an imminent financial collapse.

Around the same time, following four years of sustained opposition, often involving heavily publicized antiglobalization demonstrations directed at the IMF, the World Bank, and the World Trade Organization, the IMF bowed to international pressure and decided to try a new approach to defaults. In November 2001, the IMF produced a new policy proposal, a sovereign-debt restructuring mechanism (SDRM), a process akin to bankruptcy procedures. Almost simultaneously, but not necessarily coincidentally, the U.S. Treasury proposed an alternative approach based on collective action clauses (see below).

The IMF's proposal is statutory in nature, in that it depends on institutions similar to a court. It would allow a debtor country to request a temporary standstill on its debt repayments while it negotiates a restructuring acceptable to a majority of creditors. The consent of the majority would bind the minority creditors. (Note that the definition of the term "majority" is still being debated. Some think of it as amounting to two-thirds, though some creditor groups prefer a higher number). The restructuring plan is meant to approximate the U.S.-style chapter 11 bankruptcy code. The IMF has proposed that a "super-majority" of creditors approve the plan rather than the unanimity of creditors because of fears that a few "hold-outs" could stop a restructuring, perhaps in an attempt to extract a better deal for themselves. Critics of the SDRM have noted that the unanimity requirement originated in part from instances where a majority, or even a supermajority, approved restructuring deals that worked to their advantage but to the disadvantage of the minority. There is a concern that under the IMF proposal, this problem will resurface. The proposal has provoked a strong marketwide political backlash, so much so that the IMF has quietly put the SDRM plan on hold. Although it still officially sanctions the plan, it has also openly endorsed an alternative, voluntary plan that has been promoted by the U.S. Treasury. This is a contractual agreement known as a collective action clause (see below).

HOW WORKOUTS CURRENTLY OPERATE

The current process for workouts is many-layered, involving formal negotiation with a creditors' committee, formal or informal consultation, as well as legal structures ranging from formal amendment of existing debt contracts to exchange offers. The restructuring process is time-consuming because most bond contracts provide that their payment terms cannot be amended without the consent of "each bond affected thereby." That means that most, if not all, creditors must agree.

There are different mechanisms for debt workouts. The earliest, and by far the most comprehensive, is a scheme known as Brady Bonds.

Brady bonds. These instruments were named after U.S. Treasury Secretary Nicholas Brady, who introduced them in the late 1980s as a way of addressing the lingering problems from the debt crisis of the early 1980s. The bonds represent the restructured bank debt of Latin American and other emerging nations that over-borrowed from U.S. institutions. A Brady bond's coupon payment, and in some cases its principal, is typically backed by U.S. zero-coupon bonds. The bonds enable debtor governments to reduce their principal, interest, and interest arrears. Countries involved in Brady Plan restructurings have included Argentina, Brazil, Bulgaria, Costa Rica, the Dominican Republic, Ecuador, Mexico, Morocco, Nigeria, the Philippines, Poland, and Uruguay. These bonds were mainly used in the 1980s and have since been largely replaced by other instruments.

More recent debt work outs have included swaps, rollovers, and, more generally, a framework that has come to be known as "exchange offers."

Exchange offers. Debtor countries such as Russia, Ecuador, Pakistan, and the Ukraine have been able to restructure sizeable portions of their debt through the use of exchange offers, which replace old debt with new debt that typically grants more generous terms to the debtor country. Those terms typically take one (or a combination) of three forms: a reduction in the debt's final face value ("haircut"); a reduction in the coupon payments; and a lengthening of maturity.

A key drawback in exchange offers is that for them to be successful, a "super-majority" of bond holders needs to sign off. This permits a minority, which could be as small as one "rogue" investor, to block the exchange. In that regard, Ecuador represented a turning point in restructuring agreements because it used certain features, known as exit consents, to encourage full participation from those in the exchange. In particular, there was fear that while the majority of bondholders would participate in the deal, a group of holdouts could theoretically attempt an intensive litigation process in which the buyer of a few bonds would attempt to extract better treatment as a condition for allowing the restructuring to go through. In the event, Ecuador's exchange permitted a majority (75 percent) of bondholders to change nonfinancial terms of the old bonds. As such, the majority voted on amendments that made the old bonds unattractive to potential holdouts.

Despite the relative success of recent exchanges (e.g., Ecuador), there are still several problems with the current workout process:

- *Coordination problem*. Debt workouts are typically hampered by a broad array of claimants. Indeed, some believe that the coordination problem has become worse in recent years. For example, in the 1980s' Latin American crisis, most of the debt was held by a very few banks. Since then, sovereign debt is often held by multiple of investor classes all competing for a payout. In addition, there are often ambiguities about which creditors are senior to other creditors. For instance, international creditors are a powerful force because they are the source of much-needed capital in developing countries. Governments, by contrast, often seek to favor domestic debt holders. For one thing, the latter often form a strong vested interest. In addition, if a restructuring deal is too onerous, it can cause bankruptcies for domestic creditors, forcing the government to take them by issuing new debt.

More generally, getting all creditors to agree to a homogenous payment plan can be a difficult task. Since the onset of the "emerging-markets finance" craze in the mid-1990s, a heterogeneous and complicated creditor base has emerged, including bond holders, foreign bank lenders, domestic debtors, as well as official bilateral and multilateral lenders. Those creditors often have conflicting interests and perspectives—a plan agreed to by some bondholders can be less advantageous to others.

- *Holdouts.* In 1996, Elliott Associates LP (a New York–based hedge fund) sued Peru after it closed on a financial restructuring plan under a Brady agreement. Elliot Partners held about $21 million of Peru's commercial bank loans and did not participate in the deal. In 2000, Elliot Associates won its legal claim, unprecedented in international workouts. While the legal victory did not ultimately repay Paris debt restructuring with other creditors, it was perceived by some, including the IMF, as a warning for future restructuring. This has been one of the only "rogue creditor" case studies to date. Nonetheless, it has played an important role in the drive to establish a formal international bankruptcy solution. The IMF and others have worried that the creditor's actions threatened, although they did not ultimately disrupt, Peru's access to capital markets. The IMF's plan seeks to deal with the potential of individual creditors holding out for their own interests rather than cooperating with a broader group.

CONTRACTUAL VERSUS STATUTORY APPROACHES

Those supporting a contractual approach to sovereign bankruptcies would prefer to leave the restructuring of sovereign debt as an informal process of negotiation predominantly governed by the contractual language of the underlying bonds. Those who prefer a statutory approach would like to see some formal law or code written to guide sovereign defaults. Those resisting the statutory approach are concerned that formalizing the workout process may actually make it easier for the sovereigns to default ("strategic default").

THE CONTRACTUAL APPROACH

The U.S. Treasury is pushing for the insertion of collective action clauses in sovereign debt contracts that would, in effect, force all creditors to go along with a restructuring approved by a majority (say, two-thirds) of bond holders. Since early 2003, most new debt is now being issued with such language included in the documentation. Since the beginning of 2004, under New York law, five more countries included CACs in sovereign debt contracts for the first time: Chile, Panama, Costa Rica, and

Venezuela. The U.S. Treasury claimed that "these nations are helping make collective action clauses the market standard in external soereign bond issues under New York law, and strengthening the international finance system."

That said, there are concerns about how such clauses can be inserted into already existing debt contracts and what to do if many contracts do not yet have such clauses. Other concerns include:

DELAYS Unlike an approach in which one arbiter decides, the collective approach can cause long delays in the debt resolution process. It is extremely difficult to meet the needs of even a majority of bondholders, especially when numerous cross-classes of creditors are involved.

AGGREGATION There is also the problem of aggregation. Put differently, what is to be done if the majority of holders of one class of bonds agree to certain terms, but the majority of all bondholders do not? If there were a single class of creditors, it would be easy to define what one means by a majority of creditors, but if there are many classes, how is one to weigh the "votes" of junior and senior creditors? Or, for that matter, international and local investors?

THE STATUTORY APPROACH

The IMF has proposed an alternative approach—one based on a bankruptcy-like legal framework. However, is that there is intense dis-agreement on the design of such a framework. Such an agreement at this juncture appears unlikely. Adopting bankruptcy laws within a country has often proved highly contentious, and there is every reason to believe that an international agreement would be even more difficult.

The specific issues related to the IMF's proposal include:

ARBITER A bankruptcy framework requires an arbiter who would decide when a standstill has occurred and when it will end, whether the debtor is negotiating in good faith with its creditors, whether it is following sound polices, and whether it can receive new financing. It would also fall to the arbiter to pressure the private market to make concessions. The IMF can-not act as a credible arbiter as it is one of the key interested parties; it is already a creditor controlled by other official creditors. The position of the dominant countries often seems dictated by the concerns of their financial markets, which in turn sometimes seem dominated by creditors. Critics argue this could easily create a perception of bias that would damage the legitimacy of the process. Accordingly, there are some that suggest that there should be an independent International Bankruptcy Court, outside of the IMF.

ENFORCEMENT PROBLEMS What would happen if an international bankruptcy court tried to force a country to meet its agreed obligations, but the country reneged on the agreement? If a country defaulted and its creditors were to decide to accelerate repayment, the creditors would have limited options. That's because sovereigns have two basic assets outside their countries—international reserves and embassies. These are both exempt from attachment under sovereign-immunity law. So the only way to enforce such seizure is to take it to the home country of the debtor and try to enforce it there—an onerous prospect.

CHAPTER 11 VS. CHAPTER 9 Of these two U.S. bankruptcy laws, some critics say chapter 11 is less relevant then chapter 9, which covers U.S. municipal and state defaults. Chapter 9 recognizes the primacy of the essential state functions of the public entity, such as social security, education, and health. In other words, in satisfying creditors, the interests of other stakeholders not only have to be recognized, but, in many cases, given priority. Sovereign restructuring obviously entails far more complicated issues than are either addressed by chapter 9 or chapter 11, but these two chapters of the U.S. bankruptcy code provide intellectual frames. For instance, chapter 9 might suggest that other stakeholders, such as social security recipients, would have priority over the financial players who hold debt.

WHERE ARE WE AT PRESENT?

By late 2002, the statutory approach was losing ground relative to the contractual approach. One reason had to do with the strong resistance to the IMF's statutory approach by both governments and the private sector. Moreover, in February, Mexico issued the first Eurobond under a New York law that included collective action clauses. The bond performed relatively well and did not trade at a discernable discount relative to existing bonds. Brazil followed Mexico, and, since then, almost all new eurobonds are being issued with CACs. It would now seem that the statutory approach is well off the center stage.

Stories about sovereign bankruptcies should answer as many of the following questions as possible:

- How much external debt does the sovereign debtor have? How much interest is coming due? What about principal? What are the major classes of debt holders?

- What is the debt to GDP ratio? How does it compare to other countries within the same region?

- What is the rate of debt service being paid? Reporters should check to see how much this number has increased in recent years and whether there is a notable trend in whom this debt service is going to (e.g., foreign versus domestic; official versus private). It is also important to check to see what percent of the government's revenue is being consumed by the debt burden.

- Has the currency been devalued? If so, has that had a major impact on debt servicing? This is likely to be more of an issue if the debt is largely denominated in foreign currencies.

- How much income is the country generating from exports, and what is it paying out in imports? How does the debt stock compare to the level of exports? How does the debt service compare to the level of imports? (The latter is called "debt-service ratio").

- How did the debt originate? When were the country's debts assumed? Was there, for instance, a particular period in time where the bulk of the debts were assumed?

- What is the mix of the country's debt? How much represents public external debt, and what is the total that encompasses domestic, external, provincial, and private debt?

- Who are the major creditors—what countries have the greatest exposure? What percent of the creditors are in the private and public sectors? What banks are involved? Sometimes a few banks have very large exposures. One way of finding out is to check with international credit agencies.

- Is the debt held by foreign entities or domestic ones? This is important because a default may cause severe problems to the country's financial system, as happened in Argentina. If domestic banks have lent money to the government, will a default later require a bailout of those banks, too? What sorts of plans has the government made to deal with this kind of disruption? What would such a bailout do to the savings the government would get from the default?

- What recourse do creditors have? Does the government own any assets overseas (other than embassies) that would be attractive to creditors?

- How have other countries with such a crisis handled it? How long has it lasted? How long has it taken them to regain access to international markets? As a country goes into a crisis, economic prospects often look bleak, but in some cases recovery has occurred rapidly. Russia, for instance, had its first growth since the beginning of the transition after its crisis and regained access to international capital markets within two years. There are controversies over the factors that contribute to a quick recovery: Mexico's quick recovery is attributed to the growth of trade with the United States and the availability of credit from U.S. importers more than to the IMF bailout. In the case of Russia, the postcrisis funds from the IMF simply went to repay the IMF and thus played no role in reactivating the economy. Reporters need to ask: what are the conditions that the IMF is imposing to provide funds? What will be done with the funds?

- What steps are being taken for future crisis prevention? A criticism of the IMF's current restructuring plan is that it doesn't address crisis prevention, but given the frequency of crises in emerging markets, all such countries need to worry about whether they appear to be vulnerable.

What are the rating agencies saying? Standard & Poor's and Moody's Investor Service, both U.S.-based rating agencies in New York City, issue ratings and commentary on the debt they rate. This includes the debt of many sovereign countries. What were the rating actions leading up to the country's default?

Reporters should try to talk to local credit officials as they have the most hands-on understanding. But caution is necessary: there is often a "party-line," the validity of which needs to be probed.

Trade groups. The Emerging Markets Traders Association is the principal trade group for the emerging-markets trading and investment community and looks after investor rights and trading issues. It is based in New York City. This is a good source for gathering market statistics and commentary from the foreign investor perspective. The EMTA is dominated by banks and invest-

ment banks. The Emerging Markets Creditors Association (EMCA) represents bondholders.

Banks. Reporters should call the major creditors in question and find out if they have named anyone to head up a restructuring team. However, this process can take many months after the initial default, and it's unusual for bank executives to talk publicly about such situations early on. Local bank branches might prove more useful. Also, investors are typically more willing to talk. Meanwhile, the emerging-market research teams of the big banks are useful for gaining additional information about the country's restructuring prospects.

Reporters should talk to a variety of people from different groups. Each party will have a different perspective. Scavenger funds, long-term investors, banks and bondholders will often have different priorities and different views as to how the situation should be resolved.

LINKS FOR MORE INFORMATION

1. Institute for International Economics' papers on financial crises. www.iie.com/catalog/wp.

2. Stern School of Business Web site for emerging market news and academic papers. www.pages.stern.nyu.edu/~nroubini.

3. Introduction to Brady Bonds. www.bradynet .com/e12.html.

4. The Paris Club is an informal group of official bilateral creditors that works on resolving pay-

ment problems of the debtor nations. It does not include multilateral creditors such as the IMF and the World Bank. www.clubdeparis.org.

5. The IMF homepage. www.imf.org.

6. Ann Krueger's speech on the IMF international-al bankruptcy proposal. http://www.imf.org/external/np/speeches/2002/040102.htm.

7. Jubilee Plus home page. www.jubileeplus.org.

8. EMTA home page. http://www.emta.org.

CHAPTER ELEVEN

DEBT RELIEF AND HIPC

GUMISAI MUTUME

THE NEED FOR DEBT RELIEF

THERE IS growing consensus around the world that debt is a major obstacle to the sustainable development of poor countries. Some governments spend more than 75 percent of their revenues on debt payments, leaving them with little money for more productive expenditures such as education and health. The cost of debt payments, or servicing the debt, can also suck up much of the foreign currency a country earns from its exports, leaving little foreign currency to buy vital imports.

When the burden of external debt, or the money owed outside the country, becomes too great, countries generally try to renegotiate the terms of the debt. Over the years, more than seventy developing countries have at one time or another renegotiated the terms of their external debt. Generally, in the past, richer countries that lent money to poorer countries have agreed to delay the payments, cut interest rates, or extend the period over which the debt was paid off. These traditional mechanisms of debt relief have provided an estimated $6.5 billion in relief to more than fifty developing countries since the late 1970s. But that is a drop in the bucket compared to the total external debt of developing countries, estimated at more than $2.3 trillion at the end of 2001 by the Organization for Economic Cooperation and Development.

Responding to mounting criticism that richer countries were condemning poor countries to poverty by not easing the pressure of their debt burdens, the World Bank and International Monetary Fund in 1996 announced a new debt relief program known as the Heavily Indebted Poor Countries initiative, a plan that critics feel has not done enough to solve the problem.

Indeed, the debt of poor countries has continued to grow and so has pressure for further debt relief, including forgiving some debt altogether. Jubilee 2000, an international movement of civil society groups and religious organizations in both developing and developed countries, has been one major proponent of debt relief. Guided by biblical teachings, Jubilee 2000 proposed a one-off cancellation of the backlog of the unpayable debt of the poorest nations as a gesture of goodwill to mark the new millennium. So far, their efforts have attracted attention but have had, at best, limited success.

HISTORY OF DEBT CRISES

How do countries get themselves into a situation where debt relief is necessary? For the poorest countries, which are the subject of discussion here, there have been several sources of the problem:

- Many of the poor countries borrowed extensively from 1960 through 1990. The strategy pursued was one known as "inward looking/import substitution." Large-scale industrialization was attempted. The hope, of course, was that the economies would start to grow by more than enough to repay the debt. But for a number of reasons, growth did not materialize and the countries were left saddled with a heavy legacy of indebtedness.

- In the late 1970s and early 1980s, interest rates soared to unprecedented levels. With those increases in interest rates, debt levels that were initially serviceable suddenly became unsustainable. In the late 1990s, interest rates to emerging markets soared again. Even when countries do not have short-term debt, there is a constant need to roll over debt, and when it is rolled over, countries tend to face ever higher interest rates.

- Most debt is denominated in dollars or other hard currencies, and, accordingly, manageable debt levels become unmanageable when a country's currency is devalued or depreciates in relation to hard currencies.

- Many developing countries are dependent on exporting commodities such as agricultural products, minerals, or metals to earn money to pay off their debts. When export prices collapse, the debt burden becomes unsustainable.

HISTORY OF DEBT RELIEF

Long before HIPC, there had been a process by which countries that could not pay their debts could have them rescheduled. "Rescheduling," as a concept, should be distinguished from "restructuring." The former simply pushes debt-service payments coming due to a future date without reducing those amounts. It is meant to help countries going through a "liquidity" crisis. Restructuring, by contrast, involves an actual reduction in either the debt-service payment falling due or on the face value of the debt itself.

There is another important distinction to keep in mind. Poor countries borrowed from both the official sector (for example, the French government lending to the Ivory Coast) and from the private sector (Chase Manhattan lending to Gabon). As countries faced difficulties and needed to renegotiate their debt, they needed to deal with a counterpart. Historically, the group that encompassed official creditors took the name of the Paris Club, which mainly comprised rich creditor nations. To renegotiate commercial debt, or money owed to private creditors, countries had to deal with a group known as the London Club.

By 1996 it was widely recognized that more substantial debt relief was required. By then, forty-one heavily indebted countries owed about $205 billion in external debt, a figure that accounted for more than 130 percent of their combined gross national products. (As a rule of thumb, a debt-to-GDP ratio that exceeds 100 percent is considered very high). Until then, most debt arrangements involved rescheduling. But the problem was evidently becoming more than just one of liquidity. It had become one of solvency. Rescheduling alone was not enough. Restructuring was becoming increasingly needed. Consequently, HIPC was introduced in an attempt to do something more for countries locked in a cycle of rescheduling debt with the Paris or London Clubs. For the first time, a systematic effort at dealing with the stock of debt was considered. In addition, debt relief would cover *multilateral* debt, or loans made by the World Bank and IMF, as well as *bilateral debt*, where one country owed another, and commercial debt.

In fact, by 1999 critics pointed out that little debt relief had actually been provided. Bolivia and Uganda had debt cancelled in 1998, but within a year their debt levels had returned to unsustainable levels, forcing them to seek further relief. Mozambique received relief but found itself paying nearly the same amounts in debt service after HIPC. In 1999, conceding that the original HIPC had not delivered on its initial objective, the Group of 7 industrialized nations launched enhanced HIPC and promised to streamline the program in order to provide "faster and deeper debt relief."

But even that did not seem to work well. Even before being fully implemented, there were growing concerns over the likely effectiveness of enhanced HIPC. For one thing, the process was costly for the creditors, and resources had to be allocated by the rich countries' budgets. In addition, the program was faced with restrictions over eligibility, excessive conditionality, and cumbersome procedures. By May 2000, only five countries had begun to receive some form of debt relief under enhanced HIPC: Bolivia, Mauritania, Mozambique, Tanzania, and Uganda. Under pressure from the Jubilee 2000 movement, debt forgiveness was finally extended more broadly. For the twenty-two countries that became eligible by December 2000, a commitment of $33.6 billion in debt relief was made. It was expected that debt servicing in some of these countries would be reduced by one-third during the next few years following HIPC treatment, combined with traditional debt rescheduling and bilateral debt relief. However, even by the end of the 2000, only Uganda had reached the final stage of HIPC, when full debt relief is given.

THE PROCESS

Only low-income, debt-distressed countries that borrow from the World Bank's International Development Association qualify for HIPC. The IDA provides loans at highly concessionary rates only to countries with annual per capita incomes of less than a certain threshold—set at $885 in 2002. These countries must go through a two-stage process.

STAGE ONE

This is a three-year period during which a country carries out economic reforms prescribed by the World Bank and the IMF. Countries are expected to make changes in their economic policy in line with the IMF's Poverty Reduction and Growth Facility. And they must establish a track record of carrying out poverty-reduction programs. To do this, HIPC countries must prepare Poverty Reduction Strategy Papers with support from the IMF and World Bank. PRSPs outline a country's macroeconomic and structural-reform policies and its concrete poverty-reduction goals. The World Bank and the IMF require that PRSPs be prepared through consultation with civil society, key donors, and regional development banks, such as the Inter-American Development Bank in the case of Latin America and the African Development Bank in the case of Africa.

These reforms often require deregulation and privatization of state enterprises, reform of the taxation system and changes in the way the public sector operates to improve efficiency. At the end of this period a country reaches its *decision point*. The two institutions then decide whether the country's debt—after the full application of all forms of traditional debt relief—remains unsustainable. If it does, the institutions offer the country a relief package. But debt relief at this stage would only be partial, canceling only a small part of the debt.

STAGE TWO

During the second three-year phase of HIPC, the country has to undertake further reforms. Only after fulfilling these requirements will it reach the *completion point* and receive the full package of debt relief. Responding to complaints over the slow pace of a process that makes countries wait six years before receiving relief, donor nations have agreed to reduce the total time required to qualify and complete the process.

HIPC IN ZAMBIA

SHANTHA BLOEMEN

Zambia is one of the beneficiaries of the World Bank and IMF's Highly Indebted Poor Countries Initiative, originally set up in 1996 to assist the poorest countries by forgiving part of their foreign debts. It was designed to reduce high levels of unsustainable debt and free up resources for poverty eradication.

The reality, as Zambia has discovered, is turning out to be different. Almost four years after the land-locked country in southern Africa became eligible for debt relief, it still spends more on interest payments to the World Bank and IMF than on health and education for its 10.3 million impoverished citizens. In 2001, Zambia, spent $158 million on debt service repayments, compared to $24 million for health and $33 million for education.

Zambia's debt crisis became increasingly acute in the 1980s. Caused in part by the oil crisis of 1973 and the dramatic fall in the price of copper that followed, the newly independent state began to borrow heavily to finance development. By the 1980s, with a deteriorating economic performance and worsening balance of payments, the country entered into a structural adjustment program with the World Bank and IMF.

In 1987, in an effort to induce economic growth under the theme "Growth from Our Own Resources," former President Kenneth Kaunda restricted debt service payments to 10 percent of the country's gross domestic product and suspended relations with the IMF. The idea was to limit debt servicing and use the savings to finance desperately needed investments in industry and agriculture. But by

unilaterally cutting debt payments, President Kaunda's defiance of the World Bank and IMF cost the country greatly. Creditors slapped penalties onto the existing debt and reduced foreign aid, causing the overall debt burden to balloon.

When Zambia signed a new agreement with the IMF after a two-year hiatus in June 1989, the debt-to-GDP ratio was over 200 percent, which led to a period of hyperinflation and the virtual collapse of the currency. In the 1990s, with a change of government and the introduction of a multiparty political system, Zambia set out rapidly down a path of free-market reform, radically overturning the one-party state. As part of the World Bank and IMF's enhanced structural adjustment program, the country quickly undertook a massive privatization of government-owned enterprises, turning 80 percent of the economy over to the private sector. The kwacha, the local currency, depreciated as the exchange rate and interest rates were floated; trade barriers were lifted; civil service was restructured and downsized; subsidies were stopped; and cost-recovery measures in the social sector were introduced.

The result was that inflation fell from 93 percent in 1991 to 16 percent in 2002, and the country posted economic growth of 3 percent in 2002, according to the World Bank. The contracting economy began to rebound in the early 1990s. The social cost, though, was enormous, as hundreds of thousands of people became unemployed, and fewer people could afford even the most basic services.

To make matters worse, by December 2000 the country's debt totaled $7.3 billion, and Zambia was barely able to make its payments on its burden. With

$606 million in debt payments due in 2001, the country was accepted into the first stage of the HIPC program. On reaching what is called a "decision point," it immediately received a 50 percent debt reduction. Normally, countries are first forced to wait till they have qualified by satisfying certain conditions, usually a three-year process, before they actually get debt relief. But in Zambia's case, not only was the global debt campaign, Jubilee 2000, demanding that HIPC deliver results faster, but creditors knew that the country would simply not be able to meet the payments due in 2001. With that write-off from the multilateral creditors, such as the IMF and the World Bank, plus additional debt cancellation from bilateral creditors, Zambia's debt now stands at $6.5 billion, down from $7.3 billion, saving the country millions of dollars in debt payments every year.

Although this sounds significant, projected debt-servicing payments remain high at over $100 million dollars per year, and Zambia's economic prospects still look bleak. The total debt is equivalent to approximately $552 for every Zambian, a huge sum considering that the country's per capita gross national income is only $330. And the interest payments represent millions of dollars that will not be spent on developing the economy of a country where an estimated 80 percent of the population live under the poverty line and where, with 20 percent of the population HIV positive, life expectancy has fallen from fifty-four to thirty-three years.

LESSONS LEARNED

Zambia's case demonstrates the limitations of HIPC, which was primarily created to bring a country's annual debt payments down to an amount that could be sustained by its export earnings. If Zambia stays "on track" by adhering to World Bank and IMF prescriptions and reaches its HIPC completion point, it should receive full debt relief, cutting its debt stock by an estimated $3.8 billion. The World Bank estimates that debt payments at that level will be equal to 150 percent or less of the country's export earnings, and it will be able to sustain its debt. However, that ratio that has already proved unsustainable in countries that have reached their HIPC completion points, perhaps partly because the math does not take into account the amount a country needs to spend on social needs and development.

Zambia's experience has highlighted several factors that need to be taken into account in the HIPC process, including a country's overreliance on exporting one commodity. Like many other countries in sub-Saharan Africa, Zambia's economy has long been reliant on a single commodity export, in its case, copper. Today, copper exports still account for up to 80 percent of Zambia's export earnings. Since copper is almost the only thing that Zambia sells overseas, when copper sales decline, Zambia is left without the foreign exchange it needs to pay its debt.

Everyone agrees Zambia needs to diversify its economy, but no one is quite sure how to go about it. Under colonial rule, the country's development primarily took place along the railway lines leading to the copper mines, leaving huge pockets of the country underdeveloped. In the 1960s, financed by copper revenue, the government tried unsuccessfully to create new industries and jobs in agriculture and manufacturing.

Agriculture and tourism are now cited as the arenas where Zambia has the most "comparative advantage," but it is not clear where the needed investment will come from to modernize these sectors or, while northern countries maintain agricultural tariff barriers, which markets Zambian produce can actually reach.

Looking at Zambia, a few things are clear:

- *Including civil society groups in drawing up a Poverty Reduction Strategy forces change in economic policies.* The creation of the IMF and World Bank's mandatory Poverty Reduction Strategy Paper, a condition for HIPC, has forced governments to include a human dimension in their economic polices. This document must be drawn up in order for the country to qualify for any debt relief. It is intended to serve as a blueprint for the country's development and should be written in consultation with NGOs and civil society groups. In Zambia, local NGOs were very active in the first draft of the document, and many of their main recommendations were included in the final PRSP that was approved by the parliament in May 2002.

- *The debt relief offered often is not enough to fund poverty-alleviation plans.* Although the World Bank and the IMF have endorsed Zambia's PRSP, they still warn that the cost of the programs and too much deviation in economic policies may delay Zambia's effort to reach its "completion point" and receive full debt relief. The PRSP plan would cost $1.2 billion for 2002 through 2004, a sum far greater than the money available from debt relief. According to the PRSP, debt-service-payment relief should amount to $773 million, but, with donor assistance in decline over recent years from $539 million in 1999 to $376 million in 2001, it is not yet certain where the needed money will come from.

However, while the IMF may find the amount of spending on social needs set out in the PRSP too ambitious, for many critics it is not enough. For example, it requires an increase in spending in the education sector from 18.5 percent of the budget in 1999 to 20.5 percent in 2003. According to Jubilee Zambia, part of the global campaign to cancel debt, this hardly looks adequate to actually meet the needs. The same, they argue, is true in the health sector, where increased attention on drug availability, an HIPC condition, is welcome. But they also argue that without increased wages to health workers, who were on strike for a large part of 2001, the quality of health care will not substantially improve.

The agreed social-sector spending also does not include increases in wages, especially for teachers and health workers. And as long as unemployment remains high and the government remains the largest employer, the social and political consequences stay dire. In 2003, the government, under enormous pressure from trade unions, agreed to wage increases that resulted in the budget deficit growing to 3 percent from an initial forecast of 1.55 percent. The IMF and international donors promptly froze lending until the government recanted. The 2004 budget has imposed a wage freeze on civil servants while simultaneously increasing personal income taxes by 30–40 percent. The return to fiscal discipline has now set Zambia back on the HIPC track, and the country is set to reach its completion point in June 2004. The social cost, though, has meant the government failed to employ 9,000 qualified teachers. Unions have promised industrial action, claiming the wage freeze is illegal. As a result, debt campaigners contend that the conditionality attached to HIPC has the same deleterious effects as the structural-adjustment program that added to high levels of poverty and unemployment.

- *Transparency and the active participation of civil society and in monitoring HIPC and the PRSP are crucial.* Tracking savings from debt relief and ensuring that it does find its way to the social sector is already proving to be difficult, according to Charity Musamba from Jubilee Zambia. The HIPC Monitoring Team, set up by the Ministry of Finance, is intended to be independent of the government and report directly to the minister of finance, who will then determine what information becomes public. Although the ministry has agreed to allow civil society participation, it is still not clear what their terms of reference will be and how this process will actually work.

CONCLUSION

While the impact of drought and the AIDS pandemic continues to exacerbate the country's woes, the limitations of HIPC, whether in bringing Zambia's debt levels down to sustainable levels or in significantly reversing the current cycle of poverty, are apparent. And as long as substantially more debt is not cancelled, Zambia, like many others countries in sub-Saharan Africa, will continue to spend a large part of its precious foreign exchange on debt servicing while neglecting the needs of its people.

In its current form, HIPC is unlikely to provide the needed funds to finance development, but it has managed to put the issue of poverty on the agenda. In a significant reversal of policy, under HIPC, distinct from the enhanced structural adjustment program, countries are encouraged to increase their share of social spending. But as long as governments continue to be restricted in their ability to increase wages and there are no other sources of job creation, the political and social fallout will remain severe.

LINKS FOR MORE INFORMATION

1. HIPC news and analysis. http://www.jubileeresearch.org.

2. Justine Nannyonjo, "Uganda's Social Sector Reforms and Outcomes," November 2001. http://www.wider.unu.edu/publications/dps/dp2001-138.pdf.

3. Reports and updates on HIPC by European development NGOs network. http://www.eurodad.org.

4. This Web site focuses on development issues affecting the global South, including the Asia-Pacific, Africa, and Latin Africa. http://www.focusweb.org.

5. A Web site created by African institutions to respond to globalization. http://www.isgnweb.org.

CRITICISM OF THE IMF AND THE WORLD BANK

Some of the harshest criticism of the debt-relief process has been aimed at the multilateral institutions. The World Bank and IMF are reluctant to write off the debts that developing countries owe them. The institutions' argue that multilaterals are the lenders of last resort supporting a country when no other creditor is willing to lend. This role renders their debt "senior" and covered under "preferred creditor status." Advocates of debt forgiveness contend that these official institutions have, over the years, become by far the largest creditors to the poorest countries. Put differently, the multilateral institutions have become the problem rather than the solution.

In addition, the World Bank, unlike the IMF, raises its own funding from the capital markets and its credit has the distinction of being rated AAA—the highest rating possible for any borrower. Officials at the bank talk ominously of the damage debt write-offs would cause to its AAA credit rating. Debt write-offs would imply an acknowledgment that the bank had made mistakes in lending. Therefore, to avoid jeopardizing their financial standing and to ensure repayment of their loans, a HIPC Trust Fund was created. It finances debt relief on money owed to the multilateral institutions. The Trust Fund either purchases and cancels the debt, or services it when repayment is due. The Trust Fund is in turn financed by (rich) creditor nations, but, by the bank's own admission, it remains underfunded.

In the IMF's case, special Poverty Reduction and Growth Facility grants from creditor nations are used to cover debt relief provided by the institutions. This practice has been criticized as showing a lack of commitment by the institutions as they avoid taking losses for their lending mistakes in the past. Activists charge that the bank and the IMF are passing their losses onto their shareholders in order to maintain their high credit ratings.

THE CASE FOR NON-HIPC COUNTRIES

There are a number of countries with huge debt burdens that still do not qualify for debt relief because of their classification at the World Bank and IMF. Nigeria and Pakistan are currently considered severely indebted. However, they do not borrow from the IDA but from a fund at the bank that provides loans to middle-income countries. They therefore do not qualify for HIPC. Gabon is classified an upper-middle-income country and therefore is also not eligible, even though it is also severely indebted. Georgia is a low-income country but is considered moderately indebted and therefore not qualified. There are many other examples of countries that periodically seek debt rescheduling from the Paris Club but are not covered by HIPC.

TIPS FOR REPORTERS

■ *Pace of debt relief.* By September 2003, the World Bank reported in an HIPC review, only eight of the forty-two countries in the HIPC process at that time had reached the completion point; twenty had reached decision points; and twelve had not reached decision points. One of the reasons why many countries did not reach decision points is that they were engaged in, or had recently emerged from, conflict, or a war of some kind (e.g., Ivory Coast). There is a growing debate on how such countries can be accommodated under HIPC.

Other countries have failed to reach completion points because they have not met the preconditions for full debt relief. As a reporter, it is important to report on why countries are failing to meet these requirements. What is delaying debt relief for the country? What standards are being used, and how does the country's performance and circumstances compare with others that have received debt relief?

■ *Poverty Reduction Strategy Papers.* A reporter should examine the PRSP process in his or her country. Is it supporting or hindering poverty reduction efforts? Is it delaying debt relief? How? Increasingly, civil-society organizations are charging that the process is too complicated, requiring institutional and administrative capacity that many HIPCs do not possess. Many are complaining that they are not really consulted; in the end, the papers are little different from what they would have been without a consultation process.

Access to a country's PRSP document provides excellent information on the spending priorities of the government. What are the concrete proposals to tackle poverty that the government outlines in its PRSP? How will money saved from debt servicing be spent? Is debt relief beginning to make a difference?

It is also necessary to assess how transparent and open the PRSP process is in the country. Many governments are reluctant to make World Bank and IMF documents accessible to their citizens. That makes it all the more important to ask whether the process is really engaging civil society. Is there any debate around the PRSP and on how to improve fiscal systems so that resources released by debt relief reach the poor?

- *Government expenditure.* Debt relief opens up the budgeting process to greater involvement of civil society and the public. This brings many issues into public scrutiny—for example, how reasonable is government expenditure in areas such as defense? How does it compare with spending in the social sector? Is government spending in nonessential areas undermining planned poverty reduction? Governments may claim to be prioritizing poverty reduction in their commitments for debt relief. Is this reality reflected in their budgets?

To make the HIPC process accountable, Uganda set up a Poverty Action Fund where money released through HIPC is deposited. This fund in turn finances poverty-alleviation programs, such as building rural schools. Uganda, the first country to receive full debt relief under enhanced HIPC, is largely considered a success story. It is reportedly spending HIPC savings on poverty reduction. The IMF expects Uganda to save 0.7 percent of its gross domestic product during the first three years of debt relief under enhanced HIPC. This amounts to about 10 percent of currently projected social expenditure. Among other things, the money has been targeted towards agricultural expansion, primary education, and healthcare programs.

More recently, Honduras proposed to set up a fund for the distribution of HIPC savings along the lines of the Uganda model. As a reporter, it is important to find out if there are similar efforts in the country at issue. Once set up, how transparent is the management and auditing of such a fund?

There may also be tradeoffs between poverty reduction and other policy targets. For example, internal security is an issue with which many developing countries are grappling. Should the government spend resources solely on poverty reduction? When does it become optimal to reallocate to other areas? Reports should note the inconsistencies and tradeoffs that may exist between poverty reduction under HIPC and other broader economic objectives.

- *Is debt relief working?* Nongovernmental organizations active in the area charge that HIPC does not live up to its promise of bringing down the debts of poor countries to sustainable levels. Analyses by Jubilee 2000 UK show that the debts of many of these countries will become unsustainable again after full HIPC treatment. This is partly because the World Bank and IMF base the amount of debt cancelled on the performance of HIPC economies over the next two decades—that is, on projected levels of revenue, exports, and GDP. Jubilee 2000 UK says that because the institutions use "wildly optimistic" growth projections and project higher revenues than historical trends reveal, less relief is being provided. Subsequently, countries will find that export earnings in the future will not be able to meet debt repayments.

The institutions base their calculation of debt sustainability on the ratio of a country's debt to its exports. It is deemed sustainable if this falls below 150 per cent. Using this criteria, at least seven of the countries that have qualified for HIPC will still not achieve debt sustainability at their completion points. The Jubilee 2000 UK study, utilizing World Bank data, notes that Chad, for instance, will only attain sustainable debt in 2005. Malawi has to wait until 2013 and Niger until 2014. Bolivia's debt will not be sustainable in the next twenty years, the report notes. There is also the question of methodology. Activists argue that comparing debt to GDP is inappropriate and that a better measure would be to look at debt-service payments in relation to overall social spending.

Reporters need to analyze the situation in their countries. The levels of debt servicing compared to revenue and social spending should be monitored following HIPC. Are the HIPC assumptions indeed optimistic? Is the exercise projecting economic and export growth rate that are historically unprecedented? How do other factors, such as the vulnerability of HIPC economies to shocks, affect debt servicing? Hurricanes and earthquakes in Latin America, floods in Mozambique, and the growing burden of HIV/AIDS in sub-Saharan Africa affect economic growth and budget revenues in these countries, yet observers say HIPC does not adequately take into account such factors. Most HIPCs depend on primary products for most of their export revenue. How do falls in commodity prices affecting revenues and debt servicing?

- *Growth rates.* When estimating the amounts of debt relief to provide to 23 HIPC countries, the World Bank and IMF projected average GDP growth rates of 5.5 per cent for 2000 through 2010. However, from 1990 to 1999, the countries averaged 3 percent GDP growth. The institutions rationalized their projections by arguing that the reforms undertaken under the PRSP process will lead to a "supply response" that increases investment and exports and, by implication, economic growth rates. However, if the bank and the IMF overestimated growth in HIPC countries, they also overestimated future revenue. That may mean these countries will have to continue allocating relatively large shares of government budgets to debt servicing instead of other vital areas, such as health and education. The World Bank acknowledges that some of the projections used were unrealistic. Reporters should recalculate debt-servicing obligations as a fraction of government revenue or export earnings, using more reasonable estimates of growth. How far will HIPC go to resolve the country's problems? Will yet another debt rescheduling be required? More sophisticated analyses would look at, for instance, fluctuations in commodity prices. How large a fall in the price of the principal export commodity would be required to make the debt unsustainable? Based on historical variability, what is the likelihood of such a drop? An economist or institution that may have done studies including these calculations can help with the reporting. Paradoxically, the best source for

such simulations can come from the World Bank and IMF staffs themselves.

Under HIPC, most of the debt relief is given at the completion point, with the expectation that the amount given is sufficient to return a country's debt to sustainable levels. However, critics charge that this formula does not factor in the accumulation of new debt in the interim. Many HIPC countries find themselves forced to continue borrowing after the initial stages of debt relief—more so since the decline in official development assistance to poor countries accelerated. The General Accounting Office of the U.S. government reports that due to shortfalls in revenue and lower GDP growth than predicted, some HIPCs will require increased donor assistance. It notes that the debt levels of seven countries studied will resume rising after receiving relief because in order to have the funds necessary for poverty reduction, they must continue borrowing at the same rate as during the years prior to qualifying for HIPC. The GAO presents a scenario where Tanzania will not be able to repay its debt unless donor flows (loans and grants) increase by more than 30 percent. Yet new loans would only add to the endless debt cycle.

SOME IMPORTANT DEBT TERMS

What makes reporting on debt relief difficult is the jargon used. Here are some common terms:

- *Public sector debt.* Money owed by the government. Governments can borrow abroad from the three sources listed below.

- *Bilateral debt.* Country-to-country debt. Often, industrial countries give loans to poorer nations for development programs or to purchase manufactured goods, such as arms, vehicles, and industrial equipment.

- *Multilateral debt.* Debt owed to a multilateral institution such as the World Bank, the International Monetary Fund, the African Development Bank, or the Asian Development Bank. Many governments are "shareholders" in these institutions, which is why they are called multilateral. The level of a country's contributions determines what amount of the institution a country can control; rich nations control majority shares in the institutions.

- *Commercial debt*. Money owed to private sector lenders. Governments often borrow from commercial banks and other sources to meet budget deficits. Commercial debt should not be confused with private debt, which is borrowing done by companies within the country.

- *Private sector debt*. This is debt owed to the private sector of the country. There are many types of private sector debt in developing countries but three stand out: (i) trade credits by importers; (ii) lines of credit by domestic banks owed to international banks; and (iii) syndicate loans usually raised by large corporations in the country and destined for particular projects.

- *Sustainable debt*. To qualify for debt relief under HIPC, a country's debt must be deemed unsustainable. The World Bank, the IMF, and the debtor country determine this through a debt-sustainability analysis. The most common criteria is the ratio of a country's debt to its exports. Other criteria include debt-to-exports

and debt-to–government revenues ratios. Sustainability exercises project these debt ratios into the future, relying on assumptions for economic and export growth and interest rates. A country's debt level is deemed unsustainable if: (i) the debt ratios do not fall sufficiently fast; and/or (ii) if the debt ratios fall but, nonetheless, remain at unacceptably high levels.

LIST OF HIPC COUNTRIES

- **AFRICA (35)** Angola, the Gambia, Rwanda, Benin, Ghana, Sierra Leone, Burkina Faso, Guinea, São Tomé and Príncipe, Burundi, Guinea-Bissau, Senegal, Cameroon, Kenya, Somalia, Central African Republic, Liberia, Somalia, Sudan, Chad, Madagascar, Tanzania, Comoros, Malawi, Togo, Congo, Mali, Uganda, Congo Democratic Republic, Mauritania, Zambia, the Ivory Coast, Mozambique, Ethiopia, Niger

- **LATIN AMERICA (4)** Bolivia, Honduras, Guyana, Nicaragua

- **MIDDLE EAST (1)** Republic of Yemen

- **ASIA (3)** Republic of Lao, Myanmar (Burma), Vietnam

LINKS FOR MORE INFORMATION

- Database of developing countries' external debt. http://www.oecd.org/std/finance/debt/index.htm.

- Paris Club. http://www.clubdeparis.org.

- A primer on Brady bonds. http://www.emgmkts.com/research/bradydef.htm.

OFFICIAL HIPC SITES

http://www.worldbank.com/hipc.

http://www.imf.org/external/np/hipc/hipc.htm.

http://www.clubdeparis.org/en/index.php.

Country case study—Uganda. http://www.oxfam.org/about_us/thisisoxfam/skilled/case_studty.htm.

CRITIQUES OF HIPC

http://www.jubilee2000uk.org.

http://www.wider.unu.edu/publications/dps/dp2001–138.pdf.

http://www.eurodad.org.

http://www.focusweb.org.

http://www.isgnweb.org.

http://www.twnside.org.sg.

ANALYSES OF THE PSRP PROCESS

http://www.prspsynthesis.org/synthesis/synthesis.htm.

http://www.eurodad.org.

http://aidc.org.za/sapsn/discussion/gender_perspective.html.

http://www.focusweb.org.

■ **THE BRADY INITIATIVE.** A late 1980s plan that allowed highly indebted developing countries to convert their commercial debt into bonds backed by the U.S. Treasury. It was named for U.S. Treasury Secretary Nicholas Brady.

■ **BURDEN-SHARING.** Allows official creditors to spread out the cost of debt relief granted to heavily indebted countries onto commercial (i.e., private sector) creditors. At the limit, debt relief could include complete nonpayment (i.e., default).

■ **CONCERTED LENDING.** The infusion of new money into debtor countries, thus allowing them to continue servicing their debt obligations. Concerted lending is usually made conditional on policy measures.

■ **CONDITIONALITY.** The principle that access to new loans, rescheduling, and debt reduction, for example, should be conditional on the implementation of policy measures.

■ **CROSS-CONDITIONALITY.** When the World Bank agrees to lend money to a country only if the borrower follows certain conditions laid out in an IMF program (and vice versa). Cross-conditionality is mostly applied to policy lending rather than project lending.

■ **CROSS-DEFAULT CLAUSE.** In a loan agreement, enables creditors to treat a default by the borrower under another loan as a default under that agreement.

■ **DEBT BUY-BACK.** When a debtor government buys part of its debt from its creditors for cash at a discount to its face value.

■ **DEBT OVERHANG.** The excess of a country's external debt over its long-term capacity to pay. It usually discourages new investment.

■ **DEBT-SERVICE RATIOS.** Measures of how much money is being spent on servicing debt. For external (i.e., hard-currency denominated) debt, economists look at the percentage of export earnings that needs to be devoted to servicing external obligations. To assess the government's ability to pay its obligations, economists look at the ratio of tax revenues that need to be devoted to debt service payments. As a rule of thumb, economists consider the country as highly indebted if either of the two ratios is higher than 30 percent.

■ **DEBT-EQUITY SWAP.** A refinancing device that gives a debt holder an equity investment in a debtor country in exchange for cancellation of the debt.

■ **DEFAULT.** The failure to repay the principal and/or interest on a loan.

■ **ESAF.** The so-called Enhanced Structural Adjustment Facility was established in 1987 to provide assistance on concessionary terms to low-income member countries facing balance-of-payments problems. It was replaced in 2000 by the Poverty Reduction and Growth Facility.

■ **EXTERNAL SHOCK.** The drastic deterioration in the external economic environment facing a country. Examples include an increase in the price of a major import such as oil or a sharp fall in the price of one or more major exports.

■ **LENDER OF LAST RESORT.** Offers (usually conditional) loans to financial institutions who have no access to funds from other sources and where wider economic and financial system problems would ensue without such sources of credit. At the national level, the central bank is the lender of last resort; at the global level, it is the IMF.

■ **LIQUIDITY.** The ability of a country to meet its immediate foreign-exchange obligations (for imports and debt-service payments) from its exports and new borrowing. This concept should be contrasted with solvency (see below).

■ **THE LONDON CLUB.** The standard name given to a group of private-sector lenders who, collectively, negotiate and offer rescheduling and/or restructuring of a country's commercial bank debt. It is a concept rather than an institution and should be contrasted with the Paris Club (see below).

■ **Moral hazard.** The idea that investors or borrowers will take risks because they know they will be bailed out or protected later. An example would be an investor lending to a risky borrower knowing that the borrower is thought of as "too big to fail" and that, under stress, will receive government help. At the national level, examples include large utility and airline companies and at the global level examples include "strategically important" sovereign debtors.

■ **Moratorium.** The temporary suspension of payments of interest and/or principal on external debts. It is generally called for when a creditor faces extreme financial pressures and requires time to restructure its finances and/or its debt.

■ **Net lending.** Disbursements received by a country minus the repayment of principal it makes in a given year. Net lending represents the transfer of resources to a country from its creditors, excluding its payments of interest.

■ **Net present value.** The total value of a series of payments over time discounted at a certain interest rate. The discounting is meant to take into account the "time value of money." The NPV represents the amount that would need to be invested at a commercial interest rate at the beginning of the period so that, with accumulated interest, it would be enough to meet all the payments as they came due.

■ **Net resource transfer.** The overall transfer of resources between a country and its creditors (and sometimes foreign investors and aid donors), used as a measure of the extent to which they are making a contribution to or represent a drain on the national economy. Cf. net lending.

■ **Policy ownership.** The idea that if a country is to be genuinely committed to the terms and success of an adjustment program

(of the World Bank or the IMF), its society must collectively believe that the program is in its own self-interest rather than one which has been imposed on it by an outsider.

■ **The Paris Club.** An informal group of wealthy creditor nations whose role is to find coordinated and sustainable solutions to the payment difficulties facing debtor nations. The Paris Club only deals with government-to-government debt.

■ **Poverty Reduction and Growth Facility.** The IMF's low-interest lending facility for poor countries. This has replaced the old Enhanced Structural Adjustment Facility and in theory is aimed more at poverty reduction than on improving fiscal discipline.

■ **Poverty Reduction Strategy Papers.** Submitted by eligible countries (with support from the IMF and the World Bank) that are looking to establish a track record of carrying out poverty-reduction programs as a condition of joining the HIPC program. PRSPs outline a country's macroeconomic and structural-reform policies and its concrete poverty-reduction goals.

■ **Public expenditure.** The total spending of all branches of government and other public agencies, including the net losses of state-owned enterprises (rather than their total expenditure).

■ **Solvency.** The ability of a country to meet its foreign exchange obligation in full over the long term—as opposed to its liquidity.

■ **Structural adjustment.** The reallocation of labor and capital among sectors within an economy in response to volatile economic circumstances such as external shocks, trade policy, or changes in government policy.

■ **Track record.** A country's recent history of compliance with the conditions of its IMF programs. The IMF uses this "record" to determine, among other things, the size of lending.

■ **Trade liberalization.** The reduction of

tariffs and the removal or relaxation of policies that interfere with exports or imports.

- **WRITE-DOWN.** The reduction of a debt shown in a creditor's accounts. In theory, when sovereign debt is written down, countries are relieved of their debt burden and can then resume borrowing.

- **WRITE-OFF.** The comprehensive cancellation of debt.

CHAPTER TWELVE

ASSESSING SOVEREIGN RISK

GRACIANA DEL CASTILLO

INTRODUCTION

SOVEREIGN-RISK ANALYSIS has acquired a new importance as more and more emerging-market governments borrow in the international capital markets. Governments borrow for a number of reasons, most importantly to finance their fiscal and current-account deficits. In addition to borrowing from banks, governments borrow from the public by issuing bonds, both in domestic and foreign currency. A bond (or debt instrument) is simply an IOU that describes the terms of the contract between borrower and lender, including the cost of borrowing and the promise of repayment in full by a certain time. Sovereign risk refers to the risk that the government will not service its debt in full and on time.

While corporate rate issuers often need to pledge some asset as collateral, a government borrows based on its capacity to raise taxes and adopt other monetary and exchange-rate policies to cover its debt. Hence sovereign-risk analysis focuses on the ability, flexibility, and willingness that the government has to take appropriate policy measures to facilitate its debt servicing.

Investors purchase government bonds according to their appetite for risk. Those who are risk averse will be likely to purchase U.S. Treasury Bills, the returns on which are low because of their low risk. Those who are risk prone are more likely to be attracted to emerging-market bonds where the higher return is commensurate to the higher risk.

Investor funding is often pooled together and managed by a professional money or fund manager. These institutional investors, including pension and mutual funds, are active in government bond markets and are often subject to stringent regulations in terms of the bonds they can purchase. In some cases, for example, they require that the bonds have "investment grade" ratings by at least two of the international rating agencies, that is, until recently, Moody's Investors Service (Moody's), Standard & Poor's (S&P) and Fitch Ratings (Fitch).[1]

In making their investment decisions, investors rely on sovereign-risk analysis, including that of the rating agencies, the International Monetary Fund, and the investment banks. To evaluate risk, analysts need to place economic and financial issues in the context of the political, institutional, and social conditions in the country. Such evaluation depends critically on the data and methodology used as well as on the competence, training, and experience of the analysts. Seasoned analysts are necessary not only to interpret basic economic and financial indicators but also to assess policy flexibility and policy consistency. Policy flexibility is necessary for the government to react quickly and boldly to external and internal shocks.[2] Policy consistency refers to the need to have fiscal, monetary, and exchange-rate policies that reinforce one another rather than clashing.[3] Policy inconsistencies and the inability of governments to react quickly to shocks through policy changes are often the main cause of crises.

THE ACTORS

Different actors analyze sovereign risk differently. Although this chapter focuses on rating agencies, we shall briefly discuss the ways other actors analyze sovereign risk.

THE INTERNATIONAL MONETARY FUND

Although the IMF does not rate governments as such, sovereign-risk analysis is part of its macroeconomic surveillance functions. Surveillance, known as Article IV consultations, involves monitoring and consultations with member states on a wide range of economic and financial policies. For surveillance purposes, member states provide the IMF with all necessary information. Particularly in the wake of the Mexican financial crisis of 1994–95 and the turmoil in the financial markets of East Asia in 1997, data issues have received increasing prominence in the IMF's work. In aiming to strengthen surveillance, the IMF requires the provision of comprehensive, timely, and accurate economic data by members.

To implement its surveillance functions on a country, the IMF focuses on the accounting, analysis, and projections of each of the four interconnected sectors in the economy: the national income account (or the real sector), the balance of payments (or the external sector), the fiscal sector (or the government finance statistics), and the monetary sector. The links between the income and spending balance of a sector (or its saving-investment balance) and the associated financial transactions with other sectors are systematically described in a "flow of funds" account. A flow of funds analysis among the four sectors is carried out to ensure that projections for the different sectors are feasible and that inconsistencies do not arise. For example, if a rate of growth of 3 percent is projected for an economy, the flow of funds among the sectors will show whether the financing for the projected investment is available, either from the domestic financial sector or from abroad. Also, the flow of funds analysis would show whether the projected rate of growth is compatible with the current-account deficit that the country can expect to finance through foreign borrowing, portfolio and foreign direct investment, and international reserves, and whether it is compatible with projections for the fiscal accounts and domestic inflation.

Thus, IMF methodology ensures the consistency of available data and projections, helps to identify policy inconsistencies rigorously and facilitates macroeconomic and risk analysis. This framework is also useful in policy simulations, which is a form of forecasting that generates a range of alternative projections based on differing assumptions about future situations, specifically to answer the question "what would happen if?" In the financial programming exercise of a middle-sized country, six to ten Ph.D.'s and other well-qualified and experienced economists participate,[4] mostly from the area department, but often involving experts from fiscal, monetary and exchange, and other departments.

While emphasis is put on policy consistency, IMF sovereign-risk analysis often exaggerates policy flexibility due to the frequent inability of macroeconomists to incorporate political constraints into policymaking. This has often led them to underestimate sovereign risk. The recent case of Uruguay, which required a huge IMF program in terms of the country's GDP in 2002, is a case in point.[5] The IMF greatly overestimated the government's political flexibility in dealing with the fiscal problems and structural reforms necessary to stave off contagion from Argentina and Brazil.

INVESTMENT BANKS

Although investment banks also analyze sovereign risk, they do not rate governments. Furthermore, to facilitate investors' decisions in general, these banks focus on short-term sovereign-risk analysis rather than on more medium- and long-term perspectives. In some cases, their tools to assess sovereign risks include financial programming to evaluate macroeconomic consistency. Some of the large investment banks provide excellent publications (often on a daily basis) on sovereign-risk analysis that are widely used by investors. Investment banks employ many M.B.A.'s and some Ph.D. economists, often with IMF backgrounds. Research from investment banks, however, has been criticized because of its lack of independence from the investment-banking functions of these banks.

RATING AGENCIES

Unlike the IMF and investment banks, rating agencies translate their sovereign-risk analysis into a sovereign rating of either the government debt or specific government issues. Sovereign ratings represent just one opinion of government creditworthiness, and the impact they ultimately have on the markets depends on how investors make use of the ratings themselves, on their timeliness, and on the soundness of the economic and political explanations given to justify them. Sovereign ratings facilitate cross-country comparisons of governments' creditworthiness. In analyzing risk, rating agencies rely to a large degree on basic economic and financial indicators and a qualitative analysis of policy flexibility and political developments. There are institutional and economic reasons for which governments seek ratings—often from two or three different agencies—and pay for them. Ratings determine the terms and conditions of access to global securities markets. For regulatory reasons, ratings often allow governments to attract a larger investor group and establish risk benchmarks.[6]

For ratings agencies, sovereign ratings are an assessment of a government's ability and "willingness" to service its debts "in full" and "on time." They view the rating as a forward-looking estimate of the probability of government default.[7] As such, sovereign ratings will determine the cost of government borrowing, are a basis for the ratings of corporations, banks, local governments, and other entities in the country, and are important in the determination of country risk. Sovereign ratings normally also impose a ceiling to the ratings of government-supported institutions such as state-owned enterprises.[8]

Ratings agencies use letter-based grading systems and base their ratings on peer comparisons.[9] The rating scale applies equally to all classes of obligors, sovereign as well as subsovereigns. Ratings agencies assign long-term and short-term sovereign credit ratings as well as foreign and local currency sovereign ratings. An "outlook" is assigned to the long-term ratings (positive, stable, or negative). Local currency ratings often surpass the foreign currency ratings, reflecting the ability of governments to tax and borrow from the domestic economy on a sustainable basis.[10] In assigning long-term ratings, the agencies indicate that they try to see through economic, political, credit, and commodity cycles. This means that a domestic recession or deteriorating conditions in the global economy by itself should not be an occasion for a downgrade. Rating agencies review their ratings at specific times when particular events may have had an impact on the rating or, lacking such events, on a yearly basis.

Rating agencies' concept of default is not based on a legal definition. Agencies consider that a default takes place when debtors fail to meet a principal or interest payment on the due date or a distressed or coercive rescheduling of principal and/or interest takes place on terms less favorable than those originally contracted. In practice, however, a generalized sovereign default (default on all outstanding debts) is rare. Normally, defaults are selective and sequenced, reflecting the de facto if not de jure seniority of different types of debt instruments. S&P's SD (selective default) rating applies only to issuers but not to specific debt instruments. When a specific debt instrument is in default the rating is D.

TABLE 12.1

RATING SCALE

SCORE	S&P	MOODYS	FITCH
	INVESTMENT GRADE		
1	AAA	Aaa	AAA
2	AA+	Aa1	AA+
3	AA	Aa2	AA
4	AA-	Aa3	AA-
5	A+	A1	A+
6	A	A2	A
7	A-	A3	A-
8	BBB+	Baa1	BBB+
9	BBB	Baa2	BBB
10	BBB-	Baa3	BBB-
	SPECULATIVE GRADE		
11	BB+	Ba1	BB+
12	BB	Ba2	BB
13	BB-	Ba3	BB-
14	B+	B1	B+
15	B	B2	B
16	B-	B3	B-
17	CCC+	Caa1	CCC+
18	CCC	Caa2	CCC
19	CCC-	Caa3	CCC-
20	CC	–	CC
21	C	–	C
22	SD	Ca	DDD
23	D	C	DD
24	–	–	D

Source: Bhatia, "Sovereign Credit Ratings Methodology," 8.

DETERMINING FACTORS

In analyzing sovereign risk, rating agencies do not in general use specific models.[11] Instead, they generally focus on a number of quantitative and qualitative factors that affect sovereign default risk. The reason why they do this is that the variables that affect sovereign risk are highly interrelated (and correlated), and hence it is difficult to isolate their individual effects through econometric work.

Despite the difficulties, some empirical studies tried nevertheless to identify which factors had historically received the greatest weights in the ratings process of Moody's and S&P's. Canton and Packer's research identified high per capita income, low inflation, more rapid growth, a low ratio of foreign-currency external debt to foreign-exchange earnings, the absence of a history of defaults, and a high level of economic development as factors associated with high ratings.[12] Despite the high predictive power of the model,[13] factors such as the fiscal position and the external balance were not identified as determinants of the ratings. This, of course, can be explained by the high correlation among these variables.

In the late 1990s, econometric work was revised to take into account new variables that were affecting sovereign ratings. Juttner and McCarthy found that the variables identified by Canton and Packer continued to explain ratings up to 1997 but that the relationship broke down in 1998 in the wake of the Asian crisis.[14] In 1998, additional variables, such as the ratio of problematic bank assets to GDP and the interest-rate differential (a proxy for expected exchange rate changes), came into play.

The factors used in risk analysis are disaggregated in a number of broad categories. They include:

■ *Political factors*, including the level of democratization, the degree of plurality, the division of powers, the orderly transition of heads of government and other officials, freedom of the press, the support for policy making, the strength of institutions, public security, and geopolitical considerations are critical to sovereign ratings.

■ *The economic structure and growth prospects* of an economy are key considerations in analyzing sovereign ratings. The indicators used for this purpose include measures for income (GDP, per capita GDP, and real GDP growth and its components); savings and investment levels in relation to GDP; open unemployment; prices (CPI, WPI, GDP deflator); and exchange rates (flexible vs. fixed; real exchange rate as a measure of international competitiveness). Other factors that are more difficult to quantify are also taken into account, such as the diversification of the economy, the level of economic development and income distribution in the country, labor market flexibility, the efficiency of the public sector, and the degree of financial sector intermediation.

■ *Fiscal flexibility* is another major determinant of sovereign ratings. This includes not only an analysis of fiscal flows (revenue, expenditure, balance) but also of stocks (debt levels, debt burden) and off-budget and contingent liabilities (unreported and contingent claims on government resources such as, for example, those resulting from the up-front fiscal costs of banking-system collapses). The fiscal situation of different levels of government—that is, the central government, the general government (central government plus local governments), and the consolidated public sector (general government plus state-owned enterprises)—is often analyzed separately.

Fiscal indicators used by rating agencies for the public sector include revenues vs. expenditures; primary balance; consolidated public-sector balance (i.e., public sector borrowing requirements, or PSBR, which is a measure of increased indebtedness, the degree of the public sector's crowding out the private sector, and inflationary pressure). Other indicators include the stock of public sector assets and liabilities (on a gross and net basis) and a number of critical ratios. These include: interest payments in relation to total revenue; oil revenue as a proportion of total revenue; and net public sector debt in relation to GDP. The maturity profile and the currency composition of the debt as well as the development of local capital markets are important determinants of fiscal flexibility.

- *Monetary and liquidity factors* are used to analyze inflationary conditions and exchange-rate sustainability. Indicators used include domestic credit to the private sector, monetary aggregates (including M_1, M_2, and so on) in relation to international reserves, short-term interest rates, core and nominal inflation, and a liquidity ratio (external liabilities of banks vs. external assets). The health of the banking system is measured by the degree of nonperforming loans and capital adequacy. Consistency between exchange rate and monetary/credit policies and institutional factors such as central bank independence are also taken into account.

- *External payments and debt* is the category used to ascertain the adequacy of international reserves and the availability of foreign-exchange earnings that the country has in order to service its liabilities. This category is used to analyze both balance of payments flows and the stock of international debt. Indicators used include BOP data: trade balance (exports, imports, balance); current account (trade balance; factor payments, including interest and dividends; transfers); capital and financial account (net foreign direct investment and net borrowing). The composition of the current and capital and financial accounts are taken into consideration, as is the adequacy of international reserves and access to international capital markets. Important ratios in this category include the share of the current account deficit covered by foreign direct investment and the months of imports covered by international reserves.

Indicators for the stock of debt include total external debt, public and private, short-term and long-term, and net external debt. To calculate net levels of debt, international reserves, government deposits at the central bank, and other public and private assets are taken into account. An indicator for debt burden is total debt service (amortization and interest). Critical ratios in this category include total and net external debt in relation to foreign exchange earnings, the proportion of short-term debt covered by international reserves, and the proportion of the gross financial gap (current account deficit plus amortization payments plus short-term debt) covered by international reserves.

Until recently, only three rating agencies were "nationally recognized statistical rating organizations" or NRSROs.[15] This gives these agencies a virtual oligopoly. In addition to the sovereigns, many corporations, as well as state and local governments, require ratings by these institutions. Institutional investors often require "investment grade" ratings from Moody's and Standard & Poor's (thus creating a de facto duopoly) and putting these two agencies in a preferential position vis-à-vis Fitch.[16]

CRITICISM OF RATING AGENCIES

Because of the power of the rating agencies to determine the cost, terms, and conditions of access to global securities markets, the agencies have had a major impact on the large capital flows to emerging markets in the 1990s. At the same time, their inability to detect financial failures in Asia brought severe criticism of the ratings agencies' role in the evaluation of sovereign credit risk. Critics have argued that agencies gave too little warning before the onset of the Asian crisis and overreacted once the crisis emerged.[17] The same kind of criticism was made on subsequent crises, most recently in the cases of Uruguay and the Dominican Republic.

Since the Asian crisis, criticisms of rating agencies have been grouped into three areas: the ratings themselves and the impact they have on capital flows; the oligopolistic nature of their business and the lack of incentive for good performance; and the way the agencies finance themselves. The latter creates not only a conflict of interest but has also resulted in the inadequacy of resources devoted to establishing the ratings. The three, however, are interlinked in many ways.

PROCYCLICAL IMPACT ON CAPITAL FLOWS

Given the sharp adjustments to sovereign credit ratings in Asia in the period starting in August 1997 and as recently as last year in the case of Uruguay, sovereign ratings have often been responsible for *introducing a procyclical bias into global capital flows*. This means that as the country is doing badly, ratings collapse, and, as they do, capital outflows accelerate markedly.

Some analysts argue that downgrades are often late and that they follow the market rather than leading it.[18] For example, S&P rated Thailand A (stable) until August 1997,[19] well after the July devaluation. Korea's rating of AA minus (stable) was maintained until August 1997, and in five months it was downgraded nine notches to B plus (credit watch negative) in December of that year.[20] Russia was downgraded to B plus (stable) in June 1998 and put on selective default in January 1999. Brazil was downgraded to B plus (negative) only the day before the 15 January 1999 devaluation, when the crisis had been brewing for some time.[21]

Many analysts feel that downgrades for Argentina and Turkey from 2000 through 2002 have mostly followed the market as well. Uruguay was kept at investment grade by the three major ratings agencies until February 2002, four months before the peak of the banking crisis; these agencies ignored contagion factors from Argentina and Brazil, the lack of fiscal flexibility, and the inability of the government to adopt structural reforms that could have made the country less vulnerable to external shocks. Then the rating was brought down by six notches in less than nine months and was put in SD six months later.[22] The Dominican Republic was rated BB minus (stable) until 15 May, when the outlook was changed to credit-watch negative. On 9 June the country's rating was downgraded to B plus (negative), and its outlook changed to negative (from stable) in the last days of June 2003 on concerns that the nation's heavy depreciation and banking-sector stress would undermine its medium-term economic outlook and make external payments difficult. These rating and outlook changes came only after the mid-May collapse of the Banco Interconti-nental (Baninter).

As Helmut Reisen pointed out,

> If sovereign ratings lag rather than lead the financial markets but have a market impact, improving ratings would have euphoric expectations and stimulate excessive capital inflows during the boom; during the bust, downgrading might add to panic among investors, driving money out of the country and sovereign yield spreads up. For example, the downgrading of Asian sovereign ratings to "junk status" reinforced the region's crisis in many ways; commercial banks could no longer issue international letters of credit for local exporters and importers; institutional investors had to offload Asian assets as they were required to maintain portfolios only in investment grade securities; foreign creditors were entitled to call in loans upon the downgrades.[23]

The more recent experience in Uruguay is similar in many ways, although the visible signs of contagion and lack of progress on structural reform had been more obvious for quite some time.

OLIGOPOLISTIC NATURE

At the same time that the rating agencies were under attack throughout the world as a result of their sovereign ratings, the Securities and Exchange Commission pledged in January 2003 a "sweeping overhaul of the regulation of credit rating agencies" following criticism of their role in the collapse of Enron and the crisis in the telecommunications industry.[24] The ratings agencies were accused of being too slow in the case of Enron, keeping its rating at investment grade until just four days before it filed for bankruptcy on 2 December 2001. On the other hand, a noncertified rating agency, Egan-Jones Rating Co., which sells ratings to investors, downgraded Enron to junk a month before the big agencies.[25] In the case of the telecoms, the agencies were accused of cutting ratings too hastily and precipitating the crisis in their sector.[26]

Lawrence White of New York University argues that the protective regulations responsible for the oligopolistic nature of ratings agencies have "lured these agencies into complacency." He recommends two ways to revert this process. First, the SEC and other regulators could require that financial institutions defend their judgments about their bond holdings instead of providing the market with a list of approved rating agencies. Then the SEC could eliminate its certification process and allow other rating agencies to get into the ratings business. Second, if regulators are not prepared to do this, then the SEC should certify new rating agencies that can demonstrate competence and expertise in predicting bond defaults. In White's view "one way or the other, the creation of some fresh competition to challenge the Big Three is essential."[27] He also argued that "the NRSRO status is simply a way of coddling the three agencies and stifling competition in what should be an industry as competitive as any other."[28] Sir Howard Davies, chairman of the UK's Financial Services Authority, said at the World Economic Forum in Davos that certification should be lifted and that the participants in the credit rating business should "stand on their own feet."[29] Senator Joseph Lieberman has pointed out that tougher regulation of the ratings industry may be needed. In his view, "power of this magnitude should go hand in hand with some accountability."[30]

A study by Richard Johnson of the Federal Reserve Bank of Kansas City concluded that one reason why the rating agencies are reluctant to cut a company's creditworthiness to junk status is because of the severe consequences that usually result—often leading to a rapid default and heavy losses for the investors. Furthermore, much corporate debt is sold with "triggers," whereby a downgrading of a company's credit rating can accelerate the repayments schedule.[31]

CONFLICT OF INTEREST AND INADEQUACY OF RESOURCES

In February 2003, the G7, led by France, reported the need to agree to a set of principles to make rating agencies more transparent and accountable, both in their corporate and sovereign ratings. French officials want the G7 to recognize that the rating agencies are "privately-run, profit-oriented businesses that also run the risk of conflict of interest."[32] It is still to be seen whether such recognition would pave the way for changes to make these agencies more competitive and hence more transparent and accountable.

Some analysts have also raised the issue of conflict of interest. Former S&P analyst Ashok Bhatia noted that "each agency's sovereign ratings group remains excessively reliant on issuer-fee revenue, creating incentives for ratings generosity; and ongoing diversification into parallel consultancy business may be exacerbating conflicts of interest, strengthening incentives for ratings generosity." Furthermore, he pointed out that "each agency's sovereign ratings group faces an asymmetry in its revenue structure, with reliance on fee income from issuers creating incentives in favor of ratings generosity. This bias is especially acute in the case of new ratings, because ratings agreements typically allow previously unrated issuers to suppress their ratings, if they so prefer, and because interagency competition tends to be focused on attracting new ratings clients."[33]

The IMF also seems to be concerned about the conflict of interest affecting member states. In addition to concerns expressed in 1999,[34] on 27 March 2003, the head of the IMF's Capital Markets Department, Gerd Haeusler, announced in Frankfurt that the IMF planned to take a close look at the way international credit rating agencies work, "most importantly in the context of potential conflicts of interest, given the fact they are paid by those whom they rate." Mr. Haeusler questioned whether there is enough competition and enough expertise to look at corporations and countries in various parts of the world.[35]

The potential conflict of interest was also an issue in the House of Representatives hearing on 3 April 2003, as was the issue of regulation and competence of the rating agencies. The rating agencies remain basically unregulated despite determining borrowers' access to the debt markets and how much companies and countries have to pay to borrow. They are subject to no federal reporting requirements, and there are no written rules about the training and hiring of their employees. From this some witnesses concluded that the system is flawed and in need of reform.[36]

On 15 January 2004, Charles Dallara, managing director of the Institute of International Finance, said that "it is important for investors not to rely too heavily on the ratings agencies, but to make their own assessments of sovereign risk to differentiate between countries and classes of assets." He noted that bond spreads, or the risk premium that foreign governments and companies must pay over U.S. rates, had fallen sharply over the previous year. He argued that this was true even for countries such as Peru, the Philippines, Poland, and Venezuela, where credit quality had deteriorated.[37] The adequacy of resources of rating agencies is also questioned by Bhatia, who noted that "as profit-seeking entities, all three major ratings agencies strive to maintain streamlined operations, resulting in considerable rationing of analytical man-hours." He reckons that on average, analysts at S&P cover about five sovereign credits.[38]

Recent job announcements hint that the burden might be even more overwhelming. S&P job announcements for analysts in the *Wall Street Journal* (30 April 2002) and in *The Economist* (25 May 2002) state that, in addition to covering sovereign credits, the analysts should cover sovereign-supported issuers (state-owned enterprises including state development banks) and at times supranational issuers (including regional and international banks). This requirement overlooks the fact that to analyze risk relating to these institutions requires a different set of capabilities and expertise than for analyzing sovereign risk.[39] Furthermore, academic requirements and years of experience required seem hardly commensurate to the overwhelming task. For a sovereign analyst, graduate training in economics and only two years of experience are required. For a director of sovereign ratings—covering both Latin America and Asia—S&P requires a "master's degree in economics or international public affairs and three years in position offered [sic]." This contrasts sharply with requirements at the IMF where entry-level economists normally have Ph.D.'s from reputable universities, and many years of experience are required for more senior positions.

The number and diversity of credits, the limited academic training for conducting rigorous analysis, and the short work experience required are all factors reflected in the poor performance of sovereign ratings. In Bhatia's view,

The heavy workload at the ratings agencies may result in an element of piggy-backing, with analysts relying to varying degrees on research produced by the IMF, academia, investment banks, and—conceivably—other rating agencies as they seek to remain abreast of developments.[40] To the extent that analysis free-rides on the IMF or other entities, the agencies dilute their own contribution and so run the risk of simply joining the prevailing consensus. To the extent that analysis free-rides on market participants and their affiliates, the agencies compromise their objectivity. The relatively small action by an individual analyst of tabling selected investment bank "sell-side" or "buy-side" research literature in a ratings committee can trigger a string of errors culminating in rating failure. Despite ongoing efforts by the agencies to increase their analytical resource bases and introduce greater specificity into their ratings methodologies, it may be argued that ratings failures such as that for Uruguay in 2002 were the result of inattention, with insufficient resources devoted to data gathering, corroboration, and analysis.[41]

Because of the devastating impact that bad or untimely sovereign ratings can have on both countries and investors, the regulatory framework needs to be changed to ensure that sovereign ratings are done competitively by qualified analysts with the expertise and resources necessary to analyze the consistency and sustainability of macroeconomic policies in the framework of the political and institutional conditions of each country. In fact, governments paying for the ratings should demand that this be so.

TIPS FOR REPORTERS

- Reporters need to find out who are the rating agencies analysts for the country in question and try to get to know them. Contact should be made with analysts from the investment banks and with the IMF External Relations Department and other relevant staff.

- What are the key issues that the rating agencies/IMF/investment banks are looking at?

- Reporters should send relevant published stories on the countries covered to the rating agencies/IMF/investment banks to establish credentials as a knowledgeable source. This could help develop a mutually beneficial relationship.

- Reporters should exploit the pressure analysts feel to be "in the news."

- Who, where, and what are the sources of information for these analysts, and how reliable are they?

- What other sources of information are there that may have been overlooked or to which reporters have easier access?

- Reporters should beware of methodological differences that may lead to differences in results.

- Reporters should beware of a herd instinct by ratings agencies as a result of having the same sources of information and pressure from the markets.

- The records of analysts on particular topics should be examined closely. Reporters should return to the issues six or twelve months later to see whether the analysts proved to be correct.

- Analyses should be focused on some of the issues discussed here with the purpose of creating debate and improving the ratings.

1. Fitch Ratings Ltd. http://www.fitchratings.com.
——. "Fitch Sovereign Ratings: Rating Methodology." 2001. www.fitchratings.com.
——. "Sovereign Ratings History." 2003. www.fitchratings.com.

2. Moody's Investors Services. http://www.moodys.com.
——. *Moody's Country Credit Statistical Handbook*. 2001. 1st ed. www.moodys.com.

3. Standard & Poor's Corp. http://www .standardandpoors.com.
——. "Sovereign Credit Ratings: A Primer." 2002. www.ratingsdirect.com.
——. "Sovereign Ratings History Since 1975." 2003. www.standardandpoors.com.

4. Dominion Bond Ratings Services Ltd., a Toronto-based company. http://www.dbrs.com.

5. Japan Credit Rating Agency Ltd. http://www.jcr.co.jp/homepage.com.

6. IDEAS, an electronic database maintained by the University of Connecticut, carries many research reports and working papers on the issue of sovereign risk. http://ideas.repec.org.

7. The Emerging Markets Companion, Inc. site, run by the research firm with the same name, carries commentaries, news analyses, and research reports on emerging markets. http://www.emgmkts.com.

8. International Monetary Fund's Sovereign Debt Restructuring Mechanism. http://www .imf.org/external/np/exr/facts/sdrm.htm.

9. Defaultrisk.com, a site maintained by an individual, provides links to a host of credit researchers, their publications, and commentaries. http://www.defaultrisk.com/links.htm.

10. Many private investment banks such as Goldman Sachs Group, Merrill Lynch & Co., or Credit Swiss First Boston have analysts covering emerging markets who are often willing to talk to reporters. For a list of the largest U.S. investment banks, see http://www.top10links .com/cat.php/Finance:Banking:Investment +Banks.

NOTES

1. Fitch is the product of the merger of Fitch IBCA and Duff & Phelps Credit Rating Co. in March 2000. This allowed them to become a strong competitor to Moody's and S&P.

2. For example, if, as a result of a shock, the government needs to cut the fiscal deficit, can it raise taxes or cut expenditure easily, or would it face difficulties (political and others)? If wages and pensions represent a large share of total expenditure, the flexibility to cut expenditure will be low. If taxes are already high, flexibility to raise them will be limited. A major determinant of policy flexibility is the political support the government has in congress and how easily it can pass major policy reforms.

3. For example, the Mexican crisis of 1994 was clearly caused by incompatible exchange-rate and monetary policies. While the exchange rate was fixed, the government reacted to the fall in reserves due to an exogenous shock by increasing the money supply over and above what was compatible with the maintenance of the fixed exchange rate. Similarly, the collapse of fixed exchange rates in the Southern Cone countries in Latin America in the early 1980s was the result of inconsistencies between the fixed-exchange-rate system and the need to monetize (finance through money creation) large fiscal deficits.

4. The IMF recruits Ph.D. economists from top universities in the United States and abroad as well as senior government officials from central banks and ministries of finance. Since the Asian crisis, the IMF has also recruited economists with experience in the markets. At the same time, the IMF Institute provides constant training not only to incoming staff but also to senior and middle-level staff on a large number of issues. In this way, the IMF constantly updates

and upgrades the capacity of its staff to carry out macroeconomic and risk analysis.

5. The Uruguayan program of close to $3 billion represented about 23 percent of that country's GDP. In comparison, the much-publicized Brazilian program of $30 billion represented only 5 percent of GDP.

6. The policies of these agencies are not homogenous. For example, contrary to Moody's, S&P only rates countries at their request, and the ratings are made public only after the country has agreed. Hence, S&P is always paid for its ratings, while Moody's has rated countries without the request of the countries and without payments.

7. Thus, sovereign ratings are not "country ratings."

8. Sovereign ratings normally cap other ratings because the government could impose foreign-exchange or capital controls or any other constraint that could make nongovernmental entities default on their debts.

9. This creates the obvious problem that peer ratings have to be current at the time of the comparison for the comparison to be meaningful. Given that ratings are often revised on a yearly basis, this might not always be the case.

10. For a detailed description of rating scales, outlooks, and other characteristics of sovereign ratings, see Ashok V. Bhatia, "Sovereign Credit Ratings Methodology: An Evaluation," IMF Working Paper WP/02/170, 2002, available at http://www.imf.org/external/pubs/cat/longres.cfm?sk=16092.0.

11. See IMF, International Capital Markets 1999 (Washington, D.C.: IMF, 24 September 1999). See chapter 5, "Emerging Markets: Nonstandard Responses to External Pressure and the Role of the Major Credit Rating Agencies in Financial Markets," available at http://www.imf.org/external/pubs/ft/icm/1999/pdf/file05.pdf; and annex 5, "Credit Rating and the Recent Crises," available at www.imf.org/external/ pubs/ft/icm/1999/pdf/file11.pdf. The study also argues that up to that time, rating agencies did not generally conduct extensive scenario analyses and stress testing, and they only rarely assigned probabilities to specific risk factors and scenarios. From recent reports and

methodological notes, it does not seem that these trends have changed much.

12. R. Cantor, and F. Packer, "Determinants and Impact of Sovereign Credit Ratings," Economic Policy Review 20, no. 2 (1996): 37–53.

13. This means that the variables mentioned explain a large percentage of the variation in sovereign ratings.

14. J. D. Juttner and J. McCarthy, "Modeling a Ratings Crisis," unpublished paper, Macquarie University, Sydney, Australia, 1998.

15. A Financial Times editorial, "The Ratings Business" (10 February 2003) notes that "this arbitrary designation was introduced by the SEC in 1975, long after S&P and Moody's were founded and at a time when the business was more competitive. Since then the field has been cut to the Big Three by the series of mergers that created Fitch" and argues for the need to eliminate what "increasingly looks like a cartel."

16. In February 2003, the SEC added a fourth agency to the list, Dominion Bond Rating Service Ltd., a small Canadian firm that had been seeking status for more than three years.

17. See IMF, International Capital Markets 1999; Helmut Reisen, "Ratings Since the Asian Crisis," ICRA Bulletin 2, no. 8 (January–March 2002): 14–35; H. Reisen and J. von Maltzan, "Boom and Bust and Sovereign Ratings," Technical Paper No. 148 (Paris: OECD Development Centre), www.oecd.org/dev/dataoecd/38/44/1922795.pdf; and Carment Reinhart, "Default, Currency Crises, and Sovereign Credit Ratings," in The World Bank Economic Review 16 (2000): 151–70; and Ratings, Rating Agencies, and the Global Financial System, ed. R. M. Levich, G. Majnoni, and C. Reinhart (New York: Kluwer Academic Press, 2002).

18. For evidence of causality between sovereign ratings and market spreads, see G. Larrain, H. Reisen, and J. von Maltzan, "Emerging Market Risk and Sovereign Credit Ratings," Technical Paper No. 124 (Paris: OECD Development Center, 1997); Helmut Reisen, "Ratings Since the Asian Crisis"; and Carment Reinhart, "Default, Currency Crises, and Sovereign Credit Ratings."

19. Ratings throughout the chapter refer to foreign-currency sovereign ratings.

20. See Japan Center for International Finance (JCIF), "Characteristics and Appraisals of Major Rating Agencies," 2000, available at www.jcif.or.jp/e-index.htm; and JCIF, "Characteristics and Appraisals of Major Rating Companies," 1999, available at www.jcif.or.jp/e_index.htm. In the case of Korea, JCIF found a strong correlation between S&P and Fitch ratings changes and market fluctuations. It also noted that the S&P also changed ratings of other countries extremely frequently, as in the case of Indonesia (eight times) and Malaysia (five times).

21. JCIF, "Characteristics and Appraisals of Major Rating Companies," 2000; JCIF, "Characteristics and Appraisals of Major Rating Companies," 1999. JCIF noted differences in the way rating agencies interpreted events and the timing of ratings revisions based on those interpretations. Thus, some downgrades were timelier than others. For example, Moody's downgraded Thailand in April 1997 before the plunge in the baht. Also, while Duff & Phelps and Moody's downgraded Brazil right after the Russian crisis, showing foresight in incorporating contagion from the crisis into the ratings, Fitch IBCA and S&P did not.

22. After a debt exchange was completed, S&P updated Uruguay's rating to B minus on 2 June 2003 (from the SD rating imposed on 16 May).

23. Helmut Reisen, "Ratings Since the Asian Crisis," 21–22.

24. J. Wiggins, V. Boland, and C. Pretzlik, "SEC Pledges Overhaul of Credit Rating Agencies," Financial Times, 25–26 January 2003.

25. Amy Borrus, "The Credit-Raters: How They Work and How They Might Work Better," Business Week, 8 April 2002.

26. Financial Times, editorial, "The Ratings Business," 10 February 2003.

27. Lawrence White, "Credit and Credibility," New York Times, 24 February 2002.

28. Vincent Boland, "Rating Agencies May Lose Status," Financial Times, 3 April 2003.

29. Wiggins, Boland, and Pretzlik, "SEC Pledges Overhaul."

30. Borrus, "The Credit-Raters."

31. Vincent Boland, "Rating Agencies May Lose Status."

32. R. Graham, J. Wiggins, and A. van Duyn, "Credit Rating Agencies to Be G7 Issue," Financial Times, 5 February 2003.

33. Bhatia, "Sovereign Credit Ratings Methodology," 51 and 45.

34. IMF, International Capital Markets 1999.

35. Newsmachine, "IMF Wants to Take Close Look at Work of Credit Rating Agencies," AFP, 27 March 2003.

36. Alec Klein, "Lawmakers Criticize SEC's Oversight of Credit-Rating Firms," Washington Post, 3 April 2003.

37. Dow Jones International News, 15 January 2004.

38. Bhatia, "Sovereign Credit Ratings Methodology," 44.

39. Macroeconomics accounting, that is, the accounting of the real, monetary, fiscal, and external sector, which is critical for macroeconomic analysis and projections is quite different from corporate accounting. In fact, they normally are not only taught in different university courses but at different schools within the university.

40. Sovereign ratings by the three major rating agencies rarely differ by more than two notches.

41. Bhatia, "Sovereign Credit Ratings Methodology," 45.

CHAPTER THIRTEEN

PENSION REFORM

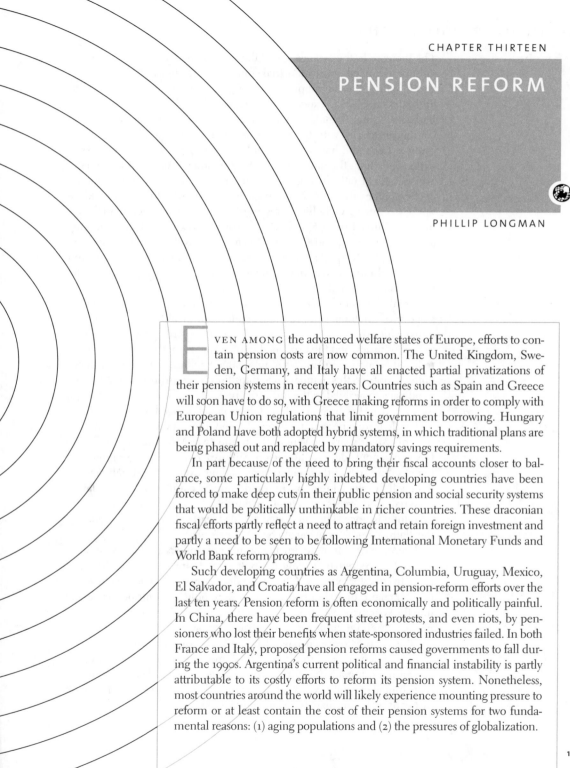

PHILLIP LONGMAN

EVEN AMONG the advanced welfare states of Europe, efforts to contain pension costs are now common. The United Kingdom, Sweden, Germany, and Italy have all enacted partial privatizations of their pension systems in recent years. Countries such as Spain and Greece will soon have to do so, with Greece making reforms in order to comply with European Union regulations that limit government borrowing. Hungary and Poland have both adopted hybrid systems, in which traditional plans are being phased out and replaced by mandatory savings requirements.

In part because of the need to bring their fiscal accounts closer to balance, some particularly highly indebted developing countries have been forced to make deep cuts in their public pension and social security systems that would be politically unthinkable in richer countries. These draconian fiscal efforts partly reflect a need to attract and retain foreign investment and partly a need to be seen to be following International Monetary Funds and World Bank reform programs.

Such developing countries as Argentina, Columbia, Uruguay, Mexico, El Salvador, and Croatia have all engaged in pension-reform efforts over the last ten years. Pension reform is often economically and politically painful. In China, there have been frequent street protests, and even riots, by pensioners who lost their benefits when state-sponsored industries failed. In both France and Italy, proposed pension reforms caused governments to fall during the 1990s. Argentina's current political and financial instability is partly attributable to its costly efforts to reform its pension system. Nonetheless, most countries around the world will likely experience mounting pressure to reform or at least contain the cost of their pension systems for two fundamental reasons: (1) aging populations and (2) the pressures of globalization.

The increase in the average age of the world's citizens is a phenomenon most pronounced in the industrial countries of Europe and Asia. But it is also rapidly gathering momentum in many parts of the Third World as birthrates fall and life expectancy increases. In the Western Hemisphere, Barbados, Cuba, Trinidad, Martinique, and Guadeloupe are among the Caribbean locales with birthrates lower than that of the United States. Tunisia, Lebanon, Iran, and Sri Lanka have likewise joined the ranks of nations in which the number of births is no longer sufficient to keep the average age of citizens from increasing or even to prevent an absolute decline in the number of working-age individuals over time. Other developing countries with birthrates currently below replacement levels include China, Russia, Kazakhstan, Bosnia/Herzegovina, Thailand, Singapore, Macedonia, and Georgia. Even in relatively "young" countries, (for example, North Africa and some nations among the Persian Gulf states), birthrates are declining, and the relative burden of supporting the elderly is increasing.

Population aging is a product of many trends most people would view as positive, including improved sanitation and health-care delivery systems, which have cut infant mortality and boosted life expectancy in many countries, and the expanded roles available to women, which have reduced economic incentives to raise large families. And in many developing countries, this demographic transition is occurring at a much more rapid pace than it did in the industrial nations. In France, for example, it took 140 years for the proportion of the population aged sixty-five or older to double from 9 percent to 18 percent. In China, the same feat will take just thirty-four years; in Venezuela, twenty-two. Moreover, according to UN projections, developing regions will experience far larger growth in the absolute size of their elderly populations over the next half century than will developed regions. In less-developed countries, the population aged sixty and over is expected to quadruple, from 374 million in 2000 to 1.6 billion in 2050. The developed world at least got rich before it got old; the Third World is growing old before it gets rich.

Unfortunately, by reducing the number of workers available to support each retiree, population aging also puts great strains on social security systems. In 1955, for example, Chile's social security system had 12 active contributors per retiree, but by 1979 there were only 2.5 contributors paying into the system for every retiree collecting a pension. As in many developing countries, the trend was exacerbated a growing underground economy that further reduced payroll tax receipts. By 1980, the system was running a deficit equal to 2.7 percent of gross domestic product, and the cost of honoring all its future pension promises exceeded the country's total annual output. Because of these pressures, Chile became in 1981 the first country to privatize its social security system.

PRESSURES OF GLOBALIZATION

Globalization, or the increasing integration of the world economy, also continues to put pressure on both developed and developing nations to contain their pension costs. This can be seen in Eastern Europe, where countries hoping to join the European Union must contain their fiscal deficits and limit overall debt burdens—feats that necessitate reducing pension spending—before they will even be considered for admission. More generally, countries with inefficient industries that are suddenly exposed to global competition often find they can no longer afford to pay for generous pensions.

This has occurred most dramatically in China and the former Soviet Union. There, poverty among the elderly exploded during the 1990s following the failure of many state-sponsored industries to compete in a market-based economy after the collapse of communism. When state-run companies had to compete in the global marketplace, many went under and were unable to pay pensions. Globalization also coincided with a push to privatize state-owned enterprises. To ensure the success of privatization, governments needed to assure investors that they would not be saddled with massive pension liabilities. Finally, globalization has also been accompanied by large flows of immigrants moving from poor to rich countries—a trend that often exacerbates the challenge of population aging in the developing world. This is particularly a problem among Caribbean countries, which have both low birthrates and high rates of emigration, leaving fewer and fewer young people available to support the aged left behind.

POLICY PRESCRIPTIONS

Even the most committed advocates of social security, such as the International Labour Organization, now concede that population aging and globalization pose huge challenges to any system of collective provision for old age. But how individual nations should go about meeting that challenge is a subject of increasingly hot debate.

In 1994, the World Bank published an influential report, entitled "Averting the Old Age Crisis: Policies to Protect the Old and Promote Growth," which highlighted the bank's deepening concern that the high and growing cost of pensions in many developing countries is a major drain on economic efficiency. In the bank's analysis, the best way for countries to manage their pension cost is to create a three-tiered system.

- The first tier, funded by payroll taxes or general government revenues, focuses on providing minimum benefits to the most needy—the so called "social safety net."

- The second tier is a so-called prefunded system, in which workers must make contributions toward their future pensions. Under these plans, future retirement benefits are no longer defined and prescribed. Instead, contributions to the pension system become definedm with benefits depending on how well, or poorly, an individual manages his or her own retirement account. By fixing contributions but rendering benefits variable, this scheme ensures that the pension system never goes into deficit (hence the term " prefunded").

- The final tier asks employees to supplement their retirement incomes by relying on voluntary savings, which allow individuals to choose how to allocate their income over their lifetime.

In broad outline, this is the blueprint adopted by pension reformers around the world, although many variations in detail are possible. Today, World Bank staffers are engaged in pension-system reform work along these lines in some thirty countries.

KEY CONCEPTS

The record of pension reforms around the world shows, however, that they often impose huge hardships and economic dislocations—at least in the short term. Argentina, for example, attempted to follow the World Bank's prescriptions for pension reforms by enacting a system of individual retirement accounts. But the cost of this transition reached 3 percent of gross domestic product by 2000—a cost the country could not bear given its other financial difficulties. Elsewhere, charges of corruption and high administrative costs have tarnished pension-reform efforts. In many of the poorer provinces of China, for example, money intended to help younger workers prefund their retirements was instead diverted to paying for current retirees, and pension fund withdrawals now exceed payments in twenty-five cities, up from just five in 1997. Journalists covering pension reform efforts need a clear understanding of the key concepts involved and also a shrewd eye for how theory may not be working out in practice.

"PAY-AS-YOU-GO" FINANCING

The rhetoric used to describe traditional social security systems often gives the impression that they operate like insurance schemes: workers make "contributions" and beneficiaries collect "earned benefits" that are paid out of "trust funds." But in reality these systems function as devices for transferring income from one generation to another. Under the so-called pay-as-you-go system, the money today's workers pay into these systems is used to pay for people who have already retired. If there is a surplus, the funds are sometimes also used to lend to other government operations, rendering future taxpayers liable for paying off these debts. The term "pay-as-you-go," though, is a misnomer. In reality, each generation pays for its elders' retirement, while in turn relying on the next generation for support in old age.

ADVANTAGES AND DISADVANTAGES The system works well so long as a country's population and economy continue to grow robustly, but it breaks down when population aging and slower economic growth set in. Increases in productivity, or the rise in wages after accounting for inflation, can help sustain pay-as-you-go systems. But so long as there are consistently fewer workers available to support each retiree, such systems will inevitably come under strain. Reporters need to find out if the country in question has a pay-as-you-go system? If so, is the population growing, or growing older? What about the country's productivity? If either of these rates are stagnant or negative, reporters should find out if any economists or institutions have calculated how long it will be before the pension system runs out of money. These same studies also calculate the present value of the future deficits, which typically represent a "contingent liability" that the government will eventually need to take over.

TRUST-FUND FINANCING

Some governments, such as that of the United States, use trust funds in their pension programs. Trust funds are best thought of as accounting exercises. Their statements of assets and liabilities are, in effect, estimates of the ratio of the future benefits the system has promised to pay to what it will take in from future taxes. This calculation enables policy makers to know whether their pension system has any long-term unfunded liabilities that will have to be paid through increases in taxes or cuts in benefits. Without going through this accounting exercise, policy makers would be hard pressed to know whether a pension system is solvent over the long term.

Unfortunately, the language used to describe trust funds can be highly misleading. Trust funds are said to contain assets and liabilities, to be in surplus or in deficit. To many people, this language makes trust funds seem analogous to bank accounts, and they imagine their contributions being safely stored up in an account that will later pay their own benefits. The reality is far different. With few exceptions, public pension plans do not have any actual assets, such as stocks or bonds, invested in wealth-producing enterprises. All the money they take in during any given year is spent in the same year, if not for pensions then for other government operations.

So what are these assets that trust funds show in their balance sheets? They are not, as one might think, funds set aside and invested or "in the bank." Instead, these numbers are estimates of contributions to the pension system expected from future taxpayers or from other parts of the government. Just as a bank would count a loan you owe as part of its assets, governments count their claims on future taxpayers as assets as well, even though these "assets" represent a drain on the future wealth and income of the citizens themselves. From the point of view of taxpayers, therefore, the assets appearing in a trust fund report are really measures of the future payments that either they or their children and grandchildren are expected to make to the system.

RUSSIAN PENSION REFORM

SERGEI BLAGOV

During the Soviet era, Russia's pension system was fully backed and guaranteed by the government—a cornerstone of a state policy guaranteeing citizens' financial stability. But things began to change under former President Mikhail Gorbachev as economic controls were eased and inflation began to erode the value of the 120-ruble monthly pension. The sacred notions of safety and stability came to an abrupt end when the USSR collapsed in 1991 and radical market reforms brought on hyperinflation, which drove the purchasing power of pensions to rock bottom levels.

Some 40 million pensioners currently live on the system's benefits, but many subsist in virtual poverty because of the inflation-led erosion of benefits. At the same time, an aging population, tax evasion, and other problems have yielded a deficit in the system that will leave it bereft of funds if not addressed.

The current system, in the process of ongoing reform, is funded by a 29 percent payroll tax and replenished from the budget if it falls short. Employees' direct contributions are minimal, placing the burden almost entirely on the employer—for decades the government, but now more commonly the private sector. This structure encourages companies to underreport payroll expenses to avoid paying taxes, and the resulting shortfall has helped feed the deficit. Another burden is the growing pool of pensioners: the over-sixty age bracket doubled as a share of the population between 1959 and 1990, to some 20 percent. And despite rising life expectancy rates, Russian retirement ages are still fifty-five for women and sixty for men, lower than in comparable Eastern European countries.

Private pension schemes have been available since the mid-1990s, and there are now more than 250 licensed pension funds with some 21 billion rubles (approximately $700 million) under management. These funds are predominantly established under corporate sponsorship, but there are some open to the public. Still, private funds represent a mere fraction of the overall system, making the public scheme's sustainability as critical as ever.

HISTORY OF REFORM

Russia has made several attempts to reform its pension system. After two initial steps that ended in failure, the government, in 1998, tried again, and the World Bank aided the effort with an $800 million loan. The project was designed to strengthen revenues through better collection and enforced compliance of larger companies. The reform was hindered by the August 1998 financial meltdown. In late 2000, the authorities again revived the pension reform, and a year later President Vladimir Putin approved three basic laws of a pension package previously approved by parliament.

This reform introduced a multipillar pension system that shifted from a defined benefit scheme to a defined contribution system comprising three levels. The first is a notional-defined contribution pay-as-you-go pension scheme in which benefits are determined by the sum of contributions paid into the plan, economic performance, and life expectancy at the time of retirement. A mandatory-funded second pillar, meanwhile, is managed by private institutions and allows individuals to direct their own investments. The final level is the basic benefit plan, which promises a specific monthly benefit that is usually based on factors like age, earnings, and years of service.

The reform aims to address several problems of the old system, including complex benefit formulas and generous eligibility conditions, such as early retirement in many occupations. It is also designed to tackle the growing financial burden produced by a sliding number of contributors and an increasing number of pensioners—the result of rising layoffs, tax avoidance, and an aging population. And the funded scheme endeavors to increase pension benefits while deepening the roots of capital markets and promoting economic growth.

LESSONS LEARNED

In spite of the reform efforts, a host of uncertainties and structural snags persist. One criticism is that the system fails to provide incentives for workers to increase contributions or to work longer, both of which are necessary to bolster the system's funds and reduce costs. A solution would be to increase the retirement age, which would encourage Russians to continue working and continue paying into the system. Other disincentives include taxes, which eat up most of workers' contributions, and a lack of inflation indexing. By law, pensions are linked to inflation, but in practice they are not increased accordingly, leaving many pensioners in poverty.

Beyond these structural issues, and even if reforms are successful, grave questions persist about the system's fiscal sustainability. The World Bank has said that if economic growth falters, the system's pay-as-you-go portion will likely fall into the red. While the basic benefit pillar is expected to post surpluses in coming years, the extra cash could not be used over the long run to offset the deficits.

The system's effectiveness also hinges on stable, functioning markets. In order for workers to contribute, they must have confidence that their money will be invested safely. Banks too must be entrusted to safeguard assets, but this idea faces hurdles in a nation where citizens keep their savings far from banks. Given the absence of trust, it is difficult to imagine how other parts of the financial system vital for the funded pension system's success—like capital market institutions—will prosper.

To bolster confidence in the system, the World Bank has recommended allowing pension funds to invest substantially in foreign assets. This would help ensure the population that its savings are not hostage to the whims of local markets, where infrastructure remains weak in spite of recent macroeconomic stability.

By the end of September 2003, the state pension fund had sent letters to millions of Russians advising them to decide whether to open new individual retirement accounts with the state-run system or with private pension funds. But it remains far from clear what kind of state-run system they would be buying into.

ADVANTAGES AND DISADVANTAGES "Trust-fund" financing forces governments to calculate long-term deficits in their social security systems, even if they do nothing to fund those deficits. The arrangement may also help build political support for social security systems by creating an impression that funds are being set aside in reserve to pay for future benefits. Yet talk of "surpluses" building up in trust funds can be highly misleading to the public and also provide governments with an excuse for spending more money than they actually have. Reporters should ask: what are the unfunded liabilities in the country's pension system? Has the government issued debt to try to account for those liabilities? Does the government's budget include this information? This information should be included when calculating the government's performance in reducing national debt or balancing the budget.

PREFUNDING

Prefunding is where each worker must make contributions toward his or her future pension; under these so-called defined contribution plans, either individual retirement accounts are created, or the government directs the investments and uses the returns to pay promised social security benefits to workers in the future.

ADVANTAGES AND DISADVANTAGES In an aging society, making the transition from pay-as-you-go financing of social security to one in which each generation prefunds the costs of its own retirement will theoretically save money in the long run and defuse the ticking time bomb of implicit pension debt. That is because each generation gets the benefit of compound interest on its investments during its working years. Yet in any effort to move from a pay-as-you go to a prefunded system, there is a key challenge to be surmounted, namely the cost of financing the transition.

If benefits are to be preserved for the current generation of retirees, current workers will have to bear that cost *plus* pay for the prefunding of their own retirement. As the World Bank acknowledges in one of its publications, "Moving from a pay-as-you-go to funding means that current workers pay twice: for both their own (funded) pensions and current retirees' (pay-as-you-go) pensions."[1] This transition cost, known as the "double burden" problem, bedevils all proposals to move toward prefunding of pension costs. In 2002, for example, the Croatian government announced it would borrow 150 million euros, at an interest rate of 6.875 percent, to finance the cost of changing its pay-as-you-go pension plans to a prefunded system. Is the country in question planning on making this change? Can it afford to make this investment without causing undue economic hardship in the short term?

KEY THINGS TO WATCH FOR

HIDDEN COSTS

Though a country's current "pay-as-you go" pension scheme may be unsustainable, political leaders are often reluctant to communicate the true costs of reform. A frequent ploy is to suggest that government finance the cost of the transition by issuing new debt. Yet if the pension debt built into the old system is simply replaced by new bonds sold to the public, how will future generations of taxpayers benefit? In effect, the debt is still there. Reporters should be wary of claims that pension reform can be achieved without any group—current taxpayers and retirees or future taxpayers and retirees—sharing in some measure of sacrifice. The IMF, for example, has recently warned European nations that they will have to run budget surpluses for the next fifteen years to fund state pensions for today's middle aged.[2] What is the overall change in the nation's savings rate and in the national debt level as a result of a change in the pension scheme? What are savings rates and debt levels doing in the short and long term? What does the government project for these levels? How much debt do independent economists think the country's economy can stand to take on?

What is the cost involved in switching to a prefunded system? During the transition, workers may, for example, earn 10 percent annually on their retirement accounts, but the same generation will be responsible for paying all or much of the cost for honoring benefits promised to current retirees. An honest reckoning of the rate of return available to participants in the new, prefunded system must take this liability into account.

RATES OF RETURN

Pension reformers also sometimes make dubious claims about the rate of return individuals or governments are likely to make through investment of pension funds in private securities such as the stock market. Historically, the long-term return on stocks in developed countries has averaged 7 to 8 percent after inflation. In contrast, unless a country has a growing population, the returns that a pay-as-you-go system can offer each gener-

BANKING AND MACROECONOMICS

ation of participants (without any future increase in taxes) will be limited to the country's underlying rate of productivity growth, or the amount wages increase after inflation, which rarely averages more than 2 to 3 percent annually. But claims that participants will get "a better deal" from a prefunded pension plan that invests in stocks than from a pay-as-you-go system can be misleading because money invested in private securities is inherently at risk and markets are volatile and past performance is no guarantee of future reward. Though pay-as-you-go systems are also vulnerable to economic depressions, losses are not born exclusively by individuals who made failed investments, as they are under defined-contribution plans, but are instead spread out across the entire pension system.

In small countries with underdeveloped capital markets, requiring citizens to invest their whole retirement nest egg in the domestic economy can be imprudent. The entire Russian stock market is worth less than a moderate-sized U.S. company, for example. A country may have a deep need for increased savings and investment, but individual savers need to hedge their risks by investing in a wide portfolio of holdings, which may not be possible so long as they are required to invest only in domestic companies. Unfortunately, this is precisely what the World Bank and many governments prescribe. Economist Laurence Kotlikoff notes: "In effect, the Bank is telling citizens of developing countries to do something it would never suggest to its own employees—namely, to invest their retirement assets in a single, small country that may default on its bonds and whose corporations do not meet western standards of accounting or corporate governance."[3] Does the country in question allow workers to invest pensions outside their own country? If not, what is the worth of the country's stock market? What is its historical rate of return and how safe are investments there?

There is also good reason to believe that the return on capital will decline in the coming decades even in advanced countries. In the long .run, interest rates paid to savers, as well as the value of stocks and bonds, are to a large extent a function of supply and demand. To the extent that both people and governments save more to prefund the cost of retirements, the world's supply of financial capital should (all else being equal) increase. This rise in supply implies a decrease in price, and thus reduced premiums, or rates of return, paid to savers. At the same time, the slowing growth of the labor force should—again, all else being equal—lead to higher wages, leaving fewer resources available to compensate investors.

The cost of administering defined-contribution plans has to be taken into account. These costs are often substantial, particularly during the early years of a transition to a prefunded system. Has the government of the country in question said how much it is paying for the administration of the pension system? Is it being done by a department of the government, or was the contract given to a private company?

ALTERNATIVE REFORMS

Reporters should consider whether pension reform can be achieved by measures short of full privatization, especially if the country is likely to struggle with the costs of making a wholesale change in the pension system. Ask if the government has considered other options such as: Including a large underground or informal work force that escapes, or is excluded from, participation in the national pension scheme, as a potential new source of funding. The United States, for example, has helped preserve its social security system to date by expanding its coverage to occupations previously excluded, such as doctors, clergy, domestics, farm workers, and public employees, as well as by embracing a dramatic increase in the number of women working outside the home and therefore paying taxes into the system.

In countries where the labor force is shrinking, has the government done anything to encourage young workers to stay at home, rather than emigrate? What government policies, corruption, and so on are driving young workers away?

In some instances, the long-term solvency of pay-as-you-go systems may also be achieved through increases in productivity. Is the government giving priority to policies promoting productivity, including effective spending on education and other measures to improve the quality of the workforce?

In countries with below-replacement-level fertility rates, it may be appropriate for governments to look for ways to encourage more childbearing. What is the cost of raising a child in the country? What programs could the government enact to ease the financial burden on parents and the strains of balancing work and family life?

NOTES

1. "Transition: Paying for a Shift from Pay-As-You-Go Financing to Funded Pensions," 2, http://www.worldbank.org/wbi/pensions/courses/february2003/readings/transition.pdf.
2. Heather Tomlinson, "Only 15 Years of Surplus Will Save Euro Pensions," *Independent on Sunday* (London), 21 September 2003, 1.
3. Laurence Kotlikoff, "Look Abroad to Solve the Pensions Crisis: Developing Nations Should Ignore World Bank Advice to Invest for Retirement at Home," *Financial Times* (London), 25 April 2000.

PART III
CORPORATE REPORTING

CHAPTER FOURTEEN

FOREIGN DIRECT INVESTMENT

DAN DELUCA

OREIGN DIRECT investment has increased dramatically in the past twenty years to become the dominant type of crossborder capital flow in both developed and developing economies. Total worldwide FDI inflows grew from $59 billion in 1982 to $651 billion in 2002, peaking at $1,393 billion in 2000.[1]

In the same period, FDI in developing countries grew from $8 billion to $205 billion. This dramatic growth both reflects and helps bring about the growing integration of the world's economies. Multinational corporations have increased their geographic scope of operations dramatically, creating the "global supply chain," where each stage of production takes place in a location most suitable in terms of costs, inputs, or other factors.

Perhaps the factor most responsible for FDI growth in developing countries has been changes in government policies regulating external investment. FDI was once viewed warily as a threat to domestic firms, and so many developing countries had regulations prohibiting foreign ownership or imposing onerous conditions. Now, however, FDI is courted aggressively around the globe. Many countries have a range of programs and policies in place to promote investment, and they often compete directly with other nations for large-scale investments such as auto assembly plants.

The principle attraction of FDI for developing countries has been, and probably continues to be, jobs directly created by the investment. But there has been a growing realization that FDI can also produce many other benefits, both direct and indirect. Michael Porter, of Harvard University, has helped promote the idea that a government's economic policies, including those designed to attract FDI, can be a powerful tool for fostering economic competitiveness and development. In his influential book *The Competitive Advange of Nations*, Porter notes that investment by multinational corporations brings a country not only capital but also world-class production, management, and technical expertise. This expertise can diffuse into the economy at large, improving the competitiveness of many firms and raising the overall level of economic growth. In addition, enhancements to physical infrastructure and the legal and regulatory environment designed to attract multinational corporations can improve the efficiency and competitiveness of all of a country's enterprises, both foreign and domestic.

For the most part, politicians and economists welcome the increase in FDI to developing economies. But there is an acknowledgement that not all FDI is equally advantageous and that certain investments can bring some risk. For this reason, it is important that the press encourage open discussion of government policies and specific proposed investments. In particular, examination of large incentives for specific investments should be encouraged by the press, since these incentives are often not made public, and it is thought that the cost of such incentives can sometimes outweigh the benefits of the investment.

The journalist covering FDI in a developing economy will have to confront this uncertainty. Familiarity with the benefits, risks, and possible side effects of FDI should help in sorting through the issues. Journalists may need to cover the benefits and risks of specific investments, as well as the overall foreign investment profile of a country.

DEFINITIONS

Crossborder capital flows generally take one of three basic forms: official development aid, debt, or equity investments. The latter (that is, equity) is further divided into two categories: equity portfolio investments and *foreign direct investment*. FDI is defined as any equity holding across national borders that provides the owner substantial control over the entity. This is generally defined as a 10 percent holding or greater. Most foreign direct investment ends up being 100 percent ownership by a multinational corporation, though certain countries like to promote joint ventures with local entities. Equity flows providing less than 10 percent ownership of a foreign entity are referred to as *portfolio equity investment*.

There are two fundamentally different types of FDI, sometimes called *"modes of entry."* The multinational corporations can either buy an existing foreign company or can create a new company. The latter is often referred to as "build" (vs. buy), or as a *"greenfield"* investment. A greenfield investment can create additional productive capacity in a country, but it may also create new competition for existing local companies.

Another important distinction is the difference between the *FDI "inflow"* and *FDI "stock."* Inflow measures the amount of FDI entering a country during a given period. The FDI stock is the total (that is, cumulative) amount of productive capacity owned by foreigners. FDI stock grows over time and is defined as including all earnings of the foreign-owned firms that are retained in the country. (By the same token, the FDI stock excludes the dividends that the company earns but distributes back to the mother multinational corporation).

Economists and policy makers often speak of "*positive spillover*" and "*negative spillover.*" These terms refer generally to the range of positive or negative effects that a particular instance of FDI can have on local firms and on the local economy in general.

TRENDS

Prior to the early 1980s, most capital flows to the developing world were in the form of either debt or official development aid. After the Mexican default of 1983, and the subsequent debt crisis throughout Latin America, debt flows to developing economies dried up dramatically, as lenders reassessed the risk of loans to developing nations.

The majority of FDI does go to the developed economies (e.g. Japanese automakers opening plants in the United States and UK), but FDI to developing countries is still large and has increased substantially. Inward FDI to developing countries increased from $8.4 billion in 1980 to $36.9billion in 1990 to $190.7 billion in 2002. This is spread throughout the globe, with substantial gains seen in many countries and in every region (see table 14.1).

This growth across regions masks the high concentration of FDI to developing nations. In 2001, about 62 percent of inward FDI to developing countries went to five countries: China, Mexico, Brazil, Hong Kong, and Poland. The least developed economies, including many in Africa, continue to receive very little FDI. These tend to be shunned by multinationals, which prefer to invest in countries known to be "safe," with relatively high levels of political stability, infrastructure, education, well-enforced property rights, and so on.

TABLE 14.1

REGION	FDI 1990 (IN BILLIONS OF DOLLARS)	FDI 2002 (IN BILLIONS OF DOLLARS)
Latin America	9.7	56.0
South, East, and SE Asia	22.1	88.6
West and Central Asia	2.1	6.4
Central and Eastern Europe	0.6	28.7
Africa	2.4	11.0

Note: All figures are inward FDI.
Source: United Nations Committee for Trade and Development, *Handbook of Statistics.* See http://www.unctad.org.

POLAND

DAN DELUCA

Poland has been very successful in attracting foreign direct investment, which has contributed greatly to the country's recent economic growth. Starting from a difficult position in the early 1990s, Poland's economy grew strongly in the second half of that decade. Over the same period, FDI inflows grew from minimal to the largest in Eastern Europe. In 2001, Poland was fifth in FDI received among developing countries, behind China, Hong Kong, Brazil, and Mexico.

Like other former eastern bloc countries, Poland is no ordinary developing economy. Economists sometimes refer to these countries as "transition economies," since each is transitioning from an economy with minimal capitalist experience, institutions, and infrastructure to a free-market economy. Several transition economies have high economic potential, with a well-educated workforce and a substantial industrial heritage. But realizing that potential has required substantial investment. For Poland, along with other eastern bloc countries, FDI has helped drive the transition to a modern capitalist economy.

Famous as the first eastern bloc country to experience a widespread popular revolt against communism, Poland formed the first noncommunist government in the eastern bloc in 1989. By then, growth was strongly negative, inflation was very high, and foreign debt had reached unsustainable levels. In 1990 Poland announced that it could not pay its external debts. The country undertook significant capitalist reforms in 1990 and 1991.

In a few years Poland's economy stabilized, and in 1994 Poland rescheduled its external debt with both private ("London Club") and official ("Paris Club") creditors. After this, FDI in Poland increased dramatically, from $88 million in 1990, to $3.7 billion in 1995, peaking at $9.3 billion in 2000. FDI dipped to around $8 billion in 2001 and to around $5 billion in 2002, accompanying a worldwide slowdown in FDI. Overall stock of FDI in Poland expanded from $3 billion in 1992 to $62 billion in 2002.

Over this period, Poland took some moderate steps to attract FDI, such as tax incentives and favorable import/export handling. But probably more important was the economic and regulatory stability that began after the debt agreements were signed, as this created an environment that appeared "safe" for potential investors. This contrasts distinctly with the Russian Federation, which has lagged behind Poland, Hungary, and the Czech Republic in attracting FDI, largely due to perceptions of criminal activity and tax and regulatory instability.

Much of Poland's FDI has been related to privatization, as the government has sold off assets to foreign investors. But FDI has also been substantial in the private economy, including a number of large "greenfield" investments. Foreign investors are represented throughout the economy. Manufacturing, telecommunications, and construction have received the most FDI, since these sectors required substantial investment to modernize. The financial sector has also received a great deal of FDI, since a thorough revamping of the financial system was required in the transition to capitalism. Key investors include France Telecom, GM, Fiat, Dae-

woo, Citibank, HVB Group, Gazprom, and Vivendi Universal.

Poland's economy grew strongly while it was receiving these large FDI inflows. Economic growth averaged 4.8 percent per year from 1995 to 2001. Gross domestic product per capita increased from $3,280 in 1995 to $4,881 in 2002. From 1995 to 2001, exports increased from $23 billion to $36 billion. The nature of exported goods changed dramatically, with manufactured goods constituting a much higher share. This points to a shift in exports from basic goods such as food and steel to more complex, value-added goods, fueled largely by foreign firms.

But note that that over the same period, imports increased even more, from $29 billion to $50 billion. Two primary factors explain this. First, firms producing for export had to import capital equipment as part of the modernization process. But perhaps more important, much FDI was of the "market-opening" type, aimed at gaining entry to the underserved local market. Such market-opening investment in transition economies has been generally as important as "efficiency-seeking" investment geared towards export.

In the last two years, economic growth in Poland has slowed to around 1 percent a year. This is partially related to the global economic slowdown, especially in Germany, which takes about one-third of Poland's exports. But other macroeconomic factors are also involved. There are still many state enterprises, especially in mining and heavy industries, which are unprofitable and inefficient. In addition, the government has been running a large deficit, currently about 5 percent of GDP, largely due to generous social welfare programs, many left over from the communist era.

Unemployment has become a problem, with the overall rate hovering between 15 percent and 20 percent since 2000. One contributing factor may be high payroll taxes and generous benefits mandated by the government, which may make firms reluctant to take on new employees. But there is no evidence that FDI has contributed significantly to unemployment by, for instance, large-scale layoffs by acquired companies.

Poland is also suffering from a growing disparity between urban and rural dwellers, with the latter experiencing higher unemployment and lower incomes. This is due in part to structural factors, such as poor rural infrastructure and education. It may also be an unintended effect of the relatively rapid industrial modernization of Poland. Investment—both foreign and domestic—has been concentrated in manufacturing and a few other industries, whereas agriculture has not

received the investment needed to modernize.

Whether current economic difficulties will lead to a further decrease in FDI remains to be seen. FDI to Poland did decrease in 2002, but it was still around 5 billion dollars, and FDI has decreased globally. What is clear is that the Polish economy has gone through a substantial, though incomplete, economic transformation, and FDI has played a substantial role in this process.

FACTORS CONTRIBUTING TO THE GROWTH OF FDI

Starting in the early 1990s, a number of factors converged to make FDI increase dramatically. The first is the increased perception of risk associated with crossborder debt. The Latin American debt crisis in the 1980s and the Asian capital crisis in 1997 and 1998 made lenders much less eager to lend across borders.

Perhaps the most important factor contributing to the growth of FDI since the late 1980s has been globalization, or the internationalization of production and the introduction of the so-called global supply chain by multinational corporations. Technological change, especially lower transportation and communication costs, has enabled multinational corporations to locate specific stages of production in different locations, taking advantage of favorable local conditions to minimize costs and improve sales.

Another substantial contribution to the growth of FDI has been changes in government policy, as countries have begun actively courting investment from overseas. Many countries have changed policies to allow investments that earlier might have been prohibited or been otherwise difficult. FDI has also come to be officially encouraged by governments, many of which have formal FDI promotion programs. Governments sometimes provide substantial incentives to companies locating in their countries, especially for facilities that will generate significant employment.

Some of the many types of programs and incentives used by governments to encourage FDI include:

- Exemption or reduction of income tax on earnings, typically for five to ten years

- Exemption from property tax or other business taxes

- New or improved infrastructure, such as roads, ports, or utilities

- Tariff exemptions, particularly for goods used as production inputs

- Creation of "export-promotion zones," with superior infrastructure and streamlined regulatory processing

- Subsidies for job creation and/or worker training

- Direct subsidies, favorable loans, land grants, or other direct financial incentives

These incentives often are not publicized and so can be hard to quantify. More open disclosure of these incentives should be encouraged, since some economists question whether in certain cases the value of certain FDI might actually be less than the value of the incentives granted.

ADVANTAGES OF FOREIGN DIRECT INVESTMENT

A good way to evaluate a particular country's inward investment portfolio is to examine the key benefits of FDI. Those are listed below.

1. *FDI can contribute to growth, higher incomes, and reduced poverty.* Growth in a developing country is the heart of the matter. But, as with many economic phenomena, there is not conclusive evidence here on what generates growth in emerging economies. The good news though is that there is empirical evidence showing that FDI often, though definitely not always, contributes to economic growth. Economic growth usually leads to reduced poverty, though not necessarily to a more equitable distribution of income.

2. *Incentive structure leads to productive investment.* FDI is generally undertaken by multinational corporations. Those companies are usually concerned with making investments that will make them profits. Therefore, the investments are usually well-targeted toward setting up successful businesses—ones that will make money and create jobs. This contrasts with aid and official loans, which have often been squandered through corruption or spent inefficiently on unneeded infrastructure or other "vanity" (also known as "white elephant") projects.

3. *FDI is less volatile than other capital flows.* Because FDI is generally spent on "hard assets" such as plant and equipment, the capital embodied in FDI cannot flee a country in times of crisis as easily as portfolio capital ("hot money"). A company cannot sell off a factory and pull out of the country as quickly as a mutual fund can sell bonds and stocks or a bank can refuse to roll over short-term loans. Even in instances where the FDI is in a service-related industry such as banking or advertising, substantial effort and time is spent to develop an ongoing business, and owners will not easily pull the plug. Thus FDI

is said to be much less likely than other forms of short-term capital (for example, debt) to exacerbate a crisis situation, as happened in the Asian crisis in the late 1990s. Experience through the 1990s showed FDI to be much less variable than debt flows. During the politically charged year of 2002, for example, Brazil remained a major destination for FDI even when portfolio investors and bank lenders fled.

4. *FDI can lead to increased tax revenues.* A successful foreign-owned firm should generate profits and hence generate tax revenue for the host country. Those taxes can then be spent on needed infrastructure, social programs, education, and so on. Fiscally challenged developing countries, as such, face a strong incentive to encourage FDI. However, this is not always the case. As noted above, governments attract FDI precisely by providing tax amnesties as incentives. FDI, unfortunately, has also been a means of tax evasion. In particular, a foreign-owned entity that produces intermediate goods typically sells those goods to its parent company (for example, car parts that are shipped to an assembly plant in another country). The price at which those intermediate goods are sold is known as the *transfer price.* However, since transfer prices are internal accounting concepts, they are subject to manipulation. A subsidiary can alter transfer prices when it sells its product at an artificially cheap price to the parent company so that it can pay lower taxes.

5. *FDI can lead to "technology transfer" and "management skills transfer."* These are important examples of "positive spillover." Because multinational corporations typically have greater technological and management expertise than local firms, such expertise can be transferred to other parts of the economy. This appears to happen most clearly when the multinational corporation has close ties to local partners, suppliers, and customers. But even in cases where the multinational is not tightly integrated with local firms, there is evidence that technology and skill transfer takes place, most likely through labor mobility, professional contacts, or a general raising of competitive pressure.

6. *FDI can improve skill and wages of a labor force.* FDI is often encouraged because multinational corporations provide training and, as such, contribute to better development of the labor force. Evidence is strong that multinationals pay better and train employees more thoroughly than domestic firms in developing economies. It is also argued that the presence of multinational corporations in the labor market provides incentive to local firms to improve the conditions and wages of workers. Note that from the perspective of local firms this can be a negative—if multinational corporations "skim" the local workforce of skilled workers, labor costs for local firms can increase.

7. *FDI may improve access to export markets.* Multinational corporations almost by definition have substantial skill in importing and exporting. Many economists and policy makers believe that a key benefit of FDI is the presence of export-oriented foreign firms in a country, which can help improve efforts by local firms to sell overseas. There is good evidence that this is the case. One way this happens is through improvements in shipping and logistics infrastructure—for example, an increased presence of international shipping firms and agents. There is probably also some knowledge transfer, where managers of local firms learn from the example of the multinational corporation how to open new export markets.

8. *FDI can provide additional demand for output by local producers.* Another key component of "positive spillover" is the increased demand for inputs from local suppliers that a new multinational corporation can create, which can lead to increased revenue and profits for local firms. Some studies have suggested that a key determinant of the benefits to national income from FDI is the extent to which the foreign enterprises sources locally rather than importing their inputs.

9. *FDI can provide lower-cost inputs for local suppliers.* Similar to the previous benefit, if a multinational corporation creates a product previously imported by local producers or otherwise in short supply, the FDI can lead to a decrease in production costs for local firms and correspondingly higher productivity and profits.

10. *FDI can improve the balance of payments and capital account.* Because exports will typically bring in hard currency, an export-oriented foreign-owned entity can improve the balance of payments and capital account of a nation. The initial FDI investment itself can also be an important source of hard currency, since multinational corporations will typically need to convert hard currency to the local currency either to purchase a local entity or contract for work and equipment in setting up a new entity. This balance of payment benefit is reduced, however, by the extent to which the firm imports its production inputs and insofar as the multinational corporations will eventually repatriate profits and retained earnings, which causes a reduction in hard currency reserves.

RISKS OF FOREIGN DIRECT INVESTMENT

1. *If FDI becomes too extensive, repatriated profits can put pressure on the balance of payments.* As foreign-owned firms become established and profitable, they begin to repatriate earnings to the home country of the owner. In this "decapitalization" process, local currency is converted to the home country's currency, and capital leaves the

country. If the base of foreign-owned companies is large enough, this can lead to a serious capital drain—especially if not offset by additional FDI. This is especially a concern in times of crisis when foreign-owned companies both reduce their FDI and, at the same time, accelerate the repatriation of earnings. The effect of this can be similar to the effect of foreign lenders refusing to roll over short-term loans—the country can be starved of capital, and a bad economic situation can be made dramatically worse. This is sometimes cited as one of the primary risks of a country becoming too reliant on FDI.

2. *FDI may create damaging competition for local firms.* This is often cited as a primary "negative spillover" from FDI. Because multinational corporations often have skill, technology, and capital that local firms cannot match, FDI can create damaging competition for local firms. This is noted as one of the most significant risks, but it is a complex one to evaluate. It is certainly true that local firms can be damaged, even put out of business, and that unemployment can result. But it is also true that in many instances competition from more efficient foreign-owned producers can be seen as a benefit to the economy as a whole, improving overall productivity and forcing local firms to modernize and improve efficiency. The question to ask here may be whether local firms will be able to improve enough to compete, or will they just be decimated by the competition from the multinational? If it is the latter, then the FDI may deserve additional scrutiny.

3. *FDI can lead to market dominance by multinational corporations.* Utilizing deep pockets and advanced technical and managemerial expertise, multinational corporations can possibly force all local competitors out of business. Once such monopoly power is obtained, the multinational can then raise prices, extracting excessive profits and potentially eliminating any overall benefit of the FDI. Monopoly power, however gained, appears to be a risk associated with FDI, one that should be closely scrutinized in most cases.

4. *Social protest and disorder can occur.* When multinational corporations are seen as exerting too much power, especially monopoly power over something considered a "public good"—for example, water, electricity, or phone service—then public resentment and protest can occur. This can lead to a hostile business environment, social disorder, and, in the worst case, political instability. This happened dramatically in Cochabamba, Bolivia, in 2000, when local water service was taken over by a multinational conglomerate led by Bechtel, which immediately doubled prices, precipitating a general strike and transportation shutdown. In this case the Bolivian government reversed the privatization, and Bechtel was forced to leave the country. A counterexample is phone service in several countries around the world, including

Mexico, Brazil, and India, where foreign entry into an industry previously controlled by the government dramatically reduced cost and improved phone service. However, in each of these cases, it is probably the introduction of competition rather than the introduction of foreign capital per se that led to such dramatic service improvements.

5. *New production facilities may lead to environmental and working-conditions degradation.* A frequent argument against FDI is that multinational corporations attempt to locate polluting facilities where environmental controls and labor-condition standards are the weakest. It is true that most developing countries have fewer such regulations, and less ability to enforce those that they do have, than developed countries. However, while there may be some instances of terrible accidents and great environmental harm being caused by multinationals (for example, the Bhopal chemical disaster, oil-related pollution in southern Nigeria), for the most part there is no good evidence of multinationals being more likely to pollute than domestic firms. The same thing applies to infamous cases of "sweat shops." If anything, evidence may actually point the other way, because multinational corporations, due to their higher profiles, may be more sensitive to environmental and social issues than local firms.

QUESTIONS AND ISSUES FOR JOURNALISTS

1. *Will the foreign-owned entity be export-oriented, or will it sell locally?* Export-oriented firms generally have the advantage of generating hard-currency income for the host country. Also, they tend to compete less directly with local firms, which may lessen negative economic spillover.

2. *Will the foreign-owned entity compete with local firms?* This is a complex issue because competition often leads to increased productivity and higher national income. But, if the local firms are significant employers or otherwise economically or socially important, displacement of these firms by multinational corporations can have significant short-term negative effects. Reporters should also investigate whether the multinational will compete with local firms for skilled labor, which might have the effect of raising labor costs for local firms.

3. *Will the foreign-owned entity buy from or sell to local firms?* The more closely a multinational corporation works with local suppliers, the more likely that the transfer of technical and management skills will occur. This is in addition to the expected increase in revenue to local firms. If the multinational sells to local firms, especially in cases where the input was previously imported, local costs of production may decrease.

CORPORATE REPORTING

4. *Is the government offering incentives? What kinds? What are the anticipated costs?* Some governments have let themselves be pulled into bidding wars, especially for high-profile investments such as auto plants. If these incentives are too generous, a country and its economy can experience a net loss from the investment. Governments often will not publicize these incentives, but they deserve public examination.

5. *Will the multinational corporation become the sole provider of an essential public good such as water or electricity?* If this is the case, the social environment may become an issue, especially if the multinational is expected to raise prices. Journalists should investigate whether any service or pricing guarantees are offered and, if not, whether there are any other countervailing controls in place to protect the public interest.

6. *Is the overall level of foreign ownership sustainable?* There are no clear guidelines as to how much foreign ownership is too much. At some point, though, there may develop a risk of "decapitalization" as mentioned above—where repatriating of capital by foreign owners becomes excessive.

LINKS FOR MORE INFORMATION

1. The United Nations Conference on Trade and Development (UNCTAD) produces a very thorough *World Investment Report* each year. The most current report is available online in English, and the forty-page overview is available in seven languages, including Russian, Chinese, French, Romanian, Spanish, and Arabic. http://www.unctad.org.

2. The Development Gateway is an online collection linking many resources on economic development and poverty reduction. Their "Foreign Direct Investment" section has many great links. http://www.developmentgateway.org/node/130616.

3. The Harvard Center for International Development (CID) has a page with many links to academic papers on mostly FDI-related investment. http://www.cid.harvard.edu/cidtrade/issues/investmentpaper.html.

4. This article from the World Bank's Web site has a good appendix summarizing dozens of studies and papers on FDI, economic growth, and poverty reduction. http://econ.worldbank.org/files/2205_wps2613.pdf.

5. Peter Nunnenkamp of the Kiel Institute for World Economics in Germany wrote an interesting paper titled "To What Extent Does Foreign Direct Investment Help Achieve International Development Goals?" http://www.uni-kiel.de/ifw/pub/kap/2002/kap1128.pdf or http://ideas.repec.org/p/wop/kieliw/1128.html.

6. The Institute for International Economics in Washington, D.C., publishes research papers on various economic and development areas, including foreign direct investment. http://www.iie.com/research/trade.htm#fdi.

7. The Center for Global Development also posts many working papers about development, privatization, and investment in developing countries. http://www.cgdev.org.

8. The World Bank's Rapid Response Unit publishes extensively on the topic of foreign direct investment. http://rru.worldbank.org/Resources/foreign_direct_investment.asp.

9. The Globalization and Poverty Web site provides researches on the impact of foreign direct investment on poverty reduction. http://www.gapresearch.org/finance/asean.html.

10. Professor Kyoji Fukao at the Hitotsubashi University in Tokyo has written many papers about foreign direct investment and trade in Japan. http://www.ier.hit-u.ac.jp/~fukao/english/publication/paper/index.html.

NOTES

1. United Nations Conference on Trade and Development (UNCTAD), *World Investment Report* 2003, 3, 249.

CHAPTER FIFTEEN

PRIVATIZATION

DEIDRE SHEEHAN

SINCE THE 1980s, when Margaret Thatcher was elected prime minister of Great Britain and Ronald Reagan was elected president of the United States, there has been a massive change in thinking about the role of the state. Part of this was a move towards privatization, as governments around the world decided to stop running businesses and let the private sector take over.

This was a fairly profound reversal in public policy. Until then, governments in both the developed and developing world had pursued a development strategy that emphasized heavy government participation in the economic cycle. Over the decades, governments accumulated a legacy of state assets. The Reagan/Thatcher "revolution" called for their divestiture. The main way of accomplishing this was for governments to sell the companies they owned, a process known as privatization.

All but a few countries—Cuba and North Korea are among the minority—have carried out at least some privatizations in recent years, and more are sure to follow. At this writing, there are about 110 countries involved in privatization programs. In many cases, they are driven by the promised rewards of privatization: higher economic growth, elimination of fiscally costly subsidies, and better companies that deliver cheaper and more efficient products and services to the people. But sometimes countries privatize because they are told it is a condition for loans from entities such as the World Bank and the International Monetary Fund. In other cases, countries choose to privatize because they want to raise money for the government treasury, not because the companies being sold off need to be privatized. As a reporter, it is important to look at why a privatization is taking place.

While privatization can result in greater "efficiency," it also causes job loss, so it is important to look at whether the government has a safety net for those workers who are put out on the street. There is some question as to whether privatization really makes companies more efficient; in some cases this efficiency comes from private owners' being able to make job cuts that governments cannot make for political reasons. Also, some studies have shown that the major gains take place before the actual privatization occurs as managers ready the companies to be sold, sometimes by putting in new business plans, or making job cuts ahead of the government sell-off. This process is referred to as *corporatization* and often means the government has to take stock of what the company's assets and liabilities are and how profitable it is or could become. These kinds of information are necessary before a company can be restructured, whether by the government or by the entity buying the state-owned enterprise.

When covering privatizations, it is important to remember that the promised rewards do not always materialize. How privatization is carried out is at least as important as the privatization itself. For developing countries in particular, without a clear legal or regulatory framework to encourage competition in the marketplace, the dangers are acute. In Russia, for example, many companies went from being badly run government-owned enterprises to being badly run privately owned enterprises. The new private-sector companies, often still run as monopolies, were no more efficient, did not deliver better services or products, and did not cut prices or even create jobs.

To follow what can be a complicated and often politically fraught process, it is vital to know not just how companies are privatized but also why they can fail.

THE PROCESS

WHAT GETS SOLD?

A government may choose to sell 100 percent of its ownership in a firm (full divestiture) or it may choose to keep a stake (partial divestiture). A commonly used rule of thumb is that a "true privatization" entails the government selling at least 51 percent of the company and giving up managerial control. A government may choose to keep a stake to reassure the public that it is still closely monitoring the country's strategic interests. Vietnam, for example, has sold off some of the hundreds of enterprises owned by the state, but has said it will not divest from "strategic" companies such as the national airline, telecom, and oil company. Or a country may decide that in order for its firm to compete abroad once it is sold, it is better to keep it in one piece rather than spinning off different divisions.

- *Vouchers*. In a mass privatization through vouchers, citizens of the country are given vouchers, which they can exchange for shares in companies when those are sold off. This method was widely used in Central and Eastern Europe in the mid-1990s, but with only limited success.

  Advantages: Vouchers can be a politically popular way of giving a typically alienated public a stake in the ownership of the company. The method is also seen as equitable in that it confers ownership across the board rather than restricting it to the moneyed elite. Vouchers have also been seen as a good way to develop budding stock markets by automatically turning members of the public into stockholders. Also, workers who are laid off during the privatization may feel they have benefited because they have been given a piece of the company.

  Disadvantages: Vouchers cut down on the amount of money received by the government for the sale of a company. Also, because the company is effectively owned by thousands of individuals, there is a risk that old managers at the company may carry on as before, with no single investor forcing the changes needed to make the company more efficient. Issuing vouchers does not necessarily create new wealth, as it does not bring new investment into the country.

  Another problem was seen when the Czech Republic used vouchers in a mass privatization program from 1992 through 1995. Investment funds bought up many of the vouchers. Large, domestic, government-owned banks controlled those funds. Those same banks often held debt owed by the privatized companies, too. In effect, the bank became the ultimate owner of the company. As a result, the funds would not punish a badly run company by pulling out because then the bank would have to write off the loans it had extended to the company. Of course, this problem, while important, is not restricted to the voucher method. Banks could, and often do, become owners of enterprises in other ways as well.

- *Direct Sales*. The government sells the company directly to large investors. These strategic investors, usually a private company or group of companies, bid against each other to buy the firm. They may bid in an open process with the highest offer accepted, or the government may choose to review potential buyers on a case-by-case basis. This process was used to privatize Kenya Airways in 1996. The government sold 77 percent of its shares in the airline in a series of competitive auctions. KLM Royal Dutch Airlines bought 26 percent of the carrier; local investors bought the remainder.

  Advantages: Competitive bidding is likely to bring the government the most revenue from the sale. In addition, the method typically

BREAKING THE BANK— BANKING PRIVATIZATION IN THE CZECH REPUBLIC

PETER S. GREEN

At two minutes before noon on 16 June 2000, a heavily armed police assault team stormed the Prague headquarters of Investicni a Postovni Banka, the Czech Republic's third-largest bank. Within minutes they had corralled the bank's top managers and seized control of the building, handing it over to government-appointed administrators. A run on the bank had emptied its coffers, threatening the Czech banking system—and, regulators feared, the entire Czech economy—with collapse. IPB's largest shareholder, a Netherlands-based firm controlled by the Japanese bank Nomura, cried foul. Within days, IPB had been sold to KBC Bank of Belgium, the owners of IPB's local rival, Ceskoslovenska Obchodni Banka, and the government agreed to swallow most of IPB's bad loans. The final bill is not yet in, but the IPB debacle is expected to cost Czech taxpayers as much as $5 billion, or about $500— more than a month's average wage—for every man, woman, and child in the land.

IPB was at the heart of the entire Czech economy, and its path from state-owned banking giant to an apparently empty shell is a microcosm of the problems the Czechs had privatizing not just their banking sector but the entire economy. Czech banks were among the last businesses privatized after the fall of communism, and, as the country's chief source of investment capital, they held extraordinary power over the Czechs' newly privatized industry. The managers of the state-owned banks were nearly all political appointees, and they opened the cash taps to political parties and well-connected firms.

The postcommunist government, believing in the magic of the market, barely regulated the banks or the stock market, and a vicious circle quickly developed. Banks loaned money to companies that were in turn owned by investment funds controlled by the banks. The firms lost money, but the loans kept flowing as companies borrowed just to cover the interest on outstanding loans. As long as no one looked too closely, the whole house of cards stayed up.

As economists Edward Snyder and Roger Kormendi pointed out in the case of IPB's state-owned rival Komercni Banka, "the opportunity to privatize a strong bank and harden enterprise-level budget constraints quickly was foregone, or at least postponed, in favor of creating a protected bank that would deal more leniently with [the bank's] politically-vested commercial clients."[1]

At IPB, as economist Zdenek Kudrna of Prague's Charles University noted in a comprehensive study of IPB that was sponsored by CSOB, before Nomura took control of the bank, management quietly bought control of the bank at the shareholders' expense. Through a series of sophisticated and highly opaque transactions, using tax havens like the Cayman Islands and a web of friends and firms allied to IPB, the management dug into IPB's deposits to effectively lend itself the money to buy shares in the bank.

By 1997, bad loans and insider deals had left the Czech banking system in crisis. A dozen small- and medium-sized banks had collapsed, and IPB, like the other large Czech banks, was in a liquidity squeeze. Police investigators had already jailed IPB's top managers, Jiri Tesar and Libor Prochzka, in a fraud investigation, later abandoning the probe.

With the fall of the center-right Klaus government in November 1997, the new cabinet moved swiftly to sell IPB. Rushing to show he was serious about privatization, finance minister Ivan Pilip sold IPB in March 1998 for half of what the government had originally hoped to net. Nomura, which had already acquired a 10 percent stake in IPB, bought the government's remaining 36 percent share for about 3.03 billion crowns, or $80 million in cash, and the promise to inject another $160 million.

Nomura said it aimed to restructure IPB, clean up its loan portfolios, and reorganize the bank's commercial-, retail-, and postal-banking operations. Then it would sell IPB to a larger but more cautious commercial bank. Under Nomura's ownership, IPB hired teams of consultants and became one of the country's most consumer-friendly banks.

Nomura's interest in IPB was not limited to consumer banking. As an investment bank, it already had several business arrangements with IPB, some involving shares controlled by IPB and its investment funds in key industries, including world-renowned Czech breweries. IPB also knew how to play its political cards. The bank itself had loans outstanding to the top two private television networks and to Mr. Klaus's party and its chief rival, the Social Democrats.

Despite its large stake in IPB and its promises to turn the

bank around, Nomura kept its distance from IPB's banking operations. Tesar and Prochazka were kept on during Nomura's ownership, even as an on-site inspection by regulators from the Czech National Bank, at the end of 1999, provisionally concluded that IPB, by then 46 percent owned by Nomura, "was not proceeding prudently and was conducting its affairs in a manner which harmed the interests of its investors and threatened the security and stability of the bank."[2] The regulators provisionally concluded IPB would need to create a further 40 billion crowns of reserves, but Nomura disagreed.

IPB's troubles had begun long before Nomura entered the picture, but even under Nomura, IPB ignored the growing holes in its reserves, many of them caused by poor loans made under Tesar and Prochazka to firms linked with the bank. Analysts say the reason was a tacit agreement between IPB's Czech management and Nomura. IPB, wrote Kudrna, provided Nomura with shares in the highly lucrative Czech beer industry, while Nomura would offer IPB a cloak of credibility as Tesar and Prochazka continued to consolidate their ownership of IPB using the bank's own deposits.[3]

In one key transaction, a Nomura-owned firm, Ceske Pivo, bought IPB's stakes in Plzensky Pivovary, maker of the world-famous Pilsner Urquell beer, and several smaller breweries for an estimated $250 million. The brewery was merged with Pivovar Radegast, the second-largest brewery in the Czech Republic, and the merged group was sold for $629 million to South African Breweries in 1999. The deal was a profitable one for Nomura, which booked the profits through a series of subsidiaries. Minority shareholders in IPB and shareholders in the IPB-run funds that sold their shares to Nomura's Ceske Pivo, say they never received fair market value for their brewery shares.

Meanwhile, IPB's banking business continued to worsen. By early 2000, IPB was beginning to bend under the weight of bad loans. Auditors estimated them at $1.1 billion, nearly a third of IPB's portfolio. A string of newspaper stories detailing the depth of IPB's troubles sent depositors scrambling to empty their accounts. Nearly $1.5 billion, a quarter of IPB's deposits, were withdrawn in less than a week. Nomura proposed refinancing the bank, but the government was under pressure from public opinion to move quickly. Talks between the government and Nomura fialed to

produce results, and on that fateful Friday, Czech regulators sent in the police. Three days later, IPB was a paper shell, its banking operations in the hands of Belgian bank KBC and its Czech subsidiary, CSOB.

"Machine guns and taxpayers' money were used to expropriate IPB and make CSOB the dominant Czech bank," Randall Dillard, Nomura's point man on the IPB transactions, told *Newsweek* in 2000. "When the smoke clears and the mirrors no longer dazzle, we will see a familiar tale of corruption, cronyism and politics."[4] Dillard is probably right. Nomura is now suing the Czech government for about $1 billion and says it was unfairly denied the bailout some state-owned banks received. The European Union scolded the Czechs for subsidizing their banking sector, but the Czech government says it will pay Nomura nothing and is countersuing for the hundreds of millions of dollars it says were lost in the beer deal. The gist of the government's argument: the smoke and mirrors were all manipulated by Nomura and its political patrons.

This article includes some changes made at the request of Nomura International PLC to avoid lengthy disputes under the restrictive free speech and expansive libel laws of the United Kingdom, which are far stricter than the laws of the United States.

brings along a "strategic investor" who, in addition to capital, provides technological and managerial expertise. Direct sale is also cheaper than offering the company for sale on the stock exchange, which often involves marketing and other costs.

Disadvantages: Direct sales may be politically unpopular since the general public has no opportunity to get a stake in the company. In addition, focusing attention on one buyer tends to raise complaints that the government is selling the country's jewels, often to foreigners. And since shares are not issued or sold, this method does nothing to help develop the stock market.

- *Public offerings*. Where the company is sold to the public on the stock exchange through an initial public offering of shares.

  Advantages: A direct sale helps to develop the stock market. It is also easier to make this a transparent process, where the public can see exactly who buys what and for how much. It is also used to phase in a sale with a first tranche (a bond series issued for sale in a foreign country) used for "price discovery" purposes before launching a more comprehensive public offering. And it prevents a single politically powerful investor from snapping up all the shares. For these reasons, this process is also more likely to attract foreign investors.

  Disadvantages: Public offerings have shortcomings similar to those of the voucher approach. They also involve a diffuse shareholdership that amkes owner control over management more difficult. Advantages accruing from technology and management-technique transfers typically associated with "anchor investors" tend to be absent when privatization is done through public offerings.

- *Mixed Sales*. This is a mix of a direct sale to strategic investors followed by a public offering, often held six to twelve months later. In the 1990 privatization of Telmex, the Mexican government sold 20 percent of the company's shares to a "strategic" investor, then sold another 31 percent through public offerings in 1991 and 1992.

  Advantages: The "anchor" investors can carry out the changes needed to make the company more efficient and profitable by the time it is offered publicly. This often raises significantly the company's value, benefiting both the government and the new partial owner. Chances of a successful public offering increase when a company has first been run by a strategic investor.

  Disadvantages: There is a cost to carrying out one type of sale and then another type, including fees to the investment banks that help organize the sales and so on. Because of this, this method is normally used on large companies that are attractive to investors. The approach can also be politically sensitive since the original ("anchor") investors typically buy shares at a cheaper price than the price eventually prevailing when the company goes public.

- *Concessions*. Citing "strategic reasons," governments sometimes decide not to give up ownership of companies in certain sectors, particularly in the case of natural monopolies such as water, electricity, or infrastructure development. Owning an asset, though, does not mean that the government needs to manage it. As such, governments will sell the rights to operate the company for a specific period of time. This method aims to give the investors the freedom they need to make money, while still protecting consumers from exorbitant price increases. It can also be seen as a way of keeping ownership of a vital national asset. In 1997, Gabon used this method to privatize its water and electricity company, Sociètè d'Energie et d'Eau du Gabon (SEEG). Interested companies bid by offering the biggest cut in water and electricity rates that they could implement if they won the concession. France's Vivendi, in a consortium with the Electricity Supply Board of Ireland, won with a proposed cut of 17.25 percent and an investment requirement of at least $200 million. A successful IPO was carried out afterwards.

WHAT SHOULD HAPPEN NEXT?

Ideally, after privatization the company should become more competitive and productive. Ultimately, if it is successful, it should create more jobs and deliver better goods and services to the people of the country at a cheaper price. In addition, the government should be able to save the money it previously used to subsidize an inefficient company and instead spend it on things the country needs, such as health care, education, or roads.

To figure out if this will happen, reporters should ask these questions:

- Who bought the company?

- What are they doing to make it work better?

- Is the government doing what it must to create the right kind of economic environment for the company to succeed?

- Even *before the privatization* has been held, reporters should be asking, What has the government done to prepare for this?

The government will likely continue to play a role even after a company is sold. They will likely perform a regulatory role and may need to set up a regulatory agency in order to do this. New legislation may need to be passed. Government officials may even serve on the board of the privatized agency.

IMPORTANT INDICATORS

- *Large amounts of debt.* Few investors will want to take over a government company that is deeply in debt. The government must usually assume the company's debt and promise to pay it off separately, in order to sell the company free of debt. The alternative is to sell the company at a very low price to tempt investors to take on the debt, too.

- *Competition policies.* Turning a government-owned telecommunications monopoly over to a private investor may simply replace one monopoly (that of the government) with another (that of the new private owner). Monopolies are not known for bringing down prices. This would require a new competitive environment. Has the government issued licenses to anyone else who wants to start up similar companies? Is there a watchdog agency that makes sure the new owner's activities mimic those of a firm working in a competitive environment? The latter could include forcing the firm to allow newly emerging competitors to use its infrastructure for a reasonable fee and ensure that consumers in rural areas where there is no competition are charged reasonable rates.

- *Property rights.* There must be a functioning system of legal property rights. There will be no buyers for a company if the ownership of the land or assets it owns is in dispute. Are there any hidden disputes over ownership before the sale? Are the country's courts strong enough to enforce contracts if there is a dispute after the sale?

- A *weak financial and economic environment.* The success of a privatization is linked to the health of the overall macroeconomy—including the health of the banking sector. Once the company is privatized, are interest rates too high for it to borrow the money? Is there a viable stock market or bond market where the company can raise money? Is the banking system strong, or is it carrying a lot of bad debt? It is also important to look at whether the new owner's plans for financing are credible and well planned. The new owners will need to restructure the company in the short term, while in the medium to long term they will hopefully want to expand. It will be difficult to do either if the new owners do not have the access to the funding they need.

Next, *after the privatization*, reporters should ask: What is the government doing to make sure the transition is as smooth and beneficial as possible?

- *Layoffs.* In the short to medium term, there are likely to be job losses both before and after a company is privatized. Governments often use state-owned companies as employment-generating machines, rendering the firms overstaffed, inefficient, and unprofitable. Jobs may have to be cut before the sell-off as the new owners will not want a company with excessive employees. Often, the new owners will find that they have too many clerical and administrative workers. Laying off large numbers of white-collar workers may be necessary for the company, but it could have harmful effects for the country's economy and political stability. Is the government making plans to soften the blow? Did the government take into account the new owners' layoff plans when it negotiated the sale? Some countries (Benin, Zambia) insert five-year "no layoff" clauses into their sale contracts. Others, (Pakistan, Madagascar) require the buyer to provide severance packages to the workers it lays off. In many cases, the country receives low-interest loans from the international development agencies for this purpose. These severance packages, varying from a few months' to more than a year's salary, give the worker support while looking for a new job or provide seed capital for a new business.

- *Shortages of skilled workers.* While there are often too many administrative workers at a state-owned company, there may also be too few skilled technical employees available in the workforce. Has the government set up any education and training programs to make sure the country is producing enough skilled workers? Has the new owner developed and implemented a training program? What about new hiring?

- *Benefits*. Many government companies include housing, education, and health and child care as part of their employees' package. Has the government set up any safety net of benefits to replace the ones these workers will lose? This issue, particularly acute in the former Soviet Union, extends beyond the divestiture of the enterprise and involves myriad issues of fiscal decentralization and institutional building of local governments. The fiscal implications of these programs are extremely important and need to be carefully examined.

- *Poor tax collection and big budget deficits*. When a government privatizes a company it receives a big influx of cash. But that is just a one-time effect. Over the long run, the government will be losing out on the profits the company may have been earning while it was state owned. To make up for that lost revenue, tax reform is often needed to introduce market-based systems that replace old-style transfers with corporate taxation of the newly privatized company. The absence of such a tax system in post-privatization Russia caused a dramatic collapse in government revenues, eventually contributing to the crisis of 1998.

- *Government interference*. In cases where the government has given up management control of the company, it should not interfere with the running of the firm. Independent regulatory boards should be the ones to monitor price and competition policy.

THE NEW OWNERS

The government is not the only party to watch. The new owners are now responsible for the running of the company. Will they make it a healthy part of the economy and create jobs for the country?

There are generally three types of new owners:

- *Foreigners*. Foreign investors pay for companies with foreign exchange. This is attractive for governments, who can use that money to pay off their foreign debt. Foreigners also bring in expertise and technology. In poorer nations, there may not be a local investor with enough money to buy the company. Foreign investors, in addition, tend to have access to capital that local investors may lack. A committed foreign owner will reinvest profits in the company to ensure its long-term prosperity. Reporters should watch for foreign owners who whisk future profits out of the country instead of reinvesting them. This will spur political opposition to the whole privatization process.

- *Insiders*. Inside owners are generally the managers and employees already at the firm. On the one hand, these kinds of owners could be seen as having the most experience at running the particular company and having the most interest in seeing it succeed. On the other hand, though, selling a company to existing managers risks their continuing with the same inefficient practices behind the initial problems. "Asset stripping"—the practice of siphoning off company assets in the guise of losses—is not unknown in companies sold to insiders. Reporters should watch for inside owners who are reluctant to make any change in the way the company is run or who keep relying on the government for financial support and bailouts.

■ *Outsiders*. These owners tend to be local entrepreneurs and business-men. In their favor, they will have a good understanding of the domestic marketplace, sufficient capital for expansion and technological improvements, and proven track records in business. Reporters should watch for outside owners with political influence who force the government to protect the company from competition.

WHAT SHOULD THE NEW OWNERS BE DOING?

■ *Incentives and training for workers*. In the short term, the new owners may have to bring in executives from their old businesses with the experience they need. But are they spotting workers with managerial talent and developing those employees? They will need to do this if they want to ensure stability and profits in the long run.

■ *Strategy*. Are the new owners identifying and terminating products or services that the company provided for purely political reasons? Are they focusing on improving those areas where the company does have a competitive advantage? Are they updating technology and labor skills? If the company is not making money in the beginning, how will it gain access to short-term cash flow? Can it sell bonds or borrow from the banks? Does the new owner have the cash to invest in the company?

■ *Reporting requirements*. Is the newly privatized company transparent—is there reasonable public access to information regarding the financial health of the firm? If it is listed on the stock exchange, is it filing reports in line with international accounting standards with the securities regulator? If it is a monopoly, is it submitting accounting reports to the government or a watchdog body? Is the company training its managers and accountants in the new accounting procedures?

■ *Profitability and efficiency*. The company should tell reporters not just what profit it made but also give some measure of its efficiency. A commonly used measure of profitability is earnings before interest and net earnings. Also important is the rate of return on assets and equity. Reporters should inquire about the level of debt both in absolute terms and relative to assets (leverage). Profit statements should be checked against cash flow—some companies hide losses by exaggerating depreciation charges and other accounting gimmickry. Do the indicators improve or worsen in the first year following privatization?

FOR MORE INFORMATION

1. The Reason Public Policy Institute publishes research papers and commentaries and maintains a database on privatization issues. www.privatization.org.

2. This Web page maintained by Universiti Putra Malaysia provides many links to online resources on issues pertaining to privatization. www.lib.upm.edu.my/iispri.htm.

3. The World Bank's Web site provides information on privatization projects and developments in about seenty countries. http://www.privatizationlink.com.

4. The World Bank's Rapid Response Unit is also a good source of resources on privatization issues. http://rru.worldbank.org.

5. Padma Desai, a professor at Columbia University, is an expert on Russian privatization and a number of her papers are available on her Web site. www.columbia.edu/~pd5.

6. Professor Ann Harrison at the University of California at Berkeley has written about privatization and her papers are published on her Web site. http://are.berkeley.edu/~harrison.

7. The Center for Competitive Government at Temple University publishes research studies on privatization issues. http://www.temple.edu/prc.

8. A case study on Bulgaria's enterprise privatization can be found on the World Bank's Web site. http://www.worldbank.bg/fpres/priv-ls.

9. The Development Gateway Web site also has useful information on many issues around privatization, such as laws, costs and benefits, and labor impact. http://www.developmentgateway.org.

10. "Bank Privatization in Argentina: A Model of Political Constraints and a Different Outcome," a paper written by George Clarke and Robert Cull of the World Bank, July 1999. http://ideas.repec.org.

NOTES

1. Edward A. Snyder and Roger C. Kormendi, "The Czech Republic's Commercial Bank: Komercni Banka," Working Papers Series 6A, William Davison Institute, University of Michigan, 1996, http://eres.bus.umich.edu/docs/workpap-dav/wp6.pdf.

2. Michal Bauer et al., *The Rise and Fall of Investicni a Postovni Banka* (Prague: The Student Research Team, 2002), http://www.historieipb.cz/doc/study-en.pdf.

3. Bauer et al., *The Rise and Fall of Investicni a Postovni Banka*.

4. "Meltdown in Prague," *Business Week*, 7 August 2000.

CHAPTER SIXTEEN

CORPORATE GOVERNANCE

HOWARD I. GOLDEN

THE DAY-TO-DAY running of a corporation is entrusted to the management, who are supposed to act in the interests of the corporation—its shareholders and other stakeholders (such as workers). Under *good corporate governance*, a publicly held corporation is managed properly (not just in the interests of managers or majority shareholders) and efficiently. This benefits its shareholders and society as a whole.

When a chief executive in the U.S. spends $15,000 of his shareholder's money to buy an umbrella stand, and millions of corporate dollars go to support a royal lifestyle, it is fair to question whose interests are being served: those of the executive or those of the shareholders. It also raises the question: Where were the directors who were supposed to be "watching the shop"? If this can happen time after time in the U.S., with its shareholders protection laws, oversight by the U.S. government's Securities and Exchange Commission, and corporate activism, how much worse can corporate waste be in the nascent capital markets in developing and transition countries? How can one recognize the issues so that good reporting can educate those in emerging markets to control and prevent similar abuses?

Effective corporate governance will not guarantee efficiency in production or distribution nor magically create a profitable company; however, its absence almost always promotes the opposite. Even if one were to disregard the fairness issue—that shareholders entrust their capital to corporate managers and directors who are supposed to act as fiduciaries—society as a whole needs protection from waste and misallocation of scarce resources. Corporate governance promotes this general good by assisting corporations to act in an accountable manner.

Benefits of good corporate governance go beyond microeconomics: they can have a major effect on the path of capital inflows and, by implication, economic growth. Take the United States, for instance. As of 2003, the country was running a current-account deficit equal to roughly 5 percent of its GDP. In dollar terms, this equates to $500 billion. Even for a superpower, this is a large number. The United States needs to finance this amount by "borrowing" abroad. Anything that curtails this borrowing—including, in recent years, corporate scandals—can have (and is indeed having) important effects on the economy and its currency, the dollar. What applies to the United States applies even more so to less-developed nations. Russia's equity market, for example, languished for years since investors had no confidence in how publicly traded corporations were being managed.

It is logical to assume that when managers and corporate boards are accountable for their actions and decisions through transparent oversight, there will be increased responsiveness to societal and shareholder needs. At the very least, this promotes the common good.

WHY IS CORPORATE GOVERNANCE NEEDED?

- *It enhances a company's returns.* Well-managed corporations can attract low-cost capital by inspiring investor confidence. This, combined with greater oversight of the use of such capital, usually provides a greater return on investment to the company and its shareholders.

- *It leads to societal gains.* In many formerly communist countries, the belief that a nation of shareholders would be helpful in promoting a healthy economic climate led to mass privatization projects in which millions of citizens also became shareholders. However, lack of corporate governance eroded these gains and, ironically, promoted greater national cynicism. Proper corporate governance precludes corruption. Corrupt managers are interested in redistributing the assets of a company to themselves, their friends, their and relations; a management governed by the proper controlling authority seeks to develop the company's competitiveness in order to survive and thrive. This means, among other benefits to society, that there is a need to invest in worker training. A company's skill in training and motivating its workforce usually leads to improved economic performance. This creates a more educated workforce, a crucial factor in the postcommunist economies, with their legacy of central planning and redundant workers.

- *It promotes restructuring.* To restructure a company and become competitive in an increasingly global market, its directors and managers have to be incentivized. It is never pleasant to fire workers. This difficulty is enhanced in a homogenous society where the manager went to school with the workers and may still live in the same neighborhood.

To carry out tough decisions and create proper incentives, a strong and independent supervising body is needed.

- *Fairness to shareholders.* A company belongs to all its shareholders, not to the largest shareholder or its president or the chairman of its board of directors. The owners have a right to expect that their money will be properly handled. This is especially important in transition economies where many privatizations created shareholders out of people in the lowest economic strata of the society. For example, in the Czech Republic about 85 percent of the adult population became shareholders as a result of voucher privatization. These new shareholders knew, and still know, very little about how to create a proper control mechanism to ensure that the company was run according to their interests; in addition, they were too dispersed to act effectively, and the governing authorities did not take their rights as shareholders seriously. This allowed the old managers to remain in power and create fiefdoms, destroying rather than creating value. One effect of this was to prevent the emergence of a real capital market and consequently the slow death of the Prague stock exchange.

A basic problem with corporate governance in formerly communist regimes is the manner in which state-owned companies became public. Their creation contrasts strongly to the manner public companies were created in Western countries. In formerly communist countries, companies sprang forth fully grown as a result of privatization. Their shareholders were "reluctant capitalists"—the butcher, the baker, and the bus driver—who became owners of a company without having the sophistication, background, or even the interest to understand their rights, and conversely their obligations, as shareholders. Further, the company did not receive any new capital as a result of its change from state to private ownership. This fact burdens the supervisory authority with guarding the treasury for a large number of relatively disinterested parties, none of which has a large enough ownership stake to make it worthwhile to assist or to even become involved in the process.

In Western countries, capital markets developed as companies sought money for growth. The need to raise capital forced the offering company to make concessions to potential shareholders, often informed institutional investors, who were parting with real cash in return for a stake in that company's future profits. Such a new or growing company made the conscious decision to be governed by the constraints of supervisory bodies (a board of directors, the S.E.C., and so on) in order to raise money. This process developed over tens of years, as financial scandals due to inadequate corporate government caused investors to flee the capital markets, which led to the business community accepting greater controls. The U.S. S.E.C. was created in 1934 as a reaction to the collapse of the stock market and the Great Depression, which itself was partially due to a speculative bubble caused by the lack of real corporate governance and adequate regulatory controls. In contrast, companies in formerly communist economies made no deals, implied or contractual, with their shareholders. They were instantly burdened with a diverse group of thousands of anonymous individuals, many of whom had no concept of what share ownership meant. Those companies certainly did not want supervision or regulatory constraints and often actively tried to avoid such supervision. This is logical, since these companies only got the burden of regulation without the benefit of new money. If these countries follow a similar economic pathway as most of the developed world did until today, the business community itself will demand better standards as it comes to understand that they are the key to creating capital-market conditions that will allow them to raise the money necessary to grow. On the other hand, in those formerly communist countries in which interest rates are high and savings are low, so that capital appears inaccessible (on reasonable terms), many managers who control firms have decided that it is better for their own financial benefit simply to divert the assets of the firm or even to let the assets gradually deteriorate over time rather than reinvesting profit to help the company grow. Thus, the economic environment provides no incentive for them to advocate good corporate governance rules: there is a cost, but little prospective benefit. This is especially true if the management is elderly, and it appears as if it will be a considerable length of time—beyond their time horizon—before capital markets will work sufficiently well to make the prospect of raising capital appear reasonable.

In other parts of the emerging world, capital markets have only recently been founded or are revitalized relics of stock markets founded under colonial regimes. As many of these new emergent economies grow, capital markets naturally develop as a home for the capital of the new middle class.

One of the most important jobs of any financial journalist is to inform the public of fraudulent activities in the capital markets in order to protect the public from losing its money to con men. To this extent, any journalist should make himself aware of the basic principles of corporate governance so he can sound the alarm when these standards are laxly applied.

When examining corporate governance issues, reporters should consider the position of the officials responsible for regulating the capital markets. First, are they independent, or do they depend on the political patronage of a governing party that may itself depend on the patronage of individuals who have interests in issuing companies? Second, do they have a true understanding of the role of the capital markets, including corporate governance issues, full disclosure, and so on, or are they relatively young, inexperienced, and basically approaching the issues from a bureaucratic, formalistic perspective instead of trying to really solve the fundamental problems facing these markets? Third, do the officials of the exchanges themselves promote and fight for better corporate governance for listed companies? When the governing regulatory body—often the board of directors of the exchange itself, who are usually closer to the problem and understand the issues better in many small emerging markets—refuses to step in, who is capable of taking aggressive action to ensure that investors on their exchange benefit from their rights? Fourth, is the court system capable of understanding and implementing the intent of the law?

Too often, the regulatory authority charged with supervising these markets is staffed by people with no capital-market experience or, worse, cronies and subordinates of businesspeople who are the major players in these markets. This situation allows pyramid schemes, such as MMM in Russia or FNI in Romania, to operate with relative impunity. While not always true, it happens often enough for a good journalist to at least question whether a regulatory agency is doing its job.

Strong and effective corporate governance is especially important in emerging economies since it promotes efficient use of corporate and societal resources in the company and the broader economy. Where resources are scarce, emerging economies will have more difficulty "emerging" if their corporations continue inefficiently to allocate resources. Debt and equity capital are much more likely to be given to corporations able to utilize it efficiently in producing goods and services.

CONTROVERSIES IN CORPORATE GOVERNANCE

The advantages of good corporate governance are so compelling that one might wonder how there could be any controversies surrounding the issue? Some of the controversy arises from the fact that there are those who benefit from *bad* corporate governance, in particular those who are stealing from their firms in one way or another (for example, through overinflated compensation systems).

But there are also some difficult trade-offs:

- One of the reasons that some have advocated making takeovers more difficult is that some firms were practicing "greenmail," threatening a takeover unless payments were made.

- One of the motivations for litigation reform in the United States was that class-action suits were filed every time a stock declined in price, with the firm (shareholders) having to pay the suing law firm, whether guilty or not, to settle out of court, due to the high cost of litigation.

There are other controversies: should firms focus exclusively on shareholder value (a presumption in the U.S.,) or pay some attention to other stakeholders (e.g. workers), as in Germany? The issue is not well settled in the economics literature.

In many developing countries, there are allegations that abuses stem not so much from majority shareholders abusing minority shareholders, but from government-controlled banks providing funds to their "cronies" in corporations and not acting to ensure that the corporations use the money efficiently. (This was the often unproven allegation in East Asia.)

It is important to realize, however, that the system of corporate governance in any economy is *not* just the board of directors but the entire set of checks and balances and includes the banks, the media, the accountants, and the regulators. A good system of corporate governance attempts to make sure not only that management incentives are aligned with the interests of the shareholders but also that those who are supposed to be providing the checks and balances have the appropriate set of incentives. The recent corporate, accounting, and banking scandals in the United States reflect a failure of corporate governance, in which management incentives were not well aligned with those of shareholders, and those who were supposed to provide the checks and balances had their incentives more aligned with the interests of management than those who they were suppose to be protecting. Good reporting of corporate governance requires monitoring all of the elements of the corporate governance system.

Are the directors' interests sufficiently aligned with, and dedicated to, creating long-term value for the company?

1. Do any board members have conflicting interests that may prevent them from effectively representing all shareholders?

   - Does a member represent the government or a union?

   - Does a major shareholder control the board?

   - Does a company affiliated with the director do business with the company?

2. Does the director's compensation encourage him or her to act in shareholders' interests?

   - Will he get paid even if he does not show up at board meetings?

   - Is the pay so low she has no incentive to do real work?

3. Do the directors have ownership positions that positively align their interests with shareholders' interests?

   - Do they own any shares?

   - Do they participate only in the up side (through options) and not bear any downside risk?

4. Are any directors dependent on the cash compensation and perquisites from their directorship to an extent that precludes responsible action on the shareholders' behalf?

   - If they sit as representatives of an investment fund, are the directors' fees considered part of their salary or do they go to the fund?

   - Is the pay so high that its loss would create an economic hardship?

5. Are directors required to show up at shareholder meetings?

   - Failure to attend such meetings shows disregard for the office.

6. Does the corporation provide appropriate reporting?

   - Are required reports provided in a timely manner?

   - Timely filed with authorities?

   - Timely sent to shareholders? Note: When reports are often late, it usually is a red flag about other problems.

   - Are the reports accurate?

   - Do they disclose proposed changes in the structure or corporate policy?

- Are there footnotes explaining general accounting points?
- Are the accounts in international accounting standards or local standards that tend to hide information in general categories?
- Are the accountants reputable, or do they have conflicts of interest (for example, consulting contracts?)
- Do they provide information about the real issues?
- Do they give investors sufficient information to make informed investment decisions? *Note*: Communist accounting was not designed to assist in analysis; it was for reporting how the managers met "projected" results.

7. Are the corporate statutes accessible to shareholders?
   - Are management salaries/incentives transparent and appropriate?
   - Does the pension reflect only actual years worked, and is it commensurate with salary?
   - Is severance pay reasonable? (No golden handshakes?)
   - Are there loans from the corporation to management (or directors)?
   - Does the incentive system really create incentives?
   - Are incentives based on relative performance? Or does the manager do well if the stock market does well?
   - What happens when the market price goes down? Does compensation increase in some other form?

How easy is it for shareholders to participate?

1. Are there obstacles to voting?
   - Legal barriers, such as the need to notarize a proxy or inability to mail in proxies. Note: Proxy voting is usually legal, but the time and expense of notarizing a proxy for a small shareholder, added to the need to have the proxy personally presented by another share-holder, effectively prevents a majority of shareholders from participating in a corporate democracy.
   - Artificial barriers such as holding meetings in obscure, distant places at inconvenient times. Note: This is a red flag.
   - How is the notice of meeting delivered? In a legal advertisement published in an official bulletin that no one reads or sent by mail and/or published in a popularly read newspaper?

2. Can shareholders initiate actions?
   - What percent ownership is required to call shareholders meeting? *Note*: The higher the percent (10 percent or more), the less the ability of shareholders to participate.
   - Is the shareholders list available to others or is it a "business secret"? *Note*: In Slovenia, one can pay a small fee and legally obtain the list; in the Czech Republic, shareholder names are considered to be a "business secret."
   - How easy is it to replace management? To engage in takeovers?
   - Would shareholders be considered to be illegally "working in concert" if two or more pooled their shares to meet the percentage threshold to call a meeting?

3. What is the company's attitude toward shareholders?
   - That they are a bothersome necessity?
   - Is the board staggered, or are all directors elected at the same time?
   - Is the company open to active participation?

4. How easy is it for minority shareholders to obtain representation
   - Is there cumulative voting?

5. Are outside "independent" directors really independent, or are they friends of the management? What role do outside directors play? How accountable are they to shareholders?

Are there other checks on the behavior of the corporation?

1. For example, does it borrow from a bank that is unrelated to the corporation? Or is the lending bank a large shareholder?

2. What recourse do minority shareholders (or bondholders) have if they are cheated?

   - How easy is it to file class action suits?

   - How easy is it for aggrieved shareholders (or bondholders) to file charges with the regulatory authority?

   - Will the regulatory authority respond promptly, or is it a nightmarish bureaucracy?

3. Are analysts provided information on the firm really independent, or are they in some way beholden to the firm (as in the United States, where those for whom the analysts worked made money effectively by keeping in good stead with the firms they were supposed to be "analyzing").

4. How effective are the regulations on insider trading? On management short-selling the firm? Other abusive practices

LINKS FOR MORE INFORMATION

1. The European Corporate Governance Institute is a nonprofit organization that specializes in developing corporate governance rules within the EU legal framework. http://www.ecgi.org.

2. The World Bank's Web page. A wide range of articles, reports, and surveys of corporate governance practices in countries all over the world. http://www.worldbank.org/html/fpd/privatesector/cg.

3. The international Corporate Governance Network is a coordinating body that contains information on corporate governance from a wide variety of different countries. http://www.icgn.org.

4. Calpers is a large U.S. institution that has been active for greater corporate governance in its portfolio and around the world. Its Web page offers a wealth of information on its efforts and corporate governance in general. http://www.calpers-governance.org.

GLOSSARY

- **CAPITAL MARKET.** An organized system where ownership rights in corporations (shares or stocks) are bought and sold. Usually called a "stock exchange," the system may have brokers present on a "floor" for hours like some commodity exchanges in the U.S., or it might electronically match buy and sell orders during a one-to-four-hour period.

- **CORPORATE ACTIONS.** Usually a motion made by a shareholder, which, if approved by the majority of voting shareholders at the meeting in which the motion is made, causes the corporation to do a specific thing. This could be a change of corporate policy, or the obligation to give employees a certain type of pension.

- **INDEPENDENT DIRECTOR.** A person who does not depend financially or through familial or business connections on the chairman of the board of the company's business.

- **NONEXECUTIVE DIRECTOR.** A director who is not actively involved in running any aspect of the company.

- **NOTICE OF MEETING.** To convoke a shareholder or director meeting, formal notice requirements must be met. These requirements are found in corporate laws and the organizing documents of the company. The purpose of the notice is to give shareholders information about what will happen at the meeting, where it will be held, and when.

- **PROXY.** A vote, almost always in writing, which is cast by a substitute in place of the shareholder.

- **S.E.C.** (Securities and Exchange Commission). A legal body set up by the government to supervise the capital market. It may be part of the Ministry of Finance, the central bank, or some other state fiscal institution or be an independent organization called by some other name, but its purpose is to make certain that the market functions smoothly and that all investors are treated equally and fairly.

- **STAGGERED BOARD.** Electing each director in a different year so that the entire board cannot be changed at one annual meeting. This prevents a takeover, or at least delays it and makes it more costly.

CHAPTER SEVENTEEN

LABOR

KRISTIN HUCKSHORN

OVERVIEW

ISSUES OF labor and workers' rights have been fertile ground for journalists since the 1800s, when thousands of impoverished Europeans and Americans left farm fields for factories. A reporter needs to look no further than the strict rules governing working girls in the Lowell, Massachusetts, textile mills in the 1850s to find antecedents for the regulations issued 150 years later to Asian workers inside foreign-controlled sneaker factories.

Today, the rush toward globalization and the accompanying exodus of jobs from industrialized to developing countries has reestablished labor as a hot-button issue. Indeed, labor is one of the chief ways in which globalization affects developing countries. Many major multinational companies that sell products in consumer economies no longer produce the products that they sell; they have become branding and marketing organizations. They contract and subcontract actual production to manufacturing firms in developing countries, with long supply chains stretching back through numerous middlemen to the production of the raw materials used to make branded goods. The fact that most newly created jobs offer low-wage, labor-intensive employment has become a rallying point for groups in the West concerned about labor conditions in developing countries, some of whom are also resisting the reduction in manufacturing jobs in developed countries. These include protectionists, trade unions, college students, human-rights organizations, environmentalists and, finally, socially concerned consumers who buy the Nestlé chocolate bars made from West African cocoa, Reebok soccer balls stitched in Pakistan, Gap T-shirts sewn by young Guatemalan women, and Nike sneakers glued together in southern China. The outcry against foreign-controlled "sweatshops" has led some corporations to establish codes of conduct for factories in their supply chains and try to monitor conditions in those factories. Others have closed factories and reopened in other countries, taking the jobs with them. Groups working to improve conditions are struggling to find a way to hold private companies accountable for the treatment their workers receive, in much the same way that governments once were held accountable.

When the United States and other industrialized countries undergo an economic downturn, consumer spending and demand for many of those made-anywhere-but-here products is expected to drop. For the workforce in developing countries, that means reduced orders, more factory closings, and higher unemployment. Add to this China's ascension into the World Trade Organization and its billion-plus supply of low-wage workers and the fact that the Multi-Fiber Arrangement exemption to the WTO rules will expire in 2005, diminishing the special quotas that many countries receive to export their clothing products to the giant U.S. and European markets, and clearly, in an increasingly competitive global marketplace, developing countries will feel continued pressure to damp down both wages and demands for better working conditions as they attempt to hold onto jobs or attract new investment. Impoverished young women will continue to abandon back-breaking work in rice paddies for indoor jobs stitching and gluing sneakers for $1.50 a day. And antisweatshop groups will continue to seek ways to hold companies accountable and responsible for their workers and factories.

THE SHIFTING INVESTMENT CLIMATE: ASIA AT CENTER STAGE

Asia is at the center of the current debate over labor and workers' rights. More than half of all textiles and apparel produced each year are made in Asia, the majority in China. These low-skill jobs—cutting, stitching, gluing—traditionally pay the lowest wages within the manufacturing sector. And factory wages in some Asian countries are among the lowest in the world, below those in Mexico and Central America. These low-wage jobs disproportionately go to young women. Indeed, as many as 85 percent of the jobs in apparel factories are held by women, most of them between the ages of eighteen and twenty-three. Asia is also home to some of the world's poorest and most overpopulated countries, including China, Indonesia, and Vietnam. In agrarian countries like these, too many people and not enough arable land lead to high unemployment and social unrest. Cash-strapped governments also desperately need foreign currency.

NIKE AND VIETNAM— A LABOR CASE STUDY

KRISTIN HUCKSHORN

In the mid-1990s, Nike was riding high, its signature "swoosh" the epitome of cool. Then, reports emerged that its subcontractors in Asia, particularly in Vietnam, were underpaying and mistreating workers. The outcry turned into a public-relations disaster for Nike, one from which it still has not fully recovered. Human-rights groups, not reporters, were the first to uncover the abuse in Vietnam. Yet reporters and Nike itself should have seen the trouble coming. The case is a textbook example of how one country's history and culture helped create a hostile environment for a company like Nike.

When Nike arrived in Vietnam in 1995, the country was just emerging from two decades of postwar isolation. Vietnam ranked as one of the world's poorest and most overpopulated countries. But it had a semiliterate work force that was already earning praise from pioneering foreign investors for diligence. Freedom of association was illegal, meaning workers could not form their own unions or strike at will. And the authoritarian, communist government was eager to manufacture for export. Nike and Vietnam looked like a perfect match. The company quickly became the largest foreign-controlled employer in Vietnam with ten subcontracted factories and 35,000 to 40,000 employees.

What went wrong? Nike made several missteps that helped turn later issues inside factories into full-blown international incidents. For starters, all of Nike's subcontractors in Vietnam were South Korean and Taiwanese. Yet there are few people more hated by the Vietnamese than the Koreans (who fought with the U.S. in the Vietnam War and were guilty of numerous atrocities in southern Vietnam) and ethnic Chinese (who made up the majority of the boat people driven out of Vietnam in the 1970s and 1980s). The Korean and Taiwanese factory managers quickly gained reputations as harsh managers—an oil-and-water match with young, reticent Vietnamese women from the countryside.

Nor did Nike understand the venerated status of blue-collar "workers" in a communist country like Vietnam, where nearly every propaganda poster features a young male or female member of the proletariat. At the local level, the workers represent the backbone of the Communist Party. When Nike's subcontractors abused some workers—one was hit with a sneaker, others were made to stand in the noon-day sun or run laps around the plant—the Vietnamese viewed the abuses as an attack on the very heart of their nation.

Nike might have expected that the lack of a free press—common in many developing countries— would keep the problems inside the factories out of the newspapers. But it badly underestimated the survival instinct of the Vietnamese government. The party, under pressure from its population to loosen political and economic control and accelerate re- forms, instead found foreign-controlled companies like Nike a perfect distraction from its own internal issues. The government instructed Vietnam's two most influential labor papers to investigate and attack Nike. The editors, both government appointees, followed through with a vengeance. Nike found itself featured almost daily in the newspapers, stirring further antipathy among the Vietnamese. One labor reporter admitted that his editor was telling him what to write and when to write it. Some of the coverage was at best exaggerated, at worst false. At one point, workers en masse complained to a reporter about the lunch food and demanded the contract go to the government-controlled labor union—a deal worth tens of thousands of dollars. But many foreign reporters picked up the story without noting the controls on the Vietnamese press.

Nike finally got fed up. Its representatives told the Vietnamese government it wanted the attacks ended or it would take the jobs elsewhere. Almost overnight, the critical coverage stopped. Labor reporters said they had been ordered to write only positive stories about Nike. They then turned their attention to the company manufacturing toys for McDonald's. The problems inside Nike factories continued for another year. But one did not read about them in the Vietnamese press.

In the case of Nike and Vietnam, the country's historical and political heritage clearly had a significant role in how the story played out.

Foreign-controlled factories offer low-skill jobs and cash. The shift in manufacturing jobs from Latin America to Asia has begun to be felt throughout Mexico, for example, where 200,000 jobs are lost every year to Asian manufacturing.

CODES OF CONDUCT AND THE RISE OF CORPORATE RESPONSIBILITY

MILA ROSENTHAL

Throughout the 1970s and 1980s, technological innovation, improved transportation systems and infrastructure, political changes, and the rapidly increasing prosperity of a handful of the world's richest nations led to a rise in the production of goods across the world by workers in poor nations for consumers in wealthy nations. In those richest nations, especially the United States, awareness of these new systems of production and the inequality that came from them gave rise to a new kind of political activism that linked workers, trade unions, community groups, and nongovernmental organizations in developing countries with their increasingly sophisticated and well-organized counterparts in the developed world. Media stories exposing terrible working conditions and blatant injustices in factories producing brand-name goods for multinational companies were often uncovered by local activists and popularized by international groups. By the late 1990s, antisweatshop activism on college campuses and communities across the United States, dovetailing with antiglobalization protests against inequalities in the international distribution of wealth and resources, had made global economic development an issue of public concern.

The multinational companies who found their valuable brand names dragged through the mud of public opinion reacted strongly, if not always constructively. Nike, when accused of sweatshop problems in its subcontractors in Vietnam, Indonesia, and China, initially denied responsibility for labor conditions in the factories. Since Nike did not own the factories, it claimed, it had no control over labor relations; Nike was just a customer of the Asian factory owners. However, with continued public pressure, Nike began to respond by hiring more local staff to mediate with workers and report problems back to the head office. Eventually, Nike became part of the corporate social responsibility effort undertaken by many apparel and footwear companies in the United States.

As part of this effort, many companies have adopted codes of business practice, codes of ethics, or what are most often called "codes of conduct." These codes spell out the standards for workers that companies promise to uphold throughout their business operations, including in the factories that produce their goods. Most corporate codes of conduct promise to protect what the International Labor Organization calls the four "fundamental" or "core" labor rights. These are: the right to freedom of association and collective bargaining (guaranteeing the right to form independent labor unions); no child labor; no forced labor; and no discrimination with respect to employment. Additionally, most codes promise that workers will receive at least the national minimum wage or "prevailing industry wage" and will be paid for overtime work; codes also usually promise basic health and safety protection and prohibit abuse and harassment. (See, for example, Adidas's "Standards of Engagement" at http://www .adidas-salomon.com/en/ sustainability/coc/default.asp.).

Although many companies have adopted these codes, working conditions in the global garment industry generally remain poor. In many countries, young female garment workers cannot adequately feed and house themselves and their children on the wages they receive. Many still work more hours per week than is legally allowable, without proper overtime pay, in unhealthy and unsafe environments, and are threatened or fired immediately if they complain. Very, very few have access to an independent trade union that can negotiate their contracts or mediate a formal complaint.

Proponents of the codes movement, including many human-rights organizations, consumer groups, and some labor unions, argue that change will happen but that it takes time. While companies might have expected their suppliers to institute fair labor practices just as they instituted quality control mechanisms and other contract demands, they are learning how hard it is to improve conditions in poor countries where managers are scrambling to wring profits from their hard-working labor force. Much more effort is needed to educate workers and managers about codes and standards and to assist them in developing complaint mechanisms, independent workers organizations, and other systems that will lead to improvements.

Additionally, some companies and activists have put effort into developing more comprehensive systems to monitor and enforce their codes of conduct in factories. Some multinational companies have established "compliance" or "human rights" departments that are responsible for checking whether the companies' codes are respected.

This involves monitoring the factories, sometimes by paying independent groups to do the monitoring, and then trying to fix problems when they are found. Companies have also joined external organizations dedicated to this kind of monitoring and improvement. The Fair Labor Association, for example, is a nonprofit organization that monitors factories, as well as evaluating the internal monitoring systems of companies for many shoe and clothing companies, including Nike, Adidas, Reebok, Liz Claiborne, and Nordstrom. Social Accountability International monitors factories and certifies them as complying with labor standards according to an SAI code of conduct called "SA8000," modeled on the codes of the International Standards Organization. The Ethical Trading Initiative, based in the UK, has some European company members and designs individual monitoring processes for companies in different industries—agriculture, textiles, flower-farming—in different countries.

These corporate-responsibility efforts are very much just the first steps toward improving labor conditions in global manufacturing. Eventually, to effect serious and continuous improvement and lift manufacturing workers out of a cycle of poverty and short-term subsistence and to achieve sustainable national development, countries will need to pass and enforce decent labor laws.

The World Bank endorsed the rush to manufacturing in the early 1990s with two comprehensive and widely quoted reports. One report, in 1990, said that labor-intensive growth provided countries with one of the main exits from poverty. The other, "The East Asian Miracle," published in 1993, largely credited the remarkable economic growth and rise from poverty in eight high-performing Asian countries to a high savings rate and the governments' decisions to manufacture for export. Emerging countries could look to countries like Japan and Korea, where workers who had once glued together sneakers or plastic toys now held high-skill, high-wage jobs, and see the rewards of manufacturing for export.

In the United States, manufacturing jobs began moving overseas in the 1950s, and that shift accelerated in the 1970s. For instance, in 1972 there were 1.42 million apparel-sector jobs in the United States. By 1996, that number had fallen 41 percent, to 837,000. During the 1990s, trade barriers continued to fall, and once-isolated countries like China and Vietnam began to open for foreign investment. Foreign-controlled companies shifted jobs to Asia to take advantage of low wages and authoritarian regimes that outlawed trade-union activity. Additionally, in 1993, the U.S. Congress passed the North American Free Trade Agreement, removing trade barriers with Canada and Mexico. The earlier rise in manufacturing in Latin America was the result of preferential trade agreements with the United States, such as the Caribbean Basin Initiative and the bilateral General System of Preferences agreements. Five-year studies on the impact of NAFTA estimated that between 200,000 and 500,000 jobs shifted from the United States to Mexico after NAFTA went into effect.

Foreign-controlled companies and their subcontractors also country-shop in Asia for lower wages. Nike is a case in point. In the 1970s, the Beaverton, Oregon, company employed subcontractors based in Japan, South Korea, and Taiwan to make their shoes. In the 1980s, its subcontractors moved to China and Indonesia, which offered lower wages. In the 1990s, Nike began producing in Vietnam and Cambodia, where workers earned thirty cents to one dollar less a day than their counterparts in China and Indonesia. Nike produces its products—not only shoes, but sports gear and clothing—at more than 900 factories around the world, in a long and fast-moving supply chain. Asian countries continue to compete against one another for jobs, a strong incentive to keep wages low and unions at bay.

COVERING WORKERS' RIGHTS: PITFALLS AND PREJUDICES

A nineteen-year-old girl stands inside a poorly ventilated factory, gluing together 2 of the 150 pieces that make up an athletic shoe. She'll repeat this same step for the next eight hours, and at day's end she'll be paid $1.30 for her work.

The image of young women bonded in sweatshop labor ignites anti-sweatshop campaigns and stirs consumers to boycott brand names. It is an emotional issue, unlike other business-related issues such as currency controls or privatization, which impact ordinary people in a more obtuse way. But the image is only part of the picture. A reporter needs to leave preconceived ideas and personal prejudices at the factory door when reporting on labor and workers' rights.

The reality is that many, if not most, workers in foreign-controlled factories desperately want these jobs. Often, the other alternative is seasonal farm work—standing knee deep in muck for long hours every day to bring in the rice harvest. For young women, whose families often leave their meager farm land only to sons, the factories truly are their only route to financial independence. In the poorest countries, such as Cambodia, a factory job can mean the difference between dignity and a life of prostitution. It is imperative for reporters to talk to the workers themselves to find out what their previous lives were like and what their employment alternatives were. It is not a reporter's job to validate or invalidate the individual feelings of a worker, based on that reporter's feelings or experiences. In short: if a worker tells you that life in a factory constitutes a better life, then, for her, it does.

- Who operates the factories? Who is the foreign investor, and who is the subcontractor? What percentage of the subcontractor's orders are for which companies (for instance, some subcontractors produce only for one company, giving that company virtually complete control over the subcontractor's factory conditions and regulations)? Does the foreign-controlled company have an on-site representative?

- What is the country's minimum wage? What are entry-level workers paid? A reporter should try to see an entry-level worker's pay stub to determine actual take-home pay. Many companies require automatic deductions for housing, social security, and lunch. How much money does the worker save per month? How much did the worker make in their previous job?

- What is the minimum working age in this country? Do workers know of anyone employed at the factory under that age?

- What percentage of the workers are women? What percentage of those in supervisory jobs or higher paying jobs are women? What happens when women become pregnant? (In Honduras and Guatemala, female workers in *maquilas* have been subjected to forced pregnancy tests or asked if they are pregnant during job interviews.) Are there any instances of sexual harassment?

- How are workers punished for transgressions?

- How many hours and days are in a typical workweek? Is overtime voluntary or required?

- Are workers allowed to organize into an independent union? Are they allowed to strike? If there is a union, who picks its leadership, and who does the union report to? Is it government controlled (as is the case in Vietnam and China)? Are any mechanisms in place to respond to problems or complaints? What happens to whistleblowers or workers who file complaints?

- Are workers given quotas for production? What happens if they fail to make their quotas?

- What safety equipment is issued to workers?

- What chemicals are used during processing? Which of these chemicals are in use in industrialized countries? Does the factory use safer, water-based adhesives or more toxic, glue-based adhesives like toluene, which is proven to cause respiratory and brain damage? Occupational health and safety is a technical field requiring extensive expertise: reporters must not assume they can answer these questions themselves. A credible, independent, external source can help assess health and safety conditions in a factory.

- Do workers know of anyone who has died at the factory or suffered serious injury? If so, was the victim or her family compensated? Did this conform with national law and company policy?

- Has the factory laid off workers? What was the compensation? How did this conform with national law and company policy?

- How did the workers land the factory job? Did they have to pay a middle man to procure the placement? Are they in debt to the management, which limits their freedom to leave or complain about unfair conditions? If workers are from another country (e.g., South Asian or Southeast Asian workers in the Middle East, Saipan, Taiwan, or Korea), have their travel documents been confiscated by management, or are they free to leave?

- Are workers given opportunities for advancement or skills training?

- Does the foreign-controlled company have a code of conduct? Is it visible in the factory?

- Who monitors the factory conditions for the foreign-controlled company? Is there an independent auditor? Are outsiders (reporters, human-rights groups) allowed to tour the factory? Have workers met with monitors or a representative from the foreign-controlled company?

- Is the foreign-controlled company or source brand a member of the Fair Labor Association, the Ethical Trading Initiative, the Social Accountability International, the World-wide Responsible Apparel Program, or another industry-wide code of conduct program? If not, does the company have its own code of conduct and implementation program (such as Gap, Levi Strauss, or Mattel)? If so, it has probably been visited by external monitors, who may issue periodic reports. It has also agreed to adhere to a code of conduct that includes rules on forced labor, child labor, health and safety, minimum wages, and work hours. Is the company adhering to its own standards as set out in its code of conduct?

- How does the factory compare to another foreign-controlled factory manufacturing the same goods? How does it compare to a locally owned factory producing those goods?

LINKS FOR MORE INFORMATION

1. Bartlett, Donald, and James Steel. "Importing Goods, Exporting Jobs." *Philadelphia Inquirer*, 9 September 9 1996; and Bartlett, Donald, and James Steel. "Endangered Label, Made in USA." *Philadelphia Inquirer*, 10 September 1996.

2. Multistakeholder initiatives bring together companies, nongovernmental organizations, labor unions, and other groups that issue a code of conduct on labor standards and implement a monitoring program. The Fair Labor Association includes North American universities, major footwear and apparel companies (Nike, Reebok, Liz Claiborne, and others), human-rights groups, and others, and it issues public monitoring reports. http://www.fairlabor.org.

3. Ethical Trading Initiative is a UK-based consortium whose members include Chiquita, Marks and Spencer, and NEXT. http://www.ethicaltrade.org.

4. Social Accountability International certifies factories as following a code of conduct. Members include Dole Food, Toys R Us, Eileen Fisher. http://www.sa-intl.org.

5. Worker Rights Consortium investigates allegations of code violations at factories producing for member universities. http://www.workersrights.org.

6. Worldwide Responsible Apparel Production was established by the American Apparel and Footwear Association without civil-society involvement and is considered the weakest of the code initiatives. Members include the Sara Lee Corporation and Osh Kosh B'Gosh. http://www.wrapapparel.org.

7. Human Rights Watch has information in the "Labor and Human Rights" section of its "Global Issues" page. hrw.org.

8. Clean Clothes Campaign is a European-based antisweatshop group that issues reports and urgent appeals on specific cases on its Web site. http://www.cleanclothes.org.

9. The Campaign for Labor Rights issues appeals on its Web site. http://campaignforlaborrights.org.

10. *Behind the Label* is the antisweatshop e-newsletter of the Union of Needletrades, Industrial, and Textile Employees. http://www.behindthelabel.com.

11. AFL-CIO is the federation of American unions. http://www.aflcio.org.

12. International Labour Organization is the specialized UN agency to promote social justice and internationally recognized human and labor rights. http://www.ilo.org.

13. National Labor Committee. www.nlcnet.org.

14. Sweatshop Watch, a coalition devoted to eliminating sweatshop exploitation. www.sweatshopwatch.org.

- **EXPORT-PROCESSING ZONES** (in Latin America, *maquiladoras* or *maquilas*). This is a term used to describe industrial zones—often with geographic barriers—in which companies manufacture for export with few restrictions and a loose regulatory environment. Often, governments impose few trade or environmental barriers to attract investors to these zones. Some countries do not impose minimum wage laws for foreign-controlled factories inside the zones. Most jobs inside the EPZs are held my women.

- **GENDER GAP.** Women hold most of the low-wage, labor-intensive factory jobs, particularly in the apparel industry where that number is as high as 85 percent. Apparel employers say that they prefer women workers for a variety of reasons: they have smaller fingers and hands than men and thus are more dexterous and better able to do delicate stitching work; they can be paid less than men; and they are less likely to cause unrest within a factory or unionize. At least one human-rights group that focuses on labor rights in China has charged that such hiring is discriminatory and calls for a mandatory increase in the number of male workers at foreign-controlled factories.

- **LIVING WAGE.** Many antisweatshop groups argue that foreign-controlled companies have a corporate responsibility to pay workers in overseas factories a "living wage" that enables those workers to live with dignity. There is wide disagreement, however, on what constitutes a living or dignity wage. Some would include all basic needs, such as housing, food, energy, clothing, health care, education, potable water, childcare, and savings for an average family. Others would include only such essentials as food, water, and housing. Because most workers in low-wage apparel jobs are young, unmarried women, some would calculate a wage based only on an individual's needs, not a family's. Advocates generally agree that there is no "one-size-fits-all" global minimum wage because of different standards of livings and costs in different countries.

- **PROTECTIONISM.** When a government places duties or quotas on imports to protect domestic industries from global competition.

- **SUBCONTRACTOR.** Many large apparel companies hire outside contractors to build and operate factories, thus removing themselves from day-to-day operations and, in some cases, responsibility for worker-related issues. The contractors serve as middle men. They take the orders from the foreign-controlled company and hire, pay, and discipline workers. For instance, Nike contracts all of its footwear and apparel manufacturing to subcontractors, most of them Korean and Taiwanese companies that have worked with Nike since the 1960s. Abusive treatment of workers by some subcontractors and a lack of oversight by foreign-controlled companies is a central issue in the debate over workers' rights.

CHAPTER EIGHTEEN

ACCOUNTING

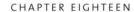

JANE M. FOLPE AND
HERBERT K. FOLPE

INTRODUCTION

U NDERSTANDING ACCOUNTING is essential to understanding what is happening in the world of business. And yet, until recently, accounting and the accounting profession did not receive much press from the mainstream media. Sure, a few journalists followed the profession and its standard-setting bodies. The U.S. financial press did some reporting on accounting scandals, including those of the mid-1990s that involved top executives at certain firms attempting to "manage earnings" in order to keep stock prices high. But more often than not, mainstream press coverage either glossed over how businesses accounted for their activities or offered the firm's own—and often incorrect—analysis and interpretation of its financial data. The healthy journalistic skepticism toward public-relations announcements found in other areas of the media was sadly lacking where accounting matters were involved.

It was the spectacular fall of two U.S. companies in late 2001 and early 2002, caused in large part by the market's reaction to the accounting scandals that engulfed each, that catapulted the topic of accounting into the media at large. Energy giant Enron and telecommunications firm World-Com revealed they had hidden liabilities, understated expenses, or employed other questionable accounting devices to maintain stock prices at artificially high levels. Outside auditors had attested to the fairness of these companies' financial statements, as auditors do for all financial statements of public companies. In Enron's case, this approval came from the Houston office of the global accounting firm Arthur Andersen. This office, and later the entire firm, was accused of obstructing justice by destroying documents that were pertinent to the government's investigation of the Enron scandal (Andersen also audited WorldCom). This led to the demise of Andersen, considered by many to be the world's preeminent accounting firm.

Enron and WorldCom were not the first companies to be involved in accounting scandals. Nor was Arthur Andersen the first accounting firm to get in trouble for attesting to the fairness of financial statements that later turned out to be questionable. It was the scope of the Enron scandal and the probing examination of "all things accounting" that soon followed that distinguished these scandals from the ones before it.

The events of the last two years have shown that every business journalist in the United States and abroad—whether he or she covers energy, equities, privatizations, or even entertainment—needs to know the basics of accounting. Using numbers instead of words, accounting chronicles the story of a company over time and at particular points in time—from its inception to its consolidation or, perhaps, its liquidation—as it grows or shrinks or simply stagnates. As with any unfolding story, it is imperative that journalists understand what is behind the elements that go into the story.[1]

This chapter will seek to provide journalists with an understanding of the varied underlying elements that ultimately define the makeup of the financial statements of multinational companies. It will also discuss the larger institutional context in which financial reporting takes place and how it is rapidly changing. This context has taken on an even more important role in the era of globalization, in which business knows no borders. The most important changes in that institutional context include

- the formation of the International Accounting Standards Board in 2000 (with a formal board taking office in January of 2001);

- the decision by the European Union to require all companies that list on European exchanges to adopt IASB pronouncements or *International Financial Reporting Standards* by 2005;[2]

- the efforts to harmonize all national accounting standards, especially those of the U.S. Financial Accounting Standards Board with those of the IASB; and

- the Sarbanes-Oxley Act, passed by the U.S. Congress in the wake of the Enron and WorldCom scandals. This legislation paves the way to tougher regulation of financial reporting, auditing, and corporate governance.

Journalists need to be aware of the full breadth of these institutional changes in order to adequately report on business matters involving international accounting.

Accounting[3] has been defined as the "process of gathering, compiling, and reporting the financial history of an organization."[4] Just as historians of any subject have developed tools and methods to establish what occurred, accountants too have developed their own tools and methods. These methods, such as double-entry bookkeeping and systems of internal accounting control, capture the information required to relate the financial history of a business, nonprofit organization, or governmental entity. Their final product is not a book or an article but, instead, the financial statements included in public reports.

A company's financial history "is distinguished by the use of economic concepts, accounting conventions, and institutional pressures that guide its construction."[5] This financial history is captured in financial statements that entities issue on a periodic basis, including yearly audited financial statements. (Full financial statements come out once a year. Interim statements, which are generally issued quarterly and tend to be unaudited, are not as complete and should not be substituted for the annual report.) With minor national variations, those financial statements generally consist of the following:

- *Balance sheet, or statement of financial position*. A balance sheet presents a picture of a company's wealth on one particular day. It shows what the company has (assets), what the company owes (liabilities), and the difference between the two, which is the equity of the owners. (Assets = Liabilities + Stockholders' equity).

- *Income statement and statement of shareholders' equity*. The income statement provides relevant information about an entity's revenues, expenses, gains, and losses that can be used to analyze how the company did in the past and judge how it might do in the future. The statement of shareholders' equity gives the amount and sources of the changes in equity that result from transactions with shareholders.

- *Statement of cash flows*. The statement of cash flows gives information about the cash receipts and cash payments of an organization, in other words, the money going in and out of a company, during a certain amount of time. It is fundamental for assessing a company's ability to pay off its debts.

- *Notes to financial statements*. The notes are an *integral* part of financial statements, often containing information about the business that is not found elsewhere. The notes include information about the nature of an entity, the accounting practices and rules followed in preparing the financial statements, and contingencies that could affect the future financial condition and performance of the entity.

Inherent in financial statements are a host of estimates, assumptions, and judgments that involve varying degrees of subjectivity. For example, the calculation of expenses such as bad debts and depreciation depends on estimates. For bad debts, such an estimate involves judgments about whether certain customers will pay all (or a portion) of the amounts they owe. In the case of depreciation, estimates must be made about the useful productive lives of buildings, machinery, and other long-lived assets. Such estimates, besides dealing with rather straightforward issues such as how long a building can stand, must also take into account much more subtle questions such as technological change that can lead to obsolescence for a machine far before it physically wears out.

Likewise, the values attached to many assets and liabilities depend on estimating fair values where no active markets (such as the New York Stock Exchange) exist for these assets or liabilities. These values also may involve estimates of the effects of future events. For example, companies that hold investments in biotechnology start-up ventures that are trying to develop cures for cancer and other diseases need to assign values to such investments. That valuation process involves, among other matters, estimates and judgments about both the scientific and commercial feasibility of any products ultimately developed in such ventures. Accountants must also deal with uncertainty in developing these estimates. In the case of liabilities, determining the ultimate amounts a company will pay pensioners some forty or fifty years in the future involves estimates based on assumptions about many future events (for example, when employees will retire, interest rates in the future, returns on investments, and so on).

As we have seen, an accountant's job is to chronicle the financial history of a business, nonprofit organization, or governmental entity. He does this by attempting to measure an entity's wealth and the changes in its wealth. This measurement is based on three fundamental concepts, namely:

- financial value

- wealth

- comprehensive income[6]

Financial value, for purposes of accounting, generally represents the amount of money a company would receive if it sold an item or the item's value in its current use to the company. For example, the value of an entity's investment in U.S. Treasury notes would be the market value of the notes based on their price in bond markets where such financial instruments are traded. The value of a plant used to manufacture computers (and that the company is not holding as investment for future sale), on the other hand, would be its value "in use," which is generally its acquisition cost minus accumulated depreciation.

Depreciation, for accounting purposes, is not intended to be a measure of how much a long-lived asset such as a manufacturing plant decreases in value. Rather, it is an accounting convention used to allocate the cost of such long-lived assets by expensing them over the periods they benefit. For example, a computer that cost $5,000 with a five-year useful life would be expensed through five yearly depreciation charges of $1,000. In those cases, however, where it is expected that the products produced by the plant are going to bring in less cash than it costs the company to carry the plant, or its acquisition cost minus accumulated depreciation, the company would record an "impairment" loss to reflect the decrease in the value "in use" of this plant.

Wealth represents the total financial values of all the things an entity owns or controls by other means minus the financial value of what it owes to others. For example, if a newly formed company had one asset, a plant costing $100,000 that was financed by $50,000 of cash invested by the company' shareholders and a $50,000 loan evidenced by a mortgage, the company's wealth would be $50,000.

Comprehensive income measures the changes in an entity's wealth over time but does not take into account any changes that come about because of what shareholders invest or receive in dividends.[7]

While the above-mentioned concepts are essential to understanding what goes into measuring an entity's wealth and changes in that wealth, they do not offer a concrete way to chronicle these changes. This is why accounting conventions, or the rules under which accountants record the financial history of an entity, are needed. Accounting conventions translate the broad abstract concepts that define wealth into concrete rules that can be applied to different types of transactions. That translation often involves compromising the intellectual purity of these concepts in the interest of producing standards that are workable and capable of being consistently applied by different preparers. Commonly referred to as *"generally accepted accounting principles,"* or GAAP, such rules have developed (generally on a national basis) to ensure some degree of consistency and comparability in reporting.

Accounting rules, or conventions, address three areas:

- measurement

- recognition

- disclosure[8]

Measurement rules specify how financial values are assigned to the items included in financial statements. For example, investments in marketable securities are generally shown at current market values, not at the cost for which they were acquired. Properties such as office buildings, on the other hand, are generally shown at what it cost to buy them, minus accumulated depreciation, or an allocation of that cost over time, even if they have since increased substantially in value.

Recognition rules govern "the process of formally recording or incorporating an item into the financial statements of an entity as an asset, liability, revenue, expense, or like item."[9] The financial statements included by multinational companies that are filed with different national securities regulators such as the U.S. Securities and Exchange Commission must be prepared using recognition rules that are consistent with the *accrual method of accounting*. Accrual accounting requires that assets, liabilities, revenues, and expenses must be recorded when the transaction actually happens and not just when the company receives the money.[10] For example, the sale of a product is generally recorded (or recognized) as an asset (for example, an account receivable) and revenue when the buyer actually receives the product and not when he or she pays for the item in cash. Similarly, a company generally must recognize a liability (or an account payable) and an expense in the period in which it receives a service or product, not in the period in which it pays the supplier.

Disclosure rules mandate additional information about the entity and its accounting conventions that must also be included in financial statements to be presented in accordance with GAAP. Many of these required disclosures are made in the notes to the financial statements.

GENERALLY ACCEPTED ACCOUNTING PRINCIPLES

Accounting standards have historically been established on a national level, resulting in major differences between the standards of different countries. At present, U.S. GAAP, issued by the U.S. standards setter, the Financial Accounting Standards Board, is more common in the United States, while International Financial Reporting Standards are more common elsewhere in the world. A number of differences exist between U.S. GAAP and IFRS that affect comparisons of financial statements of multinational corporations involved in the same industry. There is, however, a strong movement afoot to harmonize national standards and establish international accounting standards. That subject is discussed in greater detail in a later section of this chapter.

PURPOSES AND BASIC COMPONENTS OF FINANCIAL STATEMENTS

BALANCE SHEET/STATEMENT OF FINANCIAL POSITION

The balance sheet presents a picture of a company's wealth on one particular day: it shows what the company has (assets), what the company owes (liabilities), and the difference between the two, which is the equity of the owners. Information provided in the balance sheet, used with the notes and information in other financial statements, will help journalists assess the financial condition of a company. It will aid them in ascertaining its liquidity (can the company pay its bills tomorrow?) and solvency (does this company have the resources to stay in business?). Among other things, the balance sheet gives some idea of how much cash should come into the company as a result of resources the company owns or controls. It also shows, either directly or indirectly, how much cash the company needs to have on hand in order to pay the majority of its debts.[11]

One side of the balance sheet shows the resources that the company has (*assets*); the other shows how these resources are being financed, either by obligations to outsiders (*liabilities*) or by owners' *equity*. Assets represent "probable future economic benefits obtained or controlled by a particular entity as a result of past transactions or events."[12] Assets may consist of tangible resources, such as a plant or factory, intangible resources, such as a patent, or claims against others, such as accounts receivables. The common characteristic is that each such resource or claim is going to produce cash: The company's factory makes products that are sold for cash. The company's patents give it the exclusive right to produce something that is later sold for cash. A customer or supplier will pay cash to settle his or her claim.

An asset is an asset only if the economic benefit it provides is the sole property of an entity—or under its sole control. No other entity can have access to the economic benefit, or it is not considered an asset. For example, companies cannot claim as an asset access to a river that helps power a plant, even if they have helped to clean up the river.[13] In addition, for an item to qualify as an asset, the company must have it in its possession, that is, the transaction or event giving rise to the entity's control of benefit must have already occurred.

But in order to gain economic benefits, a company usually needs to make economic sacrifices. The second half of the balance sheet begins by detailing these sacrifices, or *liabilities*. Liabilities represent "probable future sacrifices of economic benefits arising from present obligations of an entity to transfer assets or provide services to other entities as a result of past transactions or events."[14] In other words, the company's future potential cash flow will be affected because of something—either cash or services—that it owes to someone else, like a supplier (accounts payable) or an employee (accrued wages).

A liability is only a liability if there is no way around the economic sacrifice that it supposes. In addition, the obligation arising from the liability must arise from a past transaction or event, such as work done by an employee or the receipt of goods or services from a supplier. Many, but not all liabilities are based on contracts and other legally enforceable agreements such as agreements to pay suppliers and employees for goods and services they provide.

After detailing assets and liabilities, the balance sheet then goes on to look at owner's equity. *Equity* is defined as the interest of shareholders in a company, represented by the difference between total assets and total liabilities.[15] The equity in a corporation (the most common form of business enterprise engaged in international activities) is generally referred to as *shareholders' equity* and includes two distinct components. The first component is the equity that results from what owners contribute to and receive from the company, that is, the purchase of shares and the receipt of dividends by shareholders in a corporation. The second component is the equity that comes about as a result of the entity's profit-seeking activities or, in other words, the revenues and gains that the company generates beyond expenses and losses.

Equity from shareholders can take the form of *common stock*, and, in certain cases, *preferred stock*. Common stock is a piece of paper that represents a "piece" of a corporation. If you hold common stock, you hold ownership in a company. Common stock holders do very well if the company does well and the price of the stock goes up because they can sell their ownership—or shares of stock—at a higher price. But, if the entity fails, common shareholders are last in line to get distributions.

Preferred stock represents a claim on the assets of the entity that takes precedence over the claims of common shareholders. The nature of the preferences given to this class of shareholders may differ from entity to entity. Usually, holders of preferred stock receive dividends at a stated rate before any dividends are paid to common shareholders. If the entity fails and has to be liquidated, preferred shareholders are first in line (after creditors) to get distributions before common shareholders.

Retained earnings represent all the equity produced by a company's operations since it began (equivalent to its accumulated profits and losses included yearly in net income) minus all the dividends that have been paid to shareholders. For example, if a company began business on 1 January 2001 and had a net income of $10,000 in 2001 and a net loss of $5,000 in 2002, its retained earnings as of 31 December 2002 would be $5,000. Distributions of dividends to shareholders generally must be made from retained earnings.

INCOME STATEMENT

The second and, in the opinion of many analysts, the most important financial statement is the *income statement*, which in certain countries is called *the profit and loss account*. The purpose of this statement, which is also known as the earnings statement, is to provide information about an entity's *revenues, expenses, gains*, and *losses*, that is, the resources that come into a company and those that go out, as well as the amount left over to add to the company's equity. This statement can help journalists analyze how a company did in the past and judge how it might do in the future. It can also give journalists certain information needed to assess the future earnings and cash flows of a company.

An income statement, which captures a company's activities during a certain time period between two balance sheets, reflects the changes in net assets in the balance sheet that result principally from the "operations" of a company. As indicated above, the income statement shows the relationship of four elements—*revenues, expenses, gains*, and *losses*.

Revenues are increases in assets or decreases in liabilities or a combination of both that result from a company's *central operating activities*.

Expenses are decreases in assets or increases in liabilities or a combination of both that result from a company's *central operating activities*.

Gains are similar to revenues, in other words, they increase assets or decrease liabilities, except that they result from *peripheral activities* of an organization.

Losses are similar to expenses—they decrease assets or increase liabilities, except that they result from *peripheral activities* of an organization.[16]

The most important thing to remember about the differences between revenues and gains and expenses and losses, respectively, is that both are directly related to a company's definition of its central operating activities. Dell describes itself as "the world's leading computer systems company" in its company overview on its Web site, so when Dell sells a laptop it considers the selling price to be revenue. But when it sells one of the marketable securities it holds as a short-term or long-term investment it considers the difference between the selling price and the amount it paid to acquire that investment as either a gain or loss. Dell considers the cost of producing the laptop sold as an expense but views the decrease in the value of a building destroyed by fire as a loss.

Unlike the balance sheet, the format of the income statement is not the same for all companies. Companies differ not only on how many intermediate items, such as *gross margin* and *operating income*, they include before showing the final total of *net income*, they also differ on how to define—and calculate—these intermediate items. For example, there is no definition of operating income in authoritative accounting literature. That means that this important measure of performance may be calculated differently for companies in the same industry. Journalists need to be aware that they might not be able to compare the operating income of two companies that appear to be in the same business.

STATEMENT OF SHAREHOLDERS' EQUITY

The principal purpose of this statement is to report the amount and the sources of the changes in equity that result from transactions with shareholders. For this reason, the statement of shareholders' equity reports the changes in each of the components of equity in the balance sheet, or the changes in common stock and preferred stock. In addition, for companies that follow U.S. GAAP, this statement also reports in most cases the changes in *other comprehensive income*. As noted in an earlier section of this chapter, comprehensive income is defined in U.S. GAAP as all changes in equity except for what shareholders invest or receive in dividends. It is a broader concept than net income.

Comprehensive income, in turn, is divided into two components—net income and other comprehensive income. The changes in equity that enter into net income are displayed in the income statement. Other comprehensive income, on the other hand, includes "revenues, expenses, gains, and losses that under [U.S. GAAP] are included in comprehensive income but excluded from net income."[17] This is where most of the effects of foreign currency fluctuations are accounted for.

Under current U.S. GAAP, two of the most important items included in other comprehensive income are (1) unrealized gains and losses on certain investments in marketable securities and (2) certain unrealized gains and losses arising from the use of derivatives as hedging instruments. The rationale for excluding such items from net income, which has the effect of including them in other comprehensive income, has been that the volatility of such items would distort the analysis of a company's performance. Not all accountants and standard setters agree with this argument. In their ongoing projects on reporting financial performance, both the FASB and IASB have tentatively decided to eliminate the option to display items of other comprehensive income in a separate financial statement.

STATEMENT OF CASH FLOWS

The statement of cash flows provides information about the money going in and out of an organization during a period of time. That statement can help journalists answer the following questions:

- How much cash have the company's operations produced?

- What are the other sources of cash besides operations, like investment and debt?

- Can this company pay its debts?[18]

When looking at the cash flow statement, it is important to remember that this is the only one of the financial statements that is calculated by the cash-based method of accounting, as opposed to the accrual method of accounting. Accrual accounting requires that assets, liabilities, revenues, and expenses must be recorded when the transaction actually happens and not just when the company receives the money. The cash flow statement shows when cash actually comes into and goes out of the company.

In order to show the different sources of cash, the statement of cash flows separates cash receipts into three distinct categories—(1) *financing activities*, (2) *investing activities*, and (3) *operating activities*. Cash receipts and payments from financing activities represent the cash that comes into and goes out of the entity as it issues and sells debt and shares of its different classes of stock. Cash receipts and payments from investing activities take into account the cash that comes into and goes out of an entity as it buys and sells long-term assets, such as property, plant and equipment, and long-term investments. Cash receipts and payments from operating activities generally include the cash that comes from carrying out the business activities that are central to operations, for example, production and sale of major products.

Many financial analysts believe that the cash flow statement presents the most accurate picture of a company's health. This is because it shows how money is moving through the business without any reflection of the different accounting treatments (such as calculations based on subjective variables like depreciation and estimate of bad debts) used in other financial statements to get the final numbers. This does not mean, however, that the numbers in the cash flow statement are foolproof. As with all parts of the financial statements, the numbers are only as good as the information behind them, which brings us to the next section.

NOTES TO FINANCIAL STATEMENTS

It is absolutely essential to read these notes in order to understand and/or analyze a company and its business. An enormous amount of information that is vital to a journalist's understanding of a company is contained in the notes. The types of notes to financial statements fall into four broad categories, namely:

- Summary of significant accounting policies

- Detailed disclosures for specific assets, liabilities, and equity

- Disclosures for specific revenue and expense categories

- Other note disclosures, such as where the company does business around the world and what percentage of the company's net revenue and operating income come from these different segments

All of the notes to the financial statements must be read carefully if a journalist truly wants to understand a company's financial statements. The first category, the note or notes that set forth the summary of significant accounting policies may, however, be the most important type, as it summarizes the various accounting policies and rules adopted by the company. (If there has been a change in accounting policy that is material, mention of this would also appear in the auditor's opinion.)

The other categories are also quite important in understanding individual asset, liability, revenue, and expense items. That importance is illustrated in the section of this chapter that examines the Dell balance sheet and income statement. Therein are continuing references to various notes to the Dell financial statements that contain important information about specific assets, liabilities, revenues, expenses, gains, and losses.

ANALYSIS OF DELL'S CONSOLIDATED STATEMENT OF FINANCIAL POSITION AND INCOME STATEMENT

This section of the chapter examines in detail actual financial statements of a well-known multinational, Dell Computer Corporation (Dell), that are prepared in accordance with U.S. GAAP. The purpose of such an examination is to illustrate certain concepts discussed in the earlier section. This section is organized in the following way: The "Consolidated Statement of Financial Position," or "Balance Sheet," is reproduced on page 211 and the "Consolidated Statement of Income" for the fiscal year ended 31 January 2003 on page 212. A letter or number reference has been added for each item on both statements. The letters and numbers refer to explanations of the nature of each item that are included in "Explanation of References" on pages 213 to 219. These statements were taken from the 2003 Dell Corporation 10K; please refer to that document for the complete Dell Corporation financial statements and accompanying footnotes.

DELL COMPUTER CORPORATION

CONSOLIDATED STATEMENT OF FINANCIAL POSITION
(in millions)

	January 31, 2003	February 1, 2002
ASSETS		
Current assets:		
Cash and cash equivalents Ⓐ	$ 4,232	$ 3,641
Short-term investments ... Ⓑ	406	273
Accounts receivable, net ... Ⓒ	2,586	2,269
Inventories ... Ⓓ	306	278
Other ... Ⓔ	1,394	1,416
Total current assets Ⓕ	8,924	7,877
Property, plant and equipment, net Ⓖ	913	826
Investments ... Ⓗ	5,267	4,373
Other non-current assets ... Ⓘ	366	459
Total assets	$15,470	$13,535
LIABILITIES AND STOCKHOLDERS' EQUITY		
Current liabilities:		
Accounts payable ... Ⓙ	$ 5,989	$ 5,075
Accrued and other ... Ⓚ	2,944	2,444
Total current liabilities Ⓛ	8,933	7,519
Long-term debt ... Ⓜ	506	520
Other ... Ⓝ	1,158	802
Commitments and contingent liabilities (Note 6) Ⓞ	—	—
Total liabilities	10,597	8,841
Stockholders' equity:		
Preferred stock and capital in excess of $.01 par value; shares issued and outstanding: none ... Ⓟ	—	—
Common stock and capital in excess of $.01 par value; shares authorized: 7,000; shares issued: 2,681 and 2,654, respectively Ⓠ Ⓡ	6,018	5,605
Treasury stock, at cost; 102 and 52 shares, respectively ... Ⓢ	(4,539)	(2,249)
Retained earnings ... Ⓣ	3,486	1,364
Other comprehensive income (loss) ... Ⓤ	(33)	38
Other	(59)	(64)
Total stockholders' equity	4,873	4,694
Total liabilities and stockholders' equity	$15,470	$13,535

DELL COMPUTER CORPORATION

CONSOLIDATED STATEMENT OF INCOME
(in millions, except per share amounts)

		Fiscal Year Ended		
		January 31, 2003	February 1, 2002	February 2, 2001
Net revenue	(A)	$35,404	$31,168	$31,888
Cost of revenue	(B)	29,055	25,661	25,445
Gross margin	(1)	6,349	5,507	6,443
Operating expenses:				
Selling, general and administrative	(C)	3,050	2,784	3,193
Research, development and engineering	(D)	455	452	482
Special charges	(E)	—	482	105
Total operating expenses	(F)	3,505	3,718	3,780
Operating income	(2)	2,844	1,789	2,663
Investment and other income (loss), net	(G)	183	(58)	531
Income before income taxes and cumulative effect of change in accounting principle	(3)	3,027	1,731	3,194
Provision for income taxes	(H)	905	485	958
Income before cumulative effect of change in accounting principle	(4)	2,122	1,246	2,236
Cumulative effect of change in accounting principle, net (I)		—	—	59
Net income	(5)	$ 2,122	$ 1,246	$ 2,177
Earnings per common share: (6)				
Before cumulative effect of change in accounting principle:				
Basic	(J)	$ 0.82	$ 0.48	$ 0.87
Diluted	(K)	$ 0.80	$ 0.46	$ 0.81
After cumulative effect of change in accounting principle:				
Basic	(J)	$ 0.82	$ 0.48	$ 0.84
Diluted	(K)	$ 0.80	$ 0.46	$ 0.79
Weighted average shares outstanding:				
Basic	(J)	2,584	2,602	2,582
Diluted	(K)	2,644	2,726	2,746

For the sake of brevity, the notes to the financial statements are not reproduced here. However, when a specific reference is made to something in the notes, an endnote appears to guide readers to this reference in documents readily available online.

EXPLANATION OF REFERENCES

CONSOLIDATED STATEMENT OF FINANCIAL POSITION

Assets

A. *Cash and cash equivalents*. All companies need to have hard currency on hand or within reach. Cash represents the actual funds available to the company in petty cash or an account at a local bank. Cash equivalents generally refer to highly liquid investments such as U.S. Treasury Bills and bank certificates of deposits that have original maturities of three months or less at the date of purchase.

B. *Short-term investments*. Those investments in financial instruments such as treasury notes and commercial paper whose maturity is more than three months at the date of purchase but less than a year.

C. *Accounts receivable, net*. The amount that the company stands to receive from customers in exchange for filling an order. "Net" means an allowance for those accounts considered to be uncollectable has been subtracted from total amount owed to Dell by customers. Normally, the amount of such allowance will be disclosed on the face of the balance sheet or in the notes to the financial statements. Dell discloses this information (allowance = $71) in note 10 to its financial statements, "Supplemental Consolidated Financial Information."[19]

D. *Inventories*. Items that a company has in stock for sale or items that are used to produce what is sold. In the case of Dell, this asset category would include both finished products—for example, desktop and notebook computers—as well as the components that go into making those finished products. The amount of each of these categories of inventory is disclosed in note 10 to the Dell financial statements.

E. *Other*. In preparing financial statements, an entity is permitted to combine accounts with smaller balances in one caption. The U.S. Securities and Exchange Commission has a general rule that any assets with balances that are equal to or greater than 5 percent of total current assets need to be listed separately on the balance sheet.[20] This caption probably includes items such as prepaid insurance, deposits, and other items that will benefit operations within one year of the balance sheet date and therefore are included in current assets.

F. *Total current assets*. The authoritative accounting literature uses the term "current assets" to refer to cash and other assets that most likely will be converted into cash within the current operating cycle. For example, inventory sold becomes an account receivable from customer, who then pays in cash, during the normal operating cycle of the business, which is generally considered to be one year.[21]

G. *Property, plant and equipment.* Office buildings, manufacturing plants, and manufacturing and office equipment that Dell owns or leases in order to conduct its business. The amounts of each of the subcategories making up this category are disclosed in note 10 to the Dell financial statements. Assets in this category must satisfy the following conditions. They must be: "acquired for use in operations and not for resale; . . . long-term in nature [i.e., they have a productive life of more than one year] and usually . . . subject to depreciation; [and they must] possess physical substance."[22]

H. *Investments.* Financial instruments such as shares of stocks and bonds. Dell discloses in note 2 to its financial statements that "all investments with remaining maturities in excess of one year are recorded as long-term investments."[23]

I. *Other non-current assets.* Again, a grouping of assets, in this case all noncurrent, or those that do not meet the definition of current assets in (F) above, that did not reach the required threshold for separate disclosure.

Liabilities

J. *Accounts payable.* What companies owe to suppliers for goods and services that have already been received. Amounts included here are generally based on bills received from suppliers.

K. *Accrued and other.* These current liabilities represent other obligations related to the current operating cycle that are disclosed in detail in note 10 to the Dell financial statements. This category includes obligations related to warranties, employees' wages, deferred income, sales and property taxes, income taxes, and so on. In many cases, the amount for each such item must be estimated.

L. *Total current liabilities.* Those obligations such as accounts payable or accrued liabilities that a company must use its existing resources, or current assets, to pay off.[24] If a company does not have enough total current assets to cover this category, it must borrow in order to do so.

M. *Long-term debt.* Any kind of formal promise to pay back notes or bonds in the future. Since these payments are not due until more than one year from the date of the balance sheet, they are classified as long-term liabilities. It is always important to read the note associated with this category for more information on the terms of the debt and its repayment. Note 2 to the Dell financial statements in a section labeled "Long-Term Debt and Interest Rate Risk Management" spells out the specific terms of this debt—that is, interest rate, repayment date(s), and other important provisions—as required by U.S. GAAP.

N. *Other.* A grouping of liabilities, all noncurrent, that do not reach the required threshold for separate inclusion on the balance sheet. Dell discloses the items that make up this total in note 10 to its financial statements.

O. *Commitments and contingent liabilities.* U.S. GAAP defines a contingency as "an existing condition, situation, or set of circumstances involving uncertainty as to possible gain (a gain contingency) or loss (a loss contingency) to an enterprise that will ultimately be resolved when one or more future events occur or fail to occur."[25]

Companies must recognize a loss and record a liability for loss contingencies when

- "It is probable that assets have been impaired or a liability has been occurred," that is, that the value of an asset has diminished or the company has incurred an obligation to another party;

and

- "The amount of the loss can be reasonably estimated."[26]

Accounting standard setters use "probable" to mean that there is more than a 50 percent likelihood of the event occurring. Companies must disclose any unrecognized losses that arise from contingencies when a somewhat lower standard is met, that is, "when it is *reasonably possible* (more than remote but less than probable) that a loss has been incurred or it is probable that the loss has occurred but the amount cannot be reasonably estimated."[27]

This is the category where companies reveal how any pending litigation, product recall, or environmental cleanup costs could affect the company positively or negatively. For example, a company that is being sued for $100 million dollars for delivering products alleged to be defective may be vigorously disputing the claim. Lawyers have advised the company that, in their opinion, it is not probable that the claim for that amount will be successful. Accordingly, the company has not recorded any liability for the claim. On the other hand, if the company's lawyers do believe it is reasonably possible that some amount will be paid to settle the action but cannot reasonably estimate that amount, then a contingent liability exists that must be disclosed. Placing a caption on the face of the balance sheet (even though no amount is shown) is intended to emphasize the importance of such contingencies to the reader of the financial statements.

In note 6, "Commitments, Contingencies, and Certain Concentrations," among other things, Dell lets investors know that the company is "subject to various legal proceedings . . . in the ordinary course of business" but underlines that it does not think that this will have any "material adverse effect" on earnings, operations, or future cash flows.[28] In other words, Dell does not think that these proceedings with affect the company's financial condition and bottom line.

Stockholders' Equity

Note 4 to the Dell financial statements, "Capitalization," describes the rights of each class of stock authorized and other important information about contributions made to Dell by owners.

P. *Preferred stock.* As we already discussed, preferred stock represents a claim on the assets of the entity that takes precedence over the claims of common shareholders. The nature of the preferences given to this class of shareholders may differ from entity to entity. Holders of preferred stock generally are not entitled to vote for directors or approve decisions of the directors. While Dell has the authority to issue five million shares of preferred stock, par value $.01 per share, no such shares have been issued.

Q. *Common stock.* Again, common stock is a piece of paper that represents one's ownership in a corporation. As owners, holders of common stock usually get to elect the board of directors of the entity and approve the decisions of that board, such as deciding how much to pay executives and approving mergers and acquisitions. Common stock is generally reflected at what is called *par value*. Par value establishes the nominal value per share and is generally the minimum amount (established by state law) that must be paid by each shareholder when stock is issued. Corporations generally sell shares of their common stock for amounts greater than its par value.

R. *Additional paid-in capital.* The amount that stockholders have paid above par value to a company to acquire common stock. This amount is generally shown separately from par value of common stock outstanding. Dell, however combines the two amounts in one caption, *Common stock and capital in excess of $.01 par value.*

S. *Treasury stock.* The cost of shares repurchased by Dell on the open market and held by it for reissue, or what it costs the company to buy back its stock and hold it. Repurchases and reissuances are made for various purposes. In note 4 to its financial statements, Dell indicates it has a share repurchase plan "to manage the dilution resulting from shares [of common stock] issued under the Company's employee stock plans."[29] This is just Dell's way of recognizing that when it issues shares, this issue dilutes everyone else's ownership and earnings per share. By repurchasing shares given to employees, Dell minimizes the effect of such dilution.

T. *Retained earnings.* This category principally represents the accumulated net income of Dell since its founding.

U. *Other comprehensive income (loss).* This category principally represents unrealized losses on certain derivative instruments.

"CONSOLIDATED STATEMENT OF INCOME"

The explanations below follow the order in which the captions appear in the Dell "Statement of Income." Letter references such as (A) refer to items of revenues, expenses, gains, and losses in this statement. Numerical references such as (1) refer to intermediate totals in the statement.

A. *Net revenues.* Note 1 to the financial statements, "Description of Business and Summary of Significant Accounting Policies," indicates that "net revenue includes sales of hardware, software and peripherals, and services (including extended service contracts and professional services)." As such, these activities constitute the major or central operations of Dell.[30]

B. *Cost of revenue.* The costs of products and services sold during the period, or how much it costs Dell to produce what it sells. This would include, for example, the costs of laptops sold and wages and other direct costs of employees performing professional services for Dell customers during the period.

1. *Gross margin.* The difference between net revenue and the cost of revenue, or sales revenue minus the cost of sales. This intermediate total may be a good indicator of the competitive pressures faced by company. For example, Dell's gross margin dropped from 20.2 percent in 2001 to 17.6 percent in 2002 and 17.9 percent in 2003, an indicator of the fierce price competition that existed in the markets for computer systems, desktops, and laptops.

F. *Total Operating Expenses.* Dell divides these expenses into the following three categories:

C. *Selling, general and administrative.* This category includes all advertising and marketing expenses as well as most corporate overhead, including accounting and legal expenses.

D. *Research, development and engineering.* This category of expense consists of two distinct subcategories: (1) research and development and (2) engineering. Note 10 to the financial statements discloses the amount of each subcategory. Generally, research and development expenses have accounted for 70–75 percent of this category.

E. *Special charges.* This category consists of expenses incurred by Dell to get out of certain business activities in fiscal 2002 and 2001. Note 8 to the financial statements, "Special Charges," details the nature of these expenses. They principally represent costs that arose from (1) severance packages and (2) closing facilities that Dell leased or owned.[31]

Because "special" charges, often characterized as "restructuring" charges, are supposed to be irregular and some companies have them year in and year out, the SEC requires extensive disclosure of the nature of such charges.

2. *Operating Income.* As previously discussed, there is no common authoritative definition of this term, so this measure of performance differs from company to company. Dell uses a straightforward notion of operating measure, which means that it includes most revenues, expenses, gains, and losses. Dell excludes three items from the measure: (1) certain revenues, expenses, gains, and losses included in the caption "Investment and other income (loss)" (details discussed below), (2) income taxes included in the caption "Provision for income taxes," and (3) the cumulative effect of a change in accounting principles.

It is only in the first area ("certain revenues, expenses, gains and losses") that Dell exercises judgment in developing an operating measure. Generally, such a measure is developed on a pretax basis and excludes income taxes. Moreover, U.S. GAAP requires the cumulative effect of an accounting change (details discussed below) to be shown separately after all other items in the income statement. Dell's operating income as a percentage of total pretax income, or income before income taxes and the cumulative effect of change in accounting principle, ranged from 83 percent in fiscal 2001 to 103 percent in fiscal 2002 and 94 percent in fiscal 2003.

G. *Investment and other income (loss), net.* Note 10 to the Dell financial statements indicates that this caption includes investment income, primarily interest; realized gains (or losses) on investments; and small amounts of interest and other expenses.

3. *Income before income taxes and cumulative effect of change in accounting principle.* The pretax income of Dell.

H. *Provision for income taxes.* Taxes on pretax income either currently payable or payable in future years. Note 3 to the Dell financial statements, "Income Taxes," spells out in great detail, as required by U.S. GAAP, the nature of such taxes.

4. *Income before cumulative effect of change in accounting principle.* The net income of Dell from activities during each of the respective years. Analysts tend to focus on this number, if it is present, rather than net income because, as explained below, the cumulative effect of the change in an accounting principle relates to matters affecting prior years.

I. *Cumulative effect of change in accounting principle.* Under current U.S. GAAP,[32] changes in accounting principles are generally recognized by including the cumulative effect of such changes as of the beginning of the year, that is, the sum of such changes if they had been made in *prior* years, as a separate item in the income statement. Note 1, "Description of Business and Summary of Significant Accounting Policies," indicates that in fiscal 2001, Dell changed its accounting for certain revenue to conform to a SEC Staff Accounting Bulletin. The note describes the nature of the change and its effect on the Dell financial statements.[33]

5. *Net Income.* The sum of revenues, expenses, gains, and losses included in items A–I.

6. *Earnings per common share.* This measure, which indicates the income earned by each share of common stock, has been widely used by journalists and others to evaluate and compare the performance of multinationals. Be careful, though. Many accountants and analysts believe that earnings per share may be an overly simplistic measure that, in certain cases, may mislead rather than inform. Where a cumulative effect of a change in accounting principle is present, as in the case of Dell, earnings per share must be shown both before and after such cumulative effect. In both instances, two measures — (J) *Basic* and (K) *Diluted* must be given. The difference in those two measures is explained below.

J. *Basic.* In this calculation, income before cumulative effect of change in accounting principle (see 3, above) and net income (see 5, above) are divided by the weighted average shares of common stock issued and outstanding during the year. A weighted average is used rather than the year-end number of shares issued and outstanding to take into account any issuances or repurchases of common stock by Dell during the year.

K. *Diluted.* In this calculation, the numerator remains the same as in the "basic" calculation. The denominator, however, is changed to show the effect on earnings per share of all additional shares that would arise if securities convertible to common stock were converted or stock options or warrants were exercised. This is a "what if" calculation, meaning, for example, what would be the effect on earnings per share if all stock options that were "in the money" (meaning that the exercise price of the option is below the market price of the stock) had been exercised during the year? In the case of Dell, such dilution is much more significant in the 2001 fiscal year than in either 2002 or 2003. As required, Dell shows the weighted average number of shares entering into both calculations of earnings per share.

The institutional context in which accounting takes place is in the midst of rapid change. Some of these changes are a natural result of globalization, which has transformed the way that companies do business and underscored the need for international accounting standards. Others have come about as a result of the recent spate of accounting scandals in the United States and abroad.

While numbers may be universal, the concepts that underlie them or the real life things that they represent are not. Culture and the particulars of a country's economic and legal development have played an enormous role in determining national accounting standards.[34] Different market cultures also play a role in determining accounting standards. In the United States, which has a long tradition of broad public-equity markets, companies are used to disclosing a good deal of information and know that they must do so in order to receive public investment. The situation is quite different in Europe, where the equity of companies, at least until recently, was closely held by a few individual families, governments, or private banks. Since the public had not invested in the fortunes of the company, there was little demand for public disclosure.[35]

So it is not surprising that traditionally each country had its own accounting standards. There was no such thing as an international accounting standard until 1973, when the International Accounting Standards Committee was established. The problem, of course, was which standard to use as the international standard. The United States, the United Kingdom, and other English-speaking countries such as Canada and Australia believed their national GAAPs to be more rigorous than European standards and the general international standards, which in certain cases were the result of numerous compromises between nations.

As this debate raged, markets were becoming more and more international, and an increasing number of companies began to list on foreign stock exchanges in order to raise money. In order to do so, companies had to reconcile their financial statements with the national accounting standards of each exchange where they chose to list. This meant that companies had to basically present two sets of numbers, which could be very different, depending on the accounting standards used. This was not only costly for the company but confusing to potential investors.

In the mid-1990s, the European Commission decided that European multinationals should follow international accounting standards.[36] This was significant because international accounting standards, or those standards created by the IASC and later the IASB, were and still are considered stricter than individual European GAAPs. In 2000, the Securities and Exchange Commission (SEC), the government body that regulates the U.S. securities markets, announced that it supported the development of a high quality set of standards to be used internationally (without referring to any specific standard) for companies that wanted to sell securities in markets other than those of their home countries, also known as cross-border offerings.[37] While this support did not translate into a requirement that all U.S. companies adopt international accounting standards, it did serve as a catalyst in the formation of the International Accounting Standards Board by accelerating cooperation among national standard setters, including the U.S. standards setter, the Financial Accounting Standards Board, and the IASC.

The IASC continued to grow in members and stature. In 1999, the International Accounting Standards Committee began a restructuring that would eventually transform it into the full-time International Accounting Standards Board. This new body came into being in January of 2001 and has begun to take the lead on moving all countries toward uniform accounting standards by 2005. This is when most companies that list on European Union exchanges will be required to adopt IASB pronouncements, or what are now known as International Financial Reporting Standards.[38] Even though the United States had not officially said that it will adopt international accounting standards by 2005, the FASB has been working closely with the IASB over the last year to converge U.S. and IASB pronouncements. [39]

While IFRS are beginning to drive the debate on a number of issues, including expensing stock options and accounting for pension liabilities, not all is smooth sailing. Even as this book goes to press, there are still many difficulties to work out before IFRS are embraced worldwide.[40]

One criticism of international accounting standards in the United States has been that they are too vague. But in some respects, the argument that U.S. standards are better than international ones has become harder to defend in the wake of Enron and WorldCom. As of October of 2003, the SEC had yet to adopt IFRS across the board or allow foreign issuers to file according to these standards without reconciliation to U.S. GAAP (and there is no guarantee that this will change). That said, the SEC has tried to make things easier for foreign issuers in a number of ways, including providing different forms for registering securities based on internationally developed principles and more generous deadlines for reporting.

REGULATORY CHANGES THAT HAVE AFFECTED THE INSTITUTIONAL CONTEXT

There have been significant changes in regulation in the United States that affect both the accounting and the auditing profession in the United States and abroad. In the wake of the Enron and WorldCom scandals, the U.S. Congress passed the Sarbanes-Oxley Act in July of 2002. This law—among other things—significantly increased the reporting requirements of both foreign and domestic companies listed in the United States. Under Sarbanes-Oxley, which made no outright distinction between domestic and foreign companies, the SEC was required to pass rules in a number of areas, including disclosure, the oversight of public accounting firms, the functioning of audit committees, and the nature of company reviews of internal controls.[41]

Equally important, if not more important, were the law's provisions that removed the oversight of independent outside auditing firms and the setting of auditing standards from the accounting profession (the American Institute of Certified Public Accountants, or AICPA) and vested those responsibilities in an independent board appointed by the SEC. This independent board, called the Public Company Accounting Oversight Board, now has the job of regulating the actions of both domestic and foreign public accounting firms that audit the financial statements of companies that issue shares to the public in the United States.

Sarbanes-Oxley is especially significant because it has greatly expanded the SEC's authority over matters of corporate governance.[42] A number of the provisions of the Sarbanes-Oxley Act have been quite controversial both in the United States and abroad because they make much greater demands on companies in terms of corporate governance and auditing and reporting requirements. These provisions also increase the legal liability of companies and senior management. In addition to being uncomfortable for companies in the United States and abroad, foreign governments viewed some of the changes as impinging on national sovereignty. They have objected to the kind of rules placed on all firms and to what they see as the U.S. overstepping its jurisdiction.[43] In cases where there is a direct conflict, the SEC has tried to make certain accommodations for foreign issuers.[44] The PCAOB has also made accommodations with regard to regulation of foreign auditors, but even as this book goes to press there are still a number of issues to be worked out.

ADDITIONAL TIPS FOR READING FINANCIAL STATEMENTS OF COMPANIES

"MANAGEMENT'S DISCUSSION AND ANALYSIS"

In addition to reading the financial statements of a company, journalists should be sure to consult "Management's Discussion and Analysis of Financial Condition and Results of Operations," located in the annual report. This document gives journalists the company's take on how the business did over the past year. In addition, it signals developments that could affect the business either positively or negatively in the upcoming year.

RATIOS

Ratios are a good way of cutting through the numbers of financial statements and putting companies in the same industry on common bases so they can be analyzed. But journalists do have to be careful that certain accounting differences are not distorting these numbers. Remember: ratios are only as good as the numbers behind them.

TIPS FOR READING BALANCE SHEETS AND STATEMENTS OF SHAREHOLDERS' EQUITY

- Inventory tends to be very specific to the business that a company is in. Some companies, by the nature of their business, have a lot of inventory. Others, like Dell, have very little. Journalists should also look at a company's inventory in relation to its sales, in order to assess how quickly the company is turning over what it has in stock. It is a good idea to look at how this number has changed from previous years. (Inventory turnover = Sales/Inventory.)

- Journalists can figure out the amount of money that a company would have after paying all its bills, or its net current assets, by subtracting current liabilities from current assets. (Net current assets = current assets - current liabilities.) Rather than looking at the absolute amount, however, a more useful figure for analyzing current assets is the current ratio, which is found by dividing current assets by current liabilities. (Current ratio = current assets/current liabilities.) There is no one correct current ratio figure, although some analysts believe a company should have twice the amount of assets as it does liabilities.[45] But this varies depending on the type of business that the company is in.

- Journalists always want to look at a company's level of debt and compare it to previous years. In order to truly understand the amount of debt that a company has, however, and how this level can affect the company's prospects, journalists should refer to the balance sheet and footnotes, which give the particulars of debt, interest rates, and maturities. By reading this information, journalists should be able to ascertain what happened during the year to increase or decrease the company's level of debt. Was the company relying on outside factors such as the stock market or acquisitions, as opposed to its core business, to maintain liquidity and solvency? Journalists should also look at the net increase in debt in the financing part of the cash flow statements.

- One way of comparing the amount of debt that two companies in the same industry have is by calculating the debt-to-equity ratio, which is total liabilities divided by total shareholders' equity. (D/E = total liabilities/total shareholders' equity.) The more debt a company has, the more highly leveraged it is. If the ratio increases over a number of years, journalists probably want to investigate if this is due to a deteriorating financial condition or a strategy for financing.

- Journalists should be sure to examine the line that refers to "Commitments and contingent liabilities." This is the category in which companies reveal how any pending litigation, product recall, or environmental cleanup costs could affect the company positively or negatively. It is important to read the note about this category because if indeed a company has to settle a claim—or stands to benefit from not having to settle a claim—this may have an enormous effect on its financial condition and bottom line. The company stands to gain or lose a lot of money.

TIPS FOR READING INCOME STATEMENTS

- The format of the income statement is not the same for all companies. This is because companies differ on how many intermediate items, such as gross margin and operating income, they include before showing the final total of net income. They also differ on how to define—and calculate—these intermediate items. For example, there is no definition of operating income in authoritative accounting literature. In addition to making it difficult to compare companies in the same business, the fact that there is no one definition of operating income means that there has been some abuse in this category. Companies want to include revenues and gains in any measure of operations but want to exclude expenses and losses—because they know that analysts focus on "recurring operations" to get an idea of future earnings.

  For this reason, it is important to try to understand how a company distinguishes a "recurring" transactions or events from "nonrecurring" ones. For example, many companies have recently taken restructuring charges, which are supposedly nonrecurring, or irregular, events. But, since many companies have these nonrecurring charges year in and year out, it is a good idea to pay close attention to these *special charges*. Journalists should be sure to read the corresponding disclosure very carefully to see what a company defines as a "special" charge.

- The intermediate total of gross margin, which is calculated by dividing gross profit by sales, shows the relationship between sales and how much it costs to produce those sales. Specifically, it may be a good indicator of the competitive pressures faced by company. Journalists should examine gross margin and compare it to past years. (Gross margin = gross profit/sales.)

- Journalists should look at a company's profit margin, which is found by dividing operating income by net sales. This figure, also called operating margin, shows how profitable a company is at performing what it calls its central operations. Are the company's operations more or less profitable than the previous year? Is the company doing something to influence profit, or are outside factors involved? (Profit margin = operating income/net sales).

- Journalists should be cautious about putting too much emphasis on earnings per share as a measure of a company's performance. Companies sometimes use repurchases of shares to increase EPS by reducing the denominator of that measure.

- *Return on equity* can be a good way to compare the profitability of a company vs. other companies in the same industry. ROE is found by dividing net income by average stockholders' equity (ROE = net income/average stockholder's equity).

REFERENCES

The American Institute of Certified Public Accountants (AICPA). Accounting Research Bulletins, Inc. 1211 Avenue of the Americas, New York, NY 10036.

Antle, Rick, and Stanley J. Garstka. *Financial Accounting*. Cincinnati: South-Western, 2002.

Atkins, Paul. "The Sarbanes-Oxley Act of 2002: Goals, Content, and Status of Implementation." Speech given before the International Financial Law Review, 25 March 2003. U.S. Securities and Exchange Commission Web site. www.sec.gov/news/speech/spcho32503psa.htm. Accessed 29 July 2003.

Bannock, Graham. "The Bottom Line: Sir Bryan Carsberg on Creating Global Accounting Standards." *The Financial Regulator* 7, no. 4 (March 2003): 22–29. Available on PriceWaterhouseCoopers' Web site: www.pwcglobal.com. Accessed 17 July 2003.

Bryan-Low, Cassell. "Modest Digs, Tough Job for an Accounting Cop." *Wall Street Journal*, 23 July 2003.

Burns, Judith. "Accounting Panel Provides Insights into its Workings." *Wall Street Journal*, 29 July 2003.

Campos, Roel C. "Embracing International Business in the Post-Enron Era." Speech given before the Centre for European Policy Studies in Brussels, Belgium, 11 June 2003. U.S. Securities and Exchange Commission Web site. www.sec.gov/news/speech/spcho61103rcc.htm. Accessed 29 July 2003.

Choi, Frederick D. S., Carol Ann Frost, and Gary K. Meek. *International Accounting*. 4th ed. Upper Saddle River, N.J.: Prentice Hall, 2002.

"Commission Approves Rules Implementing Provisions of Sarbanes-Oxley Act, Accelerating Periodic Filings, and Other Measures." 27 August 2002. http://www.sec.gov/news/press/2002–128.htm. Link valid as of 8 February 2004.

Dell Financials. http://www.sec.gov/Archives/edgar/data/826083/000095013403006596/d05041e10vk.htm#toc. And: http://www.dell.com/ downloads/global/corporate/sec/10k-fy03.pdf. Link valid as of February 2004.

Deloitte Touche Tohmatsu. *IFRS In Your Pocket*. Hong Kong: Deloitte, Touche, Tohmatsu, 2003.

FASB. FASB Concepts Statements No. 5 and No. 6 and FASB Statements No. 5 and 130 are copyrighted by the Financial Accounting Standards Board, 401 Merritt 7, P.O. Box 5116, Norwalk, Connecticut 06856, U.S.A. Portions are reprinted with permission. Complete copies of these documents are available from the FASB.

Greene, Edward F., and Linda C. Quinn. "Building on the International Convergence of the Global Markets: A Model for Securities Law Reform." Paper presented at the SEC Historical Society/U.S. SEC Major Issues Conference: Securities Regulation in the Global Internet Economy, Washington, D.C., 15 November 2001. Revised 27 December 2001.

Grosse, Thomas K. "Balancing the Books." *Time Europe*, 14 February 2000. Available at www.time.com/time/europe/magazine/2000/214/account.html. Accessed 17 July 2003.

Henry, David. "Cleaning Up the Numbers." *Business Week*, 24 March 2003. Available at www.businessweek.com/bw50/content/mar2003/a3826040.htm. Accessed 11 July 2003.

International Accounting Standards Board. References. http://www.iasb.org. Link valid as of 8 February 2004.

Investors Responsibility Research Center. "IAS vs. GAAP: IS Fight Looming Between EU and U.S." *Corporate Governance Bulletin*, August 2002.

Kieso, Donald E., Jerry J. Weygandt, and Terry D. Warfield. *Intermediate Accounting.* 10th ed. New York: Wiley, 2001.

Luesby, Jenny. "Accounting for Companies." Chapter 10 of her *The Word on Business.* 155–73. London: FT/Prentice Hall, 2001.

Matlack, Carol, with John Rossant, David Fairlam, and Kerry Capell. "Europe's Year of Nasty Surprises." *Business Week*, 10 March 2003.

Merrill Lynch. "How to Read a Financial Report." http://philanthropy.ml.com/ipo/resources/pdf/howtoreadfinreport.pdf. valid as of February 2004.

Nazareth, Annette L., Director of Market Regulation, U.S. Securities and Exchange Commission. "Remarks at the PLI Conference on International Securities Markets 2003." Speech given in New York City, 9 May 2003. SEC Web site. www.sec.gov/news/speech/spch050903aln.htm. Accessed 29 July 2003.

Postelnicu, Andrei. "A Little Breathing Space: Sarbanes-Oxley Act." *Financial Times*, 7 July 2003.

Quinn, Linda. "The SEC and International Reporting (Regulatory Infrastructure Covering Financial Markets)." The Citigroup International Journalists Seminar, 9 June 2003, New York.

Scherreik, Susan. "How Efficient Is That Company?" *Business Week*, 23 December 2002.

Sarbanes-Oxley Act of July 2002. See the SEC Web site, http://www.sec.gov/about.shtml.

SEC IAS concept release. http://www.sec.gov/rules/concept/34–42430.htm. Link valid as of February 2004.

SEC Regulation S-X. http://www.sec.gov/divisions/corpfin/forms/regsx.htm. Link valid as of February 2004.

Tafara, Ethiopis. "Addressing International Concerns under the Sarbanes-Oxley Act." Remarks before the American Chamber of Commerce in Luxembourg, 10 June 2003. www.sec.gov/news/speech/spch061003et.htm. Accessed 29 July 2003.

Tergesen, Anne. "The Fine Print: How to Read Those Key Footnotes." *Business Week*, 4 February 2002.

———. "The Fine Print: How to Spot Tax Tinkering," *Business Week*, 20 May 2002.

———. "Cash-Flow Hocus-Pocus," *Business Week*, 15 July 2002.

———. "Getting to the Bottom of a Company's Debt," *Business Week*, 14 October 2002.

Wall Street Journal. "Corporate Reform: The First Year," special report, *Wall Street Journal*, 21–25 July 2003.

White, Gerald I., Ashwinpaul C. Sondhi, and Dov Fried. T*he Analysis and Use of Financial Statements*, 3rd ed. New York: Wiley, 2003.

1. In this chapter, we will discuss auditing only as it relates to the institutional context in which accounting takes place. Although often lumped together as the same thing, auditing is a separate discipline closely related but different from accounting. Auditing is best defined as "the process by which specialized accounting professionals (auditors) examine and verify the adequacy of a company's financial and control systems and the accuracy of its financial records": Frederick D.S. Choi, Carol Ann Frost, and Gary K. Meek, *International Accounting*, 4th ed. (Upper Saddle River, N.J.: Prentice Hall, 2002), 1.

2. While the EU will require this of most companies by 2005, "publicly traded companies whose securities are admitted to trading on markets outside the EU and which, for that purpose, currently use internationally accepted standards (e.g. US standards)" may delay compliance until January 2007. Deparment of Trade and Industry, "UK Extends Use of International Accounting Standards," news release, 17 July 2003, www.dti.gov.uk/cld/pressnotice170703.pdf; link valid as of February 2004.

3. The discussion of the nature of accounting follows, in certain instances, the structure set forth by Rick Antle and Stanley J. Garstka in *Financial Accounting*, which the authors have found to be the clearest exposition of the subject. See Rick Antle and Stanley J. Gartska, *Financial Accounting* (Cincinnati: SouthWestern, 2002), 3–19.

4. Antle and Garstka, *Financial Accounting*, 4.

5. Ibid.

6. Antle and Garstka use more purely economic concepts, including different definitions of financial value, wealth, and what they call "economic income" to discuss the measurement of an entity's wealth and changes in that wealth (Antle and Garstka, *Financial Accounting*, 12–14). In the interest of simplification and space, we focus on these concepts as accountants have modified them.

7. For a more technical discussion of comprehensive income of business enterprises, see FASB Statement of Concepts No. 6, *Elements of Financial Statements*, paragraphs 70–77, December 1985.

8. Antle and Garstka break out the three areas addressed by GAAP as "accounting valuation, recognition and disclosure." The authors of this article prefer the term "measurement" to "accounting valuation." Antle and Garstka, *Financial Accounting*, 16–17.

9. See FASB Concepts Statement No. 5, *Recognition and Measurement in Financial Statements of Business Enterprises*, paragraph 6, December 1984.

10. For a more technical discussion of the accrual method of accounting, see FASB Concepts Statement No. 6, paragraph 139.

11. For a more technical discussion of the balance sheet, see FASB Concepts Statement No. 1, *Objectives of Financial Reporting by Business Enterprises*, paragraph 41, November 1978.

12. See FASB Concepts Statement No. 6, paragraph 25. For further discussion of assets, see paragraphs 25–33.

13. "General access to things such as clean air or water resulting from environmental laws or requirements cannot qualify as assets of individual entities, even if the entities have incurred costs to help clean up the environment." See FASB Concepts Statement No. 6, paragraph 188.

14. See FASB Concepts Statement No. 6, paragraph 35. For further discussion of liabilities, see paragraphs 35–42.

15. For a more technical discussion of the concept of equity, see FASB Concepts Statement No. 6 paragraph 49, paragraphs 60–63.

16. For a complete technical description of the characteristics of revenues, see *Characteristics of Revenues*, FASB Concepts Statement No. 6, paragraphs 78–79. For a complete technical description of the characteristics of expenses, see *Characteristics of Expenses*, FASB Concepts Statement No. 6, paragraphs 80–81. For a complete technical description of gains, losses, and

the concept of peripheral activities, see *Characteristics of Gains and Losses*, FASB Concepts Statement No. 6, paragraphs 82–86.

17. See Statement of Financial Accounting Standards, No. 130, *Reporting Comprehensive Income*, paragraph 10, June 1997 for this citation and a further discussion of comprehensive income.

18. The purposes of a statement of cash flows are more fully explained in paragraphs 4–6 of Statement of Financial Accounting Standards, No. 95, *Statement of Cash Flows*, November 1987.

19. Dell Computer Corporation, 10-K for Fiscal Year 2003, Notes to Consolidated Financial Statements, note 10, 53, http://www.dell.com/downloads/global/corporate/sec/10k-fy03.pdf; accessed 10 February 2004.

20. For more information on the SEC rule with regard to reporting accounts with smaller balances, see SEC Regulation S-X, http://www.sec.gov/divisions/corpfin/forms/regsx.htm; valid as of 10 February 2004.

21. For a more technical discussion of the concept of current assets, see AICPA Accounting Research Bulletin No. 43, *Restatement and Revision of Accounting Research Bulletins*, chapter 3A, paragraphs 4–6, June 1953.

22. Donald E. Kieso, Jerry J. Weygandt, and Terry D. Warfield, *Intermediate Accounting*, 10th ed. (New York: Wiley, 2001) 500.

23. Dell Computer Corporation, 10-K for Fiscal Year 2003, Notes to Consolidated Financial Statements, note 2, 40.

24. For a more technical discussion of the concept of current liabilities, see AICPA Accounting Research Bulletin, No. 43, chapter 3A, paragraphs 7–8.

25. See FASB Statement of Standards No. 5, *Accounting for Contingencies*, paragraph 1, March 1975.

26. Gerald I. White, Ashwinpaul C. Sondhi, Dov Fried, *The Analysis and Use of Financial Statements*, 3rd ed. (New York: Wiley, 2003), 18–19.

27. Ibid.

28. Dell Computer Corporation, 10-K for Fiscal Year 2003, Notes to Consolidated Financial Statements, note 6, 48.

29. Ibid., note 4, 43.

30. Ibid., note 1, 35–39.

31. Ibid., note 8, 49–50.

32. FASB issued an exposure draft late in 2003 that would alter the treatment of changes in accounting principles to harmonize them with international accounting standards, wherein such changes are generally recognized retroactively.

33. Dell Computer Corporation, 10-K for Fiscal Year 2003, Notes to Consolidated Financial Statements, note 1, 35–39.

34. As Choi, Frost, and Meek explain, countries such as France and Spain, whose legal systems are based on detailed historical codes (such as the Napoleonic code in France), tend to see accounting standards as another aspect of society to be written into law. Thus, the objective of financial reporting in these countries is not necessarily to provide detailed information for investors but instead to provide regulators with information to determine if companies have complied with laws and regulations, for example, tax laws. On the other hand, countries like the United States and the United Kingdom that share the British "common law" tradition have much less specific legislation dealing with accounting standards on the books. Financial reporting is generally intended to serve investors and creditors; how that gets done tends to be left up to nongovernmental standard-setting bodies that function in the private sector. For a discussion of this and more details on of the effect of culture on the development national accounting standards, see Choi, Frost, and Meek, *International Accounting*, 41–45.

35. As Choi, Frost, and Meek explain, instead, "in credit-based systems where banks are the dominant source of finance, accounting focuses on creditor protection through conservative accounting measurements." Ibid, 43. For a full discussion of the role of market culture, see Choi, Frost, and Meek, 41–45.

36. The term "international accounting standards" refers to those standards created by the IASC and later the IASB. These standards are now

known as International Financial Reporting Standards, or IFRS. From here on in, the terms "international accounting standards" and "IFRS" are used interchangeably in the text. The European Community adopted this so-called financial-reporting strategy in 2000, but it was not until March 2002 that the European Parliament passed a law in this regard. For information on the change, see Investors Responsibility Research Center, "IAS vs. GAAP: IS Fight Looming Between EU and U.S.," in *Corporate Governance Bulletin* (August 2002), among others.

37. See the Securities and Exchange Commission's IAS concept release, at http://www.sec.gov/ rules/concept/34–42430.htm; valid as of 10 February 2004.

38. See note 2, above, for exceptions to this 2005 deadline. According to the accounting firm of Deloitte Touche Tohmatsu, Europe is not the only region moving toward these standards. Asia is also heading that way, although there is no unified, continent-wide approach. New Zealand has decided that IFRS will replace its own GAAP by 2007. Australia, Hong Kong, and Singapore, among other countries, have adopted most of the international accounting standards as their own, although with some modifications. See Deloitte Touche Tohmatsu, *IFRS in Your Pocket* (Hong Kong: Deloitte, Touche, Tohmatsu, 2003), 17.

39. The accounting firm of Deloitte Touche Tohmatsu calculates that "by 2005, there will be an additional 500 to 600 registrants filing IFRS statements with the SEC. Currently, only about 50 foreign companies file IFRS financial statements, and reconcile to US GAAP." Ibid., 16.

40. As this book went to press, there were problems in both Europe and the United States. In Europe, battles were raging over proposed IASB standards on financial instruments and accounting for stock options, among other issues.

41. Companies are now required to discuss critical accounting policies and explain why a particular policy was chosen and what the results would have been if they had chosen a different accounting policy. Sarbanes-Oxley also requires chief executive officers and chief financial officers to certify (or swear that to the best of their knowledge) that the company's financial statements are correct. For more information on the specifics of the Sarbanes-Oxley Act of July 2002, see the SEC Web site at http://www.sec .gov/about.shtml; valid as of 10 February 2004.

42. The SEC has traditionally not regulated these issues—instead, this task was usually left to states and self-regulatory organizations like the New York Stock Exchange.

43. Conflicts with foreign governments and regulators have arisen because Sarbanes-Oxley was written in such a way that "[it] does *not* provide any specific authority to exempt non-U.S. issuers from its reach. [It] leaves it to the SEC to determine where and how to apply its provisions to foreign companies." See SEC Commissioner Paul Atkins, "The Sarbanes-Oxley Act of 2002: Goals, Content, and Status of Implementation," speech given by before the International Financial Law Review, 25 March 2003, www.sec.gov/news/speech/spch032503psa.htm; accessed 29 July 2003. See also SEC Comissioner Roel C. Campos, "Embracing International Business in the Post-Enron Era," speech before the Centre for European Policy Studies in Brussels, Belgium, 11 June 2003, www.sec .gov/news/speech/spch061103rcc.htm; accessed 29 July 2003.

44. For example, the SEC has recognized that different countries define "independent" audit committees in different ways, and has thus tried to work with individual countries to make sure that these country-specific definitions are respected. Among other accommodations, the SEC has also decided to exclude most foreign lawyers from the rules guiding the conduct of attorneys in the United States. See Atkins and Campos speeches.

45. Merrill Lynch, "How to Read a Financial Report," 22, http://philanthropy.ml.com/ipo/ resources/pdf/howtoreadfinreport.pdf; valid as of 10 February 2004.

CHAPTER NINETEEN

MONEY LAUNDERING

DAVID MARCHANT

MONEY LAUNDERING is the method of concealing the proceeds of criminal activity in order to disguise its illegal origin and create the appearance that it was generated through legitimate business activities so that the perpetrators can spend their booty with the minimum of suspicion. Governments have designated it a criminal offense in its own right, just like the underlying offense(s) that resulted in the proceeds being obtained in the first place, in an attempt to take the profit out of crime.

Different jurisdictions have historically defined money-laundering offenses in different ways. Historically, it included only those crimes that were universally considered to be "serious," such as narcotics trafficking, weapons dealing, racketeering, and murder. Tax evasion, therefore, sometimes escaped attention, as it did not meet the legal standard of dual criminality, that is, it must be an offense in both countries for judicial cooperation to kick in. For example, the judicial authorities of many offshore centers would refuse requests for assistance from foreign governments seeking information about offshore bank accounts if the requests in any way involved an investigation into tax evasion, which was not recognized as an offense in offshore centers. If the word "tax" was even mentioned in a request, it would be refused, and many were, much to the chagrin of criminal investigators in the world's major countries.

All of this has changed in recent years, however, largely as a result of an effort by the world's major countries to create a minimum international standard for the creation and implementation of a comprehensive legal, supervisory, enforcement and professional framework to combat money laundering and terrorist financing.

Spearheading this drive is the Financial Action Task Force on Money Laundering, which was established by the G7 countries in 1989 and subsequently published a number of recommendations that it is pressuring all countries to adopt. These recommendations include broadening the number of predicate offenses for money laundering to include fiscal offenses, eliminating banking secrecy, introducing greater transparency of beneficial ownership of businesses, confiscating the proceeds of crime, a requirement that financial institutions and certain nonfinancial companies report suspicious activities and the passage of legislation allowing for greater international cooperation in criminal investigations.

Offshore financial centers, which have become synonymous with banking secrecy and tax evasion, were highlighted as a particular problem by the FATF. In a report dated 14 February 2000, the FATF stated: "In today's open and global financial world, characterized by a high mobility of funds and the rapid development of new payment technologies, the tools for laundering the proceeds of serious crimes as well as the means for anonymous protection of illegal assets in certain countries or territories make them even more attractive for money laundering. Existing anti-money laundering laws are undermined by the lack of regulation and essentially by the numerous obstacles on customer identification, in certain countries and territories, notably offshore financial centers."

Setting out its aims, the FATF stated: "All countries and territories that are part of the global financial system should change the rule and practices that impede the anti-money laundering fight led by other countries. The legitimate use by private citizens and institutional investors of certain facilities offered by many financial centers, including offshore centers, is not put in question. An essential aspect of this issue is to make sure that such centers are not used by transnational criminal organizations to launder criminal proceeds in the international financial system. It is also important that they are not used by criminal organizations to escape investigation in other jurisdictions."

As of August 2003, more than 130 countries had adopted the FATF's recommendations. Those countries whose anti-money-laundering systems are reviewed by the FATF and do not come up to scratch are placed on a list of "Non-Cooperative Countries and Territories" in what is essentially a global "name and shame" process. Businesses located in jurisdictions not on the list are encouraged not to do business with those that are on it. The first list was published in June 2000 and contained fifteen countries. Since then, several countries have been added and removed from the list, and, as of 8 August 2003, those that were still on it were the Cook Islands, Egypt, Guatemala, Indonesia, Myanmar, Nauru, Nigeria, the Philippines, and the Ukraine.

The economies of many small and developing countries have been affected by the FATF's measures. For example, effective 1 August 2002, the Central Bank of Montenegro revoked the licenses of all 432 offshore banks licensed in the jurisdiction, most—if not all—of which were "shell" banks committing a variety of criminal offenses in cyberspace and around the world.

Offshore financial centers have been left with "Hobson's Choice": implement the FATF's recommendations and lose significant business because foreign clients will go somewhere else or do not implement the recommendations and lose business anyway because their names will go on a global blacklist and other types of foreign clients will be pressured into no longer doing business with them. Even those that do want to be good global citizens are faced with the problem of how to pay for the introduction of these new measures.

Some small and emerging countries have felt bullied by the world's major countries, and there is a lingering suspicion that the FATF's measures, in conjunction with a global "tax harmonization" drive by the Organisation for Economic Co-operation and Development, are as much designed to help major countries collect more taxes as they are to stamp out major crime that is not tax related.

HOW BIG IS THE PROBLEM?

Although it is impossible to know the exact figure, the World Bank Group estimates that at least $1 trillion is laundered annually around the world, and the International Monetary Fund puts the figure at between 2 and 5 percent of the world's gross domestic product.

While they are undoubtedly neck-deep in money laundering, it is nevertheless a common misconception that most money is laundered in offshore financial centers and developing countries, an impression that is cultivated by governments of major countries seeking to put the blame somewhere other than on their own doorsteps and encouraged by Hollywood blockbuster movies such as *The Firm*, which portrayed the Cayman Islands as a den of tax-dodging iniquity.

The reality is somewhat different. More criminal proceeds are laundered in New York or London than the Bahamas or Panama, and the biggest culprits within those jurisdictions are more likely to be the "elite" of world banking than a little-known "shell" bank licensed in a faraway tropical paradise. And much of the criminal proceeds received by offshore banks are sent there by banks in major countries, where the underlying criminal activity originated.

Having said that, one of the most notorious examples of money laundering did indeed involve a Cayman Islands offshore bank called Guardian Bank & Trust, which was operated in Grand Cayman by U.S. national John Mathewson. After Mathewson was arrested in the U.S. in 1996 following his criminal indictment for money laundering and fraud at the U.S. District Court for the District of New Jersey, he handed over his bank's entire computer records of clients in return for leniency. At his sentencing hearing in 1999, federal prosecutors said that bank records given to them by Mathewson had resulted in investigations into 1,500 U.S. taxpayers and could eventually recover $300 million in unpaid taxes and penalties.

Guardian Bank's liquidator, accountant Christopher Johnson, unsuccessfully applied to the court for the return of the computerized records, alleging that Mathewson had stolen them. Johnson argued that the use of the records by U.S. prosecutors would harm Cayman's offshore banking industry, which at the time included 570 banks with total deposits in excess of $425 billion, but the court ruled that "the interest of the United States in its ongoing criminal investigation" took precedence.

Assistant U.S. Attorney John J. Carney described Mathewson as the "the most singularly important government co-operator in tax haven prosecutions in the history of the Internal Revenue Service." So helpful to investigators was Mathewson that Judge Alfred J. Lechner Jr. said the number of requests for leniency he had received from prosecutors was "extraordinary and had not been equalled by any other case," according to a report in the *New York Times*. The newspaper quoted Mathewson as telling the court: "I have no excuse for what I did in aiding US citizens to evade taxes and the fact that every other bank in the Caymans was doing it is no excuse."

Mathewson's unprecedented cooperation paid off during his sentencing. Rather than face the rest of his life in prison, the then seventy-one-year-old offshore banker was let off with probation, 500 hours of community service and a $30,000 fine. Not bad for someone who set up numerous shell corporations, provided false invoices, and performed other acts to launder the proceeds of what prosecutors called "the biggest cable television piracy case in history."

HOW ARE DEVELOPING COUNTRIES AFFECTED?

Developing or transition countries are particularly vulnerable to money laundering because they generally lack the level of legal, enforcement, and professional sophistication required to effectively regulate one of the most complex areas of criminal activity. Many also lack the finances to implement a system that will meet international standards. However, if they do not meet these standards, they are likely to find themselves on the FATF's list of "Non-Cooperative Countries and Territories," which, apart from being embarrassing, may lead to a loss of revenue as companies in countries that do meet these standards shy away from doing business with them for fear of attracting the unwelcome attention of their home regulators and law enforcement agencies.

Another negative consequence of failing to control money laundering is that it encourages some of the world's worst criminals, such as terrorists and narcotics traffickers, to establish a foothold in a country, with all of the underlying problems that brings, such as threats of violence, bribery, corruption, murder, and so on.

FATF has recommended that "countries should apply the crime of money laundering to all serious offenses, with a view to including the widest range of predicate offenses." FATF has recommended that countries should—as a "minimum" measure—include a range of offenses in their legislation within each of the following "designated categories of offenses" as a basis for money laundering:

- Participation in an organized criminal group and racketeering

- Terrorism, including terrorist financing

- Trafficking in human beings and migrant smuggling

- Sexual exploitation, including sexual exploitation of children

- Illicit trafficking in narcotic drugs and psychotropic substances

- Illicit arms trafficking

- Illicit trafficking in stolen and other goods

- Corruption and bribery

- Fraud

- Counterfeiting and piracy of products

- Environmental crime

- Murder, grievous bodily injury

- Kidnapping, illegal restraint, and hostage taking

- Robbery or theft

- Smuggling

- Extortion

- Forgery

- Piracy

- Insider trading and market manipulation

HOW IS MONEY LAUNDERED?

There are three distinct phases of the money laundering process: placement, layering, and integration.

- *Placement.* The point at which criminally derived proceeds enter the financial system. This might involve breaking up large amounts of cash into smaller amounts that attract less attention and attempting to deposit it into a bank account. This is the phase when the criminal's ill-gotten gains are considered to be most susceptible to seizure by the authorities. Due to anti-money-laundering legislation in many countries that typically carry severe criminal and civil penalties, financial institutions are becoming increasingly wary of accepting large amounts of cash and have a legal responsibility to report suspicious transactions.

- *Layering.* Proceeds of crime are moved around in a series of complicated and numerous financial transactions with the ultimate goal of making it difficult, if not impossible, to trace the funds back to their criminal origin. This process typically involves setting up an array of "paper" legal entities in multiple jurisdictions, particularly those known for their bank secrecy laws.

- *Integration.* Once the proceeds of crime have been spun around in a cycle of complexity, they will reenter the legitimate economy by being invested in bona fide investments, such as stocks, business ventures, property, or luxury items.

TIPS FOR REPORTERS

- Reporters should look out for the existence of "paper" entities on a balance sheet or in ownership records, that is, companies or other legal entities that do not have any employees and do not have a bona fide office in the jurisdiction in which they are incorporated. These entities will exist only as a piece of paper in the filing cabinet of the office of a company-management firm or law firm in their home jurisdiction. Obvious questions that arise are: Why do these entities exist? What do they do? What do they own? This is an important aspect of a money-laundering investigation since the process often involves criminals' sending cash to what are, in reality, paper entities on the pretext of paying an invoice for services that the paper company is supposed to have rendered, which is an all but impossible task if it has no employees. Enron, which was headquartered in the United States, incorporated more than 600 subsidiaries in the Cayman Islands yet did not have a single listing in the local telephone directory or a local office. It turned out that Enron used these firms to hide massive losses as part of an elaborate fraud.

- How does one identify a paper entity? There are certain jurisdictions that are known for incorporating high volumes of paper entities. Jurisdictions to watch out for include Delaware and Nevada in the United States and the following offshore financial centers: Anguilla, Antigua, Bahamas, Bahrain, Barbados, Belize, Bermuda, British Virgin Islands, Cayman Islands, Cook Islands, Costa Rica, Cyprus, Dominica, Dublin (Ireland), Gibraltar, Grenada, Guernsey, Hong Kong, Isle of Man, Jersey, Labuan, Liechtenstein, Luxembourg, Malta, Mauritius, Monaco, Montenegro, Montserrat, Nauru, Netherlands Antilles, Niue, Panama, Singapore, St. Kitts and Nevis, St. Lucia, St. Vincent and the Grenadines, Switzerland, Turks and Caicos Islands, and Vanuatu. Only a tiny fraction of foreign-owned legal entities incorporated in offshore financial centers have a physical presence there. The British Virgin Islands and the Turks and Caicos Islands collectively have several hundred thousand foreign-owned legal entities registered in their jurisdictions, but probably no more than two dozen of these have a physical presence there. Even in Bermuda, which has one of the most developed infrastructures of all offshore centers, only about 300—or 2.5 percent—of its approximately 12,000 foreign-owned legal entities have a physical presence.

■ If a reporter suspects a company is a paper entity, its address should be run through a major Internet search engine such as Google at www.google.com. If it is indeed a paper company, it is likely that there will be many hits for other "shell" companies who are also using that address, which is typically a mail box operated by a company-management firm or law firm. Also, its name should be run through the local telephone directory to see if it has a listing. Reporters can access a Global Yellow Pages from http://www.globalyp.com/world.htm. The overwhelming majority of paper entities do not have telephone-directory listings.

■ Learn to differentiate between the terms "beneficial" and "nominee." A beneficial owner is the person for whose benefit an asset is held, while a nominee owner is simply a "front" for the beneficial owner. In the offshore world, the nominee is king. Many law firms and company-management firms operate nominee holding companies that show up as shareholders on corporate share registers even though the beneficial shareholder is the client. It is done to hide the identity of the client. If "XYZ Holdings Ltd." shows up as a shareholder of "ABC Telecommunications Inc.," and XYZ Holdings Ltd. is a wholly owned subsidiary of a law firm, it does not necessarily mean that the law firm has a beneficial interest in ABC Telecommunications Inc. The law firm might be holding its stake on behalf of a client who wishes to remain anonymous. It is also common for foreign-owned companies to have nominee directors, who are usually local attorneys or employees of company-management firms who have little or no idea about the underlying business of the company of which they are a director. If "Joe Public" or "John Smith" shows up as a director of an offshore

company, it certainly does not mean that he plays any meaningful role in the governance of that company, as directors are supposed to. Some attorneys and company-management employees simultaneously serve as directors of dozens or hundreds of "paper" companies. The provision of nominee directors and shareholders is done for a fee and is a highly lucrative area of offshore finance for law firms, company-management agents, and others.

■ Information about legal entities in offshore financial centers is generally difficult to obtain. In most centers, the only publicly available information about a legal entity consists of its registration number, date of incorporation, and the name and address of its registered agent. Perhaps the most open offshore center is Bermuda, where, for a small fee, you are legally entitled to look at each legal entity's file at the Registrar of Companies and view its share register and list of officers and directors, which are kept at its registered office.

■ In securities fraud, it is common for insiders to hide illegal trades in the stock of their companies by buying and selling shares through offshore entities whose ownership is hidden. The existence of offshore-registered entities as significant shareholders in regulatory filings for publicly listed companies outside of their home jurisdiction is a red flag that warrants further investigation.

■ In the world of money laundering, the underlying objective of those involved is to deceive anyone looking into their activities, and very little is as it appears on the surface. A successful investigation into money laundering requires a tremendous amount of time and effort. Reporters need to be persistent and inquisitive.

■ It is important to understand that all commercial financial institutions are used by criminals to launder money and, as a rule of thumb, the bigger the financial institution, the bigger its money laundering problem. The acid test is whether they were involved knowingly or unknowingly.

- The biggest money-laundering centers in the world are generally considered to be the United States and the United Kingdom.

- Never forget the scale of the problem. Best-selling author Jeffrey Robinson has described money laundering as the world's third-largest industry in monetary terms.

GLOSSARY

- **AML.** Anti-money-laundering.

- **BENEFICIAL OWNER.** Refers to the person or people who ultimately own or control an asset.

- **CORRESPONDENT ACCOUNT.** An account established by a domestic financial institution for a foreign bank to allow the foreign bank to receive deposits, make payments, and transact other business.

- **CORRESPONDENT BANK.** A banking relationship that covers the financial services and operations that financial institutions offer to one another, both domestically and internationally.

- **FATF.** Financial Action Task Force on Money Laundering.

- **FRONT COMPANIES.** In the context of money laundering, a front company is one that appears to be legitimate and have nothing to do with the person who is laundering the funds but, in reality, is secretly controlled by the criminal.

- **IBC.** International Business Company or International Business Corporation; routinely used to describe a foreign-owned "paper" company that is incorporated in an offshore financial center.

- **KYC.** Know your customer.

- **NOMINEE.** A person who has no beneficial interest in a company but is representing a party who wants to remain anonymous.

- **OFFSHORE FINANCIAL CENTER/TAX HAVEN.** Generally, a small country which has passed business-friendly laws designed to attract large amounts of foreign capital, largely on the basis of offering bank secrecy, protection from creditors, and low or no taxes. Only a tiny fraction of foreign-owned legal entities incorporated in offshore financial centers have a physical presence there.

- **"PAPER" OR "SHELL" COMPANY.** A company incorporated in a jurisdiction in which it has no physical presence.

- **REINVOICING.** The use of a corporate tax haven as an intermediary between an onshore business and its customers outside its home country. For example, if Company A in Russia sells goods worth $1 million to Company B in France, it can evade taxes by selling the goods for $500,000 to Company C—a "paper" offshore company that it secretly controls—which, in turn, sells the goods to Company B for $1 million and retains $500,000 in an offshore account on which it pays no taxes. In essence, this is a sham transaction that is designed to evade taxes.

- **SHELF COMPANY.** A company which has already been incorporated but has not started to trade and is available for sale for a minimal amount of money. This is the quickest way to obtain a company.

- **SAR.** Suspicious activity report.

- **SHELL BANK.** A bank incorporated in a jurisdiction in which it has no physical presence and which is unaffiliated with a regulated financial group.

- **SMURFING.** One of the most commonly used money-laundering methods in the United States and Canada. It involves breaking up criminal proceeds into amounts of less than $10,000 and depositing these tranches into many different accounts at financial institutions in order to avoid the type of regulatory scrutiny that may arise if the entire amount is deposited in a single account in one transaction.

1. Financial Action Task Force on Money Laundering. http://www1.oecd.org/fatf.

2. International Money Laundering Information Network. http://www.imolin.org.

3. Asia Pacific Group on Money Laundering. http://www.apgml.org.

4. The Egmont Group of Financial Intelligence Units. http://www.imolin.org/fius.htm.

5. Interpol. http://www.interpol.int.

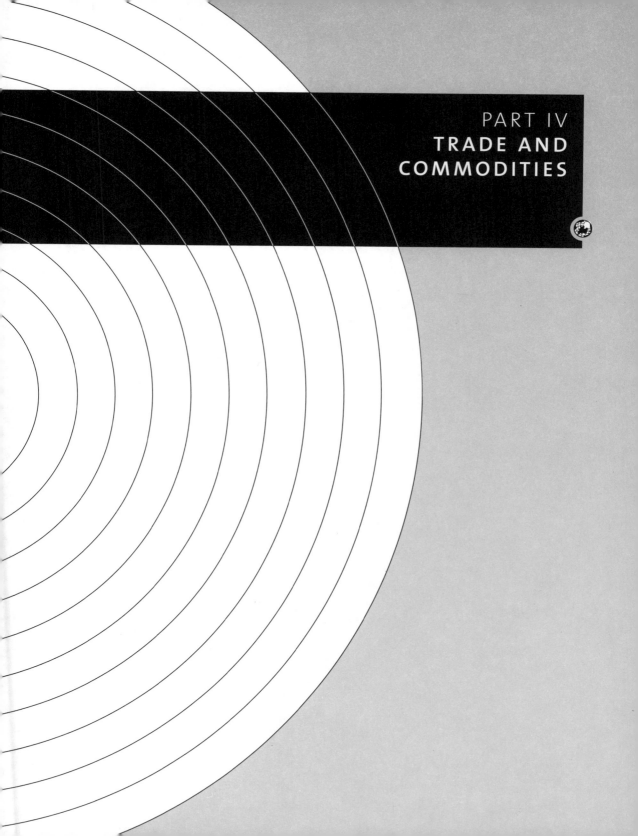

PART IV
TRADE AND COMMODITIES

CHAPTER TWENTY

INTERNATIONAL
TRADE

NICHOLAS ROSEN AND
HELEN CAMPBELL

T
RADE USED to be a dry, arcane subject best left to experts who
argued over the details of lengthy and complex international
agreements. But in recent years, the international-trade-policy
debate has become one of the hottest topics a journalist can cover. International trade—the flow of goods and services across borders—affects the
lives of vast numbers of people around the world in profound and different ways. At the national and international level, it is one of the most
important—and contentious—issues of the day. The antiglobalization
protests at the World Trade Organization Summit in Seattle (1999), and
the WTO Ministerial Conference in Cancun (2003) have put the trade
policy debate in headlines around the world. The burning questions that
government officials, nongovernmental organizations, and economists
argue about are how important trade is to overall economic development
and whether the current trade arrangements allow countries to maximize
their gains from trade. There is also disagreement about what sorts of subjects should be included in trade negotiations and unhappiness on the
part of developing countries who do not like the way the talks are conducted, as they are often pressured to sign agreements that they do not
believe they will benefit from. Related to this is the fact that developing
countries are often at a disadvantage during trade negotiations, as they do
not have the same number of trade experts and lawyers that developed
countries have.

Proponents argue that freer trade would contribute to higher overall
levels of wealth, which would benefit the global economy and its inhabi-
tants. But free-trade skeptics believe that the current trade arrangements
are unfair and will not help developing countries grow.

International trade is as old as recorded human history, dating back to ancient Mesopotamia and later the great Silk Road, which linked the Far East to the Roman Empire for the exchange of silk, perfumes, and other goods beginning around 300 B.C. After the fifteenth and sixteenth centuries, global trade soared with the advent of sea travel and exploration, which led to the establishment of colonies and the mercantile system.

Mercantile trade was based on political and military influence exercised by imperial powers over their colonies. Commerce laws were backed by military might. Imperial Europe traded its own finished goods for precious metals and raw materials from the colonies.

The Industrial Revolution in Britain created a strong demand for raw materials from overseas. This new manufacturing base, coupled with revolutions in transportation, further expanded the volume of world trade. Europe's commercial exploitation of its colonies was a contributing factor to the rise of independence movements in colonies.

Until the middle of the twentieth century, trade was mainly in primary products. The pattern of world trade has shifted in the latter half of the twentieth century; decolonialization and the development of former colonies and nonimperial powers led to the production of more complex, higher-value-added goods in many of those countries. The postwar period has been marked by accelerating international commerce.

However, this has been accompanied in recent years by widespread critique of globalization in general and trade (and the WTO) in particular. The reasons for the antiglobalization activists' concern about trade vary widely. Not all free-trade skeptics agree with one another about which are the most important objections to more free trade.

Included among the issues that critics of free trade have raised in questioning whether trade does or can potentially lead to greater economic development are:

1. *Labor and employment*. Trade can affect labor and employment in many ways. Antiglobalization activists have argued that trade liberalization can contribute to abuse of labor standards in developing countries. There have been concerns that proposals to link trade agreements to workers' rights could provide a pretext for (typically rich) countries to act in a protectionist way. For example, a government might use labor standards and environmental requirements as a way to exclude goods and services from another country that does not have the productive capacity to meet the requirements or does not share the values on which the requirements were based.

   Concern about trade flows and employment is often related to investment decisions as well. Labor organizations in wealthier countries are concerned that investors will move to countries where the cost of labor is cheaper, costing their members jobs. On the other hand, the generation of employment in other countries could benefit workers in the the country to which the investment shifted. One area that is receiving more attention internationally is the increased potential for export of service jobs from developed to developing countries. Examples include moving call centers and back-office operations to developing countries such as India and South Africa. This is, in part, an issue of service-trade liberalization. This will become an increasingly important political issue for developed countries and an increasingly important source of employment opportunities in developing countries. Trade in services is covered under the WTO agreement by the General Agreement on Trade in Services, as well as in many bilateral and regional trade agreements.

2. *Economic development.* Other criticisms directed at trade liberalization have been that the wealth generated by trade does not address the pressing economic development issues for developing countries and that trade negotiations are biased in favor of the "superpower" economies. In many cases, the critics contend, the current trading system has not delivered the development outcomes needed in developing countries. It is very difficult to generalize on these issues, though. For example, the spectacular growth of many Asian countries since the 1950s has very much been the result of export growth.

3. *The environment.* Some people regard protection of the environment and sustainable environmental outcomes as the most important single objective of trade negotiations. There are concerns that an unregulated increase in trade can accelerate depletion of natural resources and have other detrimental effects on the environment.

What do these issues have to do with trade policy? There has been considerable debate on what the relationship between trade and labor or environment should be. This has been addressed differently in different trade agreements, with varying levels of support from different countries. The WTO requires that any environmental rules adopted by WTO member-governments should be designed to address legitimate environmental issues and be the least trade-distorting measure available to policy makers. Most environmental issues are outside the mandate of the WTO and covered by a range of Multilateral Environment Agreements.

In 1992, a General Agreement on Tariffs and Trade panel ruled against a U.S. environmental law that forbade the sale of tuna caught by Mexican fisherman using methods that killed dolphins. The U.S. eventually amended its law to comply with international trade agreements, which enabled the sale of Mexican tuna in the U.S.

This raises an important technical issue that has been the subject of fierce debate. GATT and its successor (WTO) laws are based on the notion of "like products," or products that are physically the same as each other. But it does not distinguish between *how* goods are made—such as

CAMBODIA—AN ATTEMPT TO IMPROVE WORKING CONDITIONS

SHERIDAN PRASSO

Cambodia was the testing ground for an unprecedented experiment: a bilateral trade agreement with the United States that linked textile quotas to improvements in garment-factory working conditions.

In the five-year period after the agreement, Cambodia experienced a number of positive results: strong and sustained GDP growth when other Asian countries experienced stagnant growth or recession; a strengthening of labor laws to international standards; working conditions in factories that can be considered a model for developing countries; and a recognition by international retailers that garments from Cambodia were produced under fair-labor practices.

Cambodia also experienced negative effects: an increase in acrimonious labor relations resulting in strikes and violence that damaged Cambodia's reputation as welcoming for foreign investment and an increase in manufacturing costs that may deter future investors who can find cheaper and more compliant labor elsewhere.

In the deal signed on 20 January 1999, the United States agreed to increase textile imports from Cambodia in exchange for the Cambodian government's agreement to allow international monitors into garment factories to observe working conditions and certify whether they were improving. Future quota increases were conditional on improvements and on Cambodian factories being in "substantial compliance" with internationally recognized core labor standards from the International Labour Organization.

The three-year agreement, forged by the Clinton administration, was the first time the United States swapped favorable trading terms for good labor practices. It was designed to be a new U.S. foreign-policy tool and a model for other agreements around the world. It was extended by the Bush administration for an additional three years, through 31 December 2004—a date by which Cambodia expected to join the WTO and see all textile quotas for all WTO members removed on 1 January 2005. When the extension was granted, Bush administration U.S. Trade Representative Robert Zoellick called the agreement "an excellent example of the way trade agreements lead to economic growth and promote a greater respect for workers' rights."

The agreement also was a victory for U.S. trade unions. Hit by the exodus of garment jobs to less-expensive and less-regulated countries, the unions, led by the American Union of Needle Trades and Industrial & Textile Employees, had lobbied the U.S.T.R. to link labor standards to U.S. imports. They have been watching Cambodia to determine the success of the agreement, in order to push for links in future trade deals.

Cambodia had little leverage in negotiations. An impoverished country recovering from war and genocide, it had a modest $3 billion economy and an annual per capita GDP of $260 (among the lowest in the world). Dependent on foreign aid, it was keen to develop export manufacturing.

It took more than a year for the ILO to enter factories. The first report, of conditions that were better than international expectations, was issued in November 2001. Cambodians were frustrated at the slow pace, complaining that they had improved conditions and had suffered labor unrest without the promised benefits. They happened eventually: textile quotas for 2002 were increased by a 9 percent bonus (out of a possible 14 percent) on top of a minimum required 6 percent increase. (Previous annual quota increases had been 9 percent.) By 2002, Cambodia's quota exceeded production.

LESSONS LEARNED

The economy benefited, working conditions improved, foreign direct investment came in, jobs were created, and modern labor laws were passed. Before the agreement, Cambodia's economy grew 1 percent in 1998, in line with other Asian countries suffering from the regional economic crisis. Exports that year totaled $785 million, with 38 percent going to the United States. In 2001, Cambodia grew 5.4 percent and exports totaled $1.268 billion, with 66.5 percent going to the United States. The increase was almost entirely in garments. Cambodia's economy grew 6.3 percent in 2002, a rate higher than most Asian countries, with the exception of China.

Working conditions improved significantly. Many factories improved standards on their own. Others were brought into compliance under pressure. As a result, the ILO found factories to be in "substantial compliance" with international standards:

- No evidence of child labor;
- No evidence of forced labor;
- No evidence of sexual harassment;

- Improvement in the correct payment of wages;*

- Improvement with regard to ensuring that overtime work is undertaken voluntarily;*

- Improvement in ensuring that overtime hours are within legal limits;*

- Improvement in ensuring freedom of association, including protection against anti-union discrimination.*

In order to compel compliance, the government passed a modern labor code. Previous laws were a mosaic of old French laws, communist-era legislation, and statutes from the U.N. Transitional Authority in Cambodia. In other areas of law, this remains the case.

Foreign direct investment in Cambodia grew from $120 million in 1998 to $150 million in 2001. Textiles are the largest manufacturing industry in Cambodia, attracting $363 million in foreign investment in 337 projects as of 2002, and employing 250,000 people.

Cambodia may benefit from a reputation as a safe-haven for fair-labor standards for international retailers concerned about consumer "sweatshop" backlash. ILO certification that Cambodia's garments are produced under fair-labor practices gives reassurance to retailers concerned about brand image, particularly those stung by previous allegations of sweatshop practices. Gap, The Limited, Abercrombie & Fitch, Adidas, Kmart, Wal-Mart, Nike, and Reebok are some of the retailers who buy from Cambodia. Labor unions have been pushing the ILO for a stamp or insignia to certify garments as made under fair labor conditions.

Labor unrest increased, damaged the country's reputation, and raised the costs of manufacturing. Emboldened by international attention and by U.S. labor-union advisers, Cambodia's unions strengthened. They staged wildcat strikes, raising the minimum wage from forty dollars per month to forty-five dollars per month in 2000—higher than in Laos and parts of China—but not without violent clashes that damaged Cambodia's reputation. Manufacturers seeking cheap, compliant workers would need to go elsewhere.

The price of monitoring and bringing factories into compliance also raised costs for manufacturers, who paid for their own improvements. Cambodia's garment manufacturing association was required to pay for part of the monitoring program (initially, $200,000).

CONCLUSION

For the long term, it remains unclear whether the garment industry will remain a vital, thriving part of Cambodia's economy. It is possible that the resulting higher costs of manufacturing will be offset by international retailers willing to pay a premium for a labor-conditions safe haven. It is also possible that Cambodia's higher costs will drive manufacturers to other lower-cost, less-regulated countries such as China, particularly after 2005, when textile quotas for all WTO members are removed.

(* "Though this remains a problem in a number of factories": International Labour Organization, June 2003).

whether they are made by child labor or whether they were made using poor environmental-protection processes. The only issue that it does consider in this respect is goods produced by prison labor.

This is a technical factor that helps explain why labor and environmental issues have historically been outside the GATT and WTO mandate. Labor standards are addressed at the international level by the UN-affiliated International Labor Organization. Another reason environment and labor standards are outside the scope of the WTO is because many countries want them to be. Developing countries are concerned that trade actions could be taken against them if environment and labor standards are not met.

Labor, environment, and other social standards are not always met for a range of reasons. In most cases, failing to meet the standards is explained by the lack of capacity and resources, including institutional oversight.

Trade-policy retaliation does not always alleviate the situation or lead to improved commitment and enforcement of standards. Many governments think that rich countries such as the United States and members of the EU use labor and environmental standards as de facto trade barriers. Some governments argue that the attempt to link trade with nontrade issues is an attempt by some countries to meddle in the domestic affairs of others.

As the global economy becomes more interrelated, trade flows are increasingly affected by what were once regarded as domestic economic-policy tools and issues. For example, labor and environmental policies as well as animal welfare considerations have all traditionally been the domain of national governments. Governments have typically managed their own inward investment and competition policies without reference to international trade laws as embodied in the WTO.

But international trade and investment has become a more prominent part of the global economy; the value of global exports rose from $58 billion in 1948 to $5.47 trillion in 1999 (WTO). Consequently, domestic policy instruments over trade and investment have increasingly become internationalized and have come under international scrutiny. Domestic policies have also become the subject of heated debate among the various sets of interests and advocates described above. Some countries want the WTO to consider these issues; others do not.

TRADE THEORY: WHAT DO ECONOMISTS THINK?

The theoretical argument for free trade is persuasive: When countries specialize in the goods in which they have a comparative advantage, it allows them to buy relatively more goods from abroad than they would have been able to if they produced goods that did not reflect their comparative advantage. The model suggests that trade can help a country maximize its overall levels of economic welfare. Economic theory and those that support further trade liberalization argue that trade brings:

- *Cheaper goods and more choice for consumers.* Increased flows of traded goods and services can lead to lower prices than would otherwise be available to consumers.

- *Productivity gains* are achieved by exploiting comparative advantage and more efficient resource allocation. Production is organized in a more efficient manner so that more output is extracted per unit of production. Investment is directed towards more efficient industries rather than protected local industries, which may have produced more expensive products that could be imported more cheaply. Further, by concentrating production in industries they are good at, countries may benefit from economies of scale, or larger-scale production resulting in lower per-unit costs.

- *Effects on employment.* For those workers who can take advantage of these new shifts in production, trade liberalization can bring employment growth and better jobs. Who the winners end up being is difficult to predict. In developed countries, the beneficiaries are primarily higher-skilled workers. In the developing world, where labor is relatively cheap and countries tend to have a comparative advantage in labor intensive production, it is often less-skilled workers that benefit from trade liberalization. But the gains from trade can come at a price, as the changing pattern of production causes some of the old parts to collapse—what the economist Joseph Schumpeter called "creative destruction." There will inevitably be losses in some sectors, which can threaten the livelihoods of segments of the population. For instance, after signing the North American Free Trade Agreement, Mexico was inundated by corn from the United States, where large agricultural corporations produced the grain cheaper and with support from the U.S. government. The drastic drop in corn prices has jeopardized the traditional livelihoods of Mexico's 3 million families that depend on a tradition of small-scale corn production.

- *Competition.* Free trade can promote competition in the domestic economy where monopolies might otherwise control the markets. This will usually benefit consumers and smaller producers through cheaper prices.

- *Investment.* Opening to trade is often accompanied by increased investment from abroad, particularly in the form of foreign direct investment, which has exploded from $58 billion in 1982 to $865 billion in 1999. FDI is viewed by many economists as a stable and beneficial source of investment for developing countries. However, FDI flows to the developing world remain directed at countries that are thought to offer stable and less-risky business environments, including transparent and predictable patterns of governance and social stability. FDI has also traditionally been concentrated in countries with large domestic markets. This is not the case for many developing countries.

- *Technology.* The goods and FDI that flow into a country typically bring with them new technology and technological know-how. By importing technology, countries can reap the benefits of research-and-design that occurs abroad without having to pay for it—what is known as a "spillover" effect. A 1997 World Bank study determined that international trade contributes 20 percent of the total effect on productivity from foreign research and development investments.

- *"Positive externalities."* More generally, trade liberalization can bring other advantages that are not immediately associated with trade and economic policy. For instance, by increasing the economic interdependence of nations, trade can contribute to improved and more stable international relations.

THE VERDICT ON TRADE
AND ECONOMIC DEVELOPMENT

There is broad agreement that free trade is important for economic growth. But there is heated debate over what the size of the benefits are, who they benefit, and what other conditions must be present for trade to contribute to the different social and economic goals of different countries.

For many countries, economic growth can contribute to broader economic development aspirations, but it is by no means automatic. Even conventionally accepted ideas like "free trade leads to growth" are being challenged by some leading economists.[1] For instance, Harvard economist Dani Rodrik and University of Maryland economist Francisco Rodriguez argue that the evidence that foreign trade boosts economic growth is weak. Some economists point out that trade liberalization is a "one-time" gain, a positive restructuring of the economy that has little permanent and sustainable effect on growth.

Proponents of trade agree that while free trade benefits societies in the aggregate (macroeconomic gains), it contributes to important wealth redistribution that can create losers within the society. Without a doubt, restructuring can be a messy process. Those domestic industries that cannot compete with foreign imports are hit hard. People lose their jobs and may have a difficult time finding work in a new sector. And while the benefits of free trade can take a long time to be felt, the costs may be more immediate. It is not surprising, then, that free-trade policies are met with strong resistance from some parts of society. Resistance can also be attributed to the fact that losers from free trade (the already employed and the existing owners of failing companies) tend to be better organized and more vocal than those who gain (the unemployed and consumers).

It is also important to note that trade policy has been used for many policy objectives for which it is not necessarily the best policy choice. This is the fault of governments, not the policy tool itself. Governments have used trade policy to protect jobs, for example, where a well-targeted education and vocational-training policy may have been a better way to secure employment objectives. And when trade-policy protection is taken away without introducing new and more targeted policies, such as employment programs, education, or social-welfare reforms, then the costs are likely to be painful for those who lose their jobs.

MULTILATERAL TRADE-POLICY RULES: THE WTO

The rapid growth in trade has been amplified by a growing belief on the part of political leaders and economists around the world that free trade and the reduction of trade barriers is a desirable goal. Negotiations among nations have spawned numerous pacts to reduce trade barriers. The first trade agreement with extensive, global reach was the General Agreement on Tariffs and Trade, established following negotiations in Havana in 1947. Twenty-three countries signed the agreement, which resulted in massive tariff reductions affecting roughly one-fifth of global trade. Over the following decades, GATT was expanded and eventually transformed into the World Trade Organization in 1995, which now has 144 members. The WTO was created following the Uruguay Round of negotiations, in which, for the first time, agriculture, investment, and intellectual property rights were on the agenda. Before this, the GATT considered only tariffs on industrial products, which reflected the economic and commercial interests that were of greater interest to some countries.

Most countries support a multilateral rules-based trading system in which disputes can be resolved according to the rules, not the relative power of the countries involved.

The umbrella agreement establishing the WTO comprises a family of treaties that regulate:

1. Goods

2. Services

3. Intellectual property rights

These basic principles are encoded in three main agreements: GATT, GATS, and TRIPS. The details covered by these agreements and various annexes include:

- Agriculture
- Movement of natural persons
- SPS
- Air transport
- Textiles and clothing
- Financial services
- Product standards
- Shipping
- Investment measures
- Telecommunications
- Antidumping measures
- Customs-valuation methods
- Preshipment inspection
- Rules of origin
- Import licensing

- Subsidies and countermeasures

- Safeguards

- Market access commitments agreed by each member

- Countries' schedules

- Dispute settlement

- Transparency

- Trade-policy review mechanisms

The agreements themselves, GATT, GATS, and TRIPS, are a framework set of principles. It is the commitments countries negotiate and agree to that determine each country's obligations. Like the agriculture agreement, both GATS and TRIPs were only agreed as part of the formal negotiating agenda during the Uruguay Round.

The main principles governing all WTO agreements are most-favored-nation treatment—which specifies that an importing country cannot discriminate between products exported from different countries—and nondiscrimination—which specifies that countries cannot discriminate between domestically produced and imported goods and services.

Exceptions can be negotiated to these principles in specific agreements and are listed in each country's schedule. Of the annexes to the GATT, perhaps the most important exception is *agriculture*. Agriculture is the key issue on the international trade agenda and is likely to remain so for the coming years. It is the most distorted sector and the most important for most developing countries. For example, 27 percent of developing countries' GDP and export earnings come from agriculture, and the sector employs half of the developing world's workforce. The current system of subsidies, barriers, protection, and dumping leads farmers in the North—principally in the United States and the EU—to produce more food than is demanded, and excess agricultural products are dumped on world markets, making it harder for developing-country farmers to compete. In 2002, prices received by OECD farmers were, on average, 31 percent above world prices.

Services play a vital role in national economies and an increasing role in the global economy. Service sectors include financial services, education, tourism, and professional services. Unlike other agreements, obligations under the General Agreement on Trade in Services only cover sectors agreed upon by each member country and included in their schedule of commitments. GATS obligations do not apply to sectors that are not listed in the schedules. This is referred to as a "positive-list approach." Consequently, in negotiating terms, a country's "services offer" (which is the list of legal requirements for each services subsector a country is prepared to include) will reflect domestic conditions rather than minimum agreed international conditions. Other WTO members can ask for those conditions to be liberalized or the sectors expanded as part of negotiations. By contrast, a negative-list approach is used for other agreements, which only sets out the lists of measures that are prohibited.

Another important trade related issue is the WTO agreement on Trade-Related Aspects of Intellectual Property Rights. These agreements set minimum levels of protection that all WTO member countries must provide for the main categories of intellectual property rights. IPRs secure ownership and control on the use of knowledge and research and development. Without this control, companies would not spend money on research and development for new technologies. Many countries are concerned that the TRIPs agreement may limit developing countries' access to technologies that are patented especially for medicines and seeds, which are important for public health and food security. Developing-country governments can issue compulsory licenses to override patents to produce cheaper versions of (generic) drugs to address public health needs, such as HIV, malaria, and other epidemics. However, it was only at Cancun in October 2003, that agreement was reached to allow generic drugs to be exported from rich countries to developing countries that did not have the capacity to produce drugs under a compulsory license.

REGIONAL AND BILATERAL TRADE AGREEMENTS

While the WTO has been at the center of debate since Seattle, and more recently Cancun, there is a lot more to the international trade architecture than the WTO. Non-WTO agreements take the form of "bilateral" trade agreements between two countries and "regional" trade agreements between members of a region. Most agreements negotiated bilaterally and regionally by WTO members are required to be consistent with WTO principles of MFN (that is, no discrimination between products produced by different countries) and nondiscrimination (that is, no discrimination between products produced domestically or abroad).

Examples of regional trade agreements include the North American Free Trade Agreements (between the United States, Canada, and Mexico) and ASEAN FTA (between countries in South East Asia). Examples of bilateral trade agreements include the Vietnam–U.S. Bilateral Trade Agreement, Canada–Chile BTA, Australia–Singapore BTA, and the EU's trade agreements with specific African, Middle Eastern, and North African countries.

In many of these agreements, members have negotiated conditions that exceed but are not inconsistent with their WTO obligations. WTO-inconsistent agreements may be referred to the WTO. Some countries have negotiated provisions relating to investment, labor, and environmental standards in these agreements.

THE "SINGAPORE" ISSUES

The relationship between trade and sustainable development has become central to the WTO's mandate and to the current round of multilateral trade negotiations. Developing countries have pushed for development issues to be promoted in this round. Those issues have come to be known as the "Singapore Issues," reflecting the site of the 1996 Ministerial Conference in which they were first discussed. Developing countries' arguments have been reflected, to some extent, in the WTO-related negotiating agenda. Nonetheless, there are still fundamental issues on the negotiating table that reflect the lack of agreement on what the right economic path to development is and what framework these policies should have.

It is easy to characterize these debates as pitting developed countries against developing ones. It is important to remember, though, that while developed and developing countries often disagree over particular issues, there is also considerable disagreement among developing countries and among developed countries, many of whom compete directly against one another for export markets. A good example of this is the Cairns Group, comprising developed and developing countries that pushed for the inclusion of agriculture on the agenda in the Uruguay Round and continue to fight the U.S. and EU agriculture-support programs. But not all developing countries are strong agricultural-product exporters, and many feel that the group does not represent the interests of the subsistence, small-scale agricultural activity that is vital to many developing countries. This illustrates the diversity of interests among both developed and developing countries and how their domestic considerations inform their trade-policy positions with respect to trade negotiations at all levels.

The so-called Singapore issues are:

- *Transparency in government procurement* and *trade facilitation*. Intended to reduce the opportunity for corruption in international business transactions. In themselves, these have been the least contentious of the Singapore issues, as most governments recognize that higher and less-certain trade-transaction costs can damage their ability to compete in international markets.

- *Competition policy*. Intended to ensure free and fair competition between companies operating in a particular market. There typically has not been a tradition of competition policy in many developing countries, who, in addition, have resisted discussing such policies at an international level until other trade issues are addressed and they have had an opportunity to assess what the focus of competition policies should be in their domestic contexts.

- *Antidumping*. Some developing countries have noted that antidumping initiatives, while related to competition policy, have been deliberately ignored by developed countries. Many countries have accused each other of "dumping," or pricing exports below the cost of production, in order to gain market share in a foreign market—a strategy that is prohibited by WTO rules. National authorities initiate antidumping actions. If proven, the complaining country is allowed to retaliate with import restrictions, or "antidumping" measures. This is an enormously complex area and there is some concern among developing countries (and, in certain cases, developed countries), that dumping cases are fabricated so as to use antidumping measures as a form of protectionism.

- *Investment.* Perhaps the most contentious of the Singapore issues. There has been strong resistance from developing and developed countries to introducing this issue onto the WTO agenda, and indeed to considering investment at the multilateral level. While most agree that foreign investment can make a strong contribution to economic development, many do not think that having multilateral rules will contribute to increased levels of investment. Supporters of introducing investment to the multilateral agenda argue that it would be a more optimal approach than the existing (and increasingly complex) array of bilateral agreements in which powerful countries design investment agreements in their favor.

TIPS FOR REPORTERS

- Who are the losers and the winners from a trade agreement?

- Will the trade agreement boost exports? Which industries will benefit the most? What industries will be hurt most? How many jobs will be affected? What are the short-term and long-term considerations? Has the government undertaken cost-benefit analysis before promulgating the agreement? How will the government adjust its policies to address labor-market and other issues?

- What type of goods is likely to be exported? What potential do the export industries have to "spill over" and contribute to the health of other industries? For instance, technology-intensive industries typically foster sophistication and productivity in other sectors. Which countries will be the main competitors?

- Is the country's trade policy part of a broader development policy that the government has explained? The key to the success of the East Asian export strategy was an overarching plan for sustainable growth.

- What consumers will benefit from lower prices? (Consumers can be companies as well as individuals—for example, the auto industry in the United States benefits from steel imports and opposes attempts by the U.S. steel industry to limit imports.) Other beneficiaries of greater import volumes can include shippers, port operators, and distributors.

- What, if any, measures will the government take to ease the transition for those workers and businesses that will be most adversely affected? Are there educational or other retraining programs planned? What sort of social safety net does the country have in terms of welfare and unemployment insurance? In Hong Kong, about 1 million manufacturing jobs (out of a total population at the time of only 6 million) were lost when manufacturers moved across the Chinese border to take advantage of China's cheaper labor costs (a move made possible by the economic reforms that began in 1978). The Hong Kong government provided no special assistance and the then-British colony had virtually no social safety net. (It did, however have a good public-housing program and an extensive, heavily subsidized medical system; an efficient government and a good educational system also helped.) By the mid-1990s, Hong Kong companies employed an estimated 5 to 6 million workers in factories across the border. China's prosperity drove Hong Kong's growth.

- What will be the impact on service sectors such as finance (banking, insurance, securities, fund management), telecommunications, distribution, and retailing?

- What analysis has the government (or research institutes or academics) done on the impact of trade agreements for the country? Have foreign governments or business organizations published studies? (These can be a good insight into what foreign businesses see as the major opportunities in a particular market).

- Who are the country's trade negotiators? How much experience do they have, and what analytical and research resources can they draw on? What consultative mechanisms do they have with the private sector and civil society?

- What political actors (both inside and outside of government) play a role in setting trade policy? Who opposes freer trade and why? Who supports it and why?

- In what areas where the country has export competitiveness does it face export restrictions?

- Have any dumping suits been filed against the country? Does the country have antidumping policies?

- Will the country be affected by the phasing out of the Multifiber Arrangement textile quotas at the end of 2004? Many companies have set up factories in (or sourced clothing from) countries primarily to evade quotas. When the trade-distorting impact of quotas is removed, will the country be helped or hurt? Will new protectionist measures (such as "antisurge" mechanisms, which are imposed as emergency quotas to guard against sudden import floods) replace the old quota system?

LINKS FOR MORE INFORMATION

1. World Trade Organization's Web site. www.wto.org.

2. The United Nations Conference on Trade and Development. www.unctad.org.

3. A series of briefs examines the role of trade in economic development by the Center for Global Development. http://www.cgdev.org.

4. The Center for International Development at Harvard University maintains a Web site that gathers and disseminates information and research on the multilateral trade system. http://www.cid.harvard.edu/cidtrade/index.html.

5. Policy briefs, research, and working papers on trade topics released by the Institute for International Economics. http://www.iie.com/research/trade.htm.

6. Dani Rodrik, Professor of International Political Economy at the John F. Kennedy School of Government, Harvard University has published widely in the areas of international economics, economic development, and political economy. http://ksghome.harvard.edu/~.drodrik.academic.ksg.

7. "Dismantling Barriers and Building Safeguards: Achieving Prosperity in an Age of Globalization," by IMF's First Deputy Managing Director Anne Krueger. http://www.imf.org/external/np/speeches/ 2003/081303.htm.

NOTES

1. Jeffrey Sachs and Andrew Warner, "Economic Reform and the Process of Economic Integration," *Brookings Papers on Economic Activity* 1 (August 1995): 1–95.

CHAPTER TWENTY-ONE

COMMODITIES MARKETS

VINCENT NWANMA

COMMODITIES ARE a vital sector for many developing countries. Revenues from commodity exports often provide a large share of foreign-exchange revenues, as well as government income. In countries where the commodities being produced are agricultural, most of the labor force—in some cases, as much as two-thirds—is employed in the sector. This means covering commodities goes beyond merely reporting about events that influence prices on world markets. It also involves writing about economic development and the lives of the millions of people working in agriculture, mining, and elsewhere.

Anything from social unrest to bad weather can affect commodities. Good coverage of the sector includes social, labor, political, and macro-economic topics. One critical issue on this list is the impact of commodities prices on government finances. A fall in the price of a commodity often leads to fiscal imbalances as governments find it difficult to match their forecast expenses with dwindling revenues. In such circumstances, governments tend to resort to borrowing—an action that sometimes leads to excessive levels of indebtedness and, at the extreme, debt crises.

The deterioration of economic conditions in the 1980s has been partly blamed on the fall in the prices of primary commodities. Throughout Latin America and Africa, countries relied heavily on earnings from the international sales of domestically produced commodities. When prices of these commodities collapsed on the international market, government revenues fell as well. The governments found it difficult to meet basic needs at home. In theory, governments should have adjusted immediately by reducing expenditures, but this proved difficult politically. Instead, the initial response was to increase borrowing while keeping spending unchanged. Eventually, the fiscal pressure became too onerous and access to even more borrowing proved impossible. Governments throughout the developing world defaulted on their debt obligations in droves

But the impact of the decline in commodity prices goes far beyond the "formal" effect on the fiscal accounts. A fall in prices of cocoa, for instance, means a collapse in the incomes of cocoa farmers and their families as well as of workers employed on farms. This, in turn, can cause unemployment, unrest, and even violence.

COMPARATIVE ADVANTAGE

The concept of comparative advantage has often been used to justify the fact that developing countries produce commodities while other countries produce high-margin products such as computer chips. The idea is that countries should specialize in the production of commodities where they have a cost advantage *relative* to that of other countries. Developing countries, the theory goes, are endowed with the unskilled labor and land required for the production of commodities at comparatively low costs.

But developing countries worry that if they focus on commodities, they will be stuck in a low-growth trap. And comparative advantages can change over time as countries acquire the skills to produce manufactured products at lower cost; this has been the experience of East Asia. Some economists believe that learning to produce manufactured goods can only come by actually producing the goods. Limiting themselves to commodity production condemns developing countries to low-margin, less-lucrative activities. That makes it difficult for commodity producers to improve their lot, as their earnings remain low year after year.

Many developing countries start on the road to value-added activities by producing goods related to the commodities they produce, such as food processing for agricultural nations or petrochemicals for oil producers. But some countries, such as Ghana and the Ivory Coast, remain unable to process all or a significant proportion of their cocoa beans into butter, which they could export at higher prices than those they receive for cocoa beans. Nigeria and other oil producers export crude oil but not refined products.

From the perspective of some, the reliance of developing countries on commodities is reminiscent of the days of colonial rule. Then, developing countries often served as sources of raw materials that fed industries located in the developed countries. But by looking at a basic list of commodities—coffee, copper, cocoa, diamond, gold, and palm oil—it is easy to see the practice continues today. Each of these is predominantly produced by developing countries, among which are the poorest nations of the world. According to one source, Africa produces 95 percent of the world's diamonds, 55 percent of its gold, two-thirds of its cocoa, and about three-fifths of its palm oil. Yet the African continent has the largest concentration of poverty anywhere in the world.

This paradox—the coexistence of concentrated resource wealth *and* abject poverty—deserves the attention of commodities reporters. One reason for this phenomenon is the relatively low profit margins on raw materials and the heavy competition generated by many countries producing the same commodity. A buyer of coffee can buy it from Yemen, Vietnam, or Colombia, meaning it is largely a buyers' market. With the exception of the OPEC cartel, which governs the production of oil among member nations, commodity cartels like the rubber producers' association have not been very successful at restricting output and bolstering prices.

Commodity homogeneity also makes prices much more sensitive to supply considerations. When the World Bank urged developing countries to grow commodities as part of their development strategies of the last few decades, it did not think about what would happen if everyone else did so at the same time: supply rose, and, with little competition, producers had to accept ever lower prices for their commodities. A single country, Vietnam, brought down the price of coffee markedly when it increased its production of low-priced robusta coffee in the late 1990s.

The structure of the international commodity market has also rendered it vulnerable to large price swings. Periods of high prices elicit large increases in supply, which ultimately lead to a price collapse. This boom/bust cycle of commodities' prices can be very disruptive since it requires economies to continuously adjust. Many African countries have suffered from this phenomenon. During the oil price shocks of 1973–74 and 1978–79, and the boom for cocoa- and coffee-exporting countries in 1976–77, commodity price increases resulted in economic growth spurts to which governments reacted with dramatically higher expenditures. The eventual price collapse often came as a surprise, and the economic adjustment tended to be painful.

Commodity price cycles also have an impact on currencies. During boom periods, export-related hard-currency flows multiply and put upward pressures on local currencies. As currencies appreciate (that is, strengthen), they eventually become overvalued. As a result of the overvaluation, nontraditional exports become noncompetitive, and their producers gradually go under. At the same time, imports rise and external imbalances materialize. This phenomenon, the so-called Dutch disease, catches countries completely unprepared when commodity prices collapse—as they often do. The Dutch disease contributed significantly to the recurring balance-of-payments problems experienced by many developing countries in the 1970s and 1980s.

In light of these experiences and the long-term decline of commodities prices, many countries are recognizing the need to diversify their economies. Many Asian countries have been successful in this by diversifying their export bases, despite the comparative advantage they had in some commodities. Reporters should follow governments' programs or initiatives aimed at achieving this.

Unfortunately, not all of the government revenue from the sale of commodities goes to public services or economic development. Some is funneled to the officials in the state-owned enterprises or to those in the government itself.

Nigeria has earned billions of dollars from exports of crude oil. According to the World Bank, over a period of twenty-five years since the 1970s, Nigeria earned more than $200 billion from the exploitation of oil resources. But poverty is widespread, with about 70 percent of the population now living below a poverty line defined as income of less than $1 a day. Much of the money earned from oil and gas has gone to government officials, including military officers who have ruled the country for most of the period since independence. In many ways, the country today is poorer than it was a quarter century ago.

Covering commodities entails finding out about the sources and magnitude of corruption and determining what, if anything, the government is doing about it. By nature corruption is hard to detect. One way is to examine the accounts of the national treasury and uncover discrepancies between *actual* commodity revenues and the *theoretical* ones (that is, those that should have been obtained had the goods been sold at international prices). Sometimes, the problem lies with multinational companies who attempt to cheat. For instance, Alaska noted that the amounts oil companies were claiming as their "net receipts" from the disposition of Alaskan oil were less than they should be. It required hard detective work—a few pennies a barrel can add up to billions of dollars—but Alaska succeeded in forcing the oil companies to repay a substantial sum, in excess of a billion dollars.

There are other tell-tale signs of potential corruption: Was there, for instance, an open process of bidding in the auction of a contract? How many bids were submitted? Recently, there has been a major initiative to induce foreign companies to "publish what they pay," or to disclose the checks they are sending to the government. If the government does not encourage such initiatives or if there is active resistance to doing so, there are grounds for suspicion. In countries where permission from the government is needed in order to export commodities or import inputs, people may pay bribes in order to get the required permits.

SPECIFIC ISSUES

In covering commodities, it is important to focus on three key elements: government policies, the underlying forces of demand and supply, and market structure.

GOVERNMENT POLICIES

Most African countries are exporters of commodities, which in most cases form the bulk of government revenues. As a result, governments have imposed policies to regulate the commodities markets. Even with the advent of deregulation and market reforms, there is still an ongoing debate in many African countries about to the extent to which they should liberalize their commodities markets. In virtually every country in Asia, the government is involved in the local rice market, either directly or indirectly. In Vietnam the government sets a minimum price to be paid to the farmers for their crop and requires exports to go through government-run food companies. In Japan and Korea the governments subsidize local farmers and impose tariffs to keep out foreign rice. For many years in Ghana, the government-run cocoa-marketing board controlled the industry by specifying the marketing channels for cocoa beans and prescribing acceptable farming practices. But in the late 1990s—partly at the prodding of the World Bank—the government began to liberalize the cocoa industry through the licensing of privately owned buying companies, which introduced some competition in the marketing of cocoa in Ghana. In Nigeria, meanwhile, the government has partnered with multinational oil companies in the exploration and production of crude oil. Under this arrangement, the government holds an average of 57 percent in the joint venture projects and the partners contribute to the projects in proportion to their shareholding. These joint ventures account for about 98 percent of Nigeria's crude oil production, with the remaining being produced by local entrepreneurs.

Depending on the commodity produced in the country, there can be a wide range of official policies on these products. Among the key questions are the following: Why do these policies exist? Are the policies effective? Who benefits from them? Are they creating distortions in the market? Are their any pressures on the government to effect changes? What are the sources of these pressures, and what motivates them? How have such reforms worked elsewhere?

SUPPLY AND DEMAND

Commodities markets react to various supply and demand conditions found at a particular point in time. In addition to viewing how supply and demand play out immediately—something called the spot market—the markets also react to the conditions expected to prevail in the markets in the future. It is therefore important for reporters to know the current situation of a given market and what it will likely be in, say, three months' time. In each market, there are specific factors affecting demand and supply and specific sources from whom reporters can learn how the market views the current situation, as well as the future.

In covering commodities with known cycles or seasons, it is a good idea for journalists to interview farmers, agricultural ministry officials, employees of government-run market boards, port officials, and potential buyers to find out what they expect production and sales to be. Reporters should also try to find out about possible delays in shipping exports because of weather, late harvests, and so on. Also when a farmer is trying a new crop, it can take years before it becomes ready to harvest and export. Rubber, for example, needs seven years before the trees can be tapped.

In mining for commodities such as gold, the time horizon is markedly different from that of agricultural commodities like cocoa or corn. Gold mining is quite capital intensive, and every stage in securing this capital can have an impact on supply. The process starts with the award of prospecting licenses at a concession or block. During the prospecting stage, the mining company assesses, through a chemical process called assay, the quality of the ore on its concession. Through this process, it determines whether or not the amount of gold is sufficient to warrant committing workers and materials to the actual mining process, or, in other words, whether it can make money from the quantity of gold available.

Even at this stage, the reporter should pay attention to the supply story. What is the prospect of the company finding enough gold ore in the concession? What does the assay result say, although the authenticity of this result must be taken with caution since the company may be worrying about the impact of any public statement on its share value.

Mining contracts are also important commodity stories. The reporter should find out whether the mining company will undertake the actual mining by itself or if it will contract it out to another party, and if so to whom. Reporters should also pay attention to the mobilization of equipment to a mine site, since this may be affected by a number of factors, including the depth of sand to be scraped before getting to the acceptable ore quality.

Because a mine is a long-term investment, those undertaking its development must form expectations about future prices. It is important to know what those expectations are, how they change over time, and how sensitive profits are to those expectations. Will a drop of 20 percent in the price lead to the abandonment of the mine? Is the concession being bought as, in effect, an option, only to be developed if the price increases enough? Is there a contract provision that inhibits such speculative behavior, such as the forfeiture of a large deposit? At the same time, it is important to know how the mining company handles its price risk and the strength of its financial position. Is there a serious risk of bankruptcy that would interrupt the development of the mine?

MARKET STRUCTURE

Market conditions reflect the actions, and sometimes the inaction, of the chain of players that runs from the producers through the middlemen and brokers or buyers to the final consumers. These actors play different roles in markets or industries, depending on the fundamental structure of the market concerned.

A market structure can give leverage to some companies over others. In the extreme case of a monopoly, the firm has power over the level of output and the price at which it sells its product. At the other extreme of perfect competition, no one firm has market power; there are a myriad of relatively small firms. Between these two extremes lies the real world where firms operate—there is usually some competition, but it is far from perfect. The reporter should be able to understand the market structure, how it is changing, and how proposed policy reforms would affect the different participants in the market, as well as the source of market power. What factors confer market power on some firms, or countries, as the case may be? How can a firm sustain its dominant power over a period of time in the industry?

WARS OVER GEMS

Commodities have become the economic tools of wars in several countries. From Angola to the Democratic Republic of Congo to Sierra Leone to Liberia, diamonds and other precious metals have played significant roles in funding wars.

While these commodities are usually not the reasons for the wars, warlords and their supporters have found them to be a convenient way of earning resources to continue wars, sometimes against world opinion and opposition. To circumvent international financial and weapons sanctions, such military leaders target mineral-rich regions for occupation. This enables them to mine these resources illegally and subsequently export them, in spite of procedures designed to prevent profiting from these illegal activities.

This has given rise to the concept of "conflict" diamonds or "dirty" diamonds. Revenues earned from their export are used to acquire arms and ammunition that are in turn used in further prosecution of wars, many of which have been extremely costly in terms of human lives. These conflicts may not have lasted as long as they did or still do if the parties involved had not had access to such minerals.

TIPS FOR REPORTERS

- Reporters should read as much as possible about the industry covered to get a good sense of its operations.

- It is important to know the producers, intermediaries, and final consumers and how they interact in the industry.

- For commodities with known cycles, reporters should learn the cycles and what to expect in each period.

- It is necessary to both follow breaking news as it unfolds and also get a long-term picture of where the industry is headed.

- Visits to farms, mines, oil platforms, and other production sites are valuable.

- Who are the stakeholders of the industry covered? These include all the people whose lives are affected in any way by the operations of the industry.

- It is important to have good contacts among analysts who specialize in the industry covered. These may be employees of banks, consultancies, and so on.

- Reporters frequently need to be good at simple calculations.

- It is important to know the national and international regulations that affect the industry.

- What are the global prices movements and conditions in countries that produce the same commodities as the country?

- Reporters should have a good sense of the demand and supply factors in the industry. Changes in these are often at the center of most disputes in commodity markets.

LINKS FOR MORE INFORMATION

1. Basic Commodities Inc., based in Winter Park, Florida, offers full-service brokerage services for a range of commodities. www.basiccommodities.com.

2. *Commodities Now* magazine's electronic version publishes commodities and financial news, data, and research. www.commodities-now.com.

3. Sucden (UK) Ltd., a London-based commodities brokerage firm, buys and sells coffee, cocoa, and sugar, among other commodities. www.sucden.co.uk.

4. The online store owned by Halliker's, Inc., based in Springfield, Missouri, sells trading books, software, and computers. www.tradersworld.com.

5. The London-based International Cocoa Organisation is an industry group charged with administering cocoa agreements signed by forty-two member countries. www.icco.org.

6. The World Gold Council is an industry marketing and lobbying body funded by twenty-four gold companies worldwide. www.gold.org.

7. The U.S. Department of Agriculture's Foreign Agriculture Service has links to reports, trade policy and negotiations, commodities, and countries. http://www.fas.usda.gov.

8. The U.S. Department of Agriculture's commodity page has more specific information on commodities, U.S. import and export data, and market reports. http://www.fas.usda.gov/commodity.html.

9. The Chicago Board of Trade, one of the main commodities exchanges in the United States, specializes in agriculture products such as corn and soybeans. http://www.cbot.com.

10. The New York Board of Trade is where coffee, sugar, cocoa, cotton, and orange juice are traded. http://www.nybot.com.

11. Sparks, a commodities research company, offers Web links to some the most important players in that market. http://www.sparksco.com.

12. The International Rice Research Institute, a nonprofit group based in Manila, provides research and training on agricultural issues. http://www.irri.org.

13. The International Food Policy Research Institute, based in Washington, D.C., focuses on policies concerning food supply, economic growth, and poverty in developing countries. http://www.ifpri.org.

CHAPTER TWENTY-TWO

OIL AND DEVELOPMENT

PETTER NORE

THE OIL AND natural gas industries play a decisive role in the economic, social, and environmental development of countries with deposits of either fuel. While the discovery of oil or gas is usually heralded as a windfall for a country's economy, particularly a poor one, it can also be a double-edged sword. Economists term this phenomenon the "resource curse," and it is often associated with worsening income distribution and a lack of development not only on the economic front but in the social and environmental realms as well. For journalists in developing countries covering the petroleum industry, it is vital to understand the "resource curse" and what can be done to counteract it. Some oil-exporting countries have managed to spread the benefits from oil to broad sectors of their populations, primarily through mechanisms of "good governance." So there is nothing inevitable about the resource curse.

A WEAK RECORD

Historically, the petroleum industry has had a weak record in fostering development. Based on empirical data it appears that the more resources a country has, the worse its prospects for economic development. This was evident during the 1980s and 1990s, when oil-dependent developing countries posted average growth of between 2 and 2.5 percentage points less than developing countries that did not possess oil. Though the decline in real oil prices may explain part of this failure, similar results show up for resource-rich countries over a longer time frame (see table 22.1).[1] There are several factors contributing to this seemingly paradoxical result.[2]

TABLE 22.1

REAL GDP GROWTH IN OIL-INTENSIVE COUNTRIES (%)

	1983–1992	1993–2000
Developing countries	4.7	5.4
—with oil as most important source of income	2.6	3.0
—other	5.0	5.7
Industrial countries	3.3	2.7
World	3.4	3.5

Source: IMF World Economic Outlook, October 2001.

■ *Conflict*. The existence of the often huge profits, or rents (defined as returns in excess of a "normal rate of return), arising from petroleum production gives rise to conflict, and not just between the governments and the oil companies that they rely upon to extract the resources. Local and national governments in oil-producing nations often fight over oil revenues. In Russia, for example, provincial governments have historically held up expansion of the oil industry because of their dissatisfaction with the share of federal oil revenues coming their way. In Nigeria, meanwhile, the conflict has been seen in the unrest of the Niger Delta, where the population claims oil money has been squandered by the federal government or has disappeared into foreign bank accounts. With this backdrop, the oil and gas activities have in many cases done more to stall development than to foster it.

■ *Rent seeking replaces entrepreneurship*. In countries with oil and gas riches, the main commercial activity often becomes "how to rob the state" instead of how to create new wealth. Unlike other forms of enterprises, there are few direct spillovers from gas and oil production to other parts of the economy, other than through the profits generated. But the vast profits available in the oil and gas sector seem to bleed the entrepreneurial spirit of the local capitalist and merchant classes. This is nothing new, nor is it a phenomenon restricted to the oil and gas industry. In the fifteenth and sixteenth centuries, the pattern was seen in Spain following the huge inflow of gold from the new colonies in the Americas.

■ *Corruption and its consequences*. While incentives in the private sector may be undermined and misdirected toward rent seeking rather than wealth creation, the adverse effects in the public sector are even greater. The large amount of easy wealth under the control of the government often leads to corruption, and companies are tempted to bribe government officials in order to get access to the resources at a price below the fair market value. While the country as a whole loses because bribery leads to a portfolio of damaging projects, the govern-

RENT AND PROFIT

DAVID NISSEN

The term "rent" is used by economists to designate income in excess of total expenses, including "capital recovery." Another term for rent is "economic income." Economic income differs from the business-accounting concept of income in the way payments for the use of investment goods are treated. In business accounting, only the original outlay for investment goods is deducted, or "expensed," as depreciation over time. To calculate rent or economic income, a charge for the "carrying" of using the investment goods is deducted as well.

The prospective flow of rent determines the value of an enterprise in excess of the value of the investment goods it owns. The higher the expected future stream of rent, the higher the enterprise's value is today.

If an enterprise is earning rents in a particular line of business, we would expect that other investors would be attracted to enter and that in the long run, competition would bid prices down and costs up until the rents disappear and each enterprise is earning only its competitive cost of capital.

Economists identify several situations in which this long-run process does not work and in which rents continue to accrue. *Land and resource rents* arise when a critical factor of production cannot be reproduced. The price of land or resource ownership reflects the discounted value of these rents. The potential for *technical monopoly rents* arises when, at efficient scale, one firm dominates the market and can drive prices above costs unless regulated. *Political rent seeking* occurs when enterprises use political influence to find institutional benefits, such as franchises, subsidies, tariffs, or quotas, which appropriate revenue but do not add value.

In the nineteenth century, the classical economist David Ricardo elegantly worked out how to think about rent when applying the concept to land. The cost of producing a particular good, according to Ricardo's theorem, varies with the quality of land used to produce the good: the higher the land's quality, the cheaper the cost of production. However, irrespective of the cost of production, all goods of a type have the same market price. Therefore, owners of higher-quality land can keep a larger share (the "residual") of a good's price than owners of lower-quality land. This "residual" is equivalent to the rent that a landowner can charge.

The same analysis applies to oil production, where the term "rent" is used extensively. Oil prices are determined in the international market. However, the cost of extracting the oil differs markedly from region to another. Countries with low production costs (mainly in the Arabian Gulf) can extract a much higher "rent" from each oil barrel than those with higher production costs.

The above theory of rent applies to a factor of production (for example, land or oil) that is *productive* but not yet *produced*. This raises the question: What is the rent on factors of production that have already been produced but that themselves can be further used for production of other goods and services? The best example of this is an investment good such as machinery. Calculating rent on an investment good requires three steps. First, establish *free cash flow*, which is defined as the difference between revenue generated from the investment good, on the one hand, and operating expenses and required additional investment, on the other. Second, calculate *profit*, which is the difference between the free cash flow and the interest the asset's owner pays on the funding that he or she had to raise to pay for the asset. Third, economic profit, thus calculated, is defined as *rent*.

The phrase "rent seeking" is also used in another context: to describe efforts to acquire wealth without adding value. Market imperfections—including the absence of a well-structured property-rights system and a lack of efficient markets—can be abused by rent seekers to extract noneconomic profit. For example, rent seekers could use political influence to change subsidies, tariffs, franchises, regulatory measures, and the like.

ment officials gain. The corruption not only undermines good governance but fuels political and social unrest. When corrupt governments gain access to the large incomes generated by oil and gas, they often repress human rights to ensure that the revenues keep flowing without the interference of social or political unrest.

- *The Dutch disease*. Holland provides one example of the negative *financial* fallout the energy industry can unleash. In the late 1970s, the country saw a dramatic jump in its state income from the natural gas sector, which improved its financial position. As energy-related earnings flowed in, the currency strengthened, and the competitiveness of the sectors not involved in energy production eroded, causing a "crowding out" of industries not linked to the gas sector. Nigeria had a similar experience when the overvalued currency in the 1970s and 1980s crowded out the local agricultural production. The problem is particularly serious in developing countries, however: the overvalued currency impedes the creation of the *new* industries and jobs which are essential for successful development.

- *Instability*. Oil prices have exhibited enormous instability (and the same is true of the prices of other commodities), and while both developed and less-developed countries have difficulties managing the consequences of the resulting instability of revenues, the problems are particularly acute for developing countries. Typically, in good times, foreign lenders encourage them to borrow, and, given their vast needs, the countries do so with alacrity. But because of their limited capacities, much of the money is invested poorly. Then, when oil prices fall, not only do lenders stop lending, they start demanding their money back, forcing the countries into crisis.

    What is critical for any country is the difference between the price it receives for the oil and the cost of extraction. The price it receives is the international price (say the price in Europe or America), *less* the cost of transportation. A country with low extraction costs and low transportation costs has high *rents*, and a 10 percent reduction in the price accordingly has a relatively small effect on these rents compared to a country with high extraction costs and/or high transportation costs. In the aftermath of the East Asian crisis in the late 1990s, oil prices fell so low that rents were almost eliminated in some large producers, such as Russia.

GLOBAL AND LOCAL ENVIRONMENTAL EFFECTS

Oil and gas production has, in a number of well-documented cases in such places as Nigeria, Alaska, and Argentina, had an adverse effect on the local environment. That so much of the cost is often borne by local communities, including indigenous people, and so much of the revenue goes to the national governments is a major source of dissatisfaction. While this is true for most natural resources, oil and to a lessser extent gas have, in addition, adverse *global* environmental effects as a carbon-based fuel that gives off significant emissions of greenhouse gases, with the most important of these being carbon dioxide.

Some petroleum-exporting countries in the developing world such as Malaysia and Oman have not encountered the same negative effects that were described above. OECD countries like Canada and Norway have largely managed to successfully incorporate a large petroleum sector into their economies. But that being said, the overall picture for developing countries is nevertheless rather bleak. The question that arises, then, is what governments and companies can do to repair or avoid these negative consequences and encourage the more positive aspects of oil and gas production. Ideally, the extra revenues from hydrocarbons could improve living standards for the broader population, while still assuring that the interests of groups most immediately affected by the industry are met.

CHARACTERISTICS OF THE OIL AND GAS INDUSTRY

Before a discussion of such positive strategies is possible, however, it is important to understand some of the key developments in the industry and the outlook for the globe's use of oil and gas. Oil and gas are expected to remain the dominant fuels worldwide for the next thirty years. Around 62 percent of the globe's energy demand is currently supplied by hydrocarbons, a percentage that is expected to increase to about 67 percent by 2030 if demand continues to grow at the pace seen in the last decade. This increase stems from the rising use of the clean-burning natural gas, which is expected to grow from 23 percent of world energy supply to 28 percent, while oil's share is set to remain more or less unchanged.[3]

There are two principle reasons for the world's continued reliance on oil and gas. First, there are currently no alternatives to these fuels in transportation. Although a number of the world's major energy companies are pushing to advance research on hydrogen-driven fuel cells, this is unlikely to have a significant impact on petroleum demand over the next thirty years.[4] Second, natural gas is likely to continue its rapid ascent as the world's favorite fuel because of its advantages in generating electricity. Among the carbons, gas is the fuel with the lowest emissions,[5] and it yields the lowest costs per kilowatt hour of electricity produced, elements that have led to its characterization as the preferred "transitional fuel" or the "bridge to the energy future."[6] If the present concerns about global warming continue, there will be strong pressure for economies like China and India to switch from coal-based electricity to the less-polluting natural gas. Natural gas can also be used to produce hydrogen, so demand may get a further boost as hydrogen use develops.

Figures from the International Energy Agency show that even if the world pursues a more aggressive energy-saving agenda and especially increases its use of wind and solar power—renewable sources currently account for a paltry 3 percent of all global commercial energy—it would be a long time before there was a significant effect on the relative position of the oil and gas industries.

Oil and gas are also likely to remain dominant because there is more than enough of both fuels to meet expected demand for the foreseeable future. Frequently, claims are made that the world is running out of hydrocarbons, but there is little indication that the globe lacks physical resources of such fuels. The ratio of reserves to production has increased for gas and slightly decreased for oil over the last decades. The problem is more the location of the reserves—the majority are found or could be found in the Middle East, where political instability can be a hurdle to production. Gas reserves are also found at great distances from the places they are actually consumed, increasing costs of transportation. (But of course, there is no assurance that reserves will continue to be discovered.)

In addition, oil and gas have been and are likely to remain a strategic commodity, or a commodity that is so vital to the operation of the world economy that it is prone to strong political interference from both the demand and supply sides.[7] Three examples highlight this point.

- The Organization of Petroleum Exporting Countries, in existence for more than forty years, aims to adjust oil supplies in line with world demand to keep prices elevated. OPEC was also once used as a political instrument in the aftermath of the 1973 Middle East war,[8] but the organization's present policy is to stay away from such action.

- A central element of global economic development over the last fifty years has been unfettered access to relatively cheap and predictable flows of oil. The United States, as the world's main superpower, has an overriding interest in securing a stable flow of oil at such terms. Many allege that oil played a role in the country's decision to go to war in Iraq in both 1991 and 2003, while others emphasize more ideological explanations.

- International natural-gas projects are often a mixture of politics and economics since they cross national borders, requiring the cooperation and approval of various governments to become a reality. One example is the difficulty of sending gas from the Middle East and Iran to India because the planned pipeline must cross Pakistan, a country with whom India has strained relations. Another was the construction of additional pipelines taking gas from Russia to Western Europe during the late years of the Cold War in the 1980s, despite the determined opposition of the U.S. government.

Within the oil and gas industry, it is also important to understand the various players. A handful of *private multinational oil companies* currently dominate the international oil industry, companies that are known as super-majors and that include ExxonMobil, BP, the Royal Dutch/Shell Group and ChevronTexaco. Their exploration success over the recent years has been weak, and today some of these companies have developed strong interests in energy sectors other than oil, such as natural gas and, in some cases, renewable energy sources.

In spite of the dominance of the super-majors, state-owned oil companies are still powerful players in the industry, controlling a large chunk of the world's oil production. As of 2001, 60 percent of oil output was in the hands of state oil firms like Aramco in Saudi Arabia, the Kuwaiti Oil Company, the Nigerian National Oil Company, and Sonatrach of Algeria. Some countries, like Mexico, have constitutional provisions that do not allow for privatization of oil-producing assets. There is also a large group of regional private companies, whose operations are smaller in scope and who compete with the super-majors in specific niches within various markets.

Since the mid-1980s, more of the world has been opened up for the international oil companies, while there has been a growing tendency toward privatization in the oil industry.[9] This trend was partly a response to the failing performances of a number of state oil companies. Some governments, facing severe budget constraints, could not invest adequately in the sector. In part, this often reflected IMF-imposed conditions that treated all government expenditures equally, with no distinction between spending for investment purposes and spending for consumption reasons. There was also an ideological component: U.S. President Ronald Reagan and British Prime Minister Margaret Thatcher introduced the belief that the state should stay out of any kind of productive enterprises. This policy was at least initially supported by strong multilateral organizations like the World Bank.[10]

The trend toward privatization has new consequences for the way the industry traditionally has operated in places where governments control the level of production. If OPEC wants to maintain its power over the world oil market and world oil prices, it must retain the ability to control the supply levels of member states, which currently coordinate cutbacks in supplies when prices drop and supply increases when prices jump. So far, cooperation has not been a problem because production in most OPEC nations is controlled by the state, either directly or through state oil companies. But the ability to control supply may be more problematic as international oil companies strengthen their presence in the region and decisions about production levels become more investment driven. Private investors are not likely to warm to large swings in the utilization of their capital investments, even if the ultimate aim of these shifts is higher prices. This development is only in its infancy, and it is difficult to predict what will happen, especially in the Middle East. But if the trend becomes dominant it will change the way the oil industry operates.

In recent years, new powerful national firms run by the private sector have also appeared on the oil scene, such as a number of Russian companies that have opened up for closer cooperation with western companies. But their long-term fate still seems to be closely linked the Russian government, which wants to maintain strong control of Russian resources.

Finally, service companies such as the oil-technology firms Schlumberger and Halliburton are playing an increased role in the industry. Both private and public oil companies are increasingly using these types of firms to carry out complicated technological tasks. Previously, this work was given to multinational companies, which in turn subcontracted with the service companies to do the job. A possible long-term trend thus appears to be the weakening of the middlemen (the multinationals) and strengthening of the role of the service companies. This trend is today seen in Russia and parts of the Middle East.

CORPORATE SOCIAL RESPONSIBILITY

There has been extensive criticism of the industry in recent years—from oil spills that pollute the ocean (such as the Valdez spill in Alaska) to the greenhouse gases the pollute the atmosphere to involvement in abuses of human rights (as in Nigeria). During the 1980s and 1990s, nongovernmental organizations began to ask fundamental questions about the industry and the human-rights conditions in the countries in which oil companies operated. They raised concerns about the way oil operations were carried out on the ground, the impact on indigenous people of exploration and production, and the industry's position on greenhouse gases. They also questioned the conditions of the workers of the oil industry, as well as their subcontractors, in the producing countries. As the NGOs raised more and more doubts, shareholders also became restless and the share values of some companies started to come under pressure.

The corporate sector responded to these concerns, and by the mid-1990s, oil companies could no longer follow their old strategies. Shell led the way in changing its ways of operating after it was badly shaken by two incidents: the intense opposition from both consumer groups and governments to its scuttling one of its oil rigs, Brent Spar in the North Sea, and the execution of author Ken Saro Wiwa in Nigeria, which in world opinion was linked to Shell's dominant position in that country. In response, Shell developed a more aggressive policy of "corporate social responsibility," which has subsequently been copied or used as the inspiration for a number of other companies' policies. Companies attempted to deal with most or all of the questions raised by the NGOs and society at large, and while some policy statements were superficial, other firms took the issues seriously and tried to change course.[11]

The movement toward CSR was not only a result of NGO pressure. A number of the major international companies had come to believe that the questions about sustainable development and the global environment warranted a more systematic response.[12] Some of the major oil companies published goals for the reduction of greenhouse gases, and some firms began providing audited environmental and social balance sheets in addition to their financial balance sheets. BP instituted an internal trading system in a bid to reduce its emissions for greenhouse gases, and a number of oil companies are aggressively pursuing research and development into hydrogen-based fuel cells. Companies have also started to invest heavily in alternative energy sources such as wind power.

WHAT CAN BE DONE TO BRING ABOUT
SUSTAINABLE DEVELOPMENT?

In light of this recent history, there appears to be a historic opening for the global oil industry to increase its focus on sustainable development to ensure that the industry contributes more to the growth of the developing countries and that it does less to harm the environment. That at least part of the industry and some governments, regardless of their reasons, are more willing to adhere to the principles of sustainable development is to be welcomed. There are also a number of new actors in the industry that may represent a more diverse range of viewpoints than the monolithic attitudes that have characterized the industry in the past.

There are three strategies or actions that could help build a more sustainable petroleum sector. The first and most important is related to improved governance. The countries that have succeeded in overcoming the resource curse all have good records of governance. Given this, it is tempting to relabel the "resource curse" the "governance curse." One way to improve governance is to ensure better *transparency* in the spending of oil revenues, whether at the state or regional level. Transparency allows effective oversight by regulators and the public in large. It is, as such, an important way to fight entrenched corruption and helps increase the general quality of governance in a society. In countries where one root cause of the resource curse is the erratic and secretive spending of petroleum revenues by corrupt government officials, an initial step can be simply to inform the public of how much income the country earns from the activity. Incredibly, there are still a number of states in which this is not the case and in which large amounts of revenues are hidden from public scrutiny, although there has been progress recently.[13] There are a number of global initiatives to combat corruption that will contribute to improving transparency in the oil and gas sector.[14]

Another step that would guarantee increased transparency and better governance is the establishment of *petroleum-revenue stabilization funds* or petroleum funds for future generations. Such funds are found in many territories and countries, such as Alaska, Kuwait, Kazakhstan, Azerbaijan, Chad, and Norway. These funds, which store away a certain amount of oil revenues, attempt to deal with the swings in oil income and the fact that the present generation is consuming an exhaustible resource at the expense of future generations. Successful funds can also promote sustainable development by shifting petroleum resources, which will eventually run out, into new assets so that growth can be sustained even when there are no longer oil revenues. One such a fund has been set up by the government of Chad in cooperation with the World Bank to channel income from the Chad/Cameroon oil pipeline into a number of specific social fields like education and health.[15]

The Norwegian Petroleum Fund has been described as a successful example of a future-generation fund. All net petroleum-related income from the production of oil and natural gas in Norway flows into this special fund, which has reached a level equal to about 60 percent of gross domestic product. Of this money, 60 percent is placed in bonds and 40 percent in equities—all in non-Norwegian assets. Each year the equivalent of 4 percent of the fund's value is withdrawn, a level that is the expected long-term real rate of return on these assets. This arrangement ensures that the value of the fund remains unchanged if there are no new deposits into the fund while diversifying the risk of the holdings. It is, in effect, creating an *endowment* for the country.

Such funds are not a panacea. What parliaments and presidents can create, parliaments and presidents can undo. There are no guarantees that these funds, often created in periods of plenty, will continue to exist when the going gets tough. The survival of the funds ultimately depends on the strength of the political system backing it up and the ability to stick to often-difficult decisions when circumstances change. Still, these funds do force governments to be more transparent in their handling of petroleum revenues, and in this way, they encourage strengthened governance in petroleum-producing states. For many who see a basic lack of governance as the key problem in resource-rich countries, this is a good enough reason to support resource-based funds.

A second strategy to encourage sustainable development is to force the oil industry to follow the principles of "*best international practice*" when operating in developing and emerging economies. In many cases this simply means that they follow the principles the industry itself has formulated with respect to carrying out environmental-impact assessments, treating workers fairly, dealing with indigenous populations, and not paying bribes. Host governments should also follow such principles. Sometimes governments try to gain a leg up in the attraction of foreign investment by lowering environmental standards. In these circumstances, the burden falls on serious companies to refuse to invest.

A third action that would support environmentally sustainable development is an *increased use of natural gas*. Natural gas has both local and global environmental advantages over other fossil fuels, and it is the most cost-efficient way of bringing electricity to much of the quarter of the world's population currently without it. (In the past, natural gas was sometimes simply wasted, flared off, rather than captured and transported to where it could be used.) A move toward gas on a global scale is already under way, but major entities like the World Bank and the European Union could help to foster this trend.

CONCLUSION

Historically, the oil sector has seemed to have made less of a contribution in promoting sustainable development that it could have. If the sector wants to change this record and tackle some of the more pressing problems, its most important tasks involve improving governance by ensuring that petroleum revenues are more transparent and that corruption is contained. The industry should follow international "best practices" in the execution of projects, and shift more toward natural gas. If governments, industries, multilateral agencies, and civil societies work together, such actions can be implemented, and the oil and gas industry would make a more significant contribution toward sustainable development.

TIPS FOR REPORTERS

- How are oil companies living up to their own stated policies and best practices in the field of sustainable development?

- What are the responses from the financial markets to the strategies of the major companies toward achieving sustainable development?

- Is the trend toward privatizations continuing? What is driving the push for privatization? Inefficiency on the part of the state run industry? Lack of capital to investment in the state run industry? Ideology? Is the lack of investment caused in part by faulty accounting, which penalizes public investment compared to private investment? What role are international agencies like the IMF and the World Bank playing in the push for privatization?

- Is corruption in the industry being contained? Is governance improving and transparency increasing?

- What is the cost of oil extraction and transport in the country? At what price in the international markets will production become unprofitable?

- Are stabilization funds solidly anchored, or are they likely to unravel when the price of oil drops?

- Reporters should watch out for decisive technological changes in the hydrogen business, particularly in the form of dramatic decreases in storage costs, in the production costs of fuel cells, and, most important, in governments' active support of the industry.

- Is natural gas increasing its market share as expected? Reporters need to be on the look out for technological changes like the direct conversion of natural gas for air conditioning and small-scale use of natural gas for local electricity and heat generation, which will increase the local use of gas.

- Are there any signs of an increase or decrease in OPEC's power, particularly as expressed through its market share? Is the influence of the international oil companies in investment and production decisions in OPEC countries increasing?

- Reporters should be on the look out for the development of substitutes to petroleum products. Coal could become a formidable competitor and capture market share from other fuels, especially natural gas, if a way is found to decrease greenhouse-gas emissions from coal combustion. Also, closely monitor efforts at conservation and technological change that reduce the demand for energy.

- Increasing concerns about global warming may, over the next few years, lead to further efforts to reduce the energy intensity of economic growth and to internalize the full economic costs of the production and use of different fuels. This could have major effects on the price of gas and oil compared to other energy carriers.

LINKS FOR MORE INFORMATION

(with thanks to Jean-Francois Seznec)

1. Homepage of the *Oil and Gas Journal*. www.ogjonline.com.

2. The International Energy Agency, which has basic information about the world's energy scene. www.iea.org.

3. News items on the oil industry. www.oil.com.

4. Transparency International. www.transparency.org.

5. News from Bloomberg on energy matters. www.bloomberg.com/energy.

6. British Petroleum provides statistics on oil, gas, and coal. www.bp.com/worldenergy.

7. Homepage of the Petroleum Finance Ecompany, a consulting company based in Washington, D.C. www.pfcenergy.com.

8. Middle East Economic Survey. www.mees.com.

9. Homepage of the US government's Department of Energy. www.eia.doe.gov.

10. Homepage of OPEC. www.opec.org.

NOTES

This piece was written when I was affiliated with the Stern School of Business, New York University during the academic year 2002/2003. All points of view expressed are my own and do not reflect in any way the views of my employer Hydro.

1. See for example Jeffrey D. Sachs and Andrew M. Warner, *Natural Resource Abundance and Economic Growth: Leading Issues in Economic Development*, NBER Working Paper no. 5398 (1995) and (New York: Oxford University Press, 2000).

2. For an overview of the issues subsumed under the heading "resource curse" and petroleum funds, see IMF, "Stabilization and Savings Funds For Nonrenewable Resources: Experience and Fiscal Policy Implications," Occasional Paper no. 205, (Washington D.C.: IMF, 2001).

3. The facts in this section are drawn from the *World Energy Outlook* 2002, published by the International Energy Agency (www.iea.org) and BP's *Annual Statistical Review* (2002; www.bp.com/centres/energy/index.asp).

4. Hydrogen may indeed experience technical breakthroughs during this period, but because of the long lifetime of most capital assets including transport infrastructure like gas stations, the effects on the demand for other fuels will be modest.

5. In primary combustion, one kilowatt hour produced from natural gas gives rise to about half of the greenhouse-gas emissions of oil. Adopting a "life-cycle" perspective where leakage of greenhouse gases from the gas chain are included, the difference is still around one-fourth.

6. Cf. statement made by Lester Brown et al., *State of the World* (New York: W. W. Norton, 1991).

7. Daniel Yergin, *The Prize: The Epic Quest For Oil, Money And Power*(New York: Simon and Schuster, 1991), gives a comprehensive overview of the history of the oil industry and how a combination of economics and politics historically has influenced the dynamic of the industry

8. It was OAPEC (a subgroup of OPEC) that carried out the boycott.

9. For a critical overview of this trend of privatizations, see P. Stevens "The Practical Record and Prospects of Privatization Programmes in the Arab World," in *Economic and Political Liberalisation in the Middle East*, ed. T. Niblock and E. Murphy (London: British Academic Press, 1992), 114–31.

10. The bank today has a more sophisticated appreciation of the role of the state; cf. the World Bank, "The State in a Changing World," World Development Report (1997), which advocates a state that plays a "catalytic, facilitating role, encouraging and complementing the activities of private businesses and individuals" (iii).

11. The question at issue is the well-known conflict between shareholder and stakeholder value. How meaningful is a policy of CSR when the companies have a fiduciary duty towards their shareholders that takes precedence over all other interests? At the very least, a company's management should deal with situations threatening to destroy shareholder value, such as major environmental or public relations disasters, in the same way it would handle an effort to increase sales and/or margins.

12. The creation in 1991 of the World Business Council for Sustainable Development, a coalition of 165 international companies "united by a shared commitment to sustainable development via the three pillars of economic growth, ecological balance and social progress" was one such response.

13. The agreement in London in June 2003, under the aegis of "The Extractive Industries Transparency Initiative," where a number of oil-producing states pledged to make public their income from the oil sector, is a promising first step toward achieving a higher degree of transparency and hence strengthening governance in the petroleum sector. This agreement had the full support of the international oil industry.

14. Transparency International is the only international organization devoted to combating corruption. It has eighty-five independent chapters around the globe and focuses on prevention and reforming systems rather than on individual cases. See www.transparency.org.

15. For a comprehensive overview of the Chad/Cameroon pipeline project, see www.worldbank.org/afr/ccproj.

CHAPTER TWENTY-THREE

POVERTY REDUCTION

ISABEL ORTIZ

POVERTY TRENDS AND MEASUREMENTS

MORE THAN 2.8 billion people, or around half the world's population, live below the international poverty line of $2 a day. Of those, 1.2 billion live in extreme poverty, surviving on less than $1 a day. Most of the poor are in Asia and Africa. The incidence of poverty is greater in women than in men and higher in rural areas than in urban areas. Vulnerable groups such as the elderly, ethnic minorities, refugees, or the disabled are much more affected by poverty. Since 1987, the incidence of poverty has decreased, and the proportion of people living below the dollar-a-day poverty line declined from 28 percent to 24 percent of the total population of developing countries. However, in absolute terms, poverty is not decreasing. Population growth remains high in developing countries, and many are born in poverty and destitution. Using World Bank data, the number of poor people has actually increased since the late 1980s.

The definition and measurement of poverty is a highly political issue. Governments tend to hide the existence of large pockets of poverty, as they make countries look underdeveloped and show up public-policy failures. Currently, different countries use different methodologies, which are hard to compare. A commonly used approach is to consider the per capita expenditure necessary to attain 2,000 to 2,500 calories of nutrition per day, plus a small allowance for nonfood consumption. However, these measures do not adequately reflect other expenses necessary to cover basic needs—clothing, drinking water, housing, and access to basic education and health, among others. This is the reason that UN institutions started using the one- and two-dollar-a-day poverty lines. This latter approach has obvious flaws, not least the fact that a dollar in one country can buy very different amounts of goods in another. Moreover, if measurements based on a real minimum-consumption threshold were used, the number of people living in poverty would soar.

Many argue that poverty is not only income poverty. It also has noneconomic dimensions, including discrimination, exploitation, lack of control of resources, vulnerability to shocks, helplessness in the face of violence and corruption, lack of voice in decision making, powerlessness, and social exclusion. As we expand the definition of poverty, the number of people affected by it increases.

The concept of poverty is often confused in popular media. For one thing, poverty should be distinguished from inequality. Poverty measures the *absolute* number of people living below a certain income or consumption benchmark. Inequality, by contrast, refers to the *distribution* of income within an overall group. For instance, while, as an aggregate, 2.8 billion people in the world are poor (a poverty concept), it is estimated that the richest 20 percent of the world receives 89 percent of world income and the poorest 20 percent receives only 1.2 percent (an income-distribution concept). The comparison between what the rich and the poor possess raises serious questions about the adequacy of current development models ("development for whom?" has become an important slogan) and generates feelings of injustice and political claims. This is why national estimates of inequality are even less reliable than those on poverty, and UN institutions are working toward better monitoring of income distribution data. By now, there is conclusive evidence that inequality grew in the latter part of the twentieth century.

POVERTY REDUCTION IN HISTORICAL PERSPECTIVE

Poverty is not a new phenomenon. Many descriptions of Europe in the nineteenth century describe living and working conditions similar to those seen today in developing countries. Charles Dickens's stories of children's misfortunes are analogous to the lives of many working children in contemporary Africa, Asia, and Latin America. Friedrich Engels description of Manchester's river Irk industrial ghetto is similar to today's shanty-town scenes from Smoky Mountain in Manila or Nova Iguazu in Rio de Janeiro. What happened in developed countries—the progressive development of citizens' rights and welfare—can also happen in developing countries.

An example is the United States in the 1930s. After the 1929 crash and the Depression, poverty was widespread, people migrated with little more to sell than their own labor, crime rose, and citizens became powerless—once again, a similar situation to today's developing countries. After years of hardship, unemployment, and crisis, the Roosevelt administration embarked on the New Deal, mobilizing the economy, generating employment, combating crime, and creating a social safety net for the poor. It worked. The United States entered a period of prosperity.

Another good example of progressive public policies that massively raised living standards comes from the end of World War II. Politicians from the advanced Western economies were determined that unemployment and economic crises, which had provoked political crises and contributed to the rise of communism and fascism, should never happen again. They agreed that full employment and macroeconomic stability should be the primary national policy objectives. Governments also became significantly involved in education, medical care, social and housing assistance, minimum retirement levels, unemployment insurance, employment policies, and enforcement of labor laws and regulations. It worked again. These postwar Keynesian policies contributed to high productivity gains in the workforce, expanded domestic demand, and increased economic growth. The populations of Europe, Japan, North America, Australia, and New Zealand experienced prosperity virtually unmatched in history.

The lesson is that poverty reduction can be achieved quickly through concerted policy action if governments are committed. However, developing-country governments are rarely fully committed—poverty reduction is generally only one of many developmental objectives. A significant number of developing countries are starved of capital, pressured by external debt, and have limited access to developed countries' markets to export their products. Partly because of the associated costs, social development has not been a priority; it has been largely neglected, or at best addressed with inadequate resources. In many cases, public policy disproportionately benefits certain interest groups instead of ensuring development for the majority of the population. This is why the poverty-reduction debate is highly politicized and ideological.

THE POVERTY, INEQUALITY, AND ECONOMIC-GROWTH DEBATE

Many argue that poverty reduction should not be a primary objective for developing countries and that economic growth should be the first priority. Eventually, the benefits of growth will "trickle down" to the poor. Further, academics such as Simon Kuznets, the 1971 Nobel laureate in economics, say inequality is necessary in the first stages of a country's development; in a later stage, as a country becomes richer, it may invest in welfare, social development, and poverty reduction—thus those are secondary objectives. These views are old but still influential in the development debate. Numerous governments today support what has been called the "trickle down plus" approach (growth as a first priority, with some limited basic education, water supply, and other social-development projects).

This debate, though, can be a convenient way to postpone policies that benefit the poor. Of course, poverty reduction needs economic growth to be sustainable. However, a fixation on growth rates is not enough; the quality of growth matters. Different types of growth have different effects on employment, which is the surest way of reducing poverty. Ideally, poverty reduction policies aim for the kind of rapid and stable growth that creates jobs. During the last decades there have been significant cases of "jobless growth," where the trickle-down effect does not occur or occurs only marginally. That said, fast growth, even if jobless, can still be a source of increased tax revenue that can be used to finance social development and stimulate the local economy.

Kuznets's theories have been widely contested. As noted above, sustainable poverty reduction cannot happen without growth. At the same time, evidence shows that highly unequal income-distribution patterns are obstacles to growth itself. By concentrating assets and wealth in the hands of a few and maintaining high poverty levels, countries have limited domestic markets; in turn, low domestic demand depresses local enterprises and keeps them from growing. Highly inequitable societies also suffer from political tension and often social unrest. Additionally, poor living conditions, and particularly malnutrition and poverty in children, damage health, cause death, reduce intelligence, and lower productivity and opportunities for future adults, a high social tax for a country to pay. Equitable policies are an indispensable instrument for countries to raise productivity, maintain their international competitiveness, develop domestic markets, and continue economic growth.

The arguments *for* inequitable economic growth first are:

- Growth is a prerequisite for poverty reduction. The benefits of growth will eventually trickle down to the rest of society.

- The rich save more; the higher the inequality, the higher the rate of profit and the greater the incentive for investment, thus leading to faster growth in the future.

- Poverty and inequality keep the labor force cheap and thus encourage investment.

- Attention needs to be given to keeping taxation on investors and higher income groups low, thus available resources for poverty reduction or social development may be limited.

The arguments *against* inequitable economic growth first are:

- Economic growth and poverty reduction should be promoted in parallel from early development stages as part of the country's modernization strategy and the social contract between the government and citizens.

- The quality of growth matters: emphasis has to be placed on the process of growth (that is, on employment, distributive aspects, good governance, correcting market imperfections, and ensuring stability instead of volatility) with parallel investments in social development.

- Inequality fosters distorted development patterns such as dependency on cheap labor (the so-called race to the bottom, pushing salaries down to the level of the poorest competing country).

- Egalitarian distribution patterns encourage domestic demand and thus growth; greater effective demand (consumption ratios) of the lower-income groups generates a larger domestic market.

- Raising the incomes of the poor increases productivity of the work-force.

- The greater the inequality, the less the trickle-down effect, given that powerful groups are not likely to let their privileges go—inequality is often an obstacle for social progress and a catalyst of internal political conflict.

- The huge gap between rich and poor—80 percent of the world's population receives only 11 percent of the world's income—has become more worrying, since the world is facing the threat of organized terrorism from groups based in some of the world's poorest countries.

POVERTY-REDUCTION POLICIES AT THE BEGINNING OF THE TWENTY-FIRST CENTURY

Around three-quarters of the countries in the developing world have antipoverty plans incorporated in their national planning. These, however, are often underbudgeted and have no target objectives or deadlines. In 1995, the international community set some specific targets at the World Summit for Social Development. These Millennium Development Goals were later endorsed by all countries at the United Nations fifty-fifth General Assembly (2000). They include halving hunger and extreme poverty by 2015 and improving a basic set of development indicators, such as achieving universal primary education, reducing infant mortality rates, improving maternal health, promoting gender equality and empowering women, combating HIV/AIDS and malaria, supporting environmental sustainability, and consolidating development partnerships. The MDGs are ambitious but achievable, provided governments stay committed. United Nations institutions, the OECD, bilateral donors, and international NGOs have all voiced support for the MDG targets.

In this context, the multilateral development banks, such as the World Bank and the African, Asian, and Inter-American Development Banks, with the support of the IMF, changed their operational objectives from economic growth to poverty reduction—at least rhetorically. That has been an important change, full of controversy—the old "growth-versus-

TRADE AND COMMODITIES

poverty" debate reemerged and remains active in almost every country's policy dialogues. From a poverty-reduction viewpoint, even if the institutional transformation is far from perfect, it is a positive step towards achieving social progress.

The following is a summary of an internationally agreed agenda for poverty reduction:

1. *Diagnosing obstacles to poverty reduction and agreeing strategies to overcome them.* The first stage consists of understanding why poverty exists in a particular country, agreeing on a poverty line, and identifying the obstacles to poverty reduction in order to establish successful and feasible strategies. In the late 1990s, MDBs started preparing Poverty Reduction Strategy Papers to identify medium- and long-term targets and approaches for the poorest countries.

2. *National priority policies for poverty reduction.* Poverty reduction will not be achieved by charity-type safety nets alone. Poverty reduction requires structural changes at the economic, political, and social levels. Taking into consideration the different terminology used by different international institutions, the agreed priorities for poverty reduction could be summarized as follows:

    a. *Promoting pro-poor growth (growth that favors the poor).* Quality, nonvolatile growth that supports employment and well-being needs to be promoted. The private sector is the engine of growth and employment, but for private-sector growth to contribute to poverty reduction, an enabling environment and an effective regulatory framework is needed to promote competition, enforce fair practices and labor standards, and ensure that essential goods and services are affordable to the poor. Public sector investment should focus on complementing the private sector and serving the poor, for instance, investing in agriculture instead of defense, rural electrification programs instead of big power plants, farm-to-market roads instead of major motorways.

    b. *Extending opportunities for the poor* by making it possible for them to build, buy, or have access to natural assets (land, property, natural resources), financial assets (credit), or human assets (skills and training).

    c. *Ensuring good governance* by supporting efficient, accountable, transparent, and responsive public administrations, with a mandate and capacity for pro-poor interventions; ensuring legal systems that are equitable and accessible to the poor; enforcing law and order; building public management free of political distortions with decentralized mechanisms for broad-based participation in the delivery of public services and efforts to minimize the likelihood of these services being captured by local elites; promoting progressive tax systems and adequate allocations for social services; fighting nepotism and corruption.

d. *Empowering the poor and excluded groups* by enhancing their capacity to influence the institutions that affect their lives and strengthening their participation in political and economic processes. Organizing the poor and excluded groups to fight for their rights was a critical factor in promoting social progress in developed countries—social development would have not happened without of trade unions and civil rights groups' fighting. Empowerment and social mobilization are intrinsically linked to the broader agenda of good governance, transparency, and accountability of the government to its citizens.

e. *Investing in social services.* All developing countries have developed some social policies over the last decades, and ministries of education, health, and welfare exist in most countries. However, they have often failed to ensure social services to the poor. This lack of effectiveness is normally due to (1) limited coverage, that is, serving only a portion of the population, often serving the wealthiest segments of society instead of the poor; and (2) insufficient funds incorrectly distributed among programs. Typical examples are national programs subsidizing universities instead of basic education or large cardiology hospitals in the capital instead of health clinics in villages. Financing has been curtailed during the 1990s due to anti-inflationary austerity programs and debt crisis. Increasing investment in social services and reforming sectoral priorities to ensure servicing the poor are imperatives to achieve the Millenium Development Goals.

f. *Fighting gender disparities.* The increasing feminization of poverty is now a well-recognized trend. The gender division of labor and responsibilities for household welfare translate to nonpaid work and a lack of opportunities. Gender disparities frequently result in gender-based inequality in access to and control of resources and discrimination against women's basic rights, for example, education, employment, inheritance, and registration. To reduce poverty and to advance the status of half the world's population, support must be provided to the development of gender-sensitive policies and programs.

g. *Reducing vulnerability and risks to the poor.* Measuring income poverty can provide a snapshot of poverty at one point, but poverty is not a static condition. Many individuals and households with incomes near the poverty line face various risks that can plunge them into poverty. These may include covariant risks such as natural disasters, civil conflicts, economic downturns, financial crisis, or idiosyncratic household reversals such as crop failures, unemployment, illness, work injury, disability, death, and old age that threaten the future of the household and its members. A combination of social insurance, safety nets, disaster prevention and mitigation programs, and emergency relief are essential to provide security to the poor and vulnerable groups.

Critics of this agenda say it does not go far enough. The agenda, generally supported by UN agencies including the MDBs, is a necessary but not sufficient condition for fast poverty reduction. For instance, more could be added on redistribution policies. Further, the agenda focuses on national domestic topics but is very limited on external issues at the international level, such as debt relief, the effects of global finance, and a lack of access to international markets, among others. In fact, what happens is that different UN agencies and MDBs (even different departments within the same agency), develop contradictory policies—some staff members are working on the poverty-reduction agenda presented above while, at the same time, others are pushing macroeconomic decisions that may look delinked from poverty but actually cause it. Critical NGOs and think tanks are campaigning for social and economic alternatives and a new system of global governance to ensure that national and international public policy making is coherent and benefits all world citizens. Of the several proposals, there is consensus that effective poverty reduction will require international action to:

i. *Cancel Third World debt.* Despite debt-reduction attempts by the IMF and the World Bank, many developing countries remain highly indebted, and their scarce funds have to be used for debt repayment instead of for poverty reduction—NGOs like Jubilee 2000 have been fighting for a cancellation of all debt in the poorest nations.

ii. *Manage international finance and corporations.* Continual shocks and instabilities in today's financial markets, analyzed in other chapters in this volume, have led critics to talk about a "global casino" and the need to regulate it through a new financial architecture that supports development and fights short-term speculative capital flows, tax evasion, and money laundering. There is a need to establish and enforce better principles of public accountability and protect citizens and consumers from possible corporate irresponsibility. NGOs like ATTAC International and Corpwatch are fighting for these principles.

iii. *Reform international trade, including the World Trade Organization,* abandoning the present model based on supposedly free, nondiscriminatory competition among countries. The model is a fallacy given that the EU, United States, and Japan subsidize their own producers, including the agricultural sector—and agriculture is one of the few economic activities that poor countries can develop to reduce poverty. Instead, in the name of "efficiency" and "free markets," developing countries are told to open up and liberalize their economies—as a result, domestic producers cannot compete with the subsidized, higher-quality products from developed countries and close down, generating further unemployment and poverty. Abandoning this double standard ("Do as I tell you, not as I do") and the associated uncritical implementation of market-fundamentalist policies is essential to reducing poverty. Current trade policies should be replaced with a system of "fair" trade that discriminates in favor of the poorer regions, ensuring that developing countries are given a role in the world economy, as NGOs such as Focus on the Global South and the Third World Network strongly argue.

UNDERSTANDING POVERTY ON A GLOBAL SCALE

The latest thinking on poverty reduction focuses on understanding poverty on a global scale. For one thing, poverty is reemerging in developed economies and is no longer strictly a Third World phenomenon. Two decades of neoliberal policies have eroded the living conditions of citizens in the West. The end of the postwar boom in the 1970s made policy makers in developed countries abandon Keynesian approaches and replace them with supply-side policies, adhering to a "neoliberal orthodoxy" that assumed growth would revamp if companies sharpened their competitive edge. Two decades of such policies kept growth rates positive, buttressed by fairly remarkable productivity improvements. However, this did not come without costs. The structural reforms, as they came to be known, increased competition and reduced individual company profitability. Corporations reacted by shedding labor, reducing wages, and cutting back on benefits. Governments, under pressure to cut deficits, also sharply curtailed social and welfare spending. Consequently, the living conditions of many citizens in the West were eroded, while growth has remained low and unemployment and public debt high. This is because these neoliberal short-term policies do not address the long-term structural causes of the problem: overproduction and global excess capacity in a context of weak effective demand. In the meantime, until a global solution is agreed upon, poverty and unemployment continue to increase in developed countries.

It is also necessary to think globally because some of the causes of poverty in developing countries are due to international policies that national governments cannot influence, such as a lack of access to developed countries' markets; as presented in the earlier section, reducing poverty will require a concerted international effort to forgive Third World debt, manage international finance and corporations, and promote a fair system of international trade. International concerted action could also facilitate the fight against internal obstacles of development such as corruption, the vested interests of powerful domestic elites, or bad public management at the national level.

Instead, during the 1980s and 1990s, developing countries were forced to adopt the same orthodox model applied to developed economies—the so-called Washington Consensus polices (structural adjustments, reducing controls on capital and trade, curving public expenditures, privatization). This led to maintaining or deepening social deprivation instead of investing in human capital as part of national development strategies, to the point that the 1980s and 1990s have been called "the lost decades."

Globalization is shifting trade, investment, and technology and changing values; it is also generating economic interdependence and vulnerability to economic shocks and downturns. If no social policies are in place, countries may experience mounting unemployment, poverty, marginalization, and political conflict, given that populations pay the short-term costs of crisis. For globalization to be accepted, it will require better management, a "New Deal" for both developed and developing countries, in which the benefits of globalization are shared by all—instead of a few. Further, the reduction of poverty at a global scale will likely boost global demand and productivity. Thus the reduction of poverty may not only alleviate human suffering, a goal in itself, but also have a primary role in sustaining growth and well-functioning markets.

TIPS FOR REPORTERS

DISTINGUISHING BETWEEN RHETORIC AND PRACTICE

- The first question to ask is always: Who benefits? Who is truly profiting from X or Y policy? Public policy making should focus on benefiting the majority of citizens, not just a few privileged ones.

- What was the social impact of recent economic policies, including financial shocks (the impact on labor and employment, on prices of essential goods and services, on gender and vulnerable populations)?

- Where are budgetary allocations going? Does spending favor the poor (applicable to government or any development agency)? Is spending centered on sustaining administrative structures and vested interests or crowding out the private sector when the public sector is not necessary? How are government revenues collected? Is a progressive tax system enforced, that is, are upper income groups taxed at higher levels?

- Are key sectoral programs (agriculture, infrastructure, education, health, pensions, and so on) working to reduce poverty? Who are they serving? Who are the main beneficiaries? What are the major obstacles to poor people's participation in economic activities and benefiting from development?

- Are corruption and crime disrupting investment and civil activities? Do all citizens have equal access to justice, security, and services? Is the government effectively fighting discriminatory practices against gender, caste, race, or religious beliefs? Are communities organized and aware of mechanisms to protect them from abuse?

- How is progress measured? How is the poverty line calculated, and have there been any changes in the methodology? (Changes in the number of poor are not caused by lowering the poverty line.)

- How much can the country do internally? Levels of debt servicing need to be compared to social spending in the country. Has the country suffered a financial shock, and if so has economic activity fully recovered? Which of the national products find barriers to access to developed markets?

1. Millennium Development Goals. http://www.developmentgoals.org.

2. World Bank Poverty Network. http://www.worldbank.org/poverty.

3. United Nations Development Program Poverty Page. http://www.undp.org/poverty.

4. United Nations Institute for Social Development. http://www.unrisd.org.

5. DFID-sponsored site on globalization and Poverty. http://www.gapresearch.org.

6. Sussex University Eldis Poverty Resource Guide. http://www.eldis.org/poverty/index.

7. Overseas Development Institute Poverty and Public Policy Group. http://www.odi.org.uk/pppg/index.html.

8. Northwestern University and University of Chicago's Joint Center for Poverty Research. http://www.jcpr.org.

9. Jubilee, supporting economic justice. http://www.jubilee2000uk.org.

10. ATTAC International. Association for the Taxation of Financial Transactions for the Aid of Citizens. http://www.attac.org.

11. Corpwatch, holding corporations accountable. http://www.corpwatch.org.

12. The Third World Network. http://www.twnside. org.sg.

13. Focus on the Global South. http://www.focusweb.org.

14. Oxfam. http://www.oxfam.org.uk.

PART V
**REPORTING AND
WRITING**

CHAPTER TWENTY-FOUR

COVERING THE WORLD BANK

ABID ASLAM

ALL THINGS TO ALL PEOPLE?

JOURNALISTS HAVE long covered the World Bank in its many guises: lending institution, development agency, think-tank, forum for intergovernmental politics and economic diplomacy, bureaucracy, and employer of 10,000 people.

The bank was founded in 1944 to lend money to governments seeking to rebuild their economies after World War II. By the 1960s, it had redefined itself as an institution dedicated to fighting world poverty. Today, it lends and guarantees around $20 billion per year in near-market-rate loans and some $6 billion more in no-interest loans to borrowing countries in the developing world and the former Soviet Union. In turn, the bank's loans help the borrowing countries mobilize other financing from governments, commercial banks, and private investors.

The bank's policies and operations keep changing in response to pressure from member governments, activist groups, and some of its own staff. It continues to back the infrastructure projects—hydroelectric power plants, ports, and highways, for example—that once were its stock in trade. In the 1970s, however, the bank came to believe that the success of a project depended on the overall policy environment within which the project operated, among other things. As such, the institution began guiding governments on how to structure and manage their economies and social services, buttressing its advice with loans issued to finance implementation of its policy recommendations. This process, generically called "structural adjustment," has given way to so-called second-generation initiatives under which infrastructure, telecommunications, and some social services are privatized; labor, the civil service, and the judiciary are revamped; and pension systems are opened to private capital. Other facets of structural adjustment include lowering deficits and tariff barriers, opening the economy to short-term capital flows, and other aspects of liberalization and stabilization.

"Policy lending" through structural-adjustment loans and more focused adjustment loans to specific sectors of the economy has grown to account for roughly half of the bank's portfolio. The bank does not generally lend structural-adjustment money without approval from the International Monetary Fund, its sister agency headquartered across the street in downtown Washington, D.C. (The bank also is generally loath to extend significant credit for projects if the IMF suspends its programs in a given country, but there are exceptions: Ethiopia, for example, where it tripled its project loans in recent years, and Vietnam in the 1990s.)

Just as policy lending has come to account for an increasing portion of the bank's portfolio, so too has lending for health, education, and other policies and projects aimed at alleviating poverty. The shift began in the late 1960s during the presidency of Robert MacNamara and has been accentuated and amended by the current bank president, James Wolfensohn. Both have said that the bank's central mission is to fight poverty, but Wolfensohn has broadened the approach from one focused on privatization and economic liberalization (sometimes referred to as "the Washington Consensus" or described as "neoliberal" or "market fundamentalist") to what the bank terms a "comprehensive development framework" involving a wide range of players and issues.

The bank's evolving emphasis has been sustained in part by widespread criticism of structural adjustment and high-cost infrastructure projects. The former often has been seen as imposing austerity on the poor and the latter, as displacing local communities and devastating the environment.

These criticisms also spawned a number of safeguards (discussed below) to reduce the likelihood that the bank's loans would wreak environmental and social damage. The bank also has pushed for greater emphasis on corruption. For countries stuck in a high-debt, low-growth trap, the bank has come to accept the need for extensive debt relief. The latter has proceeded as the Highly Indebted Poor Country Initiative (see chapter 11, this volume).

Even so, the changes have not been free of controversy. Some critics accuse the bank of "mission creep," of arrogating unto itself roles they say should be left to the United Nations because the latter organization has greater expertise, gives developing countries more decision-making power, and grants rather than lends money. Others contend that it has not effectively implemented its safeguards. Still others worry that the bank has now lost focus.

Lending to the social sectors fell during the global financial crisis of 1997 through 1999. Under pressure especially from the United States, and over the opposition of many within the bank, the institution lent large

sums to South Korea, Thailand, Indonesia, and Brazil under international bailouts led by the IMF. (During this period, the bank strongly criticized a number of IMF policy positions, for example, its insistence that
countries open their capital markets to short-term capital flows. The IMF
appears to have acted on at least some of the complaints.)

Through its roles as financier and adviser, the bank has emerged as a
coordinator of dialogue between borrower and creditor governments and
between local businesses and foreign investors. In a number of countries,
for example, the bank chairs annual meetings of donor groups made up of
wealthy governments and international institutions (in other countries,
the UN Development Program assumes this role).

Thus, the bank has become a gatekeeper wielding considerable power,
although the extent and content of this power vary greatly depending on its
own interests, those of its wealthy member states, the political and financial
strength and tenacity of its borrowers, and the strength of the position that
the IMF takes on the economic framework of a given country.

Regardless of which of the above aspects of the bank reporters wish to
cover, they need to be able to find their way around the institution.
Although the bank is generally considered far more open than the IMF—
which was once famously described as more secretive than the Central
Intelligence Agency—critics note that it still does not recognize that citizens have a right to know about what it does and how it conducts its business. What follows is some basic information about how the institution is
governed and organized.

GOVERNANCE: WHO CONTROLS WHAT?

The bank is not a membership organization like the United Nations. It is
an international financial institution in which 184 governments hold
shares. The size of each country's shareholding, and therefore its vote, is
determined by its "subscription capital," or the amount of money it
pledged to become a shareholder. Each country is limited in the amount
it can subscribe, however. Many countries, such as China, have long been
willing to increase their subscription—and their vote—but have not been
allowed to do so because as their votes increased, others' would have to
decrease. This has meant that while subscriptions and voting were supposed to be based on relative economic strength, large discrepancies have
emerged over time.

Wealthy nations, or "Part I" countries, make up 14 percent of the bank's
shareholders but control more than 62 percent of the votes. Borrowing, or
"Part II," countries represent 86 percent of the shareholders and 38 percent of the votes. The U.S. government, the largest single shareholder, traditionally chooses the bank's president.

Most of the money the bank lends comes from selling bonds on international capital markets. Subscription capital is used as collateral to guarantee the bonds; because the bank is viewed as a safe borrower, it can

obtain funds at attractive terms. The money it takes from these investors it lends to borrowing countries at a higher interest rate. Borrowing countries service their loans, enabling the bank to pay off the investors and plow the difference into operations and reserves.

Middle-income developing countries view the bank as a credit cooperative, and since much of the bank's operations support lending and policy advice in low-income countries, middle-income borrowers have worried that they are being "taxed" by the high-income countries that control the bank to subsidize lending to low-income countries. (At various times, some middle-income countries have been able to borrow from international markets at terms more attractive than those offered by the bank.) The relatively well-off borrowing countries that do not qualify for "soft" loans have been at odds with the poorer ones that do qualify over whether the bank should concentrate on meeting the formers' needs by operating as a lending cooperative or whether it should aid the latter by increasing its "soft" loans and forgiving debt.

Representatives of the bank's shareholders oversee all this. The Board of Governors—made up of finance, development, or planning ministers from all shareholding countries—meets twice a year to review and set broad policies and priorities. The governors are ultimately responsible for the World Bank.

However, operational control rests with a twenty-four-member Board of Executive Directors, or EDs. The board meets in full session once or twice a week to approve all loans. Smaller committees meet almost daily. The bank's largest shareholders have their own, exclusive ED. Smaller shareholders organize themselves into groups and rotate the right to represent the bloc, usually every two years. Thus, forty-seven African countries share two EDs. Such "group" EDs have staffs made up of people from some or all of the countries they represent.

EDs represent shareholding governments, but they also are full-time employees of the bank, which pays their salaries and provides them with offices and secretaries. The bank's president chairs the board's meetings. In comparison, the executive boards of UN agencies meet between once and four times per year, and their members are not remunerated by the agencies they oversee. There are several controversies associated with the role of the EDs. Some worry that borrowing countries' voices often are stifled by the formula of representation based on shareholding and by executive directors' dependence on the bank for their salaries and office facilities.

There are further worries that EDs are insufficiently assertive in opposing bank plans for fear of being overturned, circumvented, or replaced. Typically senior civil servants, they rank lower at home than the cabinet ministers who serve as the bank's governors and with whom senior bank managers are frequently in touch. What's more, the bank's president and top executives enjoy direct access to borrowing countries' presidents and prime ministers. Nevertheless, some EDs from larger borrowers—China or India, for example—have been known to push through loans for projects in their home countries over environmental or other objections from Part I EDs. Legislators and government commissions in Part I countries also weigh in on these and other questions from time to time, often in response to lobbying by corporations, environmentalists, and other pressure groups.

INSTITUTIONAL STRUCTURE: WHAT'S IN A NAME?

1. Often, when we say "the World Bank," we mean the *International Bank for Reconstruction and Development*. Established in 1944, this is the core of the World Bank Group. It disburses loans at or near prevailing market interest rates and with maturities of fifteen to twenty years.

2. The *International Development Association*, created in 1960, makes "soft loans" to the bank's poorest members. These loans, called "credits," are interest-free (although they carry an administrative surcharge of 0.75 percent) and repayable over thirty-five to forty years with a ten-year grace period. Essentially, the IDA is a pool of money; it is physically indistinguishable from the IBRD and is often described as the bank's "soft-loan window."

   Insofar as there is an implicit subsidy associated with IDA loans, the facility must be replenished every three years. This is different from IBRD loans that are lent at above funding cost. In some countries, parliaments must authorize the IDA funding. In the U.S. Congress, pressure groups often lobby for the money to be tied to demands that the bank change some aspect of its work.

3. The *International Finance Corporation* was set up in 1956 to promote private investment—including its own—in businesses based in the bank's borrowing countries. Membership is limited to bank shareholders. In some ways, the IFC is a traditional investment bank, sometimes taking equity positions in projects it is involved in.

4. The *Multilateral Investment Guarantee Agency* was created in 1988 to provide political risk insurance to foreign companies making direct investments in the bank's borrowing countries. MIGA's creation reflected a view that foreign direct investment into developing countries had been curtailed by insurable risks. MIGA, consequently, provides insurance coverage against government restrictions on investors' ability to transfer currency; nationalization; war or civil disturbance; and breach of contract. Only bank shareholders can join.

5. The *World Bank Institute* arranges training for bank employees and publishes research used by the bank and its clients. It can be a useful source of information on such bank-sponsored activities as the training of civil servants and journalists in borrowing countries and is a window on bank-sponsored research. However, the more influential

research centers at the bank are the *office of the chief economist* and the *research department*, which has a Web site that often shows where bank thinking is heading (see "Links for More Information," below).

The bank also houses the *International Centre for Settlement of Investment Disputes* a legally autonomous international organization established in 1966 to arbitrate disputes between foreign investors and host governments. The Bechtel Group, for example, has sued Bolivia's government for breach of contract after officials were forced by public outrage to overturn the privatization of a municipal water company, stripping a Bechtel subsidiary of ownership.

Also housed at the World Bank are specialized consortia of donor governments, funding agencies, and research institutes. The bank plays an influential role in them but, strictly speaking, is not in charge of them. These include the *Consultative Group on International Agricultural Research* and the *Consultative Group to Assist the Poorest* which specializes in microcredit and microenterprise programs.

NAVIGATING THE BUREAUCRACY: WHO DOES WHAT?

All World Bank Group institutions have media liaison staffs, as do most units within the IBRD. Some interesting sources of information and story ideas remain obscure, however. These include:

- The IBRD's *Operations Evaluation Department*. This unit conducts postmortems of bank programs and projects. It issues findings and recommendations for changes in policy, strategy, and operations to the executive board. Reporters should seek out its draft reports—on whether bank-financed mining projects benefit poor countries, for example. However, its evaluations more often focus on operational issues (was the project completed on time, for instance) than on issues of development effectiveness.

- The bank's *Inspection Panel*. This is a good source of stories about bank projects gone wrong and efforts to put them right. This semi-independent body investigates allegations that bank policies (say, on environmental safeguards, community consultation, or indigenous peoples' rights) have been violated in ongoing or planned projects. It was set up in 1994 as an appeal mechanism for local communities and grew out of a unique probe of bank loans for the Sardar Sarovar dam on India's Narmada River. The bank eventually pulled out of that project. Critics of the inspection process have repeatedly asked the bank to give the panel power to cancel projects. Instead, they say, the agency has trimmed the unit's initial purview.

    Operating under legal constraints and immense political scrutiny from governments and the bank, the panel is extremely careful not to leak information. Its reports are made public, however, and advocacy groups tend to have foreknowledge of cases. High-profile, politically charged investigations have included those of the ExxonMobil-led Chad–Cameroon oil production and pipeline project, the Argentine–Paraguayan Yacyreta Dam, and Chinese development plans near Tibet.

- The *Fraud and Corruption Unit*. Made up of former prosecutors, this group probes allegations against staff members and companies that do business with the Bank.

- Committees of the IBRD's executive board, perhaps the most significant of which is the *Committee on Development Effectiveness*. This group handles OED reports and all other issues relating to bank operations, strategy, and evaluation.

- Top-level bank managers, who also make recommendations to the board through the *Operational Policy Committee*.

- *Operations Policy and Country Services* department. Responsible for ensuring that whatever policy or strategy changes the board enacts are implemented, this is one of the most powerful units within the bank.

STRUCTURE OF COUNTRY DEPARTMENTS

Broadly, the bank describes itself as a matrix organization, with most individuals assigned to both a region (the developing world is divided into six different regions) and a sector that represents their area of competence. Bank staff are organized in four "*networks*," each with a name that describes its work: Environmentally and Socially Sustainable Development; Finance, Private Sector, and Infrastructure; Human Development; and Poverty Reduction and Economic Management.

Under Wolfensohn, the bank has sent much of its staff to work in borrowing countries. Some country directors, overall bank administration, and key network personnel remain in Washington. Headquarters staff assigned to the networks tend to be knowledgeable about issues—say, business regulation, education, or water-resources management—and how the bank addresses them in terms of policy. They often have experience in many different countries and regions.

The *Country Department* is the unit charged with translating policy into action. Periodically, the bank, in conjunction with a borrower, formulates a *Country Assistance Strategy*, a document sometimes referred to as the bank's "master plan" for each client.

The typical Country Department includes:

1. Country Director. Manages between one and six Country Departments.

2. Resident Representative. Heads the in-country office if the Country Director is based in Washington.

3. Country Anchor or Coordinator. Staffs the headquarters country desk if the Country Director is based in the borrowing country.

4. Country Economist. Manages assembly of the Country Assistance Strategy and coordinates the macroeconomic program.

5. NGO/Civil Society Specialist or Liaison. Communicates with local civic and advocacy groups.

6. Country Officers. Monitor the bank's country portfolio of loans

7. Sector Leaders/Specialists. Identify projects within a given policy area (say, environment, health, or rural development).

8. Task Team Leaders. Overall management responsibility for specific projects (the building of a dam or highway, for example).

9. Public Information Officer/Specialist. Runs the local public-information center.

10. Country Departments may also include legal counsel, operations analysts, program staff, disbursement analysts, financial management specialists, representatives of the International Finance Corporation, and loan accounting officers.

GETTING INFORMATION ON BANK PROJECTS

The bulk of World Bank lending (all the lending that is not structural-adjustment lending) is administered through projects, though today a project may consist of "reform of the health care sector," not just the building of a dam.

The stages through which a project passes, and key sources of information, include:

1. *Project Identification*. Bank staff and government develop the project idea. The Project Team writes an initial summary, known as the "*Project Information Document*," which should be openly available. The bank's Country Department determines the amount of financing needed. (Key sources: World Bank Country Department, government ministry/agency, Project Team/Task Team Leader.)

2. *Project Preparation*. Government and bank project consultants conduct economic, technical, and other studies and produce a number of Factual Technical Documents, which reporters might have a right to see. The process should include opportunities for public consultation and participation. (Key sources: Government agency, consultants, Project Team/Task Team Leader.)

3. *Appraisal*. A bank appraisal team visits the project site, meets government officials, and evaluates the project's viability. Bank staff begins

to assemble a *Project Appraisal Document* (formerly known as a *Staff Assessment Report*), which it will eventually submit to the bank's EDs for approval. The PAD should then be made available at the bank's Infoshop in Washington, but it is not routinely accessible in borrowing countries. (Key sources: Appraisal Team [which includes Task Team Leader], consultants).

4. *Negotiation.* Bank and government officials agree on the terms and conditions of the project loan. The bank's Legal Department draws up the legal documents. (Key sources: Task Team Leader, bank Country Director, bank Legal Counsel, negotiators from relevant government ministries/agencies, borrowing country ministry of finance.)

5. *Approval.* The bank's EDs discuss the project, and, assuming they approve it, the bank and borrowing government then sign the loan. (Key sources: bank Executive Directors, Project Team/Task Team Leader or Country Director.)

6. *Implementation and Supervision.* Borrowing government implements the project under the bank's supervision, which includes site visits. (Key sources: consultants and government agency, Bank Supervision Teams, Task Team Leader.)

7. *Ex-Post Evaluation.* Borrowing government and/or bank prepare a confidential Implementation Completion Report and submit this to the EDs. The bank's Operations Evaluation Department prepares a *Project Audit Report* for the EDs. (Key sources: Task Team Leader, project staff, Operations and Evaluation Department, EDs.)

A great deal of information about projects is available online from the bank's Web site (see below). Also available is the Monthly Operational Summary a list of new and proposed loans.

Projects may be controversial because attached to the money are a variety of policies. There is a concern that Western governments entice or force borrowing governments to adopt policies based on wealthy states' interests, or their perceptions of what is good for the country, and not the borrowing country's interests and priorities. (For instance, at one time the World Bank and the IMF insisted that countries undertake "cost recovery" as part of primary-education projects; that is, charge some of the poorest children in the world fees for going to school. Subsequent experience in Uganda and elsewhere suggests that such charges, even when modest, can have the effect of forcing large numbers of families to stop or forgo schooling for their children, especially girls.) In such cases, there is said to be a "lack of ownership," and the World Bank's own research argues that local ownership and participation are important for project success.

- Reporters should cultivate sources among the EDs and their staffs in Washington and/or their civil-service or political counterparts and supervisors back home. This is especially important when covering the bank's politics and relations with shareholders. Likewise, parliamentarians or legislators with an interest in the bank should be investigated. (In Brazil and elsewhere, for example, there have been constitutional wrangles over whether agreements with the bank are the exclusive domain of the executive branch or are subject to legislative review and approval.)

- Sources among nongovernmental organizations should be cultivated. Whether they work with the bank, lobby it to change its ways, or simply oppose what it does, they often have access to people the bank or the government would rather reporters did not speak with. They also have foreknowledge of lobbying efforts, pressure campaigns, and Inspection Panel cases. Many maintain e-mail listservs for supporters and/or media; reporters should subscribe to them. Likewise, they should also keep track of what corporations and academics have to say about bank-related issues.

- Whom does the bank deal with in the countries where it works? Do bank officials speak with a wide range of people in society or just a few government officials and corporate exec-

utives? Does the bank seem to be getting accurate information, or are people telling it what it wants to hear? The questions apply equally to project and policy design and the writing of the Country Assistance Strategies mentioned above.

- Reporters need to use the Internet and any other means available—including direct contact with other journalists—to see whether and how the issues covered locally are being thought about and covered internationally or—especially when writing in a wealthy country—how global issues or policies hatched at bank headquarters or in Western capitals are playing out locally. International comparisons can be a great way of setting stories in a broader context, of overcoming local isolation or lack of data, experience, and/or expertise, and of comparing reporters' approaches and methods.

- Projects often involve procurement contracts for equipment and services. Reporters should try to see how the bidding process is working. Are payments being made under the table? Do the companies involved in the process feel it is being done fairly and openly?

- Reporters should talk to people described as beneficiaries in government or bank project or policy documents. Who benefits; who does not?

1. World Bank. Here, reporters also can sign up for access to a journalists-only site protected by password and can choose to receive information by e-mail. http://www.worldbank.org.

2. International Finance Corporation. http://www.ifc.org.

3. Multilateral Investment Guarantee Agency. http://www.miga.org.

4. Development Gateway. Web portal on development issues set up by the World Bank. http://www.developmentgateway.org.

5. World Bank Operations Evaluation Department. http://www.worldbank.org/oed.

6. World Bank Inspection Panel. http://wbln0018.worldbank.org/ipn/ipnweb.nsf.

7. Bank Information Center. Washington-based advocacy group and information clearing-house for activists, media, and researchers; good source of information, including contact details for officials and advocates involved in specific projects; "Links" page provides names and Web sites of key groups worldwide. http://www.bicusa.org.

8. Bretton Woods Project. London-based advocacy group that tracks political and bureaucratic developments as well as projects. http://www.brettonwoodsproject.org.

CHAPTER TWENTY-FIVE

INTERNET REPORTING

JANE M. FOLPE

I. HOW TO USE THE INTERNET TO COVER INTERNATIONAL BUSINESS STORIES

This section deals with Internet sourcing and research tools for journalists from developing countries. It reviews a number of Web sites that provide good general background information on the economic situation in various parts of the world, and it discusses how to get the most out of the online resources offered by governments (both the U.S. and foreign), international organizations, universities, think tanks, and activists, among others.

T IS fair to say that the Internet has transformed the job of a journalist—so much key information is just a couple of clicks away. Of course, Internet reporting should not replace traditional enterprise reporting, but it can be an enormous help in obtaining background information and contacts with which to develop a story.

Economic and business journalists can use the Internet to find anything from the latest academic thinking on currency crises and structural reform to detailed statistics on unemployment and foreign trade. Reporters can see who—academics, analysts, even journalists—is covering what and find out how to get in touch with them. Reporters can also find out more about companies working in their home countries, either through company Web sites or specific regulatory agencies. Reporters may also access the filings of foreign companies in the United States, as well as U.S. companies that do business in a particular country, for more detailed information on executive compensation, business risks, and lawsuits.

But with so much information available, it is critical to learn to distinguish between reliable and unreliable sources. Getting background for a story using the Internet requires the same skill set as reporting a story offline: intelligence, critical thinking, and analysis, as well as a healthy dose of skepticism. Reporters should think of each Web site as a potential source trying to sell his or her version of the story. Would a journalist publish a story having talked to just one source? Of course not. So why use just one Web site to get all your background information?

Everyone, including governments, businesses, analysts, academics, and activists, has an agenda or a particular story he or she wants to push. Every number, variable, chart, or graph can be shaped or molded to fit this agenda. Documents are no exception—just about anyone can publish anything on the Web these days. And in the wake of the fallout from corporate-accounting scandals like Enron's, it has become clear that even those documents filed with official government regulators like the U.S. Securities and Exchange Commission have not always been completely truthful.[1]

A reporter has to use the same critical eye to interpret information on the Web as when reporting in person. All information, even if it is obtained from the most reliable of sources, needs to be interpreted through the prism of the source. This is especially important to remember when looking at figures, which different sources will calculate in different ways. If a reporter wants to use a number from a particular source book—on the Internet or off—she needs to be able to define the components that make up this number. But most importantly, the reporter needs to decide whether this number makes sense. One example is unemployment data. Different countries may report only those people actively seeking employment, while others may report those who are partially employed. These differences can lead to artificially inflated or artificially low numbers, depending on the government's agenda.

It is also essential to know how to search strategically so as not to lose valuable time when reporting a story. There are millions of sites out there and for every one I suggest, there will be another one out there that a given journalist may already use. This guide is not conceived as a definitive list of business and economic Internet resources but instead as a way to think about reporting business and economic stories using the Internet.[2]

STARTING THE REPORTING

Reporting should always begin with a clip search to see what has been written about the particular topic. This can give an idea of the different angles from which to approach a story, as well as the angles that have not yet been covered. Reporters can also get good source ideas from clips, as well as a general panorama of the economic data available. Subscription services such as Lexis-Nexis and Factiva should always be checked, as well as the following sites:

- *BusinessWeek*, http://www.businessweek.com—a very good general business reporting site.

- The BBC, http://www.bbc.co.uk.

- The *Wall Street Journal* online, http://www.wsj.com (subscription only).

- *The Financial Times*, http://www.ft.com (subscription only).

- *The Economist* offers some of its content for free, including economic indicators and recent articles from the magazine, http://www.economist.com.

Different regions also have local magazines, newspapers, and journals that can be of enormous help when beginning to report a story. One good site from which to access periodicals from around the world is http://www.ceoexpress.com. Another is http://www.abyznewslinks.com. Here are some other sites that offer news from different world regions and are worth consulting when trying to find what has been written on a particular topic.

LATIN AMERICA AND SPAIN

The Latin American Network Information Center, mentioned below under regional gateways, offers extensive links to newspapers and magazines in the region.

- http://lanic.utexas.edu/la/region/news.

- http://lanic.utexas.edu/la/region/epub.

For periodicals in Spanish, periodista digital (http://www.periodistadigital.com) offers an annotated press diary of world events (with a heavy dosage of news from Spain), as well as links to some of the best newspapers in Spanish, Portuguese, and English worldwide. Its economic counterpart, economistadigital, (http://www.economistadigital.com) provides a similar service for economic news.

ASIA

For press links from Asia, the Asian Media Information and Communication Centre maintains a list of links at http://www.amic.org.sg/hotlinks_list.html.

- *The Far Eastern Economic Review*, http://www.feer.com.

- The *Times of India* http://www.timesofindia.com.

AFRICA

- AllAfrica describes itself as "the largest electronic distributor of African news and information worldwide." http://www.allafrica.com.

- AfricaOnline offers headline news as well as portals to different topics. http://www.africaonline.com.

MIDDLE EAST

- ArabNet offers news from the region, general country information and links to online resources in the Arab world. http://www.arab.net.

The following three sites belong to the "World News Network" and offer news and links from both the Middle East and the extended Arab world.

- http://www.arabworldnews.com.

- http://www.middleeastnews.com.

- http://www.middleeastdaily.com.

Other sites are available through regional guides, which are discussed below.

ECONOMIC AND POLITICAL BACKGROUND

In addition to reading what has been written about a given topic in the press, it is also a good idea to seek out general political, social, and economic background on the country where the story takes place. Different political, social, and even demographic contexts can mean the difference between success and failure when it comes to economic policy. Why, for example, has the currency board worked in Hong Kong but not in Argentina?

There is an ever-growing number of sites for tapping into international economic and political resources. The following offer simple and relatively direct pathways to some of the most important resources for taking a country's political and economic pulse. It is a good idea to begin by using these sites as one would a clip search—in order to get familiar with the kind of resources that are available to report a story. (A parallel Google search is also a good idea, but I will talk more about that later in this chapter.) Once a reporter knows what is available by way of resources—official sources, nongovernmental organizations, academic research, and so on—he can go to more specific sites to continue the research.

If a journalist is writing about the oil industry in Venezuela, for example, she would probably first want take a look at the country-specific resources on Venezuela, either through Global Edge, http://globaledge.msu.edu/ibrd/ ibrd.asp, or LANIC, http://lanic.utexas.edu. Looking at Global Edge, can give some of the most recent headlines out of the country, as well as an industry directory to serve as a guide to potential sources. LANIC has links to academic research sites, business and economic Web resources, and energy, oil, and gas sites, among many other resources. One would also probably want to look at the site for Venezuela's Oil Chamber, the Cámara Petrolera de Venezuela, http://www.camara-petrolera.org, as well as that of the national oil company PDVSA, http://www.pdvsa.com. The reporter can also take a look at a country analysis done by the U.S. Department of Energy and the statistics available on the Web site of the Organization for Petroleum Exporting Countries, http://www.opec.org, to which Venezuela belongs. In light of the ongoing conflict between President Hugo Chávez and his foes, one would want to search for data from the opposition, which provided its own figures on oil production during and after a two month general strike.

GLOBAL EDGE

Michigan State University has a very good international business site called Global Edge, http://globaledge.msu.edu/ibrd/ibrd.asp, with links to economic, trade, and legal resources around the world, referenced by region. Here one can find links to central banks, research institutions, regional search engines, economic indicators, export-import guides, and journals and other publications. The site also provides country snapshots, which can be useful for quick comparisons.

VIRTUAL INTERNATIONAL BUSINESS AND ECONOMIC SOURCES

This site, maintained by the University of North Carolina at Chapel Hill, offers solid (but sometimes limited) lists of international business and economic resources. It can be searched by topic, region, or nation. http://libweb.uncc.edu/ref-bus/vibehome.htm.

INTERNET PUBLIC LIBRARY

The Internet Public Library, created and maintained by the University of Michigan School of Information, is an excellent resource for finding just about anything on the Web. Both "Business and Economics" and "Regional and Country Information" offer helpful links for covering the global business environment. http://www.ipl.org.

There are also a number of regional guides that can help journalists find sources. Some examples are:

LATIN AMERICA

- Internet Resources for Latin America—La Guía Nueva. This guide, while academic in nature, provides a very good gateway into some of the most important sources for work on or in Latin America. http://lib.nmsu.edu/ subject/bord/laguia.

- Latin American Network Information Center. This excellent resource, maintained by the University of Texas at Austin, acts as an extensive gateway for resources on Latin America. There are topic directories (Economy, Education, Libraries, Internet, Media, Sustainable Development, and so on) as well as country directories for each access. http://lanic.utexas.edu.

RUSSIA AND EASTERN EUROPE

- Russian and East European Studies Virtual Library. This site, maintained by the Center for Russian and East European Studies at the University of Pittsburgh, allows users to search for electronic resources by subject, region, culture, and time period. They can also do keyword searches on specific topics. http://www.ucis.pitt.edu/reesweb/index.shtml.

- Transitions Online. This site, maintained by a Czech nonprofit organization, offers independent news and analysis from Eastern Europe. http://www.tol.cz.

AFRICA

- This site, maintained by the African Studies Librarian at Columbia University, offers business and economic information on Africa. http://www.columbia.edu/cu/lweb/indiv/africa/cuvl/bus.html.

- This site, which bills itself "the most comprehensive online resource on Africa," is maintained by the African Economics Journalists Forum. AEJ Online offers an excellent gateway from which to access information about politics, economics, and the judiciary in different African nations. http://www.afriforum.org/countryinfo.htm.

ASIA

- The Asia Pacific Resource Center at Stanford University maintains a list of general resources on Asia. http://aparc.stanford.edu/docs/global/links.html.

- Asia Source, hosted by the New York–based Asia Society at http://www.asiasource.org, offers news, maps, country guides, and other electronic resources for anyone interested in Asia. See "Asia Experts" for a link to the National Bureau of Asian Research's Access Asia project.

- Asia Business Today, another resource of the Asia Society at http://www.asiabusinesstoday.org, offers an annotated directory of electronic resources on topics ranging from agriculture and the Asian economic crisis to human rights and labor.

For a direct link to the Asia Society, go to www.asiasociety.org.

- Asia Pacific.com acts as an extensive gateway for business and economic resources from this region. Reporters can find academic research, company reports, and statistical information as well as links to the region's journals and newspapers. http://www.asia-pacific.com/links.htm. Some links are old; reporters should check updates before using data.

SEARCH ENGINES

Search engines can often point a reporter in the direction of press coverage of a subject, as well as general economic and political resources. My favorite engine and one used by scores of journalists is Google (http://www.google.com), although there are likely better ones for non-English-language journalists. But it is necessary to remember that just as important as the site chosen is the way the query is formulated. Reporters should try thinking of key words in both English and the language of the country in which the story takes place. Often by putting these terms in quotation marks—for example, "currency board" and Argentina—reporters will get more specific results.

GOVERNMENT RESOURCES

Both the U.S. and foreign governments provide an enormous amount of information about the social, political, and economic situation in nearly any part of the world. This information can provide a very good starting point from which to gather further information. Journalists need to be careful about relying too heavily on any government data, however, because in addition to not always being accurate and/or up-to-date, it tends to be presented in a way that is most flattering to the nation providing the information.

U.S. GOVERNMENT INFORMATION

- The U.S. State Department provides extensive background information on different countries. http://www.state.gov/r/pa/ei/bgn.

- U.S. embassies around the world provide reports—though they are not always useful—on the general state of the economy in the country in which they are located. http://usembassy.state.gov.

- The U.S. Census Bureau provides foreign trade statistics, current data and export information, as well as information on U.S. trade deficits and so on. http://www.census.gov/ftp/pub/foreign-trade/www.

- The U.S. Census Bureau also has an international database that offers data on demographics about a good part of the world. While a good resource to begin, again, this information should always be checked against other sources of data. http://www.census.gov/ipc/www/idbnew.html.

- The U.S. government's export portal offers country and industry market research, links to the North American Free Trade Agreement and tariff Web sites. http://www.export.gov. Reporters should keep in mind that this information represents the economic agenda of the U.S. government.

- The Foreign Agriculture Service of the U.S. Department of Agriculture offers links to industry reports, information on trade policy and negotiations, commodities, and specific countries, among other things. http://www.fas.usda.gov.

The commodities page offers specific information on all commodities, as well as U.S. import and export data, market reports, and satellite imagery. Again, keep in mind that this is a resource that reflects the interests of the U.S. government. http://www.fas.usda.gov/commodity.html.

FOREIGN GOVERNMENT INFORMATION

- Chicago's Northwestern University maintains a Web site that offers links to the official Web sites of governments around the world. From the main page one can access the Web sites of different ministries, departments and agencies as well as find relevant statistical information for each government. http://www.library.northwestern.edu/gov-pub/resource/internat/foreign.html

- For information on the European Union, the official EU Web site gives data and details in eleven different languages. One can access official documents, press communiqués, information about different ministries, and key facts about the European economic and political union. http://europa.eu.int

- Foreign embassies and consulates provide only one point of view, but they are good for getting basic political and economic information about different countries. They are especially helpful for understanding how a country wants to promote itself outside its borders. For example, the Brazilian embassy in Washington has a very good Web site with links to political and economic entities in Brazil. http://www.brasilemb.org. For a list of embassies and consulates worldwide, consult http://www.embassyworld.com

OFFICIAL STATISTICS

- Offstats or Official Statistics on the Web, a service of New Zealand's University of Auckland Library, provides links to some of the most important official statistics available on the Internet. (Be careful to check for current data.) One can search by country, region, or topic. http://www2.auckland.ac.nz/lbr/stats/offstats/OFFSTATSmain.htm.

- The European Union's official statistics agency, Eurostat, offers official economic and demographic data, among other topics, for the European Union countries. http://europa.eu.int/comm/eurostat.

INTERNATIONAL ORGANIZATIONS

The following international organizations tend to have very good document services on their Web sites, where one can access research papers, presentations, and other publications.

- The World Trade Organization, based in Geneva, Switzerland, is the international organization that oversees the rules of global trade. The WTO has a resource page, http://www.wto.org/english/res_e/res_e.htm, which is available in English, French, or Spanish. There one can find economic research as well as links to sites that contain information about trade agreements and trade law, among other topics. Also available are international trade statistics for 2002 and historical statistics from 1980. http://www.wto.org/english/res_e/statis_e/statis_e.htm.

- The Washington-based International Monetary Fund, www.imf.org, is an international organization made up of 184 countries. The IMF defines its mission in the following way: "to promote international monetary cooperation, exchange stability, and orderly exchange arrangements; to foster economic growth and high levels of employment; and to provide temporary financial assistance to countries to help ease balance of payments adjustment." The IMF offers a biannual world economic outlook report, as well as reports on global financial stability. Specific information on individual-country loan agreements is also available.

- The World Bank, the Washington-based international institution that provides resources and technical assistance to developing nations, offers an extensive database of projects and publications around the world. http://www.worldbank.org. The research department, http://econ.worldbank.org, has documentation available on different projects that the bank will be working on in the upcoming years.

- Reporters can also find information about different central banks worldwide—as well as links to these institutions and their annual reports—in the Joint World Bank–IMF Library. http://jolis.worldbankimflib.org/Special/annualre.htm.

- From the central banks of each country one can often go to the nation's finance ministries as well. One of these two entities is usually in charge of posting economic statistics on the Web. The Brazilian Central Bank, for example, has an especially good Web page. http://www.bcb.gov.br.

- Regional development banks like the Inter-American Development Bank, http://www.iadb.org, the Asian Development Bank, http://www.adb.org, and the African Development Bank, www.afdb.org, offer specifics on projects and loans in individual member countries.

- For good information on the economic situation in Latin America, try the Economic Commission for Latin America, one of the five regional commissions of the United Nations. http://www.cepal.org/acerca/default-i.asp.

ACADEMICS

Another very good source of expertise on a country or a specific topic — even if it is only for a reporter's own education and not for citation — is academia. Reporters can usually find informed professionals at the top business and international-relations schools around the world.

- The Columbia Business School is a good place to start, since many of the professors have worked in foreign countries and/or continue to advise on economic matters abroad. http://www.columbia.edu/cu/business.

Other good academic resources include the following:

- Georgetown University's School of Foreign Service. http://www.georgetown.edu/sfs/research.html.
- NYU's Stern School of Business. http://www.stern.nyu.edu/Academic/Centers.
- The Wharton Business School at the University of Pennsylvania. http://www.wharton.upenn.edu.
- Wharton has an excellent business resource site called Knowledge@Wharton, which can be found at http://knowledge.wharton.upenn.edu/about_us.cfm. Here one can access articles, research reports, and other information about topics ranging from finance and investment to marketing and public policy.
- The London School of Economics. http://www.lse.ac.uk.
- INSEAD, a renowned French business school. http://www.insead.fr.
- IESE, a Barcelona-based business school. http://www.iese.edu.

RELEVANT ACADEMIC RESEARCH ON THE WEB

- Individual faculty Web sites are a fantastic resource. An excellent site is compiled by NYU business professor Nouriel Roubini and found at http://www.stern.nyu.edu/globalmacro. Jagdish Bhagwati, an international trade economist at Columbia University, has a good Web site, http://www.columbia.edu/~jb38, as does Robert Howse, an international trade expert at the University of Michigan, http://faculty.law.umich.edu/rhowse.

- National Bureau of Economic Research. This is a great place to find journal articles, working papers, and general economic research on a host of subjects, including financial crises in emerging markets. Reporters can also look at links to other sites, including economic policy research organizations to find working papers. http://www.nber.org.

- The Federal Reserve Bank of New York has a number of good economic reports on its Web site. http://www.ny.frb.org.

- For information on global accounting standards and terms, as well as access to company annual reports, reporters should try the Rutgers University Libraries Accounting Links. This accounting Web guide, maintained by the Business Library at Rutgers University in the United States, offers an excellent starting point for research on any topic related to accounting worldwide. http://www.libraries.rutgers.edu/rul/rr_gateway/research_guides/busi/account.shtml.

- For background on international accounting standards and resources related to international financial reporting, the accounting firm Deloitte Touch Tomatsu provides an excellent Web page with updates on the most important developments in the effort to harmonize international accounting standards. http://www.iasplus.com/resource/ref.htm.

- And reporters should not forget the journalism pages of the Initiative for Policy Dialogue, Nobel laureate Joseph Stiglitz's think-tank, based at Columbia University. This Web site is aimed at helping reporters cover finance and economics in developing countries, with "backgrounders" on banking crises, dollarization, privatization, foreign-exchange crises, pension reform, capital markets, debt relief, and energy markets, among other subjects. Each section offers links to the relevant academic research on this topic. http://www.journalismtraining.net.

THINK TANKS

- For a world directory of think tanks, see http://www.lib.umich.edu/govdocs/psthink.html, and for a list of think tanks and NGOs, see http://www.worldpress.org/library/ngo.htm. Some think tanks in the United States include the Brookings Institution, http://www.brook.edu, which has a moderate political leaning and provides good background on how the U.S. government works. The Heritage Foundation, http://www.heritage.org, and the Cato Institute, http://www.cato.org, are both more conservative. Cato has a particular interest in the privatization of Social Security. The Institute for International Economics, http://www.iie.com, a more liberal think tank, has working papers on debt and development, globalization, and international economics, among other topics.

- For background on foreign policy and international affairs, reporters will also want to consult the information available on the Web site of the New York–based Council on Foreign Relations, http://www.cfr.org/index.php. Here one can access regional reports as well as material on topics ranging from economics and trade to homeland security to media and public opinion. The Council publishes *Foreign Affairs*, one of the leading international-affairs journals, which is available online at http://www.foreignaffairs.org/. (You can only access some of the articles for free, however.) *Foreign Affairs* has three international editions—in Japanese, Russian, and Spanish, and selected articles from these publications can be accessed from the Web site at http://dev.foreignaffairs.org/intl.

- The Foreign Policy Institute, based at the Washington, D.C., campus of the Johns Hopkins University's School of Advanced International Studies, http://www.sais-jhu.edu/centers/fpi/index.html, offers information on international issues and public affairs. One can also access individual scholars' homepages for specific research topics.

- The Inter-American Dialogue, http://www.iadialog.org, a policy group based in Washington, D.C., offers research reports and policy papers on topics related to Latin American and Caribbean affairs.

ACTIVIST GROUPS

The following are all good Web sites if one is looking for the so-called other side of the story, but reporters need to be careful to check all information carefully and contrast it with official sources. Activists are just as likely as official organizations to use figures or information to advance their own agenda.

- Global Issues That Affect Everyone provides links to NGOs, think tanks, and other organizations on such topics as "The Effects of Debt," "Fair Trade," "Global Warming," "Free Trade and Globalization," and so on. http://www.globalissues.org.

- OneWorld Net describes itself as "the world's . . . fastest growing civil society network online." The site has a discussion of and links to issues regarding human rights and sustainable development. Content is available in English, Spanish, Dutch, Italian, and other languages. Links are also available to other OneWorld sites such as aidschannel, which offers information on the AIDS epidemic. http://www.oneworld.net.

- Sweatshop Watch describes itself as "a coalition of labor, community, civil rights, immigrant rights, women's, religious and student organizations committed to eliminating sweatshop conditions in the global garment industry." http://www.sweatshopwatch.org.

- Union of Needletrades, Industrial and Textile Employees, AFL-CIO, CLC . This site offers good links to a host of resources on putting an end to sweatshops. http://www.uniteunion.org/sweatshops/links/links.html.

- Scholars Against Sweatshop Labor offers an extensive list of links to articles on the sweatshop controversy and to the different groups that are influencing the debate. http://www.umass.edu/peri/sasl.

- For a different take on the sweatshop debate, reporters might want to consult the Academic Consortium on International Trade's Web site at http://www.fordschool.umich.edu/rsie/acit/, where Jagdish Bhagwati and other "pro-free-trade" academics express their views and offer links to opposing points of view.

- Corporate Watch: Holding Corporations Accountable. CorpWatch is a grassroots organization based in San Francisco that keeps an eye on corporate behavior. http://www.corpwatch.org/home/PHH.jsp.

CHAMBERS OF COMMERCE

Foreign chambers of commerce in the United States and U.S. chambers of commerce abroad promote investment and are probusiness, but they can sometimes provide excellent contacts within the local business community.

- Some examples are the German American Chamber of Commerce (http://www.gaccny.com), the Argentine American Chamber of Commerce. (http://www.argentinechamber.org) or the United States–Mexico Chamber of Commerce (http://www.usmcoc.org).

- For a complete list of American Chambers of Commerce abroad, see http://www.uschamber.org/International/default.htm. For more information on international chambers of commerce, see the International Chamber of Commerce at http://www.iccwbo.org. You can also consult different regional bodies, including the Confederation of Asia Pacific Chambers of Commerce and Industry at http://www.cacci.org.tw, Eurochambres at http://www.eurochambres.be or Eurochambers' Latin America initiative, called Atlas, http://www.eurochambres.be/atlas/en/index.php.

CAPITAL MARKETS

- The New York Stock Exchange offers a list of non-U.S. companies that trade on the exchange as well as a rather complete list of links to stock exchanges around the world. http://www.nyse.com.

- The Bond Market Association's Web site offers a good way to find information on international bond markets. http://www.bondmarkets.com.

COMMODITIES

- The Chicago Board of Trade, http://www.cbot.com, is one of the principal commodities exchanges in the United States. Agriculture products—corn, soybeans, cattle, and so on—tend to trade here, while coffee, sugar, cocoa, cotton, and orange juice trade in New York at the New York Board of Trade, http://www.nybot.com.

- Sparks, a commodities research company, offers an extensive list of links to some of the most important players in and elements of the commodities market. http://www.sparksco.com.

COMPANY INFORMATION

When covering companies, information on their operations and the countries in which they do business can be found on individual company Web sites, which are easily located through a quick Google search. For information on publicly traded companies, you want to go to the regulatory agency of the country in which the company's stock trades. For example, if you are looking for a company that trades in the United States, you want to go to the U.S. Securities and Exchange Commission, http://www.sec.gov, the regulatory body for the securities markets in the United States. Every company—domestic or foreign—that wants to trade its stock on the U.S. stock exchange must periodically file documents with the SEC. These documents can also be found at the following sites: http://www.freeedgar.com or http://www.tenkwizard.com (subscription needed). Hoovers can be very useful when researching a private company that does not file, http://www.hoovers.com, but a subscription is necessary.

If a particular company does not trade on a U.S. exchange, the SEC Web site will not have information about it. In that case, a reporter must consult the regulatory body of the country in which the company's stock trades. So, for example, if a reporter is looking into a company that lists on the London Stock Exchange, he or she would go to the UK's Financial Services Authority, http://www.fsa.gov.uk. If one wanted information on a Spanish company that does not trade on the NYSE, one would want to go to the Comisión Nacional del Mercado de Valores, or the National Stock Market Commission, in Spain to examine what documents are available there. The CNMV's Web site, http://www.cnmv.es, gives financial information on Spanish companies. Until recently, however, this information tended to be more limited than what was available in the United States.

For information on particular companies that trade on other exchanges worldwide, reporters can go directly to each exchange in each particular country. The NYSE offers a list of world exchanges at http://www.nyse.com/international/p1020656068941.html?displayPage=%2Finternational%2Finternationalr.html.

II. AN INTRODUCTION TO EDGAR: HOW TO USE SECURITIES AND EXCHANGE COMMISSION DATA TO REPORT ON U.S. AND FOREIGN COMPANIES

This section explores reporting on companies using the Internet. It reviews the tools available to journalists to analyze company performance, including stock charts and company filings, available both on company home pages and the Web site of the Securities and Exchange Commission, the U.S. government agency charged with the regulation of the securities market.[3] It also discusses how reporters from developing countries can use the financial statements of U.S. companies to research industry issues within their country.

Let's first look at the site of the New York Stock Exchange, http://www.nyse.com. In addition to offering links to stock exchanges around the world, the New York Stock Exchange provides a list of non-U.S. companies that trade on its exchange.

What does this mean? Non-U.S. companies looking for foreign and American investment can raise money by selling stock in their company in the United States. But the companies' stocks do not usually trade on the U.S. exchanges. Instead, what is often traded is a certificate called an American Depositary Receipt. (Foreign stock can trade directly in the U.S. without being converted to an ADR, however.)

To find out if a company in your country trades on the NYSE, go to www.nyse.com. Look on the left side of the page. You should see a toolbar with the word "International." Double click on the "International" toolbar and you should find yourself at a page with information about foreign companies that list on the NYSE. The direct link is http://www.nyse.com/international/p1020656068941.html?displayPage=%2Finternational%2Finternationalr.html. Double clicking on the heading "Non-U.S. Listed Companies" will show what companies from a given country trade on the NYSE.

Once you know that a company trades on the NYSE, you can find out more about the operations of this company using financial information available in the United States. There are a few ways to do this. One of the best ways to begin is to write down the ticker symbol of your company. A ticker symbol is usually a three-or-four letter code, but sometimes it is just one letter, like F for Ford or T for AT&T.

Once you have the ticker of the company, you can go to a service such as Yahoo Finance, http://finance.yahoo.com, Bloomberg, http://www.bloomberg.com/analysis/index.html, or Reuters, http://www.reuters.com/financeQuotes.jhtml, that allows you to get detailed price information on the stock of publicly traded companies. Most newspapers and magazines have some kind of similar service on their Web sites. These services, however, should not be used as sole sources for an article: you must also check with the company and official documents to make sure that all information is up-to-date. But these services do offer a quick way to take a snapshot of a company.

Let's see how this is done using Yahoo Finance, for example. To begin, put in the ticker symbol to call up the company. If you do not know the ticker symbol, you can look it up. Say you want to look up the Mexican television company Televisa. Go to "Symbol Lookup" and put in the word "Televisa." Two choices come up, but only one of them trades on the NYSE, the one with the ticker "TV" for Grupo Televisa. If you click on that symbol, you will be taken to a page where you can choose from headers such as "Chart," "Profile," "News," "Historical Prices," and so on.

Let's start with the "Profile." Here you have just about everything you need to know about the company, including where its headquarters are located, the highs and lows of its stock, its latest earnings announcements, the names of its chief executives, and often even links to executive compensation. Of course, all this information must be checked for accuracy against the information offered on a particular company's Web site. It's also important to look at recent developments, or the "news" section of the Yahoo profile, to get an idea of what the company has been doing in recent weeks: changes in personnel, mergers, or a stock split, for example.

You also want to take a look at the company's market capitalization, or what the market thinks the company is worth. Market capitalization is calculated by multiplying the price of a stock by the number of shares outstanding, or the number of shares that are owned by investors. Say, for example, that Company B has thirty outstanding shares, trading at $30 each. The market would value Company B at $900. Now say that Company B reports that it has gotten rid of its chief executive, and because nervous investors begin selling shares in the company, the stock takes a dive to $15. Company B would now have half the market capitalization as before. Market capitalization, or market cap, is also important to watch because it indicates how much money people have invested in a company and thus, how much capital the company theoretically has to spend. During the dot-com boom of the late 1990s, some "new economy" companies had larger market caps than more established companies like IBM or Ford. Investors sank millions, sometimes billions, of dollars into high-tech companies, driving up their market capitalizations and, in many cases, giving a false sense of their true value. In spite of these huge market caps, many of these high-tech companies had no tangible assets.

Now let's look at the "Chart." Here you can get a good picture of how a company's stock has performed over the past year. (Yahoo and other services offer daily, weekly, and yearly charts, as well as some other combinations. You can also compare a company's stock to the stock of another company in the same industry or against a major index.) You want to pay close attention to any sudden movements. Has the stock suddenly skyrocketed? Or has it fallen into the dumps? Why? Many times the stock price can alert you to larger changes going on within the company. Have earnings been steady? Has the company just announced an unexpected loss? Does the company have any legal problems? Are they looking to merge with another company?

There are many ways to delve deeper into these questions. First, it's often good to look at the highs and lows for the past year and to write down those two dates. What happened on these dates? There are different ways to find out. If you go to "news" (or recent developments) and look for an announcement around this time, you are bound to find something that might help you understand what happened. You might also want to do a clip search using the company's name and the date when you see a significant change in the stock, or you can use the company's name and any key words that relate to the situation at hand.

Individual company Web sites, which provide more detailed information, recent financial statements and SEC filings (usually under the heading "Investor Information"), may also offer clues. By looking at SEC filings around the date that the stock rose or fell, you can usually find out what precipitated the movement. Therefore, if the stock of the company you are following suddenly fell 50 percent in one month, for example, you would want to examine the company's filings up to and following this fall. Imagine that a company disclosed that it was restating its earnings for a past year, or that management was being investigated by the SEC. These are events that have to be revealed to investors and would appear in documents filed with the SEC. Every company—domestic or foreign—that wants to trade its stock (or in the case of some foreign companies, ADRs) on a U.S. stock exchange must periodically file financial statements with the Securities and Exchange Commission.

Much of this information is available electronically on the SEC Web site at http://www.sec.gov. However, it is important to remember that until November 2002, foreign firms were not required to submit these documents electronically, according to information on the Web site. (The electronic-filing rule for foreign companies went into effect in November 2002, although it was announced six months earlier to give companies time to adjust). Therefore, while you will find electronic documents for U.S. firms prior to November 2002 on the SEC Web site, there is no guarantee that you will find electronic documents for foreign firms prior to November of 2002.

Just because you can't find information on your company at the SEC or at other financial document services like FreeEdgar, http://www.freeedgar.com (registration required), or TenK Wizard, http://www.10kwizard.com (subscription only), does not mean that the company has not filed information with the SEC. It is possible that this information exists in paper form at the SEC. This is indicated on the Web site with a corresponding code number. You can usually request a copy of the paper document from the company, and also from the SEC, but at a cost.

But remember: If the company that you are doing research on does not trade on a U.S. exchange, you are not going to be able to find information about it on the SEC Web site. In that case, you are going to want to go to the regulatory body of the country in which your particular company's stock trades.

You use also use Yahoo's International Financial Center to find information on particular companies that trade on exchanges other than the NYSE. Yahoo offers its Yahoo Finance service for a number of other countries, including Argentina, Austraila, Brazil, China, France, Germany, Hong Kong, India, Japan, Mexico, Singapore, Spain, Taiwan, and the United Kingdom, among others. Each service is customized to reflect the particulars of the national financial markets and appears in the country's native language.

In order to access these pages, go to http://biz.yahoo.com/ifc. There you will find links to economic indicators in Africa, Asia, Latin America, Europe, the Middle East, and North Africa, as well as direct links to Yahoo's international finance pages.

SEC documents can provide:

- Background on the industry

- Information on the political and economic environment of a country in which a company does business

- Background on privatizations of state-owned assets, if applicable

- Information on how certain stock exchanges work

- Company and industry risks

- Company concerns, as well as information on lawsuits

- Organization of the company, description of business units, names and locations of subsidiaries

- Details on sales, investments, and international operations

- Biographies of executives and board members

- Information on executive compensation (primarily for U.S. companies)

SEC documents are good for a number of reasons, even if you do not find all that much information about a specific company from a given country. You can almost always find information about the country in the annual reports of American companies doing business there. For example, if a large multinational has closed a plant in the country, this information would probably appear in its annual report. You can also look at American companies' SEC filings to see if they offer information about their competitors—usually under "risks," or "competitors" in the registration statement. In this way you can get a better idea of the issues that are pertinent to the sector.

But remember: The information found in these documents is information provided by the company to the SEC. It is written from the vantage point of the company and has usually tended to present the company in as favorable a light as possible. The SEC conducts reviews of company filings periodically and checks the language in these documents to make sure that it does not paint the company in an overly positive light. But the SEC does not have any control over what is filed. For this reason, SEC documents provide a good starting point from which to conduct a more thorough analysis of a company through interviews with industry analysts, competitors, clients, accountants, and company staff.

WHAT KIND OF DOCUMENTS DOES A COMPANY FILE AND WHAT DO THEY MEAN?

Foreign companies may choose to file documents designed specifically for foreign companies rather than those used by U.S. companies. If a foreign company chooses to file the foreign-only documents, in most cases it will not have to report as much information as U.S. companies. For example, foreign companies can choose to turn in a form 20-F annually, which is somewhat different from the annual report, or 10-K, that U.S. companies have to file. Some of the items that firms have to disclose in the form 20-F are only required if they have to make a similar disclosure in their home country.

For example, individual executive compensation only has to be disclosed if the regulatory body in the home country requires that it be disclosed. If not, then only the total amount that the company pays out in executive compensation has to be disclosed. This means that while in the United States you will find the individual salaries of the most important executives of a company, until recently it was impossible to find these individual figures for executives in SEC documents filed by Spanish companies. This is because in Spain individual executive compensation is not detailed in reports filed with that country's Comisión Nacional de Mercado de Valores. (This is slowly changing and should to be checked on a case-by-case basis.)

For detailed salary and compensation information for executives of a U.S. company, it is necessary to consult that company's proxy statement, which is the document mailed to shareholders before a shareholders' meeting. (This form is also known as a DEF 14A.) The proxy statement also contains information about any other kind of financial compensation that executives may have secured as part of their employment contract, as well as notice of any lawsuits that have been filed against the company. Foreign firms do not file proxy statements, but sometimes you can find similar information within a firm's registration statements, or forms F-1, F-2, F-3, and F-4 for foreign companies. (Registration statements for U.S. companies are identified by the forms S-1, S-2, S-3, and S-4. For a description of each form and how it differs from other forms of the same class, consult the SEC Web site.)

Foreign companies filing documents with the SEC do not have to turn in quarterly reports, or 10-Qs like their U.S. counterparts do unless they are so required by the rules in their home country. Foreign companies do have to file reports of significant events on form 6-K. U.S. companies file these same reports, only they are known as 8-Ks.

KEY SEC FORMS

Journalists can find more information on specific forms and what they mean at the SEC site under the heading "Guide to Corporate Filings." Go to http://www.sec.gov and then to "Descriptions of SEC forms." (There is also a separate page that explains the forms used by international issuers at http://www.sec.gov/divisions/corpfin/forms/international.shtml.) Here is a summary of some of that information.

SEC documents are generally divided into three categories: *registration statements*, *periodic reports*, and *current reports*. *Registration statements*, which are governed by what is known as the Securities Act of 1933, are filed with the SEC before a company issues new stock or goes public. Registration statements are meant to help investors decide whether to invest in a public offering. For this reason, they are especially useful for journalists wishing to learn more about a company because they include basic information about a company's business, including how the firm plans to make money, whom it believes to be its competitors, and what kind of risks it thinks it faces. Registration statements also usually provide a general panorama of the industry to which the company belongs. U.S. and foreign companies may use S-1, S-2, or S-3. Foreign companies may choose to use the forms specially designated for them by the SEC: F-1, F-2, F-3.

Forms S-1 and F-1 can be used by the broadest category of companies wishing to issue stock. The first half of forms S-1 and F-1 is usually known as the prospectus, and this is where you can find basic information about the company as well as the terms of the public offering.

Only those companies that already have publicly issued securities and filed their periodic reports according to SEC requirements may use forms S-3 and F-3. Forms S-3 and F-3 are generally much shorter documents because companies can give information simply by referring investors to documents already filed with the SEC. For example, they can direct the reader to the firm's annual report (either form 20-F or form 10-K) or to a proxy statement. In this way, there is no need to repeat this information in the registration statement. If a U.S. firm is planning on merging (or if it has to register a new issuance of stock) it uses form S-4; foreign firms use F-4.

Periodic reports, which are governed by what is known as the Securities Exchange Act of 1934, are used to provide updated annual and quarterly information about certain companies.

An annual report is an audited document that a firm must produce at the end of each fiscal year that lets shareholders—and the SEC—know its financial results for the year. U.S. firms use form 10-K, and, in addition to audited financial statements (and the footnotes to the financial statements, which journalists must read to understand the financial statements), it also includes a section called "Management's Discussion and Analysis." MD&A gives the company's take on how certain events have affected business over the past year and alerts journalists to any possible areas to watch in the year to come.

Journalists can also find detailed information on the nuts and bolts of the company's business in form 10-K—including a description of the different operating groups, information on where the company does business overseas, and a glossary of terms necessary to understand the firm's core business. In addition, there is information about top management and the salaries, bonuses, and stock options they receive from the company.

A 10-Q is a quarterly report, and this, too, can be an interesting source of information. A quarterly report contains information about how a firm has done in one particular business quarter. The financial information is usually not audited. Form 10-Q comes out three times a year, since in the fourth quarter companies must file an annual report.

Foreign firms use form 20-F to file annual reports. Form 20-F is also used as the foundation of a foreign firm's registration statement. For this reason, some of the information in form 20-F seems like it is not applicable to the annual report. Not to worry—this is as it should be. Since September of 2000, foreign firms must disclose total executive compensation in form 20-F. Although reporters will not find the kind of detailed compensation information that usually appears in a U.S. proxy statement, they can get an idea of how much a company spends on executive compensation.

For detailed salary and compensation information for executives of a U.S. company, it is necessary to consult that company's *proxy statement*. The proxy statement is a document mailed to shareholders before the annual shareholders' meeting that tells them when the annual meeting is going to be held and what they can expect to hear about at the meeting. Proxy statements, or form DEF 14As, as they are called by the SEC, usually begin with a description of the different proposals up for vote, as well as management's recommendation on how to vote. The proxy statement contains basic biographical information on top management as well as details of any compensation deals that executives may have secured as part of their employment contract. Proxies are also a good source for finding out if a company has been sued for any particular reason.

Foreign firms do not file proxy statements, but sometimes it is possible to find similar information within a firm's registration statements, or forms F-1, F-2, F-3 and F-4. Bottom line: Proxies are filled with good story ideas.

Current reports, which are also governed by the Securities Exchange Act of 1934, provide information about "material events" that fall into special categories. The SEC defines a material event as one that an investor would consider important in making a decision about buying or selling a stock.

U.S. firms use form 8-K and foreign firms use form 6-K for announcing an extraordinary event—restatement of earnings, change in management, notice of an SEC investigation, and so on. Remember: these forms—and their corresponding numerical codes—are unique to the SEC. Every country that has a stock market should have a regulatory body that sets its own rules with regard to what kind of forms a firm must file and what kind of information the firm must include in the form. Much of the information contained in these forms may be the same, but forms have different names and take different shapes depending on the different regulatory requirements and terminology of each country. For example, instead of asking firms to submit an announcement of an extraordinary event, or 8-K or 6-K, Spain's national regulatory body, the Comisión Nacional del Mercado de Valores, asks that all firms inform of "Hechos Relevantes" or "relevant events." The purpose of the form may be similar—to let investors know that something has happened that they need to know about in order to buy or sell the stock—but the similarities usually end there.

NOTES

This chapter is part of a class called Computer Assisted Reporting for Business and Economics given by the author at the Universitat de Barcelona/Les Heures journalism master's program. A number of sources have influenced the way in which the author has approached this subject, including Terri Thompson's *Writing About Business: The New Columbia Knight-Bagehot Guide to Economics and Business Journalism* (New York: Columbia University Press, 2001), in particular, the chapters on "International Business," by Dave Lindorff, and "How to Read Financial Statements," by Susan Scherreik. The author is grateful to the colleagues, students, and friends who have suggested a number of links.

1. The SEC conducts reviews of company filings periodically and checks the language in these documents to make sure that it does not paint the company in an overly positive light. However, the SEC does not have the resources to review most of the documents filed with it. It is important to realize that the SEC does not guarantee the accuracy of any document filed, even the ones it does review. It does ask people

or companies to correct mistakes if it finds them, and it can sue these parties if it finds out that they have somehow manipulated figures or other information contained in the filings. But the SEC does not have any control over what is filed.

2. The author regrets that some of these links may be outdated by the time this book goes to press and other links may have become subscription-only services. All links were valid as of February 2004. If by chance a specific link does not work anymore, journalists should try going to the home page of the organization to search for the information.

3. All information on SEC documents and filings can be found at www.sec.gov. A number of experts provided guidance on the subject through lectures that the author attended at Columbia: Linda Quinn, "The SEC and International Reporting," lecture presented at the Citigroup International Journalists Seminar, 9 June 2003, New York; Robert Strahota, "The SEC and International Reporting, lecture presented at the Citigroup International Journalists Seminar, 10 June 2002, New York.

CHAPTER TWENTY-SIX

WRITING TIPS

GRAHAM WATTS

IMAGINE HOW exciting it would have been if South Korea had made it to the finals of the 2002 World Cup. The plucky host nation—the first Asian country to get that far—against the greatest of all, Brazil. Asia vs. Latin America. Even people who know nothing about football would have loved it.

Now imagine the story was written by a reporter from the business pages:

> At the Yokohama International Stadium in Japan, attended by 76,371 specta-tors, including his excellency the President of the Federation of International Football Associations, Joseph Sepp Blatter, an encounter took place today between the two successful semifinalists to determine the ultimate victor in the Fifa World Cup of 2002, which included 32 teams, fielding a total of 637 representatives of their nations in 96 matches over four weeks.

Well, I did say imagine. And that's what you will have to do, because this lead does not even tell you who won.

Why do we do that? Why do we think when we are reporting econom-ics or business that we can forget the basics of our craft? We forget to put the news at the top of the story. We forget that our leads should not be cluttered with insignificant facts. We forget to keep it tight and tell it in plain language. Above all, we forget that while it might be about business or finance, it is still journalism.

There are, of course, many reasons. Probably the most important is that we do not know enough about the subject. So we depend on others—government officials and corporate communications departments—to tell us what the story is and to provide us with the terminology we need.

When you hear an official talking about the central bank's "net forward open position," it is safer just to use the jargon than to get tangled up trying to find words that your readers can understand. And most of the time your boss or the copy editors on the desk are not going to yell across the newsroom at you, "Hey, Junior, what's a net forward open position?" (It has to do with foreign exchange—although, talking about football, it sounds more like a good place for a goal scorer to be.) Our superiors hate to reveal their ignorance. So they too join the conspiracy that in the end leaves our readers in the dark.

Another reason we burden our stories with lots of numbers and technical language is that we think business readers are not like ordinary readers—they can take in lots of complex information, and they already know the jargon. Sometimes we want to show off to them or our colleagues, to be seen using big words. I once read a headline in a business newspaper that said: "ADR and GDR fungibility hinges on tax treatment." (I swear I did not make that up.)

Most of the time, however, it is because it is a lonely life being a business reporter. You are left there with little guidance and even less sympathy, and you have to hack your way through stuff you have never heard of and produce enough stories to keep the desk quiet. Sometimes you wonder why you do it and look enviously across the room at the political reporters or the sports desk and dream about what it must be like to be part of the real world.

Well, don't despair. This is the real world. If you have read the rest of this book, you will know by now, if you did not already, that the business and economics decisions we cover are matters of life and death. Only football reporters are able to claim with some justification that their subject is more important even than that.

Approached in the right way, we can make our subject so much more interesting and rewarding for ourselves and at the same time accessible and useful for our readers, who are not, incidentally, different from the readers of other sections. There is still the belief among too many financial journalists that their readers know what all the technical terms mean. They do not. Many readers buy and skim the financial press. And they skim it for news that directly affects what they do. The rest they leave unread, even if they have the time to read more. That is because while they might be highly paid experts in industry or government, they are only experts in one thing. A good accountant in the chemicals industry does not necessarily know anything about what is going on—or what the jargon is—in trade policy. A good agricultural economist does not necessarily know anything about how pension funds invest their money. And a good manager in the retail sector does not necessarily know how foreign exchange markets function.

If we help them all with the bits they do not know about, they will come back for more and in doing so make our publications more commercially secure. We all win.

How do we do it? By putting the journalism back into our business.

- *Make the story your own.* The biggest blight on business journalism is the habit of reporters relying on a single source for a story. Governments, companies, and nongovernmental organizations turn out a terrific number of press releases and other self-promoting material that end up in newspapers almost untouched by human hand. There is nothing satisfying in doing that. Instead, regard such information as the departure point only for what might become a story. Seek out other information, sources, and angles, and you will feel a greater sense of achievement. And when you get something that after further research and inquiry turns out to be old, boring, or inconsequential, have the courage to say, "This is not a story. I am not going to waste time with this." And then get on with a real story.

- *Get to the bottom of it.* Build real stories of greater depth. In an age where raw or basic information is instantly available on twenty-four-hour business television, online, or on a mobile phone, what readers need to know is what it means. So we have to write stories in which the significance is explicit and high up.

- *Enjoy it more yourself.* Get out of the office. Go to where the things are happening that are only abstractly referred to in the press releases and bring them alive in business features. You will find your job satisfaction improving sharply. And your readers will enjoy your stories more and understand the issues better.

- *Bring real people into it.* Search for interesting characters to give life and color to your stories. We all know that readers love human-interest stories and to read about people, yet on the business pages the people are other dull men in gray suits or not there at all.

- *Understand the subject better.* This will bring the issues alive for you. If you find it dull and mysterious, it will come across that way to your readers. But as you begin to understand the dynamics of a market or the intrigues of a boardroom or the social consequences of an economic policy, so you will understand more about how life itself works. This will allow you to connect those things you might have thought were not part of the business universe—politics, education, crime and law, and the many things that can deliver well-being or suffering.

- *And explain it well.* One of the great pleasures of the communication business is seeing people "get" something they had not understood before. ("Oh, now I see.") If you are able to deliver that understanding to your readers, it can be immensely satisfying. That means you will have to develop a sense of when it is the reader needs help in understanding technical concepts and processes—and how to craft and polish the phrases that will provide that help.

Some of these things are difficult to do. There are many conservative and insecure bosses out there who will not like it when you tell them, "This is not a story." Many of them got where they are by assuming that if it is in a press release or a government official said it, it must be news. Others just want to fill the pages and go home. Winning that fight will not be easy. But you are more likely to do so if you turn out quality journalism. So, let us look at some of the things we need to do to achieve that.

To start with, we have to go beyond the 5Ws and H. Most of us are familiar with the idea that our stories should answer the Who, What, Where, When, Why, and How questions for our readers. We should continue to do so. But we have to go much further. We must first ask ourselves what it is about the thing that has happened that our readers need to know to judge its significance. We need to measure it. Is this the biggest or the longest or the highest? Is it 10 percent or 50 percent or double? Is this the first, the only, the last, or the final? The world's biggest airline firing its chief executive is a much more important story than the fifth smallest airline firing a member of the cabin crew. Measure everything in the story—the companies, the people, the things that have happened—and give your readers a clear understanding of their scale. This in turn makes it possible for you to spell out the significance of the news.

Take the following story from a newspaper in Thailand:

FIFTEEN STATE FIRMS GO ON THE BLOCK

Fifteen state enterprises will list on the stock exchange in the next two years, boosting market capitalization by 803 billion baht, Prime Minister Thaksin Shinawatra said.

Three companies—Internet Thailand, Thai Airways International and the Petroleum Authority of Thailand—would list this year, with a value of 83.6 billion baht.

Krung Thai Bank, now over 90% government-owned, would also be divested to private investors.

Mr Thaksin said that in 2002, seven state enterprises would be listed, worth a total of 303.7 billion baht: the Telephone Organisation, the Communications Authority, the Thailand Tobacco Monopoly, the Airport Authority, the Government Housing Bank, the Port Authority, and the Government Savings Bank.

Five more would list in 2003, raising market capitalization by 309.9 billion baht: the Electricity Generating Authority, the Metropolitan Electricity Authority, the Provincial Electricity Authority, the Metropolitan Waterworks Authority and the Provincial Waterworks Authority.

"Privatisation doesn't have to wait for the economy to improve. Once the state enterprises are ready, they can list," Mr Thaksin said.

State enterprises would be grouped by sector under a new firm, the National Enterprise Holdings Co.

Finance Minister Somkid Jatusripitak said some agencies could list first, and sell shares to private investors later. Stock options would be offered to employees.

The stock exchange and the Securities and Exchange Commission would speed up listing procedures for state enterprises. Automatic listing approval would be given one year after agencies become public companies.

Even if you managed to stick with it (it's very dull), are you able to get a good sense of the importance of this story? No. You know quite a few big state companies are going up for sale, but that's about all.

To get a better idea of what is going on, the following three facts need to be added to the story:

1. The total value of all the shares on the Stock Exchange of Thailand at that time (its market capitalization) was 1,409 billion baht;

2. at its peak in 1995 it was 3,500 billion baht;

3. since the collapse of the Asian financial crisis in 1997, foreign investors have not been tempted to return to the stock market in large enough numbers to give the economy life.

This makes it possible to transform the story, which can now read:

> The government is to sell fifteen state-owned companies over the next two years in an attempt to boost the value of the stock market by more than a quarter in the hope that this will breathe life back into the economy.
>
> By selling shares in Internet Thailand, Thai Airways International, the Petroleum Authority of Thailand, and twelve others, the government hopes to attract back the foreign investors who pushed the market's value in the booming 1990s to more than twice what it is now.

The secret to getting to the essence of the story is to ignore for the time being all those details you get in company handouts—company names, the names of big shots in the company and their positions, advisers, bankers, product names, turnover figures, and all that. Make a statement with what you have left, in this case: "The government is going to sell some big companies to try to revive the stock market and the economy because both are pretty flat at the moment." You can polish up the language and fill in the details later.

The next step in the thinking is to *widen the story*. This is where you make the story your own. You start asking questions that *arise* from the story, but which are not what this specific bit of information is about. The first thing is to take it beyond the specific person or company involved (or, if you are dealing with international economic news, the specific country).

So you start asking questions like:

■ Is this the first time something like this has happened in this company or sector?

■ Is it part of a trend?

■ Or is this against a trend?

■ Or does it signal a change in the course of events?

- Now that this has happened, what might the consequences be for this company, for the sector, the country, for other things?

In our example above, we should be asking: Has the government tried to do this before? Has it been tried anywhere else in the Asia region? If so, as in the case of South Korea, what sort of success did they have? If no one else is doing it right now, why not?

When you have gone through the process of asking these "lateral" and other questions, then seek the answers. Do not think that you should know the answers yourself. This is where you begin asking the experts—using your journalistic expertise in asking questions. And the experts are, among others, the people who gave you the information in the first place, other companies in the same sector, stockbrokers' analysts, academics, and bank economists, not forgetting your colleagues (such as the person who used to cover the news beat before you) and your news editor. And never forget the archives (which used to be a library, but is probably now some online database or even a general search on the Internet). Do that and you will not end up with a single-source story. In our example above, the sources are the prime minister and his finance minister—in effect, one source. Our readers have had no help in making a judgment about this decision—nothing from economists, foreign investors, domestic investment institutions. Do you know whether something like this has much chance of working? I do not.

Your next step is to decide what numbers you need. Often you will be given lots of numbers by the original news source—too many, but not the ones you need to do the "measuring." You only want a few, but you want the ones that count, so to speak. And when you have decided which ones they are, make them reader-friendly. Do not say "32.79 percent of sales turnover" when you can say "a third." Do not say "69.36 percent of the population" when you can say "seven out of ten." If you look at our example again, the rewritten version tells us that the government is trying to "boost the value of the stock market by *more than a quarter*" and that the market's value was "*more than twice* what it is now." No need to use all those exact numbers at the top of the story.

Now you are ready to write. And the first question you have to decide on is *what details you will need for the lead*. You want to give the story real substance without cluttering the top with unnecessary details, numbers, or names, especially unfamiliar ones. In our original example above, the first paragraph is good in this respect, but very soon the story degenerates into a lifeless list of company names.

Next, either in the lead itself or soon after, *tell the readers what the story means*, why they are reading it. This is the help, the guidance, and the interpretation you offer to the busy reader who has all these questions churning around in his or her head but not enough time to put them in any order, let alone find out the answers. In our original example, there is nothing to help the reader. In the rewrite we say this is being done "in the hope that this will breathe life back into the economy." That's why we are giving you this story to read.

The *so-what element*, as this is often called, sometimes comes in the form of a paragraph that begins with a phrase such as "The decision underlines the government's determination . . . " or The announcement signals a change of policy . . . " or " . . . underlines or highlights . . . " and so on. Try to get the essence of this into the lead and then fashion a coherent paragraph that spells it out further down the story. If you have made enough calls to the right people, you should have the material to work with on this vital part of the story.

Now, as your story unfolds, make sure you *provide the necessary background and context.* Many readers of a news story are new readers—ones who have just begun to venture into reading business news or have just come back from traveling abroad or from having a baby, or whatever. So you need to write your stories in such a way that they are accessible to everyone. Develop a sense of where readers might become puzzled or lost because they do not know what has gone before. The skill is to boil down the information you have gathered from the archives and from your reporting and that you carry around in your head into phrases, sentences, and paragraphs that "remind" readers of what has happened, dropped into the story as you go. Background is more of the formal "reminders" of what has happened, and context is the wider framework within which something is happening. Again, look at our example. There is no context or background. We do not know whether this is a surprise announcement (that's a lot of privatization to come out with in one breath) or whether this has been long awaited. Nor are we told what has been going on in the stock market over the past few years or in the economy.

Next, make sure the story has life, and that means *using direct quotes.* These lend a sense of authenticity and actuality to what you write because quotes are the dialogue of real people in a nonfiction story. They change the pace and allow a story to be "heard" as well as read. They also capture things in everyday speech, which is often hard to convey in business.

And your final responsibility is to *hold the reader's hand through the technical bits.* The difficulty is deciding what you have to explain and what is generally known and understood. This will vary from publication to publication, but in my experience, most financial journalists err on the wrong side—thinking they need explain less than they should.

Holding the reader's hand need not be an obtrusive and clumsy thing. There are a number of ways in which it can be done:

■ Insert a crisp, clean, and clear definition at just that point in the story when you think readers are in danger of turning the page because they think they are running into alien territory and where their ignorance will make them feel either uncomfortable or irritated. What you are doing with this is signaling clearly to the readers that they do not have to know already what this thing means, especially when it is a new and difficult technical concept. Just stop the story and define it.

■ Rather than stopping the story and inserting a definition, use a phrase that defines the technical term as part of a sentence in the normal flow of reporting. So, instead of writing a new sentence after using the concept "trade deficit" that says, "A trade deficit is when a country imports more than it exports," construct the whole thing in a way that makes it clear what a trade deficit is: "The trade deficit rose 65 percent to a record $271 billion in 1999 as the country's strong economy pulled in foreign goods much faster than exports expanded." The skill is to make the definition part of the information.

■ Use the technical term in a normal sentence, and then in the next sentence, use the defining phrase as an alternative while giving further information. For example: "Inflation was 6 percent in 1999. This is the first time the government's measure of the change in prices for goods and services has exceeded 5 percent a year in the last decade." Again, what you are doing here is still imparting new information or background rather than stopping the story while you give a definition.

■ Give a minilecture. Sometimes what the reader needs help with is not just a technical word but understanding a process. An example is when shares fall because of a threat of an interest-rate hike. Even this reasonably widely known process could do with some explaining—that "investors fear interest-rate rises because they dampen consumer demand for the products made by the companies they invest in and increase the burden of borrowing for those companies. So share prices fall as soon as the perception of a likely interest rate rise becomes widespread among investors."

Writing clearly and simply is much harder to do than using a whole lot of technical terminology and making no effort to explain it. If you have the chance, get your hands on a copy of the *Wall Street Journal*, the biggest-selling serious business newspaper in the world. They write in a fresh and simple style, explaining things they think their readers will have difficulty with and always remembering that they have a duty to entertain as well as to inform. This is daily newspaper journalism, not writing for academic or trade journals, and it means that we should apply the same tests that any other journalist would apply: is it new, different, interesting, significant, or at times just entertaining? That's our business.

CONTRIBUTORS

ABID ASLAM broke numerous stories about the World Bank and IMF as senior finance and trade correspondent with Inter Press Service. He has covered corporate accountability, governance, and regulation for Agence France-Presse and written and edited economic and political news for magazines, Web sites, and UN agencies.

AMER BISAT is portfolio manager at UBS; he is also an adjunct professor of economics at Columbia University. Previously, Bisat worked as a portfolio manager at Morgan Stanley, as Europe's chief emerging markets economist at Salomon Brothers, and as senior economist at the IMF. He has written numerous papers on financial-sector development, private-sector financing, economic growth, and the economics of the Middle East. A Lebanese national, he received his Ph.D. in economics and finance from Colombia University.

SERGEI BLAGOV covers Russia and post-Soviet states with special attention to Asia-related issues. Between 1983 and 1997, he spent some seven years in Southeast Asia, mainly in Vietnam. Based in Moscow, Blagov has published two books on Vietnamese history and teaches Vietnamese history and journalism at the Institute of Oriental and African Studies of Moscow University.

SHANTHA BLOEMAN has worked as communications consultant for UNICEF at its headquarters as well as in Africa and South Asia. She has also worked as an independent producer. Her recent documentary, *T-Shirt Travels*, has been broadcast on PBS in the United States. She has her master's in public policy and administration with a concentration in international media and communication from the Columbia University School of International and Public Affairs.

HELEN CAMPBELL worked on trade and economic policy issues for the Australian government for twelve years. Her experience ranges from the Uruguay GATS negotiations to the negotiation of bilateral trade agreements, as well as analyses of the implications of regional trade and investment integration in Latin America and Southeast Asia. She is now exploring the relationship between economic development and responsible business behavior, as well as the implications of trade and investment policies for responsible corporate behavior in her current role at AccountAbility.

GRACIANA DEL CASTILLO is a founding partner and managing director of MAG, the Macroeconomics Advisory Group. Graciana held senior positions in the office of the secretary-general of the United Nations and at the International Monetary Fund. She has taught in graduate programs on the Latin American economy at Columbia University and has published extensively in leading professional journals on countries in both financial and postconflict crises. She received her Ph.D. from Columbia University in economics.

DAN DELUCA is a vice president in the Corporate Planning Group of the Bank of Tokyo-Mitsubishi. He was previously in product management at Citibank and also does occasional freelance writing and editing. He has an M.B.A in finance and business economics from Columbia Business School, and a B.A. in political science from Reed College.

RANDALL DODD is the director of the Derivatives Study Center in Washington, D.C. He received his Ph.D. in economics from Columbia University where he specialized in international trade and finance. He has worked at Citicorp, the U.S. Congress, and the Commodity Futures Trading Commission, and he has taught economics, political philosophy, and finance for many years.

HERBERT K. FOLPE is an adjunct professor of accounting at the Yale University School of Management and a retired partner of KPMG.

JANE M. FOLPE is a program coordinator at the Columbia University Graduate School of Journalism. In addition, she is an instructor in computer-assisted reporting at Universitat de Barcelona/Les Heures journalism master's program in Spain and has worked with Nobel

Prize economist Joseph Stiglitz's Initiative for Policy Dialogue to provide computer-assisted reporting classes to journalists from developing countries.

HOWARD I. GOLDEN, J.D., M.B.A., is president of Terra Partners, an asset-management company managing hedge funds invested in emerging economies. Terra has offices in New York, Prague, and Bucharest, and Golden spends most of his time in Prague. He has been quoted in numerous newspapers and magazines and has lectured in the U.S. and Europe about capital-market issues.

PETER S. GREEN writes on business and politics for the *New York Times* from Prague. He is a former East Europe correspondent for the *International Herald Tribune* and is currently writing a book on Vaclav Havel and the Velvet Revolution.

KRISTIN HUCKSHORN has worked as a journalist for twenty-four years, covering sports, politics, and foreign affairs. She opened the first U.S. newspaper bureau in postwar Vietnam for Knight Ridder Newspapers and served as the bureau chief from 1994 through 1998. She is an editor at the *New York Times*.

PHILLIP LONGMAN is a senior fellow at the New America Foundation in Washington, D.C. Longman is the author of the forthcoming book *The Fundamentalist Moment: Freedom and Fertility in an Aging World* (Perseus, 2004).

DAVID MARCHANT is a British journalist based in Miami, Florida, where he operates KYC News, a publisher of investigative financial newsletters, including its flagship *OffshoreAlert*, which has exposed many international, multimillion-dollar, white-collar crimes while they are in progress.

TYLER MARONEY, a Brooklyn-based writer, is a former Fulbright Scholar who has written extensively on Latin America. He was on staff at *Fortune Magazine* and has written for *The Atlantic Monthly*, *Worth*, and the *New York Times*.

GRÁINNE MCCARTHY is assistant managing editor for foreign exchange, macroeconomics, and fixed-income news at Dow Jones Newswires in New York. She was Indonesia bureau chief for Dow Jones during the period from the fall of Suharto in May 1998 through mid-2000. Gráinne has a Knight Bagehot fellowship from Columbia University and a master's in Journalism from Dublin City University. Hailing from Ireland, she has also worked for various publications in Brussels, covering the European Union.

CATHERINE MCKINLEY got her start in journalism at the BBC World Service as a production assistant for the *East Asia Today* program. She worked as a reporter for Dow Jones Newswires in Shanghai and since 1999 has been based in Hanoi where she reports on the Vietnamese economy for Dow Jones. McKinley speaks both Mandarin and Vietnamese and grew up in Singapore.

SUZANNE MILLER is a journalist who specializes in banking, finance, and economics. She was a staff reporter for Dow Jones Newswires and London bureau chief of *CBS Marketwatch* and a staff member at Knight-Ridder. She is a regular contributor to the *Banker* and has written for *Investment Dealers Digest*, *Newsweek*, and *Institutional Investor*.

GUMISAI MUTUME writes for *Africa Recovery* magazine in New York. Prior to joining *Africa Recovery*, Mutume was a correspondent for Inter Press Service in Washington, D.C., where he covered the World Bank and the IMF.

DAVID NISSEN is professor in practice and director of the program in international energy management and policy at Columbia's School for International and Public Affairs. Prior to joining Columbia, he held senior positions with Chase Manhattan Bank and Exxon Corporation. In the 1970s at the Federal Energy Administration, he directed the analysis of President Carter's national energy plan. He holds a B.S. in chemistry from the California Institute of technology and a Ph.D. in economics from the University of California at Berkeley.

PETTER NORE, a vice president of the energy company Norsk Hydro ASA in Oslo, has worked as a senior energy economist at the World Bank and as a division chief in the Norwegian Ministry of Petroleum and Energy.

VINCENT NWANMA reports on Nigeria's oil and gas industries, as well as general economic news. He had previously reported in Ghana, covering cocoa and gold, before going to Columbia University in 1998 as a World Bank Scholar on the Knight-Bagehot Fellowship in Economics and Business Journalism.

MARJORIE OLSTER was a correspondent for Reuters news agency for thirteen years, and she covered macroeconomics and Federal Reserve monetary policy for six years. She has interviewed many members of the Fed's policy-making board. She has worked in Spain, Israel, and New York.

ISABEL ORTIZ has a Ph.D. from the London School of Economics. She has worked in Brussels at the European Union (1992–19), the Spanish High Council of Scientific Research's Department of International Economics (1993–1994) and lectured on public policy at University of Madrid (1994–1995). From 1995 through 2003, she worked at the Poverty Reduction and Social Development Units of the Asian Development Bank (Manila, Philippines), where she has been team leader/manager of both project and policy initiatives. She has field experience in around twenty developing countries of Asia and Latin America. Recent publications include: *Social Protection in Asia and the Pacific* (2001), and *Handbook for Poverty and Social Analysis* (2001, with N. O'Sullivan et al.).

SHERIDAN PRASSO is a contributing editor at *BusinessWeek* magazine. She has been writing about economic and business issues for more than a decade.

NICHOLAS ROSEN is a journalist and consultant who has covered a wide range of issues—the Colombian civil war, the anti-globalization movement in Central Europe, Brazilian filmmaking, and Mexican immigration to the United States, to name a few. He holds a master's degree in international relations from Columbia University.

MILA ROSENTHAL is an advocate for international labor rights and corporate social responsibility. She is currently director of the Business, Environment, and Human Rights Program at Amnesty International USA and was formerly director of the Workers Rights Program at the Lawyers Committee for Human Rights. Her Ph.D. from the London School of Economics focused on women workers in the Vietnamese textile industry, and she is the author of several publications on globalization and labor.

ANYA SCHIFFRIN is the codirector of the media program at Columbia University's School of International and Public Affairs. She has worked as a financial and business journalist for eight years. A former Knight-Bagehot Fellow, she was a bureau chief at Dow Jones Newswires in Amsterdam and Hanoi and has worked as a reporter in Turkey, Pakistan, Spain, and the UK. She teaches a journalism class at Columbia University and has a Web Site, www.journalism-training.net.

DEIDRE SHEEHAN, a former staff writer at the *Far Eastern Economic Review* and bureau chief at Dow Jones Newswires, has worked as a foreign correspondent in Madrid, Sydney, and Manila.

SARA SILVER, a staff writer for the *Financial Times* in Mexico City, has an M.B.A from Columbia Business School and was formerly employed by the Associated Press as a reporter in New York and Mexico City.

JOSEPH E. STIGLITZ is professor of economics and finance at Columbia University. He won the Nobel Prize for economics in 2001. He was chief economist at the World Bank until January 2000. Before that he was chairman of President Clinton's Council of Economic Advisors.

GRAHAM WATTS is the editor of the *Financial Times* weekend section and worked for seventeen years on the world news, where he edited news features and special pages. He runs training courses at the *Financial Times*, in developing countries, and on an Internet-based journalism school he set up himself.

capital flight, 33, 37, 40, 98
capital flows, 5, 139–40
capital-market liberalization, 7, 10, 12, 56. *See also* capital controls; capital markets
capital markets, 5, 189, 312; bond (debt) market coverage, 22–26; bond markets, 19; bubbles, 22; corporate governance and, 184–85; disclosure, 21–22; emerging markets, 17, 32, 113, 132; equity market coverage, 19–22; foreign investors and, 27; glossary, 27–30; government ownership in listed stocks, 20–21; high volatility, 22; insider trading, 21; investment and mutual funds, 22; limits on trade, 20; regulatory and accounting systems, 20, 27; reporting issues, 20–22; secondary market, 21, 23, 30; sovereign-risk analysis and, 138; stock exchanges, 31; technical problems, 21; tips for reporters, 27
capital stock, 28
Carney, John J., 233
cash and cash equivalents, 213
Cayman Islands, 232–33
central banks, 42–43; board of directors, 42, 47, 49; crisis management, 48; decision-making process, 46; dollarization and, 48, 66–67; foreign exchange markets and, 36, 37, 38; glossary, 50; independence, 42, 47; inflation and, 43–44, 49; interest rate predictions, 43, 46–48, 49; interest rates, 44–45; key issues in covering, 45–46; links, 50–51; mandates/objectives, 43–44, 49; markets and, 42, 45; monetary policy, 43; research staff, 43, 49; supervision and regulations, 99; tips for reporters, 49; tools used, 44–45
Chad, 271
Chicago Board of Trade, 74
Chile, 38, 59
China: capital controls, 57, 60; capital markets, 20–21; labor, 192, 253
civil society groups, 123, 124
closed-ended investment fund, 28
Cold War, 9
collective action clauses (CACs), 111, 113–14
Colombia, 70
colonialism, 256
commercial debt, 120, 122, 123–24, 128
commitments and contingent liabilities, 215–16, 223–24
commodities markets, 255–56, 313; comparative advantage, 256–57;

government policies, 258–59; links, 262; market structure, 260–61; supply and demand, 259–60; tips for reporters, 261–62
commodity price cycles, 108, 257, 261
common stock, 28, 207, 216, 219
company-management firms, 236
comparative advantage, 256–57
competition: foreign direct investment, 167–68; international trade and, 247, 252
Competitive Advantage of Nations, The (Porter), 160
comprehensive income, 203, 204, 208–9, 217
concerted lending, 129
concessions, privatization and, 176–77
conditionality, 129
consumer confidence, 46
convergence trades, 86
convertible bonds, 28, 77
corporate actions, 189
corporate governance, 11, 182–83, 283; capital markets and, 184–85; controversies, 186–87; directors, 182, 185–86, 187; financial scandals and, 183, 184, 187; glossary, 189–90; links, 189; reasons for, 183–85; reporting, 185, 187–88; shareholders and, 184, 188; tips for reporters, 187–89
corporate restructuring, 183–84
corporate social responsibility (CSR), 270–72, 275
corporatization, 172
correspondent bank, 237
corruption, 10–11, 96, 103, 258, 264–65
cost of revenue, 217
counterfeiting, 70
coupon, 19
courtesy crises, 97, 98
crawling pegs and trading bands, 36, 39
credit derivatives, 77
crisis accelerators, 80
critical thinking, 13–14
cronyism, 10
cross-border capital flows, 160. *See also* foreign direct investment
cross-conditionality, 129
cross-default clause, 129
Cuba, 64
cumulative effect of change in accounting principle, 218, 219
currency, 32, 35, 119, 257; banking crises and, 97, 98; devaluation, 33–34, 40; foreign direct investment and, 166–67; overvalued,

37, 39, 40. *See also* dollarization; foreign exchange markets and foreign exchange crises
currency board, 36–37
currency crises, 33–34
currency instability, 108
currency mismatch, 56, 59, 104
currency substitution, 64
currency union, 65
current account, 38, 40, 52, 53, 138
current-account liberalization, 53
current assets, 213–14, 223
current liabilities, 213–14, 223
Czech Republic, 173, 174–75, 184

daisy chain risk, 78
Dallara, Charles, 142
Davies, Howard, 141
debt: accounting and, 223; bilateral, 120, 127; commercial, 120, 122, 123–24, 128; long-term, 214–15; multilateral, 120, 127–28; private sector, 128; privatization and, 177; public sector, 127; sovereign-risk analysis and, 138; subordinated, 101; sustainable, 128. *See also* debt relief and HIPC; sovereign debt crises
debt buy-back, 129
debt-equity swap, 129
debt overhang, 129
debt relief and HIPC, 118, 283; case of, 125; completion point, 121, 123; decision point, 121, 122, 125; eligible countries, 120–21; GDP growth rates and, 127; glossary, 129–31; government expenditure and, 126; HIPC Trust Fund, 125; history of, 119–21; links, 128; list of countries, 128; process, 121–25; sustainable levels, 123–24, 126, 127, 128; terms, 127–28; tips for reporters, 125–27; Zambia, 122–24. *See also* Poverty Reduction Strategy Papers; sovereign debt crises
debt-service ratios, 116, 129
debt-to-equity ratio, 223
decapitalization, 166–67, 169
default, 107–8, 113, 129, 135
deflation, 44–45
Dell Computer Corporation, 208; accounting analysis of, 210–19; consolidated statement of financial position, 210–19; consolidated statement of income, 212, 217–19
deposit insurance, 101
depreciation, 28, 35, 203–4
derivatives, 39, 73–74; abuse of, 73, 78–79; capital and collateral requirements, 79, 80; links, 81; markets, 76; policy solutions, 79–80;

foreign investors, 4, 23, 27, 179
forward contracts, 39, 74
free cash flow, 265
free float regime, 35–36
Free Press, 14
free trade, arguments for, 246–47
front companies, 237
fungibility, 75
futures, 45, 74–75

Gabon, 176–77
gains, 207
gender gap, 199, 282
General Accounting Office (GAO), 127
General Agreement on Tariffs and Trade (GATT), 248–50
General Agreement on Trade in Services (GATS), 243, 249–50
generally accepted accounting principles (GAAP), 204–5, 208, 220
Germany, 48
Ghana, 259
global capitalism, 5
global depository receipts (GDRs), 28
Global Edge, 304
global institutions, 4–7. *See also* International Monetary Fund; World Bank; World Trade Organization
globalization, 5, 149, 191, 201; critics and supporters, 3–4; poverty reduction and, 284–85. *See also* antiglobalization
global supply chain, 159
global warming, 5, 273, 274
glossary: capital markets, 27–30; central banks, 50; corporate governance, 189–90; debt relief and HIPC, 129–31; foreign exchange markets, 40; labor, 199
gold mining, 260
gold standard, 32, 52–53
gray market, 28
Great Depression, 53, 99, 101, 184–85, 277–78
greenfield investment, 160
Greenspan, Alan, 46
gross domestic product (GDP), 8–9, 100, 122, 127, 137, 264
gross margin, 208, 217, 224
Group of 7 (G7), 120, 141, 231
Guardian Bank & Trust, 232–33
Guatemala, 68
Gutierrez, Lucio, 67

Haeusler, Gerd, 141–42
hawks and doves, 47, 50
Heavily Indebted Poor Countries initiative, 118, 120–21, 290; Zam-

bia, 122–24. *See also* debt relief and HIPC; Poverty Reduction Strategy Papers (PRSP)
hedge funds, 83–84; definition, 84; economic crises and, 88–90; interconnectivity and contagion, 89–90; leverage, 83, 84, 85–86, 87; links, 92; management, 88; market and idiosyncratic components, 84–85; naked shorting, 86, 91; operation of, 84–86; regulation of, 90–91; shorting (short selling), 84–85, 86, 87, 91; stabilizing role, 90; tips for reporters, 92; types of, 86; unique features, 87–88
herd activity, 88
hidden agendas, 12
HIPC. *See* debt relief and HIPC
HIV/AIDS, 122, 124, 127
holdouts, 111, 113
Holland, 266
Honduras, 126
Hong Kong, 253
House of Representatives, 142
human rights organizations, 194–95
hybrid instruments, 74

IBC (International Business Company), 237
Inacio Lula da Silva, Luiz, 36
incentives, 9, 10
income, net, 208–9, 219
income before cumulative effect of change in accounting principle, 218
income before taxes, 218
income measures, 137
income statements, 202, 207–8, 224
independent director, 189
index, 28
India, 8
Indonesia, 98–99, 103
industrialization, 119
Industrial Revolution, 242
inflation, 5, 50; central banks and, 43–44, 49; dollarization and, 65, 66–67, 70, 71; exchange rate regime stands, 35–37
inflation indicators, 46, 49
information asymmetry, 18
information-based manipulation, 79
information density, 13
initial public offering (IPO), 21, 28–29
inside information, 10
insiders, privatization and, 179–80
Institute of International Finance, 142
institutional investors, 29, 132–33
integration (money laundering), 235

intellectual property rights (IPRs), 4, 251
Inter-American Development Bank, 121
interest rate predictions, 46–48, 49
interest rates: banking crises and, 97, 104; capital controls and, 56; central banks and, 44–49; real, 33, 40; sovereign debt crises and, 109, 119
International Accounting Standards Board (IASB), 201, 220–21
International Accounting Standards Committee, 220, 221
International Bank for Reconstruction and Development (IBRD), 293, 294, 295
International Business Company (IBC), 237
International Centre for Settlement of Investment Disputes, 294
international contract law, 19
International Development Association (IDA), 121, 125, 293
International Energy Agency, 267
International Finance Corporation (IFC), 293
International Financial Reporting Standards (IFRS), 201, 205, 221, 229
International Labor Organization (ILO), 245
International Monetary Fund (IMF), 4; advice to developing countries, 9–10, 55; banking crises and, 98–99; capital controls and, 54, 55; criticism of, 124–25; dollarization and, 66; formation of, 53; HIPC and, 118, 121–25; interest rate rise and, 97; Paris Club and, 26; Poverty Reduction and Growth Facility, 125, 129, 130?121; privatization and, 171; sovereign debt crises and, 109–11, 114–15, 116; sovereign-risk analysis and, 133–34, 141–42, 144–45; World Bank's relationship with, 290–91
international organizations, Internet sources, 308–9
international reserves, 38
international trade, 11–12, 241; agriculture and, 250, 252; antidumping initiatives, 252–53; Cambodia, 244–45; competition and, 247, 252; economic development and, 243, 248; economic theory, 246–47; employment and, 242–43, 247, 248; exports, 33, 35, 166; historical context, 242–46; links, 254; multilateral trade-policy rules, 248–53; poverty reduction and, 283–84; production of goods,

national income account (real sector), 133
nationally recognized statistical rating organizations (NRSROs), 138, 141
Neiss, Hubert, 98
neoliberal approaches, 284, 290
net asset value per share, 29
Netherlands, central banks, 48
net income, 208–9, 219
net lending, 130
net present value (NPV), 130
net resource transfer, 130
net revenues, 217
New York Stock Exchange, 14, 19, 20, 314
Nigeria, 256, 258, 259, 264
Nike, 193, 194, 195–96, 199
Noboa, Gustavo, 66
nominal comparisons, 35
nominee owner, 236, 237
Nomura, 174–75
nonbanking institution, 24
non-current assets, 214
nonexecutive director, 189
nongovernmental organizations (NGOs), 8, 123, 126, 270, 283, 284
nonperforming loans (NPL), 34, 40, 95–96, 103, 105
North American Free Trade Agreement (NAFTA), 195, 247, 251
Norwegian Petroleum Fund, 271–72
notes to financial statements, 202, 210
notice of meeting, 190

official debt, 26
offshore financial centers, 231–32, 235–36, 237
oil and development, 263; characteristics of industry, 267–70; conflict, 264; corporate social responsibility (CSR), 270–72, 275; corruption, 264–65; cost of extraction, 266; Dutch disease, 266; environmental effects, 266–67, 270, 273; instability, 266; links, 274; natural gas, 267, 272, 273; oil-technology firms, 269–70; privatization, 269; rent seeking, 264; state-owned oil companies, 269; super-major companies, 268–69; tips for reporters, 273; weak record, 263–66
oil price shocks, 122, 257
open-ended investment fund, 29
open foreign-exchange position limits, 100
operating activities, 207–9
operating expenses, 217
operating income, 208, 218
operating margins, 224

option premium, 76
options, 76
orderly market rules, 79, 80
Organisation for Economic Co-operation and Development, 232
Organization of Petroleum Exporting Countries (OPEC), 257, 268, 269, 273
outsiders, privatization and, 180
overnight bank-lending rate, 50
over-the-counter markets, 76, 78
over the counter (OTC) trading, 19, 29
overvalued currency, 37, 39, 40

Panama, 68
paper (shell) entities, 235–36, 237
Paris Club, 26, 109, 120, 125, 130
par value, 29
pension reform, 147; aging populations, 148; globalization pressures, 149; hidden costs, 154; key concepts, 150–54; key things to watch for, 154–56; pay-as-you-go financing, 150–51, 152–55; policy prescriptions, 149–50; prefunded system, 149–50, 153–54; rates of return, 154–55; Russia, 152–53; trust funds, 150; trust-funds financing, 151–53
per capita income, 121
Peru, 64
petroleum industry. See oil and development
petroleum-revenue stabilization funds, 271
Pilip, Ivan, 174
placement (money laundering), 234–35
Poland, 162–63
policy lending, 290
policy ownership, 130
policy rates, 44, 45
policy simulations, 134
political rent seeking, 265
Porter, Michael, 159–60
portfolio foreign investment, 160
portfolio investment, 57
positive-list approach, 250–51
poverty, 122–24, 152; income distribution, 277, 280; vulnerability to, 282–83
poverty reduction, 121; corporate governance and, 283; empowerment of poor, 282; gender disparities, 282; good governance, 281–82; historical perspective, 277–78; international trade and, 283–84; links, 286; multilateral development banks and, 280–81; policies at beginning of twenty-

first century, 280–84; poverty, inequality, and economic-growth debate, 278–80; poverty trends and measurements, 276–77; pro-poor growth, 281; reducing vulnerability and risk, 282–83; social services, 282; Third World debt, 283; tips for reporters, 285; understanding on global scale, 284–85
Poverty Reduction and Growth Facility, 121, 125, 129, 130
Poverty Reduction Strategy Papers (PRSP), 121, 123, 125–26, 130, 281
preferred stock, 29, 207, 216
price discovery, 176
price-earnings (PE) ratio, 22, 29
price manipulation, 27
price signaling, 102
price stability, 42
primary market, 29
private placement, 29–30
private sector debt, 128
private sector foreign creditors, 26
privatization, 11, 13; banking, 174–75; competition policies, 177–78; Czech Republic, 173, 174–75, 184; direct sales, 173, 175; employment issues, 171–72, 178–79; government role, 179; indicators, 177–79; links, 181; new ownership, 179–80; process, 172–79; reasons for, 171–72; results, 177; sales, 173–77; unemployment and, 171–72, 178; vouchers, 173, 184
Prochzka, Libor, 174, 175
productivity, 246
profit and loss account, 207. See also income statement
profit margins, 224
profit-sharing arrangements, 87
profit taking, 30
property, plant and equipment assets, 214
property rights, 178, 265
proprietary trading platform market, 76
prospectus, 30
protectionism, 199
protests: antiglobalization, 241, 242; foreign direct investment, 167–68, 169
provision for income taxes, 218
proxy, 190
public expenditure, 130
public offerings, 21, 28–29, 176
public relations departments, 6–7
public sector borrowing requirements (PSBR), 137
public sector debt, 127
putable bonds, 77
Putin, Vladimir, 152

put option, 76–77
pyramid schemes, 18, 24–25, 186

Quantum fund, 88–89

rate of return, 30
rating agencies, 117, 133, 134–36; criticism of, 139–43
ratios, 222
Reagan, Ronald, 54, 171, 269
real comparisons, 35
real interest rates, 33, 40
recapitalization, 102–3
recessions, central banks and, 44
recognition, 204–5
recurring operations, 224
reform measures, 12
regional trade agreements, 251
registration and reporting requirements: derivatives, 79, 80; hedge funds, 91
reinvoicing, 237
Reisen, Helmut, 140
relative-value hedge funds, 86, 92
rents, 264, 265
rent seeking, 265
repo operation, 85, 92
reporting: biased, 8–9; hidden agendas, 12; incentives for sharing information, 9, 10; information asymmetry, 18; information density, 13; lack of knowledge, 5–9; media, 10, 13–14. *See also* tips for reporters
repurchase agreements, 85, 92
rescheduling, 119
research, development and engineering, 217
reserves, international, 38
resource curse, 263, 271
restructuring, 119–20
retail investor, 30
retained earnings, 207, 217
return on equity (ROE), 225
revenues, 207
Ricardo, David, 265
rights issue, 30
risk management, 73
Robertson, Julian, 86
Robinson, Jeffrey, 237
Rodriguez, Francisco, 248
Rodrik, Dani, 59, 248
Rogoff, Kenneth, 55
rogue creditors, 112, 113
Russia, 22, 48, 56, 89, 139, 172, 269; pension reform, 152–53; sovereign debt crisis, 110, 116

Sarbanes-Oxley Act, 201–, 221–22, 229
Saro Wiwa, Ken, 270

SAR (suspicious activity report), 237
savings, private, 18
savings and loan associations, 56, 96, 97
Schumpeter, Joseph, 247
SDRM (sovereign-debt restructuring mechanism), 111
Seattle riots (1999), 3
secondary market, 21, 23, 30
Securities and Exchange Commission (SEC), 31, 91, 140, 145, 184, 190, 229; documents filed by foreign countries, 318–19; international accounting standards, 220–21; Internet reporting and, 314–21; key forms, 319–20
securities fraud, 236
securities regulation, 31
security, 30
seignorage benefits, 69–70
self-fulfilling prophecies, 12, 89
selling, general and administrative, 217
Sen, Amartya, 14
September 11th 2001 terrorist attacks, 48, 68
services, international trade and, 250–51
shareholders, offshore entities as, 236
shareholders' equity, 206–7, 216–17; statement of, 202, 208–9, 223–24
shelf company, 237
Shell, 270
shell bank, 237
shorting (short selling), 84–85, 86, 87, 91
short options position, 77
short-term investments, 30, 213
Singapore issues, 251–53
skepticism, 10
smurfing, 237
Snyder, Edward, 174
Social Accountability International, 195
socialism, banking crises and, 95–96
social security systems. *See* pension reform
social services, 282
solvency, 107–8, 130
solvency indicators, 23
Soros, George, 39, 83, 86, 88–89
South America, 47, 65. *See also individual countries*
sovereign bonds, 23–26, 107
sovereign debt crises, 106–7, 119; bailouts, 109–11; bonds and, 109, 110, 111–12; Brady bonds, 111–12; contractual *vs.* statutory approaches, 113–15; coordination problem, 112–13; enforcement

problems, 114–15; exchange offers, 112; interest rates and, 109, 119; links, 117; procedure, 109; reasons for default, 107–8; rescheduling, 108; tips for reporters, 116–17; workouts, 111–13. *See also* debt relief
sovereign-debt restructuring mechanism (SDRM), 111
sovereign rating, 23–25
sovereign risk, 132
sovereign-risk analysis, 132–33; actors, 133–36; conflict of interest and inadequacy of resources, 141–43; criticism of rating agencies, 139–43; determining factors, 136–39; economic structure and growth prospects, 137; external payments and debt, 138; fiscal flexibility, 137–38, 144; investment banks, 134; junk status, 140–41; letter-based rating systems, 135; links, 144; monetary and liquidity factors, 138; oligopolistic nature of rating agencies, 140–41; political factors, 137; procyclical impact on capital flows, 139–40; rating agencies, 134–36; surveillance, 133; tips for reporters, 143
Soviet Union, former, pyramid schemes, 24
special charges, 217–18, 224
speculation, 5, 30, 38–39
spillover effects, 161, 165, 166, 167, 168, 247
spot market, 259
spot rates, 39
staggered board, 190
Standard & Poor's (S&P), 133, 135, 136, 138–39, 142, 145
state-directed lending (policy lending), 96
statement of cash flows, 202, 209
statement of shareholders' equity, 202, 208–9, 223–24
stock dividend, 30
stock exchanges, 31
stock markets. *See* capital markets
stocks, 19; capital, 28; common, 28, 207, 216, 219; derivatives and, 77; FDI, 160–61; treasury, 216
stock split, 30
strategic default, 113
strike (exercise) price, 76
structural adjustment, 130, 289
structured securities, 77
studies, 7
subcontractor, 199
subordinated debt, 101
subsidies, 11
sudden stop, 56

Suharto, 98, 99
Sukarnoputri, Megawati, 99
Sumitomo Bank (Japan), 78
super-margin, 80
supplier delivery time, 46
sustainability: debt relief and HIPC, 123–24, 126, 127, 128; foreign direct investment, 166–68, 169; oil industry and, 271–72
sustainable debt, 128
swap contracts, 75–76, 82n.1
sweatshops, 168, 192, 194, 245

tariffs, 11
taxes, 12, 59, 165, 179, 237?
tax evasion, 78, 91, 165, 230
tax haven, 237
Taylor rule, 50
technical monopoly rents, 265
technology, 58, 163, 247
technology transfer, 165, 168
Tesar, Jiri, 174, 175
Tesobonos, 39
Thailand, 139
Thatcher, Margaret, 54, 171–72, 269
think tanks, 310–11
Tiger Fund, 86
tips for reporters: banking crises, 104; capital controls, 61; capital markets, 27; central banks, 49; commodities markets, 261–62; corporate governance, 187–89; debt relief and HIPC, 125–27; derivatives, 81; dollarization, 71; foreign exchange markets, 40; hedge funds, 92; international trade, 253–54; labor issues, 197–98; money laundering, 235–37; oil and development, 273; poverty reduction, 285; sovereign debt crises, 116–17; sovereign-risk analysis, 143; World Bank, 298
total current assets, 213–14
total current liabilities, 214
total return vehicles, 87
track record, 130
trade. See international trade

trade agreements: GATS, 243, 249–50; GATT, 248–50; NAFTA, 195, 247, 251; TRIPS, 249, 250, 251
trade balance, 38
trade-based manipulation, 79
trade liberalization, 130–31
Trade-Related Aspects of Intellectual Property Rights (TRIPS), 249, 250, 251
traditional dealer market, 76
transfer price, 165
transparency: capital markets, 17–19; categorizing loans, 102; central banks, 42, 46, 47; derivatives, 78; hedge funds, 91; international trade, 252; oil and development, 271
treasuries, 30
treasury stock, 216
trickle-down approach, 278
TRIPS (Trade-Related Aspects of Intellectual Property Rights), 249, 250, 251
trust funds, 151–53
Turkey, 56, 139

Uganda, 126
unemployment, 9–11, 50, 163, 279; privatization and, 171–72, 178
unilateralism, 5
United Kingdom: capital controls, 54; exit from European Monetary System, 34, 39, 83, 86, 88–89
United Nations, 280
United States, 4, 183; capital markets, 22, 53; derivatives and, 78, 79; dollarization and, 65, 69, 71; Federal Reserve, 43, 44, 45–46
Uruguay, 134, 139, 140, 145
Uruguay Round, 4, 249, 250
U.S. Treasury, 10, 23, 30; sovereign debt crises and, 111, 113–14

Value Added Tax (VAT), 12
vanilla interest rate swap, 75
Vietnam, 4, 18, 26, 46, 60, 172, 259; banking crisis, 95–96, 104; coffee exports, 4, 257; labor, 193, 194

volatility, 30
Volcker, Paul, 58
volume, 30
voting right, 30
vouchers, 173, 184

Washington Consensus, 5, 285, 290
wealth, 203, 204
White, Lawrence, 140–41
Wolfensohn, James, 290, 295
worker skills, 178–79, 183
World Bank, 4, 7; banking crises and, 101; Board of Executive Directors (EDs), 292–93; Board of Governors, 292; bureaucracy, 294–95; country departments, 295–97; criticism of, 124–25; governance, 291–93; HIPC and, 118, 121–25; IMF and, 290–91; institutional structure, 293–94; International Development Association, 121, 125; labor and, 195; links, 299; pension reform and, 149–50, 152–53, 155; policy lending, 290; privatization and, 171; projects, 289, 296–97; second-generation initiatives, 289–90; structural adjustment policies, 289–90; subscription capital, 291–92; tips for reporters, 298
World Bank Institute, 293–94
WorldCom, 200, 201, 221
World Summit for Social Development, 280
World Trade Organization (WTO), 4, 192, 242; agreements, 249–50; General Agreement on Trade in Services, 243, 249–50; multilateral trade-policy rules, 248–53; umbrella agreement, 249
write-down, 131
write-off, 131
writing tips, 322–29

Zambia, 121, 122–24
zero coupon bonds, 23, 30, 112
Zoellick, Robert, 244